S0-AYG-901

Intelligent Information Systems – Vol. 2

E-BUSINESS IN THE 21ST CENTURY

Realities, Challenges and Outlook

INTELLIGENT INFORMATION SYSTEMS

Series Editors: Da Ruan *(Belgian Nuclear Research Centre (SCK.CEN) & Ghent University, Belgium)*
Jie Lu *(University of Technology, Sdyney, Australia)*

Vol. 1 Advances in Artificial Intelligence for Privacy Protection and Security
edited by Agusti Solanas & Antoni Martínez-Ballesté (Rovira i Virgili University, Spain)

Vol. 2 E-Business in the 21st Century: Realities, Challenges and Outlook
by Jun Xu (Southern Cross University, Australia) & Mohammed Quaddus (Curtin University of Technology, Australia)

Intelligent Information Systems – Vol. 2

E-BUSINESS IN THE 21ST CENTURY

Realities, Challenges and Outlook

Jun Xu
Southern Cross University, Australia

Mohammed Quaddus
Curtin University of Technology, Australia

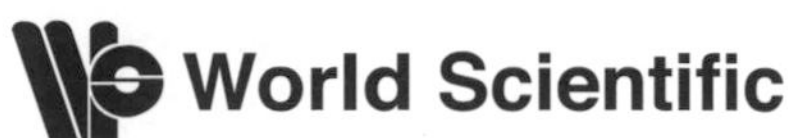

World Scientific

NEW JERSEY • LONDON • SINGAPORE • BEIJING • SHANGHAI • HONG KONG • TAIPEI • CHENNAI

Published by

World Scientific Publishing Co. Pte. Ltd.
5 Toh Tuck Link, Singapore 596224
USA office: 27 Warren Street, Suite 401-402, Hackensack, NJ 07601
UK office: 57 Shelton Street, Covent Garden, London WC2H 9HE

British Library Cataloguing-in-Publication Data
A catalogue record for this book is available from the British Library.

Intelligent Information Systems — Vol. 2
E-BUSINESS IN THE 21ST CENTURY
Realities, Challenges and Outlook

ISBN-13 978-981-283-674-8
ISBN-10 981-283-674-8

Printed in Singapore by World Scientific Printers

INTRODUCTION

The Internet has changed the way we conduct business and the way we see the world and ourselves in it. It has rewritten the rules for business and transformed many industries, e.g., book, travel, music, accommodation, internet phone, real estate, among many others. It has also brought profound changes to individuals, organizations, and society. In line with the rapid development of internet technologies and the increase in competition and other business pressures, E-business, which includes buying and selling of goods and services, servicing customers, collaborating with business partners, conducting transactions within an organization on the net, is getting more and more popular and expanding dramatically. This book titled "E-business in the 21st century: Realities, Challenges, and Outlook" aims to offer comprehensive analysis of concepts, models and infrastructures of e-business. It also intends to present unique observations of current e-business practices for different organizations in different economies; and provides insights on the future of current leading businesses on the net and the trends of e-business. This book will serve as an effective and indispensible reference book for professionals who are interested in or dealing with e-business and businesses that are embarking on e-business.

The book consists of 15 peer-reviewed chapters and is divided into three sections. The first section includes two chapters with regards to an overview of current status and current practices of e-business. In chapter 1 Jun Xu and Mohammed Quaddus discuss foundation of e-business and e-business technologies and in chapter 2 they present some different types of e-businesses.

Eleven research projects on electronic business are presented in the second section of the book. They cover areas such as online auction, online advertising, e-learning, e-ticketing, e-tailing, evaluation of e-business, web 2.0 platforms, mobile business, and e-business in small & medium enterprises, and report results from various countries in different continents (i.e., Algeria, Australia, China, Indonesia, Saudi Arabia, Tunisia). In chapter 3 Mohammed Quaddus and Jun Xu present findings of an empirical study surveying 240 participants in China that explores attitudinal, social and behavior factors explaining the Chinese consumers' intention to use online auction. In chapter 4 Jan Hailigtag, Jun Xu and Mohammed Quaddus identify factors influencing online advertising among small and medium enterprise by referring to results of a national survey among 1,000 Australian small and medium enterprises. In chapter 5 Imed Ben Dhaou and Foudil Abdessemed report three case studies of e-learning in three countries of Algeria, Saudi Arabia and Tunisia. In chapter 6 Anis Allagui and Mohamed Slim Ben Mimoun discuss factors influencing adoption of electronic ticketing among Tunisian consumers by analyzing 160 surveyed responses. Weibing Xuan, Jun Xu and Mohammed Quaddus, in chapter 7, provide us a case study of e-tailing in one of the largest retail group in China. In chapter 8 Chad Lin and Yu-an Huang develop a framework of challenges and critical success factors in business to business e-commerce evaluation. In chapter 9 Tobias Kollmann, Christoph Stöckmann and Carsten Schröer discuss the problem of oscillating degrees of utilization associated with the diffusion of web 2.0 platforms. Xiangzhu Gao, in chapter 10, describes some applications of wireless technologies in mobile business. In chapter 11 Sabah Addullah Al-Somali, Roya Gholami and Ben Clegg review relevant literature on theories and factors affecting electronic commerce/business adoption in small and medium enterprises. In chapter 12 Vera Pujani, Jun Xu and Mohammed Quaddus report results of a research studying website site success in 550 small and medium enterprises in Indonesia. In chapter 13 Jahjah Hallah, Jun Xu and Mohammed Quaddus discuss factors influencing adoption of electronic commerce among small enterprises by analyzing the data collected via surveying 1085 Australian small enterprises across the nation.

The future of e-business and e-business opprtunities are discussed in third section of the book. There are two chapters in this section. Both chapters are authored by Jun Xu and Mohammed Quaddus. In chapter 14 they discuss the future of e-business, e-business success factors, and e-business opportunities arising from emerging business trends, and in chapter 15 they present a model of e-business adoption, success and sustainable success. The future of some current leading e-business organizations is also analyzed by partially applying the model in this chapter.

A great number of colleagues and researchers deserve our thanks in connection with this project. We would like to thank Professor Jie Lu, University of Technology Sydney, Australia and Professor Da Ruan, Belgian Nuclear Research Center & Ghent University, Belgium for their support and for the opportunity of working on the book; Associate Professor Shankar Sankaran, University of Technology Sydney, Australia and Dr Chad Lin, Curtin University of Technology, Australia for their kind assistance in reviewing our book proposal; Mr Mahmud Hassan and a number of researchers for their kind assistance in reviewing the book chapters. Finally we would like to thank Mr Steven Patt, Editor at World Scientific, for overseeing the publishing processes and for giving us such a wonderful publishing experience.

Jun Xu and Mohammed Quaddus
Tweed Heads and Perth, Australia
April 2009

CONTENTS

Section 1

Overview of Current Status of E-Business

CHAPTER 1

OVERVIEW-PART I: FOUNDATION OF E-BUSINESS AND E-BUSINESS TECHNOLOGIES

Jun Xu

Graduate College of Management, Southern Cross University, Australia

Mohammed Quaddus

Graduate School of Business, Curtin University of Technology, Australia

This chapter presents foundation of e-business and discusses technologies for e-business. The foundation of e-business is discussed from the perspectives of global internet adoption and e-business growth, e-business definition, e-business categories, e-business models, impacts of e-business, security, privacy, and governance issues associated with e-business, and e-business strategy planning and implementation. E-business related technologies covered in this chapter include e-business information technology infrastructure, enterprise applications/systems, data warehouse & data mining, and technologies for addressing security & privacy concerns. The integration issue associated with e-business technologies is also addressed.

1. Foundation of Electronic Business

1.1. The Rapid Growth of the Internet and Electronic Business

In the last decade, a rapid growth and adoption of the internet has been observed in all the continents of the world (see Table 1.1). As shown in Table 1.1, all the regions in the world have achieved more than 100 percent growth for the period of 2000-2008, with 129.6% in North America, 165.1% in Oceania/Australia, 266.0% in Europe, 406.1% in Asia, 669.3% in Latin America/Caribbean, 1031.2% in Africa and

1176.8% in Middle East. In the meantime, North America has the highest adoption rate of the Internet (73.6% of its population have adopted the Internet) while Africa has the least adoption rate of the Internet (only 3.5% of its population are connected to the Internet). The differences in economic development may contribute to the variances in adoption rates of the Internet between developing and developed regions. The world has more than 14 million Internet users (or 21.9% of the world population) in the first half of 2008, and has achieved over 300 percent growth for the period of 2000-2008.

Table 1.1: Global Internet adoption

World Regions	Population (2008 Estimates)	Internet Users (Dec 31, 2000)	Internet Users (June 30, 2008 Data)	% of Population	% of World Internet Users	User Growth (2000-2008)
Africa	955,206,348	4,514,400	51,065,630	5.3%	3.5%	1031.2%
Asia	3,776,181,949	114,304,000	578,538,257	15.3%	39.5%	406.1%
Europe	800,401,065	105,096,093	384,633,765	48.1%	26.3%	266.0%
Middle East	197,090,443	3,284,800	41,939,200	21.3%	2.9%	1176.8%
North America	337,167,248	108,096,800	248,241,969	73.6%	17.0%	129.6%
Latin America/ Caribbean	576,091,673	18,068,919	139,009,209	24.1%	9.5%	669.3%
Oceania/Australia	33,981,562	7,620,480	20,204,331	59.5%	1.4%	165.1%
World Total	6,676,120,288	360,985,492	1,463,632,361	21.9%	100.0%	305.5%

(Source: adopted from www.internetworldstatistics.com with permission)

Some top countries in terms of the number of Internet users are (in the order): China (253 million or 17.3% of total world Internet users), United States (220.1 million or 15.0% of total world internet users), Japan (94 million), India (60 million), Germany (52.5 million), Brazil (50 million), United Kingdom (41.8 million), France (36.15 million), South Korea (34.8 million), Italy (34.71 million), Russia (32.7 million), Canada (28 million), Turkey (26.5 million), Spain (25.6 million), Indonesia (25 million), Mexico (23.7 million), Iran (23 million), Vietnam (20.16 million), Pakistan (17.5 million) and Australia (16.35 million) (see Table 1.2). As displayed in Table 1.2, while China has the largest number of Internet users the penetration/diffusion rate of the internet is quite low (only 19% Chinese are using the internet). Similarly India's Internet penetration rate also quite low (with 60 million users and 5.2% internet penetration rate). On the other hand countries like

Canada (84.3%), Australia (79.4%), Japan (73.8%), and United States (72.5%) are some countries with the highest internet penetration rates. At the same time, developing countries (such as China (1024.4%), India (1100.0%), Iran (9100.0%), Vietnam (9979.8%), and Pakistan (12969.5%)) have dominated the user growth for the period of 2000-

Table 1.2: Top countries of Internet users

Country or Region	Internet Users (June 30, 2008 Data)	Penetration (% of Population)	% of World Users	Population (2008 Estimates)	User Growth (2000-2008)
China	253,000,000	19.0%	17.3%	1,330,044,605	1024.4%
United States	220,141,969	72.5%	15.0%	303,824,646	130.9%
Japan	94,000,000	73.8%	6.4%	127,288,419	99.7%
India	60,000,000	5.2%	4.1%	1,147,995,898	1100.0%
Germany	52,533,914	63.8%	3.6%	82,369,548	118.9%
Brazil	50,000,000	26.1%	3.4%	191,908,598	900.0%
United Kingdom	41,817,847	68.6%	2.9%	60,943,912	171.5%
France	36,153,327	58.1%	2.5%	62,177,676	325.3%
South Korea	34,820,000	70.7%	2.4%	49,232,844	82.9%
Italy	34,708,144	59.7%	2.4%	58,145,321	162.9%
Russia	32,700,000	23.2%	2.2%	140,702,094	954.8%
Canada	28,000,000	84.3%	1.9%	33,212,696	120.5%
Turkey	26,500,000	36.9%	1.8%	71,892,807	1225.0%
Spain	25,623,329	63.3%	1.8%	40,491,051	375.6%
Indonesia	25,000,000	10.5%	1.7%	237,512,355	1150.0%
Mexico	23,700,000	21.6%	1.6%	109,955,400	773.8%
Iran	23,000,000	34.9%	1.6%	65,875,223	9100.0%
Vietnam	20,159,615	23.4%	1.4%	86,116,559	9979.8%
Pakistan	17,500,000	10.4%	1.2%	167,762,040	12969.5%
Australia	16,355,388	79.4%	1.1%	20,600,856	147.8%
TOP 20 Countries	1,115,713,572	25.4%	76.2%	4,388,052,548	284.5%
Rest of the World	347,918,789	15.2%	23.8%	2,288,067,740	391.2%
Total World-Users	1,463,632,361	21.9%	100.0%	6,676,120,288	305.5%

(Source: adopted from www.internetworldstatistics.com with permission)

2008. Also it can be seen from the Table 1.2 that the top 20 countries have accounted for more than 70% (76.2%) of the world's total number of internet users while the remaining world (with more than 140 countries) only accounted for 23.8%. Therefore in world scene most of the e-business activities come from these countries and they form the massive head of the Internet world.

Some most used languages on the Internet include (in the order): English (430.8 million or 29.4% of all Internet users or 21.1% of all English speaking population have interacted in English online), Chinese (276.2 million, 18.9% & 20.2%), Spanish (124.7 million, 8.5% & 27.6%), Japanese (94 million, 6.4% & 73.8%), French (68.15 million, 4.7% & 16.6%), German (61.2 million, 4.2% & 63.5%), Arabic (59.85 million, 4.1% & 16.8%), Portuguese (58.18 million, 4.0% & 24.3%), Korean (34.82 million, 2.4% & 47.9%), and Italian (34.71 million, 2.4% & 59.7%) (see Table 1.3). The two dominant internet languages are

Table 1.3: Top Languages on the Internet

Top Ten Languages on the Internet	% of all Internet Users	Internet Users by Languages (June 30, 2008 Data)	Internet Penetration by Language (% of World Population for the Language)	Language Growth on the Internet (2000-2008)	2008 Estimated World Population for the Language
English	29.4%	430,802,172	21.1%	203.5%	2,039,114,892
Chinese	18.9%	276,216,713	20.2%	755.1%	1,365,053,177
Spanish	8.5%	124,714,378	27.6%	405.3%	451,910,690
Japanese	6.4%	94,000,000	73.8%	99.7%	127,288,419
French	4.7%	68,152,447	16.6%	458.7%	410,498,144
German	4.2%	61,213,160	63.5%	121.0%	96,402,649
Arabic	4.1%	59,853,630	16.8%	2063.7%	357,271,398
Portuguese	4.0%	58,180,960	24.3%	668.0%	239,646,701
Korean	2.4%	34,820,000	47.9%	82.9%	72,711,933
Italian	2.4%	34,708,144	59.7%	162.9%	58,175,843
Top 10 Languages	84.9%	1,242,661,604	23.8%	278.3%	5,218,073,846
Rest of the Languages	15.1%	220,970,757	15.2%	580.4%	1,458,046,442

(Source: adopted from www.internetworldstatistics.com with permission)

English and Chinese. It can be seen from Table 1.3 that some online languages have realized fastest growth include: Arabic (2063.7%), Chinese (755.1%), Portuguese (668.0%), French (458.7%), and Spanish (405.3%). In the meantime, internet users of the top 10 Internet languages account for 84.9% of all internet users.

In addition, the growth of broadband users is also increasing faster even though worldwide usage is uneven in different regions. For example, broadband subscriber lines (per 100 people) are 29.5 in Western Europe, 27.9 in North America, 26.7 in Japan, 9.2 in Eastern Europe & Russia, 6.7 in Latin America, 5.7 in Asia and Australasia, and 2.2 in Middle East and North America (Economist Intelligence Unit 2009). Furthermore according to IDC (reported in Economist Intelligence Unit 2009), there will be 600 million mobile users accessing the internet via their mobile devices in 2009. And the number of devices with internet connections will double to 3 billion over the next few years. Countries also have different readiness for e-business. Economist Intelligence Unit & IBM Institute for Business Value (2007) study the e-readiness of 69 countries by examing factors such as connectivity & technology infrastucture, business environment, social and cultural environment, legal environment, government policy & vision, and consumer & business adoption. As per their criteria, top ten countries of e-readiness (in the order) are: Denmark, the U.S., Sweden, Hong Kong, Switzerland, Singapore, the U.K., Netherlands, Australia and Finland.

In line with a rapidly changing market, i.e., increasingly intense competition, the trend of globalization, more demanding customers, dramatic advancement of technologies (changes almost every 18 months or less), the increasing affordability of technologies and the rapid diffusion of the Internet globally, electronic business (conducting business online) is getting more and more popular and expanding dramatically. According to Economist Intelligence Unit (2009) around half of the approximate 1.5 billion Internet users will shop online in 2009 and further 400 million more internet users will purchase on the Internet by 2012. The projected over 1 billion online shoppers by 2012 will make the transaction value of business to consumer (B2C) e-business market reaching US$ 1.2 trillion. But by then B2B e-business will be worth

US$ 12 trillion (10 times of B2C e-business transactions) (Economist Intelligence Unit 2009).

1.2. Understanding E-business

E-business is a term that is used very widely, but the term means different things (i.e., online catalogue, online buying and selling, serving customers online, e-learning, e-government, e-research, e-supply chains, among many others) to different people in its relatively short history. In the meantime, there exists a debate on the similarities and differences of the two terms of e-commerce and e-business, which could be partially explained due to the lack of well-established literature. In this chapter, the concepts of e-commerce and e-business are used interchangeably. E-business/e-commerce has a broad meaning and encompasses all types of electronic transactions (i.e., B2B, B2C, C2C, Mobile commerce, E-government, E-learning, E-publishing, Online communities and Social networks) and communications within organisation and between organisations as well as with consumers. Organisations can be involved in e-business in different degrees – varying from no involvement at all (i.e. using only traditional, brick and mortar premises to sell physical goods) through partial involvement (i.e. mixing electronic and traditional distribution channels-click and mortar e-business) to full involvement (i.e., pure online businesses).

There are different ways of categorising e-business/e-commerce. One way is to classify according to the type of system involved. Under this approach, there are four types of e-business/e-commerce systems (see Figure 1.1), including electronic markets (i.e., online marketplaces), inter-organizational systems (i.e., electronic data interchange, extranets), intra-organizational systems (i.e., intranets), and service delivery systems (i.e., online banking, online learning and other online services). Electronic markets and inter-organisational systems are terms which have been used for many years. Some differences between these two types of systems include the nature of the relationship among the participants (i.e., in inter-organisational systems the participants have an existing relationship before entering into electronic transactions; in electronic markets there can be a relationship but it is more likely that the participants do not know each other before the transaction takes place) and technology deployed (i.e., inter-organisational systems are made of proprietary systems or closed systems (providing entry only to approved suppliers and customers) while in electronic markets (essentially platforms for trading) anyone can gain access and can participate in transactions).

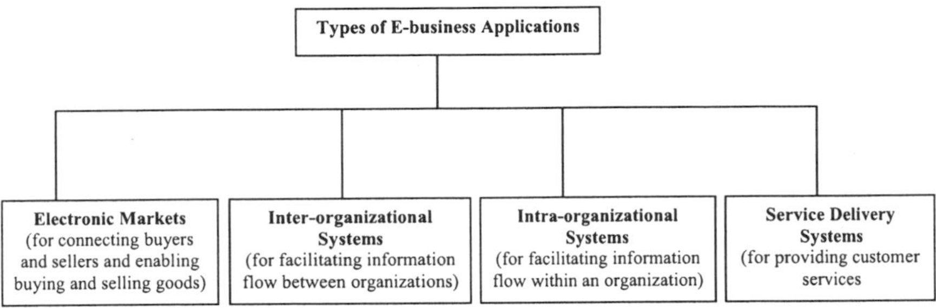

Figure 1.1: Categorising e-business according to type of application (Source: developed from Turban et al. 2008)

A different way of categorising e-business, which is the approached favoured by the authors, focuses on the type of transaction taking place (Turban et al. 2008, p. 8). With this approach, transactions may be conducted among businesses (business-to-business), between an organisation and its retail customers (business-to-consumer), within an organisation (intra-business), and between consumers (consumers-to-consumers). Other types of transactions include mobile commerce, e-government, e-learning, e-publishing, consumer-to-consumer, peer-to-peer applications, social networks & online communities, among many others. The two major types of e-businesses so far are business-to-consumer (B2C) and business-to-business (B2B).

Another important concept is the business model of electronic business, which basically refers to ways organizations can employ to generate sufficient revenue (i.e., via different approaches of (1) sales-generating revenue from selling merchandise or services online; (2) transaction fees-earning a commission based on the volume of transactions made or fees per transaction; (3) subscription fees: fixed amount, usually monthly for services provided; (4) advertising fees;

(5) affiliate fees: receiving commissions for referring customers to others' sites; (6) payment for usage, (7) donations & voluntary contributions) to sustain themselves (Turban et al. 2008, p. 18; Laudon & Trevor 2008, p. 70; Rappa 2008). Another important component is value created from the e-business for customers, organizations and other relevant parties. Like any other businesses, business model is very critical to the viability of an electronic business. In addition, many e-business failures have resulted from failed business models (i.e., relying too much on generating revenue from online advertising). While there are many similarities between Internet business models and traditional business models, the characteristics of the Internet have offered the capacity to present new Internet business models and reinvent existing business models (i.e., online auctions, search engines, mass customization, etc) (Rappa 2008). Even though there are no unified views on the classification of e-business models, some common Internet business models include: merchant (i.e., selling from B2C sites such as amazon.com, landsend.com, bestbuy.com), marketplace-matching sellers and buyers (i.e., ebay.com for transactions between consumers, alibaba.com for transactions between businesses), affiliate marketing by referring users of one website to other websites (many e-business websites have adopted it), community & social network (i.e., redhat.com, wikepedia.org, facebook.com, myspace.com, youtube.com), portal and search engine (i.e., yahoo.com, google.com, ask.com, live.com), subscription (i.e., truste.com, aol.com), utility-only paying for usage (i.e., slashdot), direct selling by manufacturers (i.e., dell.com, sony.com), content providers (i.e., wsj.com, cnn.com, espn.com), informediaries working on consumer data (i.e., doubleclick.com, netiq.com), transaction brokers (i.e., etrade.com, paypal.com, wotif.com) (Rappa 2008, Turban et al. 2008; Laudon & Trevor 2008, Rayport & Jaworski 2004).

1.3. Impacts of Electronic Business

The Internet has changed the way we conduct business and the way we see the world and ourselves in it. It has rewritten the rules of business and transformed many industries (i.e., book, travel, music, accommodation, internet phone, real estate, among many others). It has brought profound changes (including both negative and positive impacts) to individuals, organizations, industries, governments and societies (see Table 1.4).

Table 1.4: Some positive and negative impacts of electronic business

Impacts	Positive Impacts	Negative Impacts
To Individuals	Convenience; Personalised & customised products & services; Ubiquity & mobility; Better and more affordable communication and interaction (i.e., in real-time and multimedia way); Greater flexibility and better freedom of publishing ideas and views; Better connection with other members of communities; Access to products, services and information from all over the world (normally with cheaper prices); Making fulfilling the dream of being your own boss and of managing an international business much more easier; among many others.	Privacy issues; Security issues (i.e., online fraud, viruses, spam, etc); Individuality issues (i.e., passwords and user names are used to represent human beings on the internet); The lost balance between work and leisure arising from the use of lap tops, mobiles and other mobile devices; The loss of writing and other language skills resulting from overly using computer and the internet; The lost human interaction with others by excessively relying on e-mail, VoIP, instant messaging, online chatting and other electronic communication tools; etc.
To Organizations	An additional distribution channel; New opportunities in existing and new markets; Better/ new products and services; Enhanced efficiency & effectiveness; Time & cost reductions; Better relationships with customers, with suppliers and business partners, with government agencies, with competitors and with employees; Enlarged market share, Increased revenue; Improved profit, Better image, among many others.	Channel conflict when doing both online and offline operations; More intense competition from existing competitors and new entrants; Losses due to network failures and security breaches; The wide and quicker distribution of negative news on the organization; The difficulties in maintaining 24/7 reliability and accessibility of online operations; etc.
To Industries	More effective and efficient industries and industry supply chains more efficient & effective; Enhanced cooperation and collaboration within and across industries; Creation of new industries and addition of new elements to existing industries; among many others.	Increased competition in many industries (especially in service-oriented industries); Changed structure of many industries (i.e., many traditional intermediaries will either disappear or change their roles (e.g., providing more value-added services and focusing more on

Table 1.4: *Continued*

Impacts	Positive Impacts	Negative Impacts
		knowledge) while some new online players (i.e., online aggregators and distributors) will enter the market; etc.
To Governments	Better services to citizens, Reduced time and costs of operations; Better relationships with citizens, businesses, other government agencies, and employees; Quicker and Better responsiveness to national security issues and unfortunate events; Enhanced transparency of their operations; Improved engagements from citizen, businesses, other government agencies, and employees; Improved cooperation and collaboration with relevant parties; Diversified campaigns and propaganda activeties; among many others.	Security issues (both inside and outside threats); The wide and quicker distribution of negative news on the government; The difficulties in maintaining 24/7 reliability and accessibility of e-government operations; Unclear and inconsistent, and unexperienced governance of and policies for the Internet; etc.
To Societies	Better availability and accessibility of products, services, information & knowledge from all over the world; Better living (i.e., convenience of online shopping): Better understanding of the world and its history; Exposure of ideas to the global audience; Faster distribution of information and knowledge; Easier, less expensive and more flexible education (i.e., via e-training/learning, online universities); Improved health services and medical advances; Reduced risks associated with performing dangerous tasks; Better crime prevention and control; Better environment protection and sustainability; among many others.	Digital divide (i.e., between developing and developed countries); Health issues arising from using the computer and access the Internet; Job losses arising from automation; Public welfare issues (i.e., Online gaming/-gambling addiction); Public safety issues (i.e., Online pornography, especially child pornography); The loss of face-to-face social networking to social networking sites and other online applications; The e-waste (disposing computing and internet equipments); The difficulties in controlling and reducing carbon emission from computing and Internet equipments, as more and more people buying more and more computing and Internet gears; etc.

(Source: developed for this study)

1.4. Security, Privacy, Policy and Governance Issues Associated with E-business

Security and privacy are two key challenges of e-business. Many individuals are still having difficulties in trusting e-business organizations for the fears of cyber crimes and misuses of their personal & confidential information. Organisations continue to experience various cyber attacks from inside and outside of the organisation. We are also seeing more and more security threats every day. For example, there could be up to 20,000 new malicious programs ever day (Ward 2008). Any type of e-business involves a number of players who use a variety of network and application services that provide access to a variety of data sources. A perpetrator needs only a single weakness in order to attack a system. While some attacks require sophisticated techniques and technologies (i.e., denial of services, phishing, malicious software, hacking), most attacks are not sophisticated (i.e., preying on poor security practice and human weaknesses, social engineering) (Turban et al. 2008, pp. 523-524; Laudon & Trevor 2008, p. 260). Meanwhile, Insiders' breach could be more frequent and more harmful than that of outsiders. The financial losses from a cyber attack can be substantial (i.e., out of the business) for e-businesses. According to a survey conducted by McAfee cited in Chapman (2009), the estimates of the global damage from data loss could be up to US$ 1 trillion. Various parties from small, medium, large, and very large firms, individual consumers, government organisations, military/defence departments, and universities are victims of online security breaches. Security is and will remain a major issue for e-business participants. Generally speaking, security concerns can be found in communication, server and client perspectives. Some basic e-business security issues in the communication aspect include (Turban et al. 2008, p. 522; Laudon & Trevor 2008, p. 264):

- authentication: 'Does this message indeed come from the person/ organisation it claims to come from?'
- privacy: 'Is the message secure and used only by the sender and the receiver?'
- integrity: 'Does the message contain exactly what the sender sent?'
- non-repudiation: 'Can the sender deny that this message was sent?'

These issues resemble the off-line requirements for security, i.e., buying goods at a shop with a credit card. The challenge is to ensure that these issues are addressed when the two parties have no face-to-face contact. Some security issues in the server and client areas include: denial-of-service (DoS) attack, malicious software (i.e., virus, worm, trojan horse), adware, spyware, etc), social networking, online breaches and security threats by insiders.

Security concerns everyone involved in the e-business. A systematic and integrated approach is needed to address e-business security issues. Good e-business security must take into consideration of relevant technologies, organizational policies and procedures, laws and industry standards. Furthermore given the fact that a large number of security breaches are committed by insiders, education and prevention programs should be heavily emphasized. It must be remembered that people are the first defence line, and Technology is the second defence line (Haag et al. 2008).

When the Internet makes it easier and more affordable to collect, store, organize and disseminate information, it has brought great privacy concerns. The individuals' right to privacy may include – to be left alone and to be free from any interference and surveillance from any individuals and organisations (Laudon & Trevor 2008, p. 486). Privacy breaches may occur in various ways, for example (O'Brien & Marakas 2008, p. 506):

- monitoring individuals' private e-mail conversations and computer records, and collecting, sharing information about individuals by tracking their online movement
- monitoring people's location by mobile and paging services
- unauthorised collection and use of personal information.

Another major privacy issue is spam, which has been around for a long time and for which we haven't found an effective solution. According to a report by CISCO cited in News.com.au (2008), about 90% of emails are spam. Another recent privacy concern comes from the increasing use of so called "the human flesh search engine", in which many volunteers on the Internet come together online to expose the personal details of perceived wrongdoers (O'Brien 2008). Solutions to privacy issues have to come from the combined force of users themselves (they have to protect their personal information with more caution), e-business organizations (they need to strictly comply with their privacy policies which are in line with government's privacy-related legislations/laws), industry associations (they can produce industry standards of privacy and encourage e-business organizations within the industry to embrace), governments (they need to establish, update and enforce privacy laws such as Privacy Act Australia (www.privacy.gov.au)), and technological solutions.

Any business faces a number of legal, ethical, and regulatory issues. E-business adds to the scope and scale of those issues as a result of the very connected world we are living in. In many cases legal involvement by the governments is desirable. Many ethical (normally including privacy and other issues such as intellectual property rights, free speech, online fraud, etc) issues require not only national government's involvement, but also need international cooperation and global legislation. The Australian government takes the stance that electronic transactions are legally the same as traditional, paper-based transactions (As a result, e-businesses have to put up with 10% goods and services tax while in the U.S. online transactions will not occur sales tax until 2014). Singapore has passed a similar law. Such a position facilitates e-business because it provides a clear legal framework for transactions. The United States approved the Electronic Signatures in Global and National Commerce Act in 2001. UK's E-Commerce Regulations were published in 2002. Several other European and Asian countries have also established similar e-business/e-commerce laws.

Being relatively new form of business, regulations and policies in regard to e-business are still evolving. It is highly desirable that an international legal framework is developed to guide e-business. There are various ethical issues that relate to e-business, and they could be difficult to deal with. Ethical issues are always tricky. Sometimes activities may be unethical but not illegal, so there is no way that people can be officially stopped from carrying out such activities. Also, activities may be considered unethical by some people or by some cultures, but not by all. Hence it is difficult to establish a clear, well-accepted, international code of e-business ethics. Even though so far there is a lack of established international laws for e-business, progress has been made (i.e., many companies, professional organisations and industry bodies have established and implemented relevant codes, standards, and policies).

Currently we are in a mixed mode policy environment where self-regulation, through a variety of Internet policies, protocols, and standards, and technical bodies (i.e., Internet corporation for assigned names and numbers (ICANN), Internet society (ISOC), the Internet engineering taskforce (IEFT), number resource organization (NRO), international telecommunication union (ITU)), co-exists with some government regulation. In addition, there is a lack of clear Internet governance structure in place. However it is not true that the Internet cannot be controlled. In fact, the internet can be very easily controlled, monitored, and regulated through a central approach (such as done by China, Singapore, North Korea, Thailand, Saudi Arabia and others) (Laudon & Trevor 2008, p. 526). Apparently at present there is a lack of an internationally agreed governance framework which should provide guidelines on why, who, how, when, what aspects of the governance of the Internet and online businesses.

1.5. E-strategy Planning & Implementation

In today's knowledge economy (also called digital or networked economy), organizations need to take into consideration of the impacts and the potential roles of the Internet and the emerging Internet technologies when they are designing their business strategy. Many Internet-based and pure online businesses design their organizational structure and business strategy (i.e., using the Internet for competitive advantages) around the Internet. Other businesses have tried to adjust their business strategy and organizational structure with the assistance from the Internet (i.e., expanding into overseas markets). One of the most difficult aspects of e-business is translating innovative ideas into a framework of specific projects. E-business can be discussed at a high level, but actual implementation in the day-to-day operation is a major challenge. The process is long and complex and is generally not well understood. Academic journals, business magazines, and newspapers contain things such as stories of successful applications, present checklists for web design, and identify providers of various online services and products. However, there is no clear model for turning identified e-business opportunity into a fully operational e-business organisation. This could be the most challenging and lest understood area in e-business. And there is a lack of clear message and well established literature on this area. There are some available tools and techniques associated with strategic planning and implementation, but those tools and techniques could be very confusing to many people. Such confusion reflects the new and relatively immature nature of e-business strategy at present. There is no magic formula for e-business strategy planning and implementation. While there is no agreed framework on e-business strategy planning, we would suggest a framework presented by Turban et al. (2008), which includes activities of (1) initiation, (2) strategy formulation, (3) implementation, and (4) assessment. At the same time, e-business strategic planning process should be a two way street by taking advantages of both top-down and bottom up approaches (i.e., longer term view and more consistence for top down approach, and better understanding of environment, business and customers from people in the front line for bottom up approach) and by avoiding disadvantages of both approaches (i.e., disconnection between strategy formulation and implementation stages which in turn leads to poor plans and failed implementations for top down approach, and short-term focus as well as a fragmented strategy with many separate e-business projects without an integrated plan that links the individual projects for bottom up approach).

Strategy Initiation

The first step and a very important activity in the strategy initiation phase is analyzing the internal and external environments of a business. A convenient way of analysing the firm and the environment is SWOT analysis (O'Brien & Marakas 2008, p. 419), which identifies strengths (S) and weaknesses (W) within the firm and scans for opportunities (O) and threats (T) in the industry and its external operating environment. Another useful tool is Porter's (1985) Five Forces Model, which examines an industry's external operating environment by looking at rivalry of competitors within its industry, threat of new entrants into an industry and its markets, threat posed by substitute products which might capture market share, bargaining power of customers, and bargaining power of suppliers.

After knowing its external operating environment and internal conditions, a firm needs to develop a list of potential e-business initiatives, which exploit opportunities and deal with external threats in light of its strengths and weaknesses. Some broad strategic issues and initiatives the firm may look at include (Turban et al. 2008; Laudon & Traver 2008; The Authors' Own Knowledge):

- keeping the current status (no online business at all or no e-business improvement)
- being a first-mover or a follower
- choosing born-on-the-net or move-to-the-net approach
- having a separate online company? having a separate online brand?
- adopting online advertising & e-marketing
- using the internet for customer relationship management
- using the internet for supply chain management
- adding in an additional online channel to complement existing distribution channels
- establishing an online business

Strategy Formulation

There are four main activities in the e-business strategy formulation stage, namely evaluating specific e-business opportunities, conducting cost/benefit and risk analyses, and selecting an appropriate e-business strategy.

Based on the results of analyses of its internal and external environments, the company is ready to evaluate potential e-business opportunities and select appropriate one for implementation. Generally speaking, companies will look at e-business opportunities when:

- E-business can provide a solution for its internal problem or enable it to exploit the market opportunities (i.e., an additional distribution channel, a global operation)

- E-business can enhance its operations and business performance (i.e., enhancing customer relationships, improving supply chains, streamlining business processes, optimizing internal communication, etc)
- Certain internet technologies or e-business applications have become industry standard or have been adopted by their competitors, industry leaders, and have become a strategic necessity (in this case, a business may face the choices of either participating in e-business or going out of the business)
- They have already possessed advanced Internet technologies which will be a waste if they are not utilized
- There are requirements of compliance imposed by the government and/or industry associations. So businesses have no option but to invest in e-business
- When the existing systems cannot cope with the demands and challenges of networked individuals, society, and economy.

Finding suitable e-business opportunities is not easy as there are a multitude of choices and many uncertainties involved in the e-business (after all e-business is still relatively new phenomenon for many industries and businesses). There are no universal views or commonly-agreed methods so far. Turban et al. (2008, p. 655) introduce a systematic approach: the internet portfolio map. Tjan (2001) created it by adapting the Boston Consulting Group's approach. Instead of trading off market potential and market share, the Internet portfolio map is based on company fit and project viability, both of which can be either low or high. Viability can be assessed by various criteria such as market value potential, time to positive cash flow, time to implementation, and funding requirements. The Internet portfolio map can be a very effective tool for selecting an appropriate e-business strategy.

Like many other investments, an e-business project has to go through the assessment of cost-benefit analysis and risk analysis before final decisions can be concluded. To properly evaluate an e-business investment, a multiple-perspective and a balanced approach should be adopted, which should look at: (1) both tangible and non-tangible costs and benefits; (2) both qualitative and quantitative dimensions;

(3) both financial and non-financial perspectives; (4) strategic, tactical, operational & other factors.

At the same time, risk is inherent in all business activities (especially for entering new territory), and there is no exception for e-business projects. Managing e-business risk is a process of identifying the potential risks, analyzing the potential impact of the identified risks, and taking appropriate actions to deal with identified risks associated with proposed e-business projects (Turban et al. 2008, pp. 656). There are some good guidelines on risk management around, an example is AS/NZS-4360 Risk Management Standard 2004 for organizations in New Zealand and Australia, which includes steps of (1) establishing the context: what part of the organisation are we talking about?, (2) identifying risks: what could cause harm or is a threat or has unknown consequences?, (3) analysing risks: is it likely to happen?, (4) evaluating risks: what would its impact be? and (5) treating risks: what can we do about it?.

When a firm is deciding on its e-business strategy, a number of factors (i.e., industry, firm, customer, technology development, society, economy) needed to be considered. Two techniques which can be used to help identify specific e-business strategic applications among many others are:

- Critical success factors (O'Brien & Marakas 2008, p.380): Critical success factors require managers to identify the most important factors which help achieve organisational goals. This approach focuses on the particular part of the business which should be addressed first and foremost. It highlights the part of the business, which might benefit most from e-business.
- Value chain analysis (Porter & Miller 1985 cited in O'Brien & Marakas 2008, p. 53): Value chain analysis focuses on the internal activities of the firm and identifies where e-business can contribute to improve its performance and help achieve its strategic objectives/goals.

Furthermore, there are other issues involved in e-business strategy formulation stage, including online pricing strategy (i.e., how to price effectively for products and services sold in the online and offline channels?), channel conflicts (i.e., how to handle online and offline channels?), and so on.

Strategy Implementation

Some activities involve in the implementation stage may include:

- allocating/securing sufficient capital and resources to the e-business projects
- establishing an e-business project team and assign responsibilities: The team is responsible for implementation of the e-business project. Tasks are identified, responsibilities are assigned, and project leaders & champions are appointed. A good project plan should be developed and closely followed. In the meantime, effective change management is essential when organizations are adding e-business initiatives into their existing operations.
- deciding a development approach: Organizations can choose from a number of options. Each of them has advantages and disadvantages (see Table 1.5).
- deciding a conversion approach: Organizations can choose among four options (McKeown 2000, p. 263) of implementation: pilot implementation (installing and testing with one of the organization until it is evident that the new system performs correctly and then spread to other parts of the organization), parallel implementation (using both the old and the new system until it is evident that the new system performs correctly), direct/plunge implementation (discarding the old system completely and immediately starting to use the new system), and phased implementation (implementing the new system in phases).
- addressing security & privacy issues: Security and privacy issues must be considered throughout the development process. Appropriate levels of security and privacy policies should be implemented.
- working on integration issues: For many businesses integration issues (i.e., being able to communicate with business partners' systems; the integration with existing systems) are also needed to be addressed when they are developing their e-business systems.

Table 1.5: Comparison of development options

Development Options	Advantages	Disadvantages
Internal Development	o Competitive advantage o Complete control over final systems o Builds technical skills and functional knowledge of developers	o Requires dedicated effort of in-house staff o Development can be slow o Costs may be higher than working with other approaches o Systems may not work when completed or may not provide desired functionalities
Outsourcing	o Cost savings o Ease of transition to new technologies o Better strategic and business focus o Better management of information systems/ information technology (IS/IT) staff – vendor has the knowledge and skills in effectively managing IS/IT staff o Handles peaks with greater capacity of vendor o Consolidates data centres, which is very difficult to be done by an internal group o Infuses cash via selling equipment to the outsourcing vendor	o Loss of control o High switching cost o Lack of technological innovation o Loss of strategic advantage o Reliance on outsourcer o Security and reliability o Evaporation of cost saving, i.e., perceived costs may never be realised due to factors such as out-of-date processes, costs arising from software upgrades, unspecified growth and new technologies not anticipated in the contract. And some savings may be hard to measure
Acquisition	o Could purchase a complete system from a vendor o Could purchase different systems from various vendors o Fastest approach of all	o Little competitive advantage o Must accept functionalities of purchased systems o May not integrate well with existing systems o May require modification and customization to meet needs
Use of Application Service Providers (ASP)	o Firms, especially small and medium enterprises, will enjoy the benefit of reduced need for internal IS/IT staff o Saving money on internal	o Less control over the applications (i.e., on issues such as when applications should be upgraded? how access to applications is facilitated?) o Applications from ASP tend to

Table 1.5: *Continued*

Development Options	Advantages	Disadvantages
	infrastructure and initial capital layouts o Some companies find it easier to 'rent' software from an ASP and avoid the problems associated with installing, operating and maintaining complex systems like enterprise planning systems o Easier to walk away from unsatisfactory systems and solutions o Quicker to respond to market with applications available from ASP	address routine problems, there is not much attention on how particular problems the organisation is facing are addressed o ASP solutions tend to be rather generic (i.e., normally allowing only 20% customisation for any given company)

(Sources: developed from McKeown 2000, p. 251; Peralson & Saunders 2004, pp. 198–199; Hoffer et al. 2005, pp. 32–33, 38–39, 40–41; The Authors' Own Knowledge)

Project and Strategy Assessment

As for any project, post-implementation evaluation of the e-business project is important. It helps unveil problems in the planning and implementation process so that those problems could be avoided in future e-business projects. It can measure the execution of e-business strategy, ensure projects are delivering what they were supposed to deliver, determine if the e-business strategy and projects are still viable in the current environment, reassess the initial strategy in order to learn from mistakes and improve future planning, identify failing projects as soon as possible, and determine why they failed to avoid the same problems on subsequent projects. It can also help identify realized benefits and costs of the project. Strategy assessment should look at beyond metrics (i.e., some widely used metrics of net present value, internal rate of return, return on investment, payback period, total cost of ownership, click-through rate, conversation rate, speed, web traffic, availability, response time, etc) and evaluate from multiple dimensions (i.e., evaluating as per strategic, tactical, operational considerations by looking at all the tangible, intangible, financial and non-financial costs, benefits, and risks as suggested by Gunasekaran et al. (2001), which could assist in dealing with difficulties in measuring tangible & non-financial benefits and costs of e-business projects.

1.6. Launching a Successful E-Start-up

The internet has provided fantastic opportunities for people who are interested in being an entrepreneur and make their dream of being their own bosses more affordable and much easier. One can start running your business overnight from your home. The basic ICTs needed are: a computer, an internet connection, and a website (or even web pages if not decided to have own website). The successful stories of e-start-ups (i.e., Microsoft, Yahoo, Google, YouTube, E-bay, Amazon, Dell, Facebook, Flickr, Seek, Wotif, Realestate.com.au, Paypal, Skype, MySpace, among many others) have inspired many people's interest to become an e-entrepreneur, and has changed young generation's perceptions of top jobs. When being a lawyer or a doctor or a highly-paid white collar professional is still attractive to many young people, more and more young people also would like to start up their own e-businesses and become mega rich in a few years time.

While there do have some very successful businesses online, it is not easy to succeed in the online world. What are the success factors? Unfortunately there is no clear answer here; and not everyone can make his/her e-dream come true and become successful like Bill Gates (the founder of Microsoft), Michael Dell (the founder of Dell Computer), Larry Page & Sergey Brin (the co-founders of Google), Jerry Yang (the founder of Yahoo), Jack Ma (the founder of Alibaba), and Mark Zuckerberg (the founder of Facebook).

On top of the e-business strategy planning and implementation process discussed in the previous section, on the individual level, e-entrepreneurs (like other entrepreneurs) need to have or equip themselves with certain personal qualities and some critical success factors. Some of them could include:

- passion towards e-business (have an e-dream)
- persistence (never give up)

- the ability of executing your ideas (don't just dream and you need to do it)
- advanced analytical skills (excellent at finding opportunities and gap)
- innovativeness, willingness to take risk
- excellent decision-making capacity (making tough decision when necessary)
- strong communication skills
- flexibility & adaptability to changes and new environments
- very strong self-learning ability (since you need to get a new e-business up and running)
- discipline (willingness to sacrifice a lot of enjoyment and comfort)
- the ability of integrating resources from different sources
- adequate knowledge in all areas of running a business
- a good management team and sufficient financial resources are also very critical
- a good business plan
- sufficient capital and resources
- to some extent, a bit of good luck (i.e., knowing right people, at right place, at right time) also will enhance the success chance of your e-dream.

2. E-Business Technologies

2.1. E-Business Information Technology Infrastructure

E-business activities are supported by various technologies (i.e., hardware, software, networks). Some technologies existed and were in use before being applied to e-business; other technologies were developed specifically to enable e-business activities. This section looks at the technology infrastructure that supports and enables e-business activities. All e-business activities rely on specific technologies for support. It is important to understand that e-business applications are built on top of a number of technologies. The underlying technologies provide a layered, integrated infrastructure which enables e-business applications to be deployed. The layered structure means that each layer depends on the layer below and cannot function without the lower layers. Table 1.6 include some important layers of e-business IT infrastructure.

2.2. Enterprise Applications/Systems

Many companies have moved from mainframe legacy systems, which focus on traditional business functions or internal business processes, to integrated cross-functional enterprise applications, which emphasise accomplishing fundamental business processes in concert with customers, suppliers, partners, and employees. Integrated systems, such as enterprise resource planning systems, knowledge management systems, supply chain management systems, and customer relationship management systems, allow the same data to be used for multiple applications; information output from one function can easily become data input to another function. Very often only one integrated/centralised database needs to be maintained. Many organisations view cross-functional enterprise systems as a strategic way to use IT to share information resources and improve the efficiency and effectiveness of business processes, thus helping an e-business organization achieve its strategic objectives.

Enterprise resource planning (ERP) systems focus on improving the efficiency of a company's internal business processes, such as production, distribution, and financial processes. Customer relationship management (CRM) systems mostly deal with acquiring and retaining customers, especially profitable customers. Supply chain management (SCM) systems primarily provide an organization with solutions in optimising the efficiency and effectiveness of its supply chain and enhancing its relationship with its suppliers. Knowledge management systems (KMSs) aim at organising, sharing and applying knowledge within and outside the organisation and creating new knowledge. Even though there enterprise systems have different emphases, they complement and enhance each other. For example, without quality products, which are largely influenced by effective internal operations facilitated by ERP systems, CRM systems become meaningless. In the meantime, without accurate and timely information on customers

Table 1.6: E-business information technology infrastructure

Basic Technologies	Functions	Application Examples
E-business Applications	Support business processes of organizations (i.e., B2B, B2C, and intra-organizational communications) and activities of individuals (i.e., communications, networking, community building, knowledge sharing, online shopping, online selling, online information search) as well as the government's functions	E-marketplaces, E-procurement applications, Sales Force Automation applications, E-tailing, Online Banking, Online Publishing, E-learning, Online auctions, Search engines, Social networks, Online communities, E-government, etc.
Interfacing, Sharing, Integration & Aggregation Applications	Tie different services together and integrate with business partners' applications	Service oriented architecture (SOA), Web Services, Virtualizations, Grid Computing, Semantic Web, Web Science, Middleware, Enterprise Application Integration (EAI), etc.
Common Business Services Applications	Provide services required for online transactions and website functions	Online security, Online authentication, Web addresses, Storage repositories, Electronic payment systems, Smart cards, etc.
Transportation Services Technologies	Publish and distribute information in different formats (i.e., in text, audio, fax, video) on the internet	Hyper text transfer protocol (HTTP), Transmission control protocol/Internet protocol (TCP/IP), Electronic Data Interchange (EDI), E-mail, World Wide Web (WWW), Hypertext markup language (HTML), Java, Extensible markup language (XML), Virtual reality modelling language (VRML), etc.
Telecommunication Networks	Connect different devices together and Enable online communications	The Internet, TV Networks, Telephone Networks, Wireless Networks, Intranets, Extranets, Virtual Private Networks (VPNs), Local Area Networks (LANs), Wide Area Networks (WANs), etc.

(Source: developed from Turban et al. 2008; Watson et al. 2000; McKeown 2000; Kalakota & Whinston 1997; Laudon & Traver 2008; The Authors' Own Knowledge) recorded and analysed in CRM systems, ERP and SCM systems cannot work properly. Furthermore without knowledge stored, organized and disseminated by knowledge management systems, the organization's efforts of implementing enterprise-wide (also called cross-functional information systems) will not succeed easily since many costly mistakes will be repeated again and again and many wheels will be reinvented again and again. These systems themselves can be interconnected with enterprise application integration (EAI) software so that the business users of these applications can more easily access the information resources they need to support the needs of customers, suppliers, and business partners.

2.3. Data Warehouse and Data Mining

Technologies such as data warehouse and data mining allow organisations to gain vast amount of business intelligence, which basically is information for decision-making. The focus of data warehouse and data mining applications in many organizations is to have better understanding of customers and thus develop more targeted marketing and better products and services. A data warehouse extracts current and historical data from both internal and external data sources and reorganises those data into a central database for management reporting and analysis via various tools (i.e., online analytical processing (OLAP), data mining). While databases normally contain information in a series of two-dimensional tables, which means that one can only view two dimensions of information at one time, the information in a data warehouse is multi-dimensional and consists of layers of columns and rows (Haag et al. 2008, p. 83). Dimensions could include such things as products, promotions, stores, category, region, stock price, date, time, and even the weather. The ability to look at information from different dimensions can add tremendous business insight. A critical factor for the successful use of data warehouse and data mining is maintaining high quality information in the data warehouse all the time (i.e., via certain cleaning processes and tools). Without high quality information the organisation will be unable to make good business decisions and will face a situation of garbage in and garbage out.

Data mining is a major use of data warehouse databases. Data in data warehouses is analysed to reveal hidden correlations, associations, patterns, and trends and make better predictions (O'Brien & Marakas 2006, p. 147). Through data mining, firms can search for valuable business information and business opportunities. Online analytical processing (OLAP) is another important data analysis tool, and it supports manipulation of and real-time analysis of large volumes of data from multiple dimensions and perspectives (O'Brien & Marakas 2006, p. 147). An organization can capture its customer information from all customer touch points (i.e., face-to-face channels, online channel, call centres, video channels (even including information in the security surveillance cameras and videos), mail and fax services, suppliers & business partners) as well as other data sources. The captured data can be organized into a single customer data repository or data warehouse. Data mining allows managers to analyse aggregated customer behaviour to identify profitable and unprofitable customers as well as customer activities (e.g. purchasing patterns, etc.) while online analytical processing (OLAP) allows them to dynamically analyse customer activities to spot trends or problems involving customers (Laudon & Trevor 2008).

2.4. Integration

For an organization to participate in e-business effectively, its e-business applications must integrate with the organisation's existing internal infrastructure and applications (e.g. CRM, SCM, ERP, KMS, servers, databases, etc.), and with external servers, applications and databases of its customers, suppliers and business partners. Such internal and external integrations are not easy to achieve. For example, many large organisations have heavily invested in in-house systems and have streamlined internal operations by purchasing and implementing enterprise resource planning (ERP) systems. In many firms the ERP system is the core of logistics and planning and it contains a wealth of valuable information. Those organisations now face the challenge of incorporating their expensive ERP operations with e-business. Integrating online payment systems could be another challenge for many e-business organizations. Furthermore organisations often take the approach of best-of-breed for the reason that no one vendor can respond to an organisation's all needs (Haag et al. 2008, p. 138). As a result, many organisations have various systems and applications from multiple vendors.

Sharing and organising information sitting in multiple databases and applications internally and externally could be very time-consuming and inefficient. Fortunately, many applications and approaches are available in the market to help organizations' integration efforts. Some of them include: Service oriented architecture (SOA), Web services, Virtualizations, Grid Computing, Cloud Computing, Semantic Web, Web Sciences, Middleware, Enterprise Application Integration (EAI), etc. And standards such as electronic data interchange (EDI)/Internet-based EDI and XML could also greatly assist e-business organizations' integration efforts.

2.5. Addressing Security & Privacy Concerns through Technology

Each of the basic security issues in the communication perspective mentioned previously (namely authentication, privacy, integrity and non-repudiation) can be addressed by certain technology tools and practices, such as encryption (the process of scrambling (encrypting) a message in such a way (i.e., making the size of a key bigger with more bits) that it is difficult, expensive, or time-consuming for an unauthorized person to unscramble (decrypt) it), digital certificates (normally issued by third parties (i.e., verisign.com) to verify the authenticity of the engaging parties), digital signature to identify authenticate the sender of a document, secure socket layer (SSL) (a protocol invented by Netscape to provide secure online credit card transactions for both consumers and merchants and a major standard for online credit card payments), and secure electronic transaction (SET) (an open standard and protocol designed to provide secure online credit card transactions for both consumers and merchants; developed jointly by Netscape, Visa, MasterCard, and others). The following Table 1.7 shows in the first column a variety of technological tools while in the following columns the ticks indicate the use of these tools to help solve security problems

Table 1.7: Technologies to address basic security issues

	Authenticity	Privacy	Integrity	Non-repudiation
Digital Certificates	√			
Digital Signatures	√			√
Encryption		√	√	
SSL	√	√	√	
SET	√	√	√	√

(Source: developed from Turban et al. 2008; Laudon & Trevor 2008; The Authors' Own Knowledge)

associated with authenticity, privacy, integrity and non-repudiation. It is noted that not all the tools can deal with all four issues.

Some technologies for securing e-business network (client and server focus) include (a) firewall to monitor incoming traffic, (b) proxy servers to handle all the outgoing communications, (c) virtual private network (VPN) for low-cost and secure point-to-point communication via public internet, (d) intrusion detection systems (IDSs) to watch for suspicious activities and take automated action based on what it sees, (e) anti-virus & anti-spam software (such as Symantec's Norton 360, PCTools' Spyware Doctor, McFee's anti virus package), (f) authentication and biometric control applications (i.e., login user names & passwords, keystrokes, voice recognitions, iris scans, finger prints, faces, palm patterns), among many others. For security issues associated with insiders, the best approach is probably education and training coupled with relevant policies and procedures.

When most of thc tcchnologies and measures discussed for addressing security concerns of e-business could deal with or assisting in dealing with privacy issues suggested in the previous section 1.4, some specific technologies include spyware blockers (i.e., Spyware Doctor, ZoneAlarm), pop-up blockers (i.e., those pop-up blockers embedded in various browsers), E-mail encryption (i.e., Safemessage.com, Pretty good privacy(pgp.com)), Cookie manager (i.e., Cookie Crusher, Cookie control functions embedded in various browsers), Privacy Policy Reader (P3P) (i.e., embedded in Internet Explorer 6.0 and above) (Laudon & Travor 2008, p. 501). Some specific anti-spam technologies and techniques include: Authentication of E-mail, Sender-policy-framework (SPF) and/or Sender-ID, Message Enhancements for Transmission Authorization (META), Existence of the senders' domain and eliciting a response, Existence of a point record (PTR), Blacklists, Filtering (i.e., via Keyword filters, Bayesian filters, Behavioural filters, Fingerprint filters, Heuristic filters), among many others (OECD 2006).

For internet fraud, individual consumers and buyers need to ensure they only access online businesses that are known or have good reputation (they can check themselves with local commerce or fair trading or consumer protection authorities or with third party assurance services providers (i.e., Best Business Bureau (BBB), TRUSTe.org) or through their peers). On the other hand, the sellers and merchants, can protect themselves by accessing online databases (i.e., www.cardcops.com, for credit numbers with chargeback history), using the five tools of digital certificates, digital signatures, encryption, SSL, SET discussed earlier in this section, using intelligent software to identify possibly questionable customers and identify warning signals for possibly fraudulent transactions, and making better efforts in verifying the customer (i.e., investigating inconsistency in addresses, contact numbers, account details, identifications), among many others.

Finally good e-business security and privacy practices must take into consideration of technology solutions, people (both users and managers), organizational policies and procedures, laws and industry standards.

3. Conclusions

This chapter presents an overview of E-Business and E-business technologies. It first presents the exponential growth figures of Internet across the globe. It is interesting to observe how various regions of the world have embraced Internet and how it has penetrated into individual's life and working environment. The chapter then presents various e-business models and sheds some light on the impacts of e-business (positive and negative) on individuals, organizations, Governments etc. After touching on e-business strategies and implementation issues the chapter moves into giving some basic understanding on e-business technologies. The security and privacy issues are also discussed.

This chapter sets the basic scene on e-business. It will help the readers to understand the basics and move on to some newer concepts and applications of e-business in subsequent chapters.

References

AS/NZS 4360 (2004) Risk Management, Standards Australia International Ltd, GPO Box 5420, Sydney, NSW 2001 and Standards New Zealand, Private Bag 2439, Wellington 6020, 2004.

Chapman, G. (2009) Cybercrime losses up to $US 1 trillion, The Australian, Februray 03, 2009, Online, Available at: http://www.australianit.news.com.au/story/0,24897,24997483-24169,00.html (accessed on February 4, 2009).

Economist Intelligence Unit (2009) The World in Figures: Industries (E-commerce), The World in 2009, The Economist, pp. 120.

Economist Intelligence Unit & IBM Institute for Business Value (2007) The 2007 e-readiness rankings: raising the bar, The Economist, pp. 1-25.

Emily, R. & Holland, A. (2007) 50 Great e-Business and the Minds Behind them, Random House Australia.

Guanasekaran, A. Love, P. Rahimi, F. & Miele, R. (2001) A Model for Investment Justification in Information Technology Projects, International Journal of Information Management, Vol. 21, No. 5, pp. 349-364.

Haag, S., Baltzan, P. & Phillips, A. (2008) Business Driven Technology, 2nd edition, McGraw-Hill Irwin, Boston, U.S.A.

Hoffer, J.A. , George, J.F. & Valacich, J.S. (2005) Modern Systems Analysis and Design, 4th edn, Prentice Hall.

Laudon, K.C. & Laudon, J.P. (2005) Essentials of Management Information Systems: Managing the Digital Firm, 6/E, 2005, Prentice Hall.

Laudon, K.C. & Traver, C.G. (2008) E-commerce: Buisness, Technology, Society 2008, 4th edn, Addison Wesley, Boston, USA.

Kalakota, R. & Whinston, A.B. (1997) Electronic Commerce – A Manager's Guide, Addison Wesley, Reading, MA.

Kalakota, R. & Robinson, M. (1999) E-Business – Roadmap for Success, Addison Wesley, Reading, MA.

McKeown, P. (2000) Information Technology and the Networked Economy, Boston: Thomson Learning.

News.com.au (2008) 90 percent of email is spam, Online, Available at: http://www.news.com.au/technology/story/0,24808797-5014239,00.html (accessed on January 23, 2009).

O'Brien, C. (2008) The human flesh search engine, Forbes, November 21, 2008, Online Available at: http://www.forbes.com/2008/11/21/human-flesh-search-tech-identity08-cx_cb_1121o (acccessed on November 22, 2008).

O'Brien, J.A. & Marakas, G.M. (2006) Management Information Systems, 7th edn. Boston: Irwin/McGraw-Hill.

O'Brien, J.A. & Marakas, G.M. (2008) Management Information Systems, 8th edition, McGraw-Hill Irwin, Boston, U.S.A.

OECD (2006) Element IV: Anti-spam technologies, Online Available at: http://www.oced.antispam.org/article.php3?id_article=241 (accessed on January 2, 2009).

Porter, M.E. (1985) Competitive Advantage, Free Press, New York, 1985.

Pearlson, K.E. & Saunders, C.S. (2004) Managing and Using Information Systems: A Strategic Approach, 2nd edn, Wiley, Danvers.

Rappa, M. (2008) Business Models on the Web, Online Available: http://digitalenterprise.org/models/models.html (accessed on Jan 17, 2009).

Rayport, J.F. & Jaworski, B.J. (2004) Introduction to E-commerce, 2nd edn, McGraw-Hill, Boston, USA.

Tjan, A.K. (2001) Finally a Way to Put Your Internet Portfolio in order, Harvard Business Review, Vol. 79, No. 2, pp.76-87.

Turban, E., King, D., McKay, J., Marshall, P., Lee, J. & Viehland, D. (2008) Electronic Commerce 2008: A Managerial Perspective, International edn, Prentice Hall, Upper Saddle River, NJ.

Ward, M. (2008) 'Boom year' for high-tech criminals, BBC News, Online Available at: http://newsvote.bbc.co.uk/mapps/pagetools/print/news.bbc.co.uk.2/hi/technology/77 (accessed on December 30, 2008).

Watson, R.T., Berthon, P., Pitt, L.F. & Zinkhan, G.M. (2000) Electronic Commerce, The Dryden Press, Fort Worth, TX.

CHAPTER 2

OVERVIEW-PART II: B2C, B2B AND OTHER TYPES OF E-BUSINESS

Jun Xu

Graduate College of Management, Southern Cross University, Australia

Mohammed Quaddus

Graduate School of Business, Curtin University of Technology, Australia

This chapter looks at various types of e-business, including B2C, B2B, C2C, Blogs, Wikis, Social Networks, and Mobile Business. The emphasis of this chapter is on two most dominating e-business types: B2C and B2B. B2C e-business is presented from the aspects of e-tailing, online services provision, online B2C payment systems and Internet marketing. Dimensions of B2B e-business discussed in this chapter include types of B2B e-business, online payment systems for B2B e-business, and B2B e-business for managing supply chains.

1. B2C E-Business

1.1. E-tailing

Electronic retailing (also called e-tailing, online retailing) refers to selling retail goods and services online. This type of e-business is highly visible and has received much attention by the popular press (especially success stories such as amazon.com and dell.com). The Internet has provided opportunities for new, fully online retail and distribution businesses, and is making many existing, brick-and-mortar retailers wonder to what extent they ought to put their own operations online.

While there exist different ways of categorizing e-tailing models (i.e., general purpose vs speciality, global vs regional, or classification as per revenue models), a popular approach is classifying e-tailing according to distribution channels. Under this approach e-tailing can appear in the following formats (Turban et al. 2008, pp. 100):

- Mail-order retails that go online (i.e., www.landsend.com)
- Direct selling from manufactures (i.e., www.dell.com, www.jaguar.com)
- Pure online retailers (born-on-the-net retailers) (i.e., www.amazon.com, www.dealsdirect.com.au)
- Click-and-mortar retailers (online retailers have both offline and online operations, i.e., www.walmart.com, www.target.com, www.coles.com, www.woolworth.com. Most of online retailers are click-and-mortar retailers and are embarking on the Internet for leveraging the benefits of it and creating an additional or complementary channel for its existing operations)
- Internet (online) malls (online shopping malls) (i.e., http://smallbusiness.yahoo.com and www.choicemall.com)

While there are different ways of conducting retail online, some common factors of successful e-tailing do exist. Table 2.1 presents some of such factors.

Table 2.1: Some success factors of E-tailing

Success Factors	Brief Explanation
Speak with one voice	Provide customers with consistent information and services from online and offline channels.
Empower the customer with high quality services	Provide customer with services with 24/7 available channel, secure and smooth online shopping system, extensive information on products and services, assistance in purchasing decision, flexible order fulfillment methods (such as common carrier, overnight delivery, and pickup in the nearby store), personalized & customized services.
Leverage the multi-channels	Offer the advantages of each channel (i.e., picking up items ordered online from shops, returning items purchased online to physical stores), especially when many customers use the web (or the Internet we use them interchangeably) for information before they purchase in the shop (also called "web-influenced store sales") (Economist Intelligence Unit 2009).

Table 2.1: *Continued*

Success Factors	Brief Explanation
Align online and offline channels	Balance resources and support for online and offline channels.
Create strategic alliances	Set up strategic alliances with traditional retailers and other business partners (i.e., parties along the supply chain of the business). Such move is especially important for online start-ups and small & medium retailers.
Establish online communities and social networks	Establish online communities (e.g., forums, chat groups) and explore the opportunities in social networks. Online retailers should utilize the power of network and the free knowledge (also called mass intelligence, collective intelligence/wisdom, public knowledge) on the Internet.
Don't ignore profitability	Online retailers usually are not profitable for various issues in the areas such as revenue model, cost control and pricing strategy.
Practise risk Management	Manage risks (i.e., cultural, financial, legal, technological, competition-related, consumer-related risks and Internet crime) effectively.
Establish and maintain trust between customer and the online retailer	Work hard on security, privacy, order fulfilment, customers' complains, and warranty, exchange & refund issues.
Watch the cost of marketing	Watch for the cost for the marketing since it can be very expensive. Most customers (especially customers for Internet start-ups), especially long-term loyal customers come from affiliate links, search engines, or personal recommendations not from big spending advertising activities.
Secure sufficient finance and work on cost control	Start with sufficient funds while working hard on cost control: Online retailers should have enough capital to achieve sufficient size and maturity. In the meantime, the flexibility and 24/7 availability can be a double-edged sword (i.e., while customers enjoy never-closed online shops they will react strongly when the site is not available. And how about communication and maintenance costs for 24/7 services?).
Build effective web site	The web site must have excellent technical performance and functionalities, reliability, consistency, flexibility, and availability.
Ensure user friendliness and usefulness of the web site	Keep the web site user friendly and useful (i.e., ease of use, simple design, comprehensive and updated information).
Have effective order fulfilment process	Many online retailers collapsed because of the failure in delivering ordered products to customers timely (i.e., the collapse of furniture.com)

Table 2.1: *Continued*

Success Factors	Brief Explanation
Address problems timely and effectively	Address problems timely and effectively when they occur (i.e., talking to customers directly immediately, having fair policies & procedures, offering compensations and apologies). It will cost a business much more resources to acquire a new customer than selling to an existing customer. And the damage caused by a unhappy customer could be much bigger than it looks-the negative part of the effect of word-of-mouth.
Manage relationship with customers	Actively acquire, engage and retain customers via great content, high quality information, regularly emerged new products & services, user friendly marketing & promotion, excellent customer services, value-added services (information from multiple sources, total solutions by combining services from different vendors, certification, trust and evaluation services), memberships/clubs/ online communities, and other online applications (google.com, adidas.com, nike.com, microsoft.com, ford.com are some good examples of top consumer websites according to Accenture's Marketing Science Group (2007))

(Source: developed from Turban et al. 2008, pp. 136-140; Collier & Bienstock 2006; Accenture 2007; The Authors' Own Knowledge)

While online retailers enjoy such benefits as wider product selection (there is no limitation of physical space for product display), 24/7 availability, convenience, cheaper prices, easier comparison of prices and vendors, better personalisation, the ability of mass customisation, the capability of mass customization, up-to-date information, global reach, an additional business channel, a unique opportunity to test new products and services and to obtain customer feedback, not all the products are suitable for the online channel. Some popular online goods include: computers & software, electronics (i.e., MPS players, USB drivers, mobile phones, digital cameras), small tools for home improvement, books & magazines, food, sporting goods, office supplies, music, CD & DVDs, videos & video games, toys, baby stuff, health & beauty products, entertainment, apparel, shoes, services (e.g. travel, accommodation, stock trading, Internet banking, real estate, insurance), and specialized & niche products (such as antiques) that are not able to sell in the physical world since it is difficult to reach critical mass to earn the profit (Turban et al. 2008, pp. 95-97; www.amazon.com; www.dealsdirect.com.au; The

Authors' Own Knowledge). Some characteristics of goods for successful e-tailing are: (Turban et al. 2008, pp. 98: The Authors' Own Knowledge):

- products from established brands or well-known vendors (i.e., Lands' End, Dell, Sony)
- digitized format (i.e., software, music, virtual goods, journal articles and other e-publications)
- relatively inexpensive items (i.e., office supplies)
- frequently purchased items (groceries, food)
- commodities with standard specifications (i.e., books, music CDs, airline tickets): for such products physical inspection is not important
- well-known packaged items that cannot be opened even in a traditional store (i.e., vitamins, wines, chocolates, under-wears, contact lenses)
- not so bulky items which can be transported and delivered easily and cheaply: Furniture is not a favourable choice for e-tailing.

Except the legal/regulatory concerns (i.e., selling prescribed drugs online), more and more retailers are embarking on the Internet as a result of competition, changing customers & their needs, wide adoption of the Internet , and rapid advances of technologies. At the same time, when e-business organizations are facing issues such as security, privacy, the lack of tangible elements of online transactions (i.e., cannot smell and touch products), and the lack of human interaction online, more and more people are shopping online. And the more experience people have with online shopping, the more likely they are to buy from online retailers. On the other hand, the prospect of participating in e-tailing is both tempting and intimidating. Organisations considering embarking on online selling should evaluate the advantages and disadvantages, specifically tailored to their own business context. What is the future trend of B2C e-business? According to Jupitermdia.com (2006) (cited in Turban et al. 2008 (pp. 97)), many offline transactions are heavily influenced by research conducted online, with approximately 85 percent of online shoppers reporting that they used the Internet to research and influence their offline shopping choices. According to eMarketer cited in Economist Intelligence Unit (2009), Internet -influenced store sales will reach US$ 667 billion while online retail will achieve the volume of US$ 179.6 billion in the U.S. in 2009. Another trend in B2C e-business is the use of rich media in online advertising. For example, we will see more applications such as virtual reality being used in online shopping. The use of cell phones to shop online is also increasing rapidly. Lastly the difference between B2B and B2C sometimes could not be very clear (For example, Dell and Amazon also sell the products to corporations).

1.2. Providing Services Online

E-business is not purely the domain of organisations which have a product to sell. In fact, the service industries (in particular, the financial industry) were among the very first to embrace electronic transactions among business partners. Many services can be delivered very effectively on an online basis, for example, banking (i.e., www.netbank.com.au), stock trading (i.e., www.e-trade.com), travel and tourism services (i.e., www.qantas.com.au), employment services (i.e., www.seek.com.au), real estate services (i.e., www.realestate.com.au), entertainment (i.e., www.cinemanow.com, www.games.yahoo.com), learning (i.e., www.univertas21.com), publishing (i.e., www.academicglobalpublishing.com), government services (i.e., E-government initiatives in Hong Kong, Australia and other countries). All these industries have embraced the Internet as an outlet for their services and a means to reach customers. Speed of services and convenience are the main drivers of e-business development in these industries. And cost reduction is another major motivation.

1.3. B2C Online Payments Systems

When products and services are sold electronically, there has to be a means of paying for the transaction electronically. Paper-based payments cannot support the speed, security, privacy and internationalisation needed in the online environment. The benefits of electronic payment systems include the reduction in transaction costs, increased speed of transactions, and increased geographic reach in transactions. So far the overwhelming majority of online purchases are made with credit cards.

This may change in future. The use of debit cards, Paypal and other peer-to-peer payment services are getting very popular. In fact, many online businesses are accepting payments via credit cards, Paypal, debit cards, direct deposit to the bank account (via Internet transfer). The adoption of Paypal payment system is quite noticeable, especially when many popular online payment businesses failed (i.e., the very recent examples of Bitpass who closed down on Jan 19, 2007 and Peppercoin who was acquired on April 16, 2007). On top of its user-friendliness and usefulness, its use in E-bay has played an important role in its popularity. From this perspective, Google Checkout and Microsoft Points (online payments systems from Google and Microsoft respectively) may have better chance of success than those standalone electronic payment systems.

While credit card payments are very popular in online transactions for the reasons of the ease-of-use and the ability to use the existing credit card infrastructurc, c-business organizations need to deal with trust and security challenges associated with using credit cards online. Also, there exist deficiencies in credit card payment systems. Many users come from countries where the use of credit cards is not common-place. And many younger users don't have access to credit and debit cards. In addition, there is a lack of online payment systems for micropayment purchases (purchases less than US$ 10).

B2C e-business online payment methods include: credit & debit cards from financial institutions, virtual credit cards (i.e., virtual credit card from Citibank, http://www.citibank.com/us/cards/tour/cb/shp_van.htm), e-wallets (or e-purses) (i.e., Qwallets, http://qwallet.com/), smart cards (i.e., visa smart card containing an embedded microchip that enables predefined operations or the addition, deletion, or manipulation of information on the card), electronic/digital cash for low-priced items (i.e., Digital cash from clearbit, http://www.clearbit.com/), stored-value cards (i.e., National Australia Bank's NAB gift card), online loyalty programs (i.e., www.mypoints.com), person-to-person payment methods (i.e., Paypal), and so on. The wireless payment systems (i.e., paying from your mobile phone) are emerging. For example, a number of phone-based transaction systems have been developed in Europe. And in the United States, development of Wi-Fi and Bluetooth is expected to drive growth of wireless payments. Even though mobile payment (m-payments) systems have not really taken off, with growth in Wi-Fi, Bluetooth and 3G cellular phone systems, this is beginning to change (Turban et al. 2008, pp. 436). Furthermore, in countries where the Internet penetration is low the penetration rate of the mobile phone could be relatively much higher (because the lower cost and mobility).

1.4. Internet Marketing

The Internet is a powerful tool for marketing and selling to consumers. However, there are many competing service providers and retailers with a presence on the Internet. One way of creating a competitive advantage over online competitors is to leverage one's knowledge of consumer behaviour and act on the gained knowledge. For example, supermarket operators can have good knowledge of customers who are willing to purchase grocery online (i.e., people who are time poor, people who don't enjoy shopping in the stores), and have more targeted marketing campaigns. Some important areas associated with consumer and consumer behaviour on the Internet include:

- understand consumer behaviour and ways in which web tools can assist consumers in the buying process
- online market research (including gathering, storing and analyzing information about consumers)
- maintain good relationship with customers online
- promoting products and services to consumers online (online advertising)

Understanding online consumers

Consumers have not universally embraced the choice and convenience offered by the Internet. Some of the criteria that consumers use to make their online purchase decisions could include (Turban at al. 2008; The Authors' Own Knowledge): (1) product selection (i.e., Can I find what I am looking for), (2) convenience (Can I avoid the trouble of doing shopping in the store by shopping online? Can I save time by shopping online? Can I pay online with flexible payment options?), (3) user friendliness (Is it easy to use the online shopping system?), (4) price (Is the online price cheaper?), (5) customer services (Am I being treated as someone unique? Am I receiving consistent services across online and offline channels?), and (6) trust and reputation (Can I trust the web site? Does the web site have good reputation? Is it safe to use the web site? Can I receive the item I ordered on time?). Nowadays web sites and online tools (i.e., shopping portals, shopping robots, business ratings sites and trust verification sites) could greatly assist consumers' online purchase decision making.

It would be very difficult to build a successful online retail web site without paying close attention to the various factors (i.e., consumer characteristics, product/services characteristics, external environmental factors, online retailer factors, and e-tailing web site characteristics) influencing consumer' online buying decision (i.e., to buy or not to buy, what to buy, where, when and how much to buy) (Turban et al. 2008, p. 158). Online retailers also need to understand purchasing process of online customers (i.e., from initial inquiry/ information search to purchase to post-purchase services and evaluation) and thus develop better tools to facilitate each step of their online shopping process and enrich their online shopping experience with their sites.

Online market research

The Internet can be used as a tool to gather marketing information. The purpose of gathering consumer data is to learn more about the visitors to an e-business organization's web site and their behaviour. This information can be used to help organizations have better marketing efforts and develop better products and services. Gathering consumer information on the Internet can be done by asking web site users to provide information voluntarily (e.g. an online survey) or by tracking their online movement and activities (with or without the web user's knowledge). "Cookies" are normally used for noting and tracking users of websites. So the website can remember the user, show appropriate content to him/her, and facilitate his/her quick log-on to website with restricted access. Other tools for tracking customers' online movements include web logs, click-stream data, web bugs, and spyware. Once online data is collected it is stored in data warehouses or centralised databases, tools such as data mining and online analytical application (OLAP) as we previously discussed in Chapter 1 can be applied to analyze the collected data for better understanding of consumers and for better decision making. The major limitation of online market research is the sample size and characteristics of Internet users. Those researched Internet users may not represent the population at large, so marketers must ensure that they are aware of the demographics of those they are researching.

Maintain good relationship with customers online

E-business enables companies to collect individual information about their customers. This enables firms to better understand individual customer's needs and spending habits. The detailed information provides the opportunity for developing a one-to-one relationship with customers, which could be very expensive and nearly mission-impossible for traditional brick-and-mortar retailers. It is important to create and maintain one-to-one relationships with customers, especially on the Internet, customers can switch to another supplier with a click of mouse. Customers are more likely to remain with one organisation if it develops a bond with the customer. The Internet has facilitated and made the personalization (delivering matching products and services to customers as per their online profiles) and mass customization (tailored products and services to every customer) a reality. Amazon's collaborative filtering is a powerful personalisation tool, which provides personalised recommendations of products and services to customers (i.e., customers who purchase item A also buy item B). Dell Computer allows individual customers to customize their preferred personal computers online.

Attracting and retaining loyal customers remains the most important issue for any retailer, including online retailers. Increased customer loyalty can bring cost savings to a company in various ways, including lowering marketing and advertising costs, reducing transaction costs, cutting down customer turnover expenses, and lowering failure costs such as warranty claims. Customer loyalty also strengthens a company's market position because loyal customers are kept away from the competition. It can also assist in enhancing resistance to competitors, reducing price sensitivity, and promoting the company and its products and services (i.e., through customers' sharing of their positive experience). Companies can foster online loyalty by learning about their customers' needs, interacting with customers, and providing excellent customer services.

Developing trust between an online retailer and its customers is very important in attracting and retaining customers. Some measures retailers online could consider include:

- having user authentication procedure (i.e., using password and user name)
- using secure transaction systems (e.g. SSL, or SET)
- providing the third-party assurance services (i.e., CA (Certificate Authority), VeriSign, or TRUSTe) to guarantee safety of customers' data
- informing customers on collecting their personal data and how such data will be stored and uscd
- asking permission for other uses of customers' data
- providing clear transaction rules, frequently asked questions section, refund policy, and procedures of dispute resolution.
- having a comprehensive and visible privacy policy

In the meantime, great attention has to be paid to customers' satisfaction which is evidenced by customers' repeat visits and repeat orders. Two important factors are usefulness (i.e., online shopping and payment facilities, online services, online communities, comprehensive, clear, accurate and updated information) and user friendliness (i.e., easy to use, fast speed, good reputation, quick response to online inquiries). In addition, users' satisfaction could be enhanced by their positive experiences with and gained trust towards the web site (Delone & McLean 2004; Molla & Licker 2001).

Online advertising

The Internet is a new medium which has been enthusiastically embraced as an advertising outlet. Online advertising has been growing rapidly in recent years. According to Laudon & Travor (2008, p. 419) who predict the online advertising growth based on the information from various sources (i.e., eMarketer, IAB/PricewaterhouseCoopers, Universal McCann), the annual growth of online advertising is about 20% that is three times faster than the whole advertising market, and the percentage of online advertising spending of all advertising spending will increase from 3.3% in 2000 (the total ad spending was less than US$ 10 billion) to more than 13% of total advertising spending in 2011 (the projected total spending is more than US$ 40 billion). By citing the data from IAB/PricewaterhouseCoopers, they also suggest some top industries in adopting online advertising (accounting for more than 75% of online advertising) include: consumer (including retail, automotive, travel, and packaged goods), financial services, computers, telecommunication, and media (television, radio, and print publishing). They also state that compared to traditional advertising methods (i.e., magazines, newspapers, radio, TV, bill boards, catalogues, flyers, retail stores, shopping malls, among many others), online adverting appears to have such advantages of (Turban et al. 2008, pp. 185; Bruner 2005; The Authors' Own Knowledge):

- lower costs (cheaper and smaller updating costs)
- richness of format (including text, audio, video, graphics, animation, games, entertainment)
- more targeted marketing as a result of good understanding of customers online
- quicker release
- great linking ability (with a click of mouse customers can go to the online businesses)
- more powerful branding and more supplier's market for some players (i.e., Google, Microsoft and Yahoo dominate online search market and businesses are willing to pay for premium prices for placing ads with them)
- more control for viewers (users basically can decide whether they want to see the ads or not), and better accountability for investment on advertising (i.e., via better online track capabilities)

Furthermore online advertising has grown at a faster speed than traditional media (i.e., taking cable TV 25 years while online advising

13 years to reach advertising sales of US$ 20 billion) (Egol & Vollmer 2008).

Advertising on the Internet can take many forms (i.e., banners, pop-ups & similar ads, e-mail advertising, newspaper & classified ads, search engine advertisement, advertising in chat rooms, blogs, and social networks). The most common is the use of banners and search engines. Search engine marketing has grown to about 40% of all online advertising and has become the most popular online advertising approach (Laudon & Travor 2008, p. 421). Table 2.2 and Table 2.3 present advantages and disadvantages of major advertising methods and some major web advertising strategies respectively.

Table 2.2: Advantages and disadvantages of online advertising methods

Advertising method	Advantages	Disadvantages
Banners	link direct buying opportunity; wide reach; effective targeting	limited by their cost, space for information and customer indifference
Pop-up & Similar ads	catch users' attention; link to buying opportunity	can annoy users
Search engine	good credibility; good position available; significant audiences	high competition; information overload
E-mail	an effective method of advertising to large groups	may cause SPAM issues
Video & Rich media	serves up customised ads to users in real time	difficult to execute well; can annoy users

(Source: developed from Turban et al. 2008; The Authors' Own Knowledge)

Table 2.3: Major web advertising strategies

Specific web advertising strategy	Brief description
Affiliate marketing & advertising	Uses another entity to advertise and sell products or services for a commission, and is most effective in generating a user base for a new site.
Ads as a commodity	Customers are paid to read ads by the advertisers.
Viral marketing	Word-of-mouth marketing by which consumers promote a product or service by telling others about it.
Customizing ads	Advertisements are customized by comparing users' preferences to available products or services. Products or services that fit a user's preference are then used as the advertisement is displayed/sent.

Table 2.3: *Continued*

Specific web advertising strategy	Brief description
Online promotion	Some of the most popular Internet promotions are give-aways and discounts. The use of Admediaries, which are third-party vendors that conduct promotions, especially large scale ones, is also quite popular.

(Source: developed from Turban et al. 2008, pp. 194-195)

In the meantime, various measures are used to evaluate the success of online advertising. Table 2.4 presents some measures which can be used to evaluate online advertising performance. On top of those measures presented in the Table 2.4, a balanced and multi-perspectives measurement system, looking at both quantitative and qualitative dimensions and including such criteria as customer satisfaction index, repeat purchases,

Table 2.4: Some online advertising performance measures

Casual term	Specific measure
Number of surfers	Number of people with web access
Number of aware surfers	Number of people aware of the site
Number of web site hits	Number of hits on the site
Number of active investigators	Number of active visitors to the site
Number of buyers	Number of purchases
Number of repeat customers	Number of customers who repurchase
Click through rates	Percentage of times an advertisement is clicked
Number of page views	Number of pages viewed
Stickiness (duration)	Average length of stay of a web site (or a web page)
Unique visitors	Number of unique visitor during a period
Impressions	Number of times an advertisement is served
Recency	Time elapsed since the last action taken by a buyer, such as a visit or purchase
Conversation rate	Percentage of visitors who become customers
Abandonment rate	Percentage of shoppers who begin a shopping cart purchase but then leave the site without completing a purchase
Attrition rate	Percentage of customers who do not return during the next year after an initial purchase

(Source: developed from: Watson et al., 2000, p. 83; Laudon & Traver 2008, p. 450)

market share, on-time deliveries, returned orders, new customer acquisitions, and perceived value for money are also suggested by Davey (2008).

Organisations want to know performance of online advertising since it helps identify appropriate web advertising methods and strategies. It also helps determine the appropriate price to charge (or pay) for online advertising. However, even though the Internet presents e-business organizations better measures and approaches for accountability for return on their online adverting spending, there are various problems with the established quantitative measures of online advertising performance as a result of its relative newness and thus a lack of established knowledge and standardized approach to deal with it.

Offline advertising (i.e., traditional media such as television, print media) is so far still the primary advertising means even though the spending on print media is declining and the traditional print industry's move to the Internet, as a result of the wide adoption of online applications of wikis, blogs, social networks, online communities and search engines. And so far successful marketing campaigns have combined both offline and online tactics. Online companies have learned how to use traditional marketing communications to drive sales to their web sites (i.e., TV & radio advertisements for websites). Online companies also should look at traditional mass advertising channel, such as bill boards, displaying in the public places such as airports train stations, bus stops, sports stadiums, shopping centres to utilize the advantage of never-turning-off while other media including the Internet, radio, TV can be switched off any time by consumers (Nunes & Merrihue 2007). For many organizations the combined approach is so far the most effective way of communicating with their customers.

2. B2B E-Business

Business-to-business (B2B) e-business refers to transactions between businesses conducted electronically over the Internet, extranets, intranets or private networks (Turban et al. 2008, p. 219). B2B and B2C e-business are different in various areas (see Table 2.5).

Table 2.5: B2B vs B2C E-business

Dimensions	B2C E-business	B2B E-Business
Tangibility of benefits	Tend to be smaller potential savings and more difficult to be justified	Tend to be larger potential savings and easier to be justified
Required E-business infrastructure	Normally need to develop new B2C applications	More established infrastructure for B2B EC
Type of industry adopting e-business	More retail and services industries	Aerospace, defence, healthcare, utilities, computer & electronics industries are heavier users (they already have significant use of EDI and large investments in information technology).
Transaction values	Low value transactions	High value transactions
Number of interacting parties	Two (a business and its customers)	Multiple (i.e., could be in the forms of one to many, many to one, and many to many and could involve a business' suppliers, customers & business partners)
Complexity of transactions	Simple transactions	Complex transactions
Payment method	Payment by credit cards, debit cards, Paypal, Online bank transfer/deposit, etc.	Purchase cards, E-checks, etc
Negotiation	Not so much	Extensive
Integration and cooperation with customers and business partners	Limited (e-tailers may not need to integrate into customers' systems)	Strong
Switching costs and customer retention costs	Low switching costs and customer retention	High switching costs and customer retention
Importance of order fulfilment	Fulfilment is important, but not critical	Fulfilment is critical
Impact of network effects	Small to medium network effects	Huge network effects

(Source: developed from Turban et al. 2008; Laudon & Trevor 2008; CIO 2007; The Authors' Own Knowledge)

In spite of all the hypes about e-tailing and consumers' online participation, the vast majority of e-business concerns business-to-business transactions. In addition, the size of the market for business-to-business e-business is far greater than the market for business-to-consumer e-business. B2B e-business/e-commerce is, by far, the most successful form of e-commerce and accounts for over 90% of all e-commerce transactions (Economist Intelligence Unit 2009). B2B e-business covers a broad spectrum of applications that enable businesses to form electronic relationships with their distributors, resellers, suppliers, customers, and other business partners. So far improving supply chain management has been a core focus of B2B e-business activities, and multinational large corporations have been the biggest users.

2.1. Basic Types of B2B E-Business

There are different classifications of B2B e-business (i.e., as per types of materials (direct for production or indirect for maintenance, repairs and operations (MRO)), direction of trade (vertical marketplaces dealing with one industry or segment or Horizontal marketplaces for different industries, etc.), types of transactions (spot buying or strategic sourcing), parties to the transaction (directly or online intermediary), number and form of participation, and degree of openness (private and public). The categorizing e-business according to number and form of participation is adopted in this chapter. Under this approach, three basic types of B2B e-business include (Turban et al. 2008, p. 220):

- the company-centric model: one to many (sell-side) and many to one (buy-side)
- exchange: many-to-many market places
- collaborative commerce.

The most common of these models is the company-centric model, which can either be a sell-side marketplace (one seller-to-many buyers) or a buy-side marketplace (many sellers-to-one buyer). Intel, Cisco and Dell, who sell IT products to various customers via their websites, are good examples of sell-side marketplaces. Organizations also can sell to other businesses through intermediaries and via forward auctions (i.e., selling from E-bay's marketplace which is a forward auction market). E-procurement via reverse auction is a typical example of buy-side marketplace e-commerce.

Company-centric marketplaces focus on a single company's purchasing needs or selling needs and are generally private entities owned by that company. A B2B exchange is a many buyers-to-many sellers e-marketplace, usually owned and run by a third party, in which many buyers and sellers meet electronically to trade with each other. Private exchanges are e-marketplaces (which are company-centric marketplaces) that are owned and operated by one company while public exchanges are open to all interested parties (both buyers and sellers). Collaborative commerce can support activities such as communication and sharing of information, design and planning among business partners via applications such as Internet -based electronic data exchange, electronic hubs, and extranets. In addition to the trading products via B2B e-business, services, such as travel services, real estate, electronic payments, online stock trading, online financing and other online services, can also be supplied through B2B e-business.

2.2. B2B E-payment Systems

B2B e-business payments usually are much larger and significantly more complex than the payments made by individual consumers (in terms of dollar values, number of products, shipments, etc) in B2C e-business due to the difficulties in creating systems that fit both buyers' and sellers' internal existing accounting and finance systems and the lack of transparent information sharing in the supply chain. Major electronic payment methods for B2B e-business include e-checks, purchase cards (for the purchase of non-strategic materials and services up to a preset dollar limit and act in much the same way as standard credit cards, with the exception that they are issued by a company and are to be used for specific types of purchases), e-letters of credit, electronic fund transfer (EFT), and so on.

2.3. B2B E-business and Supply Chain

The supply chain is a complex network of relationships that organisations maintain with trading partners to source, manufacture and deliver products and services. A firm's supply chain can be generally divided into three parts: (1) upstream supply chain (including activities of a business's activities with its suppliers and in this part of the supply chain the major activity is procurement), (2) internal supply chain (including in-house processes for transforming the inputs from the suppliers to the outputs. Some major concerns are production management, coordination between business units, manufacturing and inventory control); and (3) downstream supply chain (including activities involved in delivering the products to the final customers and focus on distribution, warehousing, transportation and after-sales services). The major issues in the supply chain are the lack of information sharing and trust.

Business-to-business e-business is generally used in existing supply chains to make them more efficient. The four types B2B e-business discussed previously, namely one-to-many, many-to-one, many-to-many, and collaborative-commerce, can make significant contributions to organisation's supply chains. B2B e-business can render the supply chain more efficient and effective or it can change the supply chain completely, eliminating one or more intermediaries. B2B e-business could contribute to all three parts of a firm's supply chain. Meanwhile other technologies also can enhance a firm's supply chain. Table 2.6 presents B2B e-business applications and other technologies for enhancing a firm's supply chain.

Table 2.6: B2B e-business applications and other technologies for enhancing a firm's supply chain

Parts of a firm's supply chain	B2B e-business applications and other technologies for enhancing supply chain
Upstream	o Purchase via B2B buy-side web sites and exchanges (independent or consortia) o Share information and collaborate with suppliers and business partners in demand forecasting and planning via B2B collaborative commerce applications (i.e., Internet -based electronic data exchange, collaboration hubs, extranets, virtual private networks, supply chain planning systems) o Integrate external systems via applications such as XML, Web Services, Grid Computing, Cloud Computing, Service Oriented Architecture, Semantic Web, Web Sciences

Table 2.6: *Continued*

Parts of a firm's supply chain	B2B e-business applications and other technologies for enhancing supply chain
Internal	o Purchase via internal marketplaces o Communicate between business units via applications such as intranets, virtual private networks o Use enterprise resource planning systems to improve internal efficiency o Share information and collaborate internally via tools such as email, internal wikis, blogs, online communities, discussion forums, instant messaging, online conferencing RSS, podcast, vodcast, groupware, knowledge management systems, workflow management systems, electronic calendar o Integrate internal systems via applications such as XML, Web Services, Grid Computing, Cloud Computing, Service Oriented Architecture, Semantic Web, Web Sciences
Downstream	o Sell via B2B sell-side web sites and exchanges (independent or consortia) o Better understand customers by applying customer relationship management systems o Apply radio frequency identification and other similar applications to track movements of customers' orders o Share information and collaborate with retailers, distributors, and wholesalers via tools such as Internet -based electronic data exchange, collaboration hubs, extranets, virtual private networks, supply chain execution systems o Integrate external systems via applications such as XML, Web Services, Grid Computing, Cloud Computing, Service Oriented Architecture, Semantic Web, Web Sciences

(Source: developed from Turban et al. 2008; Haag et al. 2008; O'Brien & Marakas 2008; The Authors' Own Knowledge)

3. Other Types of E-business

3.1. Consumer-to-Consumer E-business

Besides B2B and B2C e-business, another popular e-business model is consumer-to-consumer (C2C) e-business, which basically concerns the transactions and communications between individual consumers. Some major applications of C2C e-business include (Turban et al. 2008, pp. 400-401; The Authors' Own Knowledge):

- C2C auctions (i.e., buying and selling items in E-bay)
- Classified ads (i.e., listing and selling items in Craiglist, TradingPost) .
- Personal services (i.e., online dating services such as Aussiematchmaker)
- C2C exchanges (i.e., file sharing via peer-to-peer networks such as Bittorrent)
- Selling virtual properties (i.e., selling and buying weapons and other virtual properties in online game and virtual worlds such as Second Life)
- Support services (i.e., online payment system Paypal)

One of the most notable C2C e-business is E-bay, which is the largest online marketplace (or flea market to some extent), connects buyers and sellers all over the world, and has expanded into many parts of the world. One of the major concerns in peer-to-peer network supported C2C e-business applications is copyright issue. Two famous cases are MP3.com and Nepster.com. Both of them distributed music and digital content online without paying loyalties to producers, distributors, and artists who had the legal rights to the content. Both of them was shut down by the U.S. government and later reopened by charging fees.

3.2. Blogs, Wikis & Social Networks

The most interesting e-business applications in recent years have been the emergence of blogs, wikis, and social networks (also called online communities). Even though these applications have different emphasis and functions, they have one thing in common: connecting people together and letting them do something they have common interest in (i.e., giving comments, sharing knowledge & exchanging experiences, making friends & networking, collaboration, participation & building communities online). Meanwhile, they all are part of the Web 2.0 revolution, which focuses on everyday people (you and me) using the Internet/the web for communication, collaboration, and creation and on conversation (listen, read, watch, and participate/respond). By 2007, no one had more power to influence society than Web 2.0 communities. For example political figures in the UK, the US, and Australia (i.e., Queen Elizabeth II, Barrack Obama, Kevin Rudd) have embarked on Youtube and other social websites for their political campaigns. One of the most significant differences between Web 2.0 and the traditional World Wide Web (could be viewed as Web 1.0) is the former emphasises on collaboration among users, content providers, and enterprises.

Blogs & Wikis

Blogs and Wikis are two kinds of online publishing applications. A blog is a published personal weblog (or an online personal diary for some people) while a blogger is the author or editor of the blog. A blog is differentiated from regular web page by its personal nature, unique content (i.e., focusing on certain niche areas), frequent updating, and quick responding. Organizations can use blogs for public relation purposes as well as soliciting information from the mass on the Internet (i.e., MBA schools could set up weblogs on topics such as good & bad MBA programs/schools to solicit views from Internet users all over the world in a cheaper and more comprehensive way). On the other hand, posts in a blog may not be as well thought or expressed as desired resulting from its quick responding.

A wiki is an online application that can be updated at any time by any members of the community. A very popular wiki application is Wikipedia (www.wikepedia.org). Many wiki applications (including Wikipedia) have openly accessible content developed collaboratively by a global community of contributors who work voluntarily. The supply of knowledge and shared experience is unlimited. They are always some people and organizations for free. Wiki applications offer a compelling value proposition for both individuals (i.e., free access to the knowledge, global knowledge sharing) and organizations (better communication, cooperation and collaboration both internally and externally) even though quality control of a large amount of information could be an issue. Some values wikis can create for their users consist of:

- focusing on democratization of knowledge rather than monetization of knowledge

- providing a conversational knowledge management approach for breaking the knowledge acquisition bottleneck
- having an encyclopaedia of the people, by the people, and for the people
- enabling users to use the Internet to save money and time on a wide range of information products and services
- creating value from leveraging its information and knowledge (about customers, business environment, processes, etc) within and outside organizations thus provide more valued added services, more personalized & customized services to users, etc.
- maintaining and enhancing its strategic alliance with information suppliers and other business partners (i.e., Google, Yahoo, Microsoft)
- creating values for users in the value-chain of publishing process (i.e., creating a page, uploading a page, quality control, free-updating and changing, reaching out to the general public, links with outside, admin support, IT, quality of editors, etc)

What roles can Wiki applications play in collaboration? Can companies innovate and succeed using the knowledge, resources, and computing power of millions of self-organizing/ voluntary contributors into a massive collective force and achieve Wikinomics proposed by Tapscott & Williams (2006)?. These are some of interesting questions to be answered. Like wiki some other similar concepts include collective intelligence, crowd intelligence, mass intelligence, collective mind, free public knowledge, public knowledge management systems, and so on.

Social networks

Social networks such as Youtube, Flickr, Facebook, Classmates, and Friendster connect people with specified interests and provide them with a suite of tools to allow them to more easily interact and sharing online with other individuals from all over the world with similar interests (i.e., exchange information, sharing videos & photos, sharing professional and personal experiences). Social networks have dramatically changed the way how people are connected and challenged the understanding of how human beings connect to each other (i.e., theory of six degrees separation proposed by Stanley Milgram may become redundant as suggested by Gary 2009). Scientists from British Science Association have suggested that social networks as one of the top ten inventions that changed the world (Gary 2009).

Financial viability is the biggest challenge for social networks as a result of its newness and uncertainties in the online world. When a few of them were very lucky to get support from Internet giants (i.e., Google's US$ 1.65 billion purchase of Youtube, Microsoft's acquisition of Webfives and its US$ 240 million investment in Facebook (but only 1.6% of the company), Yahoo's US$ 30 million takeover of Flickr, News Corporation's US$ 580 million buy of MySpace, etc), most of social networks need to work very hard to keep the business going. Furthermore these lucky ones just mentioned have been struggling with generating sufficient revenue and paying off the investments made by their parent companies (Ellis 2008). Winning public popularity is not equivalent to the success. The online world is full of opportunities (i.e., you may become someone, and a business may make its name rapidly) and challenges (i.e., the costs of building web site and for bandwidth are intangible and perishable-You burn the money basically, and you won't be seeing any assets once you fail).

Some ways social networks can generate revenue include (Turban et al. 2008, pp. 29; Turban et al. 2008, pp. 827):

- using social networks for advertising, selling, and shopping (but it will take some time for business figure out how to do it properly since it is still a new online advertising model and the issues of unpredictability and control of freely uploaded content)
- offering premium service for a monthly or per service fee
- earning a monthly service fee by partnering with other organizations
- earning some income from members' offline gathering and other social activities (some social networks have a network of thousands of local physical venues where members can meet. These venues, like coffee shops, may choose to pay a fee to be affiliated with the social network).

When there exist arguments about the future of emerging and interesting e-business systems like blogs, wikis, and social networks (i.e., whether they are going to survive in the long run since we have seen so many dot.com failures (some even with billions of dollars in losses)), organizations need to explore these applications to see how they can help them perform better (i.e., having internal wikis and blogs for knowledge sharing, establishing online communities and blogs to solicit customers' views on products and services).

In the meantime, the debate about Web 1.0, Web 2.0 and Web 30 has been going on for sometime. Even though there is no agreement on this matter, we reckon (1) Web 1.0 applications emphasize on connecting people to the information; (2) Web 2.0 application focus on connecting people-using the web for communication, collaboration, and co-creation, and (3) Web 3.0 applications and beyond may concentrate on delivering a new generation of on-demand business applications (i.e., your online personal assistant who can understand you very well through your online behaviour and thus being about to act like a good human-being friend or personal consultant who provides you with some personalized services (e.g., answers for what I should wear/eat/to/see, where should I go for movies, etc). The concept of the whole web/ Internet is your personal computer (facilitated by applications such as cloud computing advocated by Google and others) will be greatly pushed forward. In addition, we can run everything at home from one single device (all-in-one), which is also able to communicate with people all over the world via different communication appliances.

3.3. Mobile Business

As a result of wide availability and continually declining prices of wireless devices (i.e., mobile phones, PDAs, smart phones, I-phones, wireless laptops), and rapid development of telecommunication and Internet technologies and benefits arising from using wireless devices (i.e., ubiquity, mobility, convenience, instant connectivity, pervasiveness, localized services), mobile business (M-commerce or M-business) which is any e-business done in a wireless environment (especially via the Internet), is emerging as the next major development in e-business. In many places, mobile phones have become a part of people's lives. According to a survey by Microsoft reported in News.com.au (2009), which surveyed 2,500 mobile users across Australia, China, India, Japan, and Taiwan, 80 percent of survey participants told they would use their phones while eating a meal with others, 62 percent while driving, 48% while trying to sleep. And 66 percent Chinese and 48 percent Australian participants used their phones in the toilet. At the same time, 24 percent of male participants and 11 percent female participants said that it is acceptable to use mobile phones to propose to their loved ones.

Mobile business applications can integrate and enhance all perspectives of e-business: (1) retailers, government agencies and other types of businesses can provide various products & services and market to their customers (or citizens) via wireless devices; (2) businesses can optimize their supply chains (i.e., via timely, more accurate, more up-dated information and better collaboration with suppliers and business partners along the supply chain) and thus enable organisations to better manage their supply chains and respond faster to changes in the supply chain; (3) enhance communication between individuals via functions such text messages, multi-media communication; (4) improve intra-organizational communication; among many others. By applying location-based applications (i.e., GPS and GIS that have the functions of location, navigation, tracking, mapping and timing (Turban et al. 2008, pp. 446)) and pervasive computing (i.e., Bill Gate's full wired smart house, automatic lighting & water control at home, smart cars, controlling air conditioners and other electronic appliances at home via mobile phones, etc), members of societies can enjoy a more safe, healthier and happier life.

Even though the future of m-business is certain, its growth could be slowed down by the usability of current mobile devices (i.e., small screen & key board), technical limitations (i.e., lack of a standardized security protocol and as a result of its newness, insufficient bandwidth which could cause slow transfer speed, integration with existing information technology infrastructure), and potential health hazards associated with mobile devices (i.e., the concern of the impact of radio emission). Given the fact that there are various mobile data services from different vendors in the market, organizations (such as open mobile alliance (www.openmobilealliance.com), mobile phone companies, and telecommunication operators) are working together on open standard for interoperability to give consumers and business users seamless interoperable services and access to information and transactions regardless of their devices, network types, operators or geographical locations.

4. Conclusions

This chapter presents two fundamental types of e-business: B2C and B2B. After discussing various issues related to these two fundamental e-business, we move into more advanced and popular social and collaborative e-business including wikis, blogs, social networks. While these e-business applications are very popular among individuals and groups, organizations must see how they can benefit from these types of e-business. Innovative business models need to be dcvcloped and trialled to this end. Finally, we briefly discuss mobile business/mobile commerce. M-commerce, as it is popularly known, has great promises. However, as we have pointed out, some of the technological issues arc acting as barriers for M-commerce to diffuse widely.

References

Accenture's Marketing Science Group (2007) http://www.cio.com/article/127850 (accessed on 16/01/2008).

Bruner, R. E. (2005) The Decade in online advertising (1994-2004), online, available at: http//doubleclick.com/knowledge (Accessed on May 25 2007).

CIO (2007) ABC: An introduction to E-Commerce, CIO, March 6, 2007, Online Available at: http://www.cio.com/article/print/40298 (accessed on January 21, 2009).

Collier, J. E. & Bienstock, C.C. (2006) How do customers judge quality in an e-tailer?, MIT Sloan Management Review, Vol. 48, No. 1, pp. 35-40.

Davey, N. (2008) Customer metrics: What should you measure? Online, Available at: http://www.mycustomer.com/cgi-bin/itemcgi?id=133564&id=printheader&f=printfooter (accessed on March 4, 2008).

Delone, W. H. & McLean, E. R. (2004) Measuring e-commerce success: Applying the DeLone & McLean Information Systems Model, International Journal of Electronic Commerce, Vol. 9, No. 1, pp. 31-47.

Economist Intelligence Unit (2009) The World in Figures: Industries (E-commerce), The World in 2009, The Economist, pp. 120.

Egol, M. & Vollmer, C. (2008) Major media in the shopping aisle, Strategy + business, Issue 53, Winter 2008, pp. 1-12.

Ellis, S. (2008) Big money chasing social network sites may be in for small returns, The Australian, June 19, 2008, Online Available at: http://www.australianit.news.au/story/0,24897,23837194-5013640,00.html (accessed on June 26, 2008.

Gary, R. (2009) Top ten inventions that changed world, Online, Available at: http://www.telegraph.co.uk/scienceandtechnology/science/4981964/Top-10-inventions-that-changed-the-world.html (accessed on March 23, 2009).

Laudon, K.C. & Traver, C.G. 2008, E-commerce: Buisness, Technology, Society 2008, 4th edn, Addison Wesley, Boston, USA.

Molla, A. & Licker, P. S. (2001) E-commerce System Success: An attempt to extend and re-specify the DeLone and McLean mode of IS success, Journal of Electronic Commerce Research, Vol. 2, No. 4, pp. 131-141.

News.com.au (2009) Aussies chat on the loo-Microsoft mobile phone survey, Online, Available at: http://www.news.com.au/technology/story/0,28348,24930571-5014239,00.html (accessed on January 19, 2009).

Nunes, P. F. & Merrihue, J. (2007) The continuing power of mass advertising, MIT Sloan Management Review, Vol. 48, No. 2, pp. 63-71.

O'Brien, J. A. & Marakas, G. M. (2008), Management Information Systems, 8th edition, McGraw-Hill Irwin, Boston, U.S.A.

Tapscott, D. & Williams, A. D. (2006) Wikinomics: How mass collaboration change everything, Penguin Books, New York, p. 324.

Watson, R.T., Berthon, P., Pitt, L.F. & Zinkhan, G.M. 2000, Electronic Commerce, The Dryden Press, Fort Worth, TX.

Section 2

Studies of E-Business Issues and Challenges

CHAPTER 3

FACTORS INFLUENCING ONLINE AUCTION ADOPTION: A CHINA STUDY

Mohammed Quaddus

Graduate School of Business, Curtin University of Technology, Australia

Jun Xu

Graduate College of Management, Southern Cross University, Australia

There has been tremendous growth of online auction over the last several years. However, what makes consumers adopt and use online auction has not been researched deeply. This chapter aims to fill this gap. Based on extensive literature review, we developed a comprehensive online auction adoption model. The developed model is empirically tested by using Partial Least Square (PLS) based structural equation modelling approach. The primary data was collected via questionnaire survey in china, which is undergoing rapid internet adoption and e-commerce development, and is becoming the largest online marketplace in the world. The results indicate that subject norm, trust and behavioural control have significant impact on the buying intention via online auction but personal innovativeness and attitude don't.

1. Introduction

Electronic Commerce (EC) is changing the way organizations perform their tasks, interact with the customers and, in general, do their business. Among the many activities of EC e-shopping/e-purchasing has seen tremendous growth in recent years. In one of the surveys conducted by CNNIC (2008) in 19 cities in China, the volume of online sales reached 16.2 billion yuan in the first half of 2008. One of the many ways customers can purchase over the net is via online auction. Online auction sites are essentially the "market places" where customers (consumers, businesses and other types of purchasers) can participate in on line bidding for a product over a specified period of time following a particular auction model (rule) (Wang et al. 2002, Lucking-Reiley 2000). Online auction is sometime preferable to traditional mode of online buying as customer feel that he/she is controlling the price of the product.

China, with its 1.3 billion potential online customers, is undergoing dramatic development in e-commerce and related areas. According to CNNIC (2009) survey, by the end of 2008 there are some 298 million internet users (270 million with broadband internet access), 287.7 million websites (registered under CN) in China. 117.6 million mobile phone users in China have accessed the internet via their mobile phones. The bandwidth of international connection in China has reached 640286.67 million. And there are more than 74 million online shoppers and 11 million online sellers in China. After one decade of rapid development, Internet in China has evolved from an isolated industry to a popular communication and distribution channel for many people. People are using the internet for more diversified purposes. Apart from the email, online Internet services, such as online trading, online shopping, online banking, online advertisement, online banking, online trading, online advertisements, online game, etc, are getting more and more accepted and popular.

A number of auction sites have appeared in China in last few years. Some Chinese Auctions sites are: Paipai (www.paipai.com), Eachnet (www.eachnet.com), Youa (http://youa.baidu.com), Taobao (www.taobao.com), Atrade (http://www.artrade.com/), China Auction Net (www.a123.com.cn), among many others. Online trading via auction is one of the rapidly growing areas in China. For example, the volume of online auction transaction for Taobao.com alone reached 100 billion yuan (Chinaview 2008). With the large Internet users in China (e.g., 298 million by the end of 2008) (CCNIC 2009), online auction development attracts a lot of attention not only from online buyers and sellers but also from businesses. Following the joint ventures of E-bay and Eachnet.com (www.eachnet.com) and Yahoo and Sina (http://1pai.com), which is now a part of taobao), Chinese leading online businesses Alibaba, Tencent, and Baidu.com have also established their own online auction sites of taobao.com, paipai.com and youa.baidu.com respectively.

Despite its tremendous growth and coverage in public and the popular press (Lucking-Reiley 2000) deep research on online auction is somewhat limited overall and more so in China. There has been a lack of empirical studies on identifying the determinants of on-line auction from consumer's point of view. Primary aim of this research is therefore *to identify attitudinal, social, and behavioural factors of Chinese consumers that are significant in explaining the intentions of buying products via online auction.*

This chapter is organized as follows. The next section presents a brief background literature to identify the dominant research work in on-line auction domain, which further identifies the lack of adoption research in on-line auction. Our research model is then presented which has been developed based on extensive literature review on both academic and commercial papers/reports/websites etc. The hypotheses are also presented in this section. The target sample, measures and the data analysis method, based on partial least square, are presented in research method section. The findings are next presented. Finally, this chapter concludes with the discussion of results and implications.

2. Background

As mentioned earlier, deep research on the adoption of online auction is almost non-existent. A number of studies deal with various aspects of online auction, including factors influencing auction prices (i.e., Gilkeson & Reynolds 2003, Kamins et al. 2004, McDonald & Slawson 2002), issues and concerns associated with online auction (i.e., Beam et al. 1999, Ku & Malhotra 2001), advantages/benefits of online auction (i.e., Van Heck & Vervest 1998; Bakos 1998, Jaap 2002, Emiliani & Stec 2002), fundamental issues of online auction (i.e., Lucking Reily 2000), online auction in specific markets (i.e., Wang et al. 2000), field studies (e.g., Beam & Segev 1998), implementation (e.g., Neo 1992), assessment of online auction (e.g., Turban 1997), specific auction models (e.g., Heezen & Baets 1996, Lee 1997, Segev & Beam 1998), dispute resolution for online auction (e.g., Lansing & Hubbard 2002), analysis and design of online auction (Bapna et al. 2002; Bapna et al. 2003), efficiency of online auction (e.g., Bapna et al. 2001), the impact of social facilitation on online auction (e.g., Rafaeli & Noy 2002), trust in online auction (e.g., Ba & Pavlou 2002, Ba et al. 2003), price issue of online auction (e.g., John et al. 2002, Budish & Takeyama 2001), among many others. However, we could not find any formal studies on the adoption/diffusion aspects of online auction.

2.1. Theoretical Foundation

Two underlying theories underpin our online auction adoption model. These are: "theory of planned behaviour (TPB) (Ajzen 1991) and "diffusion theory" (Rogers 1995).

In short the TPB emphasizes that adoption of any phenomenon takes place through a series of deliberate planned decisions. TPB draws on "theory of reasoned action" (TRA) developed earlier by Fishbein and Ajzen (1975). TRA proposes that there are causal relationships linking beliefs, attitudes, and intentions, and that attitudes and subjective norms determine behavioral intentions (for example adoption of online auction). However, in a number of situations the resources and opportunities available to the adopter to some extent dictate the possibility of achieving the intended behaviour. The Theory of Planned Behavior (TPB) addresses this limitation and thus is an extension of the TRA (Azjen 1991). TPB thus has additional constructs, namely control beliefs and perceived behavioural control. According to Ajzen (1991), these constructs relate to a person's beliefs about the resources and opportunities at his/her disposal that are required to facilitate a particular behaviour. That is, the resources and opportunities would provide enough control to the adopter to perform the behaviour (ie. adoption of online auction).

The TPB theory covers both internal and external behavioural controls. An internal control is an individual's confidence in their ability to perform or undertake a particular behaviour. An external control relates to the facilitating conditions that provide the resources that allow the individual to engage in certain behaviour (Triandis 1980). From this perspective it is argued that TPB would be extremely applicable to model the adoption of online auction.

The Theory of Planned Behaviour has been applied to explain adoption behavior in areas such as marketing and consumer behaviour (Berger 1993), leisure behaviour (Ajzen & Driver 1992), caffeine avoidance (Madden, Ellen and Azjen 1992), wastepaper recycling (Cheung, Chan & Wong 1999) and medicine (Randall and Gibson 1991). Cheung, Chan and Wong (1999) found that the TPB has better explanatory power than the TRA. Taylor and Todd (1995) unveiled that the TPB could be applied to study the adoption of new technologies; however, use of the TPB to explain the adoption of online auction is lacking in the literature.

The "diffusion theory", on the other hand, says that there are a number of consequences which help in deciding to adopt and subsequently use the phenomenon in question or innovation (for example online auction). In his seminal work Rogers (1995) suggests five perceived attributes of an innovation, namely relative advantage, compatibility, complexity, trialability, and observability. Relative advantage is "the degree to which an innovation is perceived as better" (Rogers, 1995, p. 15) and measures both explicit and implicit advantages. Compatibility is defined as "the degree to which an innovation is perceived as being consistent with the existing values, past experiences, and needs of potential adopters" (Rogers 1995, p. 15) and measures how compatible an innovation is with the existing culture, structure, infrastructure, and previously adopted ideas. Complexity is defined as "the degree to which an innovation is perceived as difficult" (Rogers 1995, p. 16) and measures how difficult an innovation is to understand, learn, and use. Trialability is "the degree to which an innovation may be experimented with on a limited basis" (Rogers 1995; p. 16) and describes how easy an innovation is to try out or test. Observability is "the degree to which the results of an innovation are visible to others" (Rogers 1995, p. 16) and reflects how explicit are the results and outcomes of an innovation.

Rogers' diffusion theory has been applied in a number of studies relating to the adoption of innovations (i.e., Grover 1993; Agarwal & Prasad 1998; Thong 1999). In this chapter it is argued that consequences of online auction will be an important construct of the online auction adoption model. Aspects of Rogers' "diffusion theory" will thus be adapted for online auction adoption phenomenon.

3. The Proposed Research Model and Hypotheses

3.1. The Proposed Research Model

Figure 3.1 shows the online auction adoption research model which is primarily based on two previously discussed underlying theories, namely 'theory of planned behaviour' (TPB) (Ajzen 1991) and 'diffusion theory' (Rogers 1995). The model possesses seven constructs/factors which are interacting in a complex way. The constructs "BuyIntent_P7", "SNorm_P5", "Attitude_P4" and "BControl_P2" have been adapted from TPB (Ajzen 1991), while the construct "Conseq_P3" has been adapted from diffusion theory (Rogers 1995). As trust and personal innovativeness play dominant roles in overall E-commerce the construct "Trust_P1" has been adapted from Ba and Pavlou (2002) and Ba et al. (2003) and the construct "Innov_P6" has been adapted from Limayem et al. (2000).

The intention to buy via on-line auction (BuyIntent_P7) is proposed to be influenced by subject norms (SNorm_P5) (i.e. indirect pressure from friends, family, media etc), attitude (Attitude_P4) (i.e. one's overall attitudes towards online auction), personal innovativeness (Innov_P6) (i.e. willingness to try new innovative things), trust (Trust_P1) (i.e. Trust, expectations and reliability of online auction), and behavioural control (BControl_P2) (i.e. existence of internal and external resources which control/facilitate one's behaviour towards various aspects of online auction). Trust is also proposed to influence attitude, behavioural control, and consequences (Conseq_P3) (i.e. various consequences of buying via online auction). On the other hand, attitude is also expected to be influenced by consequences and personal innovativeness. Our model thus shows that online buying intention is influenced directly and indirectly by a number of factors.

3.2. Hypotheses

The links among the factors in Figure 3.1 represent various hypotheses. However we have categorized the hypotheses as being primary or secondary as follows.

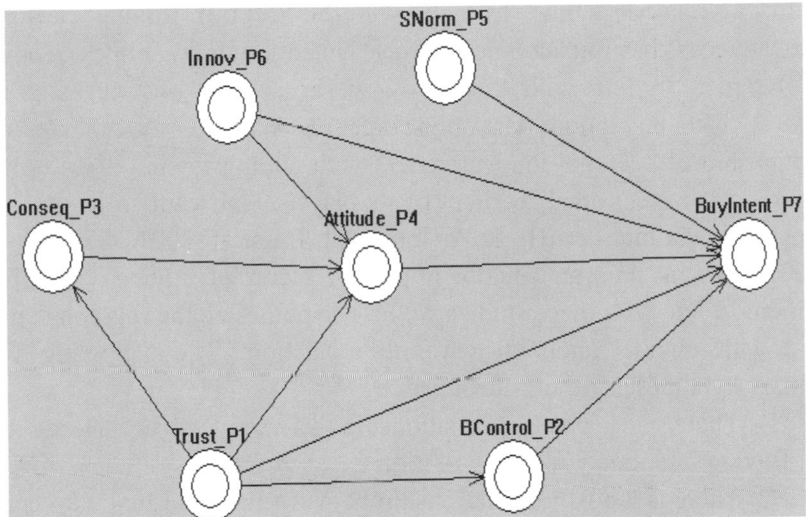

Figure 3.1: Online Auction Adoption Research Model

Primary Hypotheses

Since intention to buy via online auction is the ultimate dependent factor any hypothesis relating "BuyIntent_P7" is termed as primary hypothesis (Figure 3.1). Behavioural intention (buying intention via on-line auction in our case) is the ultimate dependent factor in any TPB based application (Ajzen 1991). As reviewed earlier TPB has been applied in various adoption intention behaviour studies (i.e., Berger 1993, Ajzen & Driver 1992, Madden, Ellen & Azjen 1992, Cheung, Chan & Wong 1999, Randall & Gibson 1991). TPB has also been applied in farm management. Beedell and Rehman (1999, 2000) have applied TPB in understanding farmers' behaviour of managing wildlife and landscape features. These applications however do not deal with adoption phenomenon. In all these applications subject norm, attitude and behaviour control have been hypothesized to influence the behavioural intention of the specific application. In line with these empirical studies and using the underlying theory of planned behaviour (Ajzen 1991) we also hypothesize the relationship of subject norm, attitude and behavioural control with buying intention via online auction.

In a related study Limayen et al. (2000) found personal innovativeness has impact on consumers' intention to do online shopping via Internet. In line with this study we argue that one needs to be innovative to buy goods via online auction. We thus hypothesize the relationship of personal innovativeness with buying intention via online auction. As mentioned earlier trust plays significant role in any transaction via internet (Ba & Pavlou 2002, Ba et al. 2003, Gefen et al. 2000). Trust is thus an equally important factor of buying via online auction. In line with these studies we also hypothesize the relationship of trust with buying intention via online auction. The following five primary hypotheses are thus formulated:

- H1: There is a positive relationship between Subject Norm and Buying Intention via online auction
- H2: There is a positive relationship between Personal Innovativeness and Buying Intention via online auction
- H3: There is a positive relationship between Attitude and Buying Intention via online auction
- H4: There is a positive relationship between Trust and Buying Intention via online auction
- H5: There is a positive relationship between Behavioural Control and Buying Intention via online auction

Secondary hypotheses

The secondary hypotheses are the hypotheses which link other factors except "BuyIntent_P7" in Figure 3.1

As mentioned earlier trust is an important factor in any form of transaction via internet. Trust is also likely to play significant role in influencing behavioural control, attitude and consequences of buying via online auction (Ba & Pavlou 2002, Ba et al. 2003, Gefen et al. 2000). The consequence construct in Figure 3.1 has been developed based on diffusion theory (Rogers 1995). Basically it deals with a range of advantages and disadvantages of buying via online auction. Higher level of trust with online auction is likely to have positive impact on perceived consequences of buying via on-line auction (Liyayem et al. 2000, Ba et al. 2003).

The attitude construct is one of the main constructs of TPB (Ajzen 1991), in our study it represents attitude toward online auction. In TPB attitude construct is influenced by various beliefs (Ajzen 1991), in our model attitude is suggested to be influenced by personal innovativeness (Liyayem et al. 2000), perceived consequences (Liyayem et al. 2000, Lucking-Reiley 2000) and trust (Ba & Pavlou 2002, Ba et al. 2003). As per the above discussion the following five secondary hypotheses are formulated:

- H6: There is a positive relationship between Trust and Behavioural Control
- H7: There is a positive relationship between Trust and Attitude
- H8: There is a positive relationship between Trust and Consequences
- H9: There is a positive relationship between Consequences and Attitude
- H10: There is a positive relationship between Personal Innovativeness and Attitude

4. Research Method

4.1. Measures

The seven constructs (factors) described earlier (see Figure 3.1) have been measured with great care. Most of the items have been adapted from the existing literature. Seven point likert scale ranging from 'strongly disagree' to 'strongly agree' has been used in all the items. The reliability and validity have been assessed based on the standard procedure of Partial Least Square (PLS) technique (Chin 1998; Chin & Newsted 1999; http://www.plsgraph.com). It is noted that PLS is specially appropriate for small sample analysis (Chin & Newsted 1999). According to Barclay et al. (1995) PLS requires a minimum sample size that is ten times the greater of: (i) the number of items comprising the most complex formative construct, or (ii) the largest number of predictors leading to an endogenous (dependent) construct. We don't have any formative construct in our research model and in our case the largest number of predictors leading to an endogenous construct (BuyIntent_P7) is five (see Figure 3.1). Thus this study requires a minimum sample size of 50. Therefore 126 usable responses in our case are appropriate for data analysis using PLS.

4.2. Sample and Procedure

The research subjects of our study were the students of MBA and BBA programs from a University in the eastern state of Australia. These students are based in China and doing their MBA degrees offshore in China. Primary data was collected via questionnaire based survey. Prior to that, the complete questionnaire was evaluated by a group of four researchers knowledgeable in e-commerce and online auction system. The questionnaire was revised several times to improve its face validity and readability.

Students have been used as subjects in various information system research, for example see Gefen et al. (2000) among many others. Gefen et al. (2000) call it "free simulation experiment". Taking part in our simulation experiment was completely voluntary. It was not part of any course assessment. Being MBA and BBA students our subjects had wealth of experience in using the internet and many had previously purchased online. Even then the participating students were asked to get exposure to on-line auction system by trialing some auction sites (i.e., Paipai (www.paipai.com), Eachnet (www.eachnet.com), Youa (http://youa.baidu.com), Taobao (www.taobao.com), Artrade (http://www.artrade.com/), China Auction Net (www.a123.com.cn)). This practice is admissible in free simulation experiment, for example see Gefen et al. (2000). Before the main survey a pre-test was conducted with five students knowledgeable in online auction. The main objective of the pre-test was to improve the face validity and readability of the questionnaire. As a result of the pre-test minor adjustment was done in the layout of the questionnaire to improve its flow. Decision was taken not to use the pre-test sample in the main analysis of data.

In the main survey the questionnaire was sent to 140 MBA students and 100 BBA students. 137 students returned their responses. 11 of them were not valid responses due to missing data. We thus got 126 usable responses (52.5% response rate).

The profiles of the respondents are as follows. 63.5% of them are female. 19.8% are in the age bracket of 15-20. 56.3% are in 21 to 29 bracket, 22.2% in 30 to 39 bracket, 1.6% in 40 to 49 bracket. 18.3% have completed high school, 10.3% have diploma degree, 53.2% of the respondents have bachelor's degree, 7.1% have graduate diploma, and 11.1% have masters degree. 31% of the respondents have annual income of more than RMB 60,000. The respondents are also quite internet literate as 85.7% of them regularly use the internet. 43.2% of the respondents used online auction system before to buy product and services. Among them the number of products that they bought from online auctions varied from a low of 1 (18.5%) to 50 (2%). And 41.2% of the respondents said their current usage of online auction is moderate to high. The most popular products bought from on-line auction are Books/Comics/Magazines, Movies & DVDs/Clothing & Accessories/PC & Video Games, Computers & IT, Toys, Hobbies, Crafts, Music & Instruments, Cameras & Accessories, Consumer Electronics, Phones, Sporting Goods, Dolls & Bears in that order.

4.3. Operational Measures of the Constructs

Most of the items of seven constructs in the model have been adapted from the existing literature as described below.

Trust

This construct measured a respondent's trust with online auction system. Nine items, which were adapted from Ba & Pavlou (2002), Pavlou (2002) and Gefen et al. (2003), were used to measure this construct.

Behavioural Control

This construct measured a person's beliefs about the internal and external resources and opportunities at his/her disposal that are required to control/facilitate various aspects of online auction. Seventeen items, which were adapted from Ba and Pavlou (2002), Pavlou (2002), Liyayen et al. (2000), Lucking-Reiley (2000), and Ba et al. (2003), were used to measure this construct.

Consequences

This construct refers to perceived advantages and disadvantages of online auction. The construct was based on Rogers (1995). It had ten items adapted from Rogers (1995), Liyayem et al. (2000) and Lucking-Reiley (2000).

Attitude

This construct measured a respondent's attitude toward online auction. It had seven items adapted from Liyayem et al. (2000) and Pavlou (2002).

Subject Norm

This construct refers to direct and indirect influences that the respondent is subjected to use online auction. It had four items adapted from Liyayem et al. (2000) and Pavlou (2002).

Personal Innovativeness

This construct measured how innovative a respondent is to try new things and ideas. It had four items adapted from Liyayem et al. (2000).

Buying Intention

As the name implies this construct measured a respondent's buying intention via online auction. It had eight items adapted from Gefen et al. (2003), Hartwick and Barki (1994), and Karahanna et al. (1999).

It is noted that all seven constructs of our research model (Figure 3.1) are reflective in nature (Chin 1998b). The model has a total of 59 items. Table 3.1 presents survey instruments and their literature support.

Table 3.1: Survey instruments

Trust		
Variables	**Measures**	**References**
Product Delivery	An online auction site should deliver to me the product I purchase according to the posted delivery terms and conditions	(Ba & Pavlou 2002; ACCC 2009)
Matched Products	An online auction site should deliver to me a product that matches the posted description.	(Ba & Pavlou 2002; ACCC 2009)
Reliability	An online auction site should be reliable/ should have reliable infrastructure to support the activities of buying and selling	(Pavlou 2002)
Trustworthiness	An online auction site should be trustworthy	(Pavlou 2002; Gefan, Karahanna & Straub 2003)
Caring about Customers	An online auction site should care about customers	(Gefan, Karahanna & Straub 2003)
Not Being Opportunistic	An online auction site should not be opportunistic	(Gefan, Karahanna & Straub 2003)
Good Customer Services	An online auction site should provides good services	(Gefan, Karahanna & Straub 2003)
Knowing the Market	An online auction site should know its market	(Gefan, Karahanna & Straub 2003)
Disclosure of Information	An online auction site should disclosc all the relevant information about its products and terms of sale	(ACCC 2009)

Table 3.1: *Continued*

Variables	**Measures**	**References**
Perceived Behavioural Control		
Control of Transaction	I should have full control over a transaction with the online auction site	(Pavlou 2002)
Control of Information	I should have the opportunity to control the information shared during a transaction with the online auction site	(Pavlou 2002)

Control of Elements	I should have the resources to control the elements of a transaction with the online auction site	(Pavlou 2002)
Ability to Navigate on the Web	I am able to navigate on the online auction site without any help	(Liyayem, Khalifa & Frini 2000)
Webpage Loading Speed	The loading speed of the web pages of the online auction site should be appropriate	(Liyayem, Khalifa & Frini 2000)
Site Accessibility	The site of online auction should be easily accessible, e.g., through search engines, cyber malls, and web ads	(Liyayem, Khalifa & Frini 2000)
Product Description	Appropriate and comprehensive information of products of the online auction site should be provided	(Liyayem, Khalifa & Frini 2000)
Navigation Effect	The online auction site should be easy to navigate	(Liyayem, Khalifa & Frini 2000)
Transaction Efficiency	Transaction processing of the online auction site is efficient (i.e., fast payment processing)	(Liyayem, Khalifa & Frini 2000)
Government Assistance	In China, there are laws and government organizations in place to protect the interests of online auction consumers.	(ACCC 2009)
Website Fraud Policies	The online action websites should actively discourage the fraud and have policies in place to prohibit the fraud	(ACCC 2009; Lucking-Reiley 2000)
Feedback & Rating Systems	The online auction should have a feedback and rating systems in place	(Lucking-Reiley 2000)
Social Norm	There is social norm of honesty in the online auction site	(Lucking-Reiley 2000)
Fraud Insurance/ Protection Program	A free or low cost insurance or fraud protection program should be available to protect buyers if they are proven to be victims of fraud	(Ba, whinston & Zhang 2003)

Availability of Escort Services	An escort service, which acts as trusted third party, should be available	(Ba, whinston & Zhang 2003)
Easy to Use	The site of online auction should be easy to use (i.e., simple to find information)	(Davis, Bagozzi, & Warshaw 1989)
Lower Auction Fees	The fees of buying via online auction is much lower than that of traditional auction houses	(Lucking-Reiley 2000)

Table 3.1: *Continued*

Variables	Measures	References
Perceived Consequences		
Cheaper Prices	Purchasing through the online auction allows me to save money, as I can buy the same or similar products at cheaper prices than regular stores	(Liyayem, Khalifa & Frini 2000)
Convenient Shopping	Buying through the online auction is more convenient than regular shopping, as I can do it anytime and anywhere	(Liyayem, Khalifa & Frini 2000)
Comparative Shopping	Buying via the online auction facilities comparative shopping, as I can easily compare alternative products online	(Liyayem, Khalifa & Frini 2000)
Risk of Security Breach	Security breach is a major problem for purchasing through online auction	(Liyayem, Khalifa & Frini 2000)
Improved Customer Services	I can get a better service (pre-sale, sale, and post sale) from online auction than from regular shopping and auction	(Liyayem, Khalifa & Frini 2000)
Saving Time	I can save time by shopping through online auction	(Liyayem, Khalifa & Frini 2000)
Risk of Privacy Violation	Privacy violation is a major problem for purchasing through online auction	(Liyayem, Khalifa & Frini 2000)

Geographic and Temporal Convenience	The online auction provides more convenience, both geographic (e.g., being able to bid from anywhere) and temporal (e.g., more flexibilities about when to submit bids), comparing to traditional auction	(Lucking-Reiley 2000)
Easy to Find Information and Products	The Internet has made it easier and more convenient for buyers to find the goods they are looking for	(Lucking-Reiley 2000)
More Varieties of Trading Goods	Online auction is able to trade more and different types goods than ever before and than the traditional auction	(Lucking-Reiley 2000)

Table 3.1: *Continued*

Variables	Measures	References
Attitude		
Good Idea	Purchasing through online auction is a good idea	(Liyayem, Khalifa & Frini 2000; Pavlou 2002)
Likeness	I like to shop through online auction	(Liyayem, Khalifa & Frini 2000)
Being Enjoyable	Purchasing through online auction is enjoyable	(Liyayem, Khalifa & Frini 2000)
Being Exciting	Purchasing through online auction is exciting	(Liyayem, Khalifa & Frini 2000)
Being Pleasant	Transacting with the online auction system is pleasant	(Pavlou 2002)
Favourable Attitude	My attitude toward the online auction system is favourable	(Pavlou 2002)
Realization of Benefits	Transacting via the online auction is beneficial to me	(Pavlou 2002)
Subject Norms		
Family Influence	The members of my family (e.g. parents, spouse, children) think I should make purchases through online auction	(Liyayem, Khalifa & Frini 2000)
Media Influence	The media frequently suggest us to make purchases through online auction	(Liyayem, Khalifa & Frini 2000)

Friends' Influence	My friends think I should make purchases through online auction	(Liyayem, Khalifa & Frini 2000)
People Who are Important to Me	Those people who are important to me (including friends and family) support my use of online auction	(Pavlou 2002)
Intention		
Purchase via Credit Card	I would use my credit card to purchase from online auction site	(Gefan, Karahanna & Straub 2003)
Providing Information	I am very likely to provide required information to the online auction site for it to better serve my needs	(Gefan, Karahanna & Straub 2003)
Use When Available	I intend to use online auction when it is available	(Hu et al. 1999)
Use as often as Needed	I intend to use online auction to purchase goods as often as needed	(Hu et al. 1999)
Use Frequently To the Extent Possible	To the extent possible, I intend to use online auction to do shopping frequently	(Hu et al. 1999; Hartwick & Barki 1994))
Use Whenever Possible	Whenever possible, I intend to use online auction to buy goods	(Hu et al. 1999)
Heavy User	I intended to be a heavy user of online auction	(Hartwick & Barki 1994)
Preference over the Regular Methods	I would use online auction rather than the regular methods for purchasing goods	(Agarwal & Prasad 1998)
Adoption Intention	I intend to adopt online auction to purchase goods within next three months	(Karahanna, Straub & Chervany 1999)
Intention of Regular Use	During the next three months, I plan to experiment with or regularly use online auction for my purchases	(Karahanna, Straub & Chervany 1999)

Table 3.1: *Continued*

Variables	Measures	References
Personal Innovativeness		
Accepting and Trying New Ideas/New Things	I am generally willing to accept and try new ideas/new things	(Liyayem, Khalifa & Frini 2000)

Being Original in Thinking and Behaviour	I find it stimulating to be original in thinking and behaviour	(Liyayem, Khalifa & Frini 2000)
Challenge of Ambiguities and Unsolved Problems	I am challenged by ambiguities and unsolved problems	(Liyayem, Khalifa & Frini 2000)
Following Other People	My consideration to use new things is not a result of seeing other people using them	(Liyayem, Khalifa & Frini 2000)

(Source: developed for this study)

4.4. Data Examination

Before the data were analysed, it was necessary to assess its properties. The raw data showed some missing values, which then was imputed using Estimated Means (EM) method. Next, the data were tested for assumption of multinormality. Although the Kolomogorov-Smirnov normality test showed the distribution anomalies in all items, the skewness and kurtosis of each item fell within the acceptable range (± 2).

5. Results

5.1. Assessment of Measurement Properties

As per Barclay et al. (1995) item reliability, internal consistency and discriminant validity were used as criteria to make sure that the model has acceptable measurement properties. The initial model with 59 observed variables was tested first using PLS.

The individual item reliability was assessed by examining the loadings of the items. A minimum value of 0.4 was used as criterion to accept the reliability of individual items (Igbaria et al., 1997). Results of the initial model showed that four items under 'behavioural control' construct had loadings less than 0.4. These items were thus dropped from further analyses in order to improve the item reliabilities. Table 3.2 shows the final item loadings. T-values of the items were also found to be high, indicating that the items are loaded significantly with their corresponding constructs.

Table 3.2: Item loadings

Items (observed variables)	Loading	Items (observed variables)	Loading
Trust_P1a	0..72	Conseq_P3g	0.41
Trust_P1b	0.85	Conseq_P3h	0.80
Trust_P1c	0.76	Conseq_P3i	0.78
Trust_P1d	0.67	Conseq_P3j	0.80
Trust_P1e	0.82	Attitude_P4a	0.64
Trust_P1f	0.56	Attitude_P4b	0.83
Trust_P1g	0.76	Attitude_P4c	0.90
Trust_Pli	0.66	Attitude_P4d	0.85
BControl_P2a	0.60	Attitude_P4e	0.85
BControl_P2b	0.73	Attitude_P4f	0.79
BControl_P2c	0.66	SNorm_P5a	0.84
BControl_P2e	0.81	SNorm_P5b	0.83
BControl_P2f	0.82	SNorm_P5c	0.88
BControl_P2g	0.77	SNorm_P5d	0.87
BControl_P2h	0.80	Innov_P6a	0.82
BControl_P2i	0.67	Innov_P6b	0.90
BControl_P2k	0.75	Innov_P6c	0.83
BControl_P2l	0.75	Innov_P6d	0.60
BControl_P2m	0.60	BuyIntent_P7a	0.63
BControl_P2n	0.66	BuyIntent_P7b	0.55
BControl_P2o	0.66	BuyIntent_P7c	0.82
BControl_P2p	0.82	BuyIntent_P7d	0.82
BControl_P2q	0.44	BuyIntent_P7e	0.87
Conseq_P3a	0.78	BuyIntent_P7g	0.80
Conseq_P3b	0.69	BuyIntent_P7h	0.75
Conseq_P3c	0.71		

Internal consistency of the latent variables was measured following the procedure of Fornell and Larcker (1981). The cut-off point for internal consistency is normally taken as 0.7. Table 3.3 shows that all the latent variables have internal consistencies above 0.7, indicating that the constructs are internally consistent and hence reliable.

Table 3.3: Internal Consistencies

Latent Variables	Internal Consistencies
Trust_P1	0.90
BControl_P2	0.94
Conseq_P3	0.87
Attitude_P4	0.92
SNorm_P5	0.92
Innov_P6	0.87
BuyIntent_P7	0.90

Discriminant validity of the latent variables was tested using the procedure of Fornell and Larcker (1981). Average variance extracted (AVE) was found for each latent variable. Square roots of AVE were then compared against the correlations among the latent variables (see Table 3.4). Square roots of the AVEs are shown in the main diagonal of Table 3.4. The off-diagonal elements are the correlations among the latent variables. For adequate discriminant validity square root of the AVE should be greater than the off-diagonal elements in the corresponding rows and columns (Barclay et al. 1995).

Table 3.4: Correlation of Latent Variables & Square Roots of AVE

	Trust _P1	BControl _P2	Conseq _P3	Attitude _P4	SNorm _P5	Innov _P6	BuyIntent _P7
Trust_P1	**0.73***						
BControl_P2	0.72	**0.71**					
Conseq_P3	0.59	0.62	**0.71**				
Attitude_P4	0.20	0.23	0.54	**0.82**			
SNorm_P5	0.13	0.14	0.38	0.63	**0.86**		
Innov_P6	0.49	0.68	0.68	0.57	0.51	**0.79**	
BuyIntent_P7	0.12	0.41	0.41	0.54	0.71	0.52	**0.75**

(* the bold elements in the main diagonal are the square roots of AVE)

5.2. The Structural Model and Tests of Hypotheses

Table 3.5 shows the results of the structural models. It is observed that among the primary hypotheses H1, H2, and H5 are supported (significant t-values) while hypotheses H3 and H4 are not supported (insignificant t-values). The model explains 55% of the variance of BuyIntent (see Figure 3.1 and Table 3.5), which is quite good. Among the five secondary hypotheses (H6, H7, H8, H9 and H10), all of them are supported. 40% of Attitude, 34% of Consequences, and 52% of Perceived Behavioural Control are explained by the model (see Figure 3.1 and Table 3.5).

Table 3.5: Tests of Structural Models

Hypotheses	**China Study**	
	Standardized path coefficients	t-value
H1: SNorm_P5 → BuyIntent_P7	0.54	6.20***
H2: Innov_P6 → BuyIntent_P7	0.26	2.39**
H3: Attitude_P4 → BuyIntent_P7	0.09	0.82
H4: Trust_P1 → BuyIntent_P7	0.03	0.33
H5: BControl_P2 → BuyIntent_P7	-0.17	1.93*
H6: Trust_P1 → BControl_P2	0.72	14.03***
H7: Trust_P1 → Attitude_P4	-0.23	2.47**
H8: Trust_P1 → Conseq_P3	0.59	7.55***
H9: Conseq_P3 → Attitude_P4	0.40	4.61***
H10: Innov_P6 → Attitude_P4	0.41	4.22***
R Square	R^2 for BuyIntent_P7 = 0.55 R^2 for Attitude_P4 = 0.40 R^2 for Conseq_P3 = 0.34 R^2 for BControl_P2 = 0.52	

(*p<0.05, ** p <0.025; ***p<0.01)

6. Results and Implications

The structural model analysis unearths some interesting findings. Our ultimate goal was to find the antecedents of buying intention via online auction (BuyIntent). It is observed that there are three direct significant factors of BuyIntent which are: subject norm, innovativeness and behavioural control. This is in line with previous literature. These factors have also been found to be significant in overall e-commerce activities.

Subject norm is a combination of various indirect pressures a consumer would be subjected to buy goods and services in online auction. Our results confirm the significant impact of Subject Norm on the BuyIntent, which in line with the notion that Chinese consumers will not feel comfortable to be left behind. If their neighbours and friends have tried the product or service, they will follow soon. In China, referral (word of mouth) is the most powerful way of opening the market for new products and services (Yang 2004). Our model postulates that subject norm does not have any antecedents. It works by itself influencing the BuyIntent. On the other hand, 'Attitude' has three significant antecedents as Innovativeness, Trust and Consequences. This implies that attitude of a consumer towards buying via online auction is formed primarily by his/her perceived innovativeness, trust toward online auction and consequences of buying via online auction. It is interesting to note that the first two are internal (personal) and psychological attributes (innovativeness and trust) and the other is an outcome oriented attribute which depends, among many other things, on 'good' online auction site.

Table 3.5 also shows that Innovativeness directly influences BuyIntent (H2). Even though it is not in line with the high avoidance of uncertainty in Chinese culture (Schneider & Barsoux 1995; Chow 1994; Hofstede 1993) or "reluctance to pioneer" (Yang 2004), young or educated people (i.e., MBA and BBA students in this case) are more likely to try new products and services, who are doing foreign business degrees and have been influenced by the western culture since China opened its door to the rest of the world in 1979. Liu (2004) and CNNIC (2004) suggest that Chinese consumes typically don't want to be among the first to try new product and services, especially when credibility and trust on the Internet remain the biggest obstacles of e-commerce in China. The results of only 43.2% of respondents have used online auction before lending support to this their argument. Given the Chinese consumers' limited experience with online auction, they will more likely to rely on reputable brands and track records. According to Yang (2004), brands could accounted for one-third to one half of all Chinese consumers' expressions of interest to purchase. In a survey conduced by Shanghai iResearch, the majority of the respondents have used EachNet before (Liu 2004), which is the eBay of China.

The non-significant relationship between Attitude and BuyIntent can be explained as follows. Even though Chinese consumers have positive attitude towards buying via online auction, they will not do shopping via online auction until they believe it is safe enough to trade online, along with the influence from important people and visible benefits of using online auction. At the same time, online trading in China still suffers from problems such as:

- *Security for online trading*: Security is a concern for all the consumers across the globe, this issue is greater for Chinese online shoppers resulting from the Chinese culture of avoiding uncertainty and not being a pioneer as well as their preferable experience with face-to-face deals (Tan & Wu 2002; Chen & Ning 2002; Anonymous 2005). This issue is also a result of the unavailability of well-established technological and transaction systems in China (Efendioglu & Yip 2004).

- *Payment inconvenience*: In China there is a lack of effective, standardized and widely adopted online payment systems and a lack of nationwide credit and processing system (Tan & Wu, 2002; Zhao, 2002; Chen & Ning, 2002; Anonymous, 2005; Bin et al., 2003). Also there is a low (about 1%) penetration rate of credit card rate in China (Ortolani, 2005). But the situation is changing with increased popularity of Paypal in China (used in eachnet.com) and other similar payments services (i.e., Tenpay (used in paipai.com), Alipay (used in taobao.com), and Baifubao (used in youa.baidu.com)).
- *Online trading credibility*: Issues such as lack of quality products & services, lack of accurate and timely information, and the failures of payments for transactions and on-time delivery need to be addressed (Tan & Wu 2002; CNNIC 2004; Liu 2004; Anonymous 2005).
- *Inherent values and attitude of Chinese people*:
    - *Anti-trust for credit cards*: Chinese consumers won't trust plastic (i.e. credit cards) as a secure form of payment, and they believe having debt is not good (Fannin 2003; Tan & Wu 2002).
    - *The tradition of face-to-face meeting*: Many sellers would use online auction site to advertise their products and select buyers in their hometowns and then settle the deal via face-to-face meetings. But today situation is changing as a result of improved postal services, banking facilities, and the emerging next-generation online payment systems as we discussed earlier on in this chapter (Fannin 2003; Efendioglu & Yip 2004; Clark 2000).
- *Legal infrastructure*: There is a lack of well-established legislation for online trading in China (CNNIC 2004; Efendioglu & Yip 2004).

Our research findings also show the importance of trust issue, which is an important issue across the globe (Efendioglu & Yip 2004).

Particularly security is one of the major concerns among Chinese online buyers (Tan & Wu 2002; CNNIC 2004; Anonymous 2005). In the meantime, even though Chinese consumers may like to purchase online, they don't feel comfortable when their personal details are asked by e-commerce sites (Anonymous 2005; Efendioglu & Yip 2004). They also would like to make sure what they are buying is what they want, which is easier to be done in a physical shop (Efendioglu & Yip 2004). Chinese consumers may not buy into "western honor system" (Efendioglu & Yip 2004, p. 59). In addition, Chinese consumers may believe "never let out your hawk until you see the hare" (Bin et al. 2003). However our results suggest while trust can have positive impacts (i.e., forming positive attitude towards online auction, developing more positive perceptions of benefits/ consequences of online auction, and enhancing consumers' confidence and comfort in using online auction), Chinese consumers will not embark on online auction just because they trust the online auction site. Factors such as personal innovativeness, influence from important people, security, online payment systems, online trading credibility, legal infrastructure as we discussed earlier on are playing important roles in their decision-making.

Among the secondary hypotheses all five hypotheses (H7-H10) are supported (see Table 3.5). Overall it is observed that each factor (latent variable) of Figure 3.1 has either a direct or indirect influence on the Buying Intention. Furthermore, this study has proved the model to be valid as evidenced by the good R square values (55%). However, more research is needed to further test those links which are not supported in this study.

The results of this study have significant implications for online auction practices. This research presents a practical model of online auction adoption, which will assist online auction sites in understanding Chinese customers' decision in taking part in online auction. The mediating effects of attitude between customer-related factors (e.g., innovativeness, trust, consequence, etc) and intention to buy suggest that online auction sites probably should put more emphasis on shaping and forming the favourable attitude towards online auction. Their efforts of promoting their online auction services might be more fruitful when their attention focuses on the "development" of pro-online auction attitude.

Successful adoption will take place if the formation of attitude is properly handled (Agarwal & Prasad 1999). The findings that innovativeness, trust and consequences have significant impact on attitude suggest that when online auction sites are dealing with developing customers' attitude toward using online auction, they should provide free trial (let customers themselves see how the online auction site works and see the benefits), deliver trustworthy services and target at such market segments where people are willing to take risks and try new things (i.e., people who are young, well-educated, having good income, and very busy).

This research also identified subject norm, innovativeness and perceived behaviour control have significant and positive effects on buy-intention. The implication is that online auction sites should provide users more control in their online activities and encourage more transparency in the process of online bidding, the use of information, and the way of dealing with frauds and disputes. Online auction sites probably should first target at segments of young and educated consumers, who normally are more willing to try new products and services like online auction. In the meantime, incentives should be provided for introducing peer customers, relatives, friends, colleagues and the like to use online auction since influence from others (e.g., word-of-mouth effect) can play an important role in people's decision of adopting online auction in China.

Given the potential largest online market in the world (1.3 billion people) and the largest number of internet users in the world (298 million by the end of December 2008), China has everything that any e-commerce business can dream of. In order to succeed or tap into the huge Chinese online marketplace, online auction sites have to form some good strategies. Some recommendations, on top of the discussions in the above two paragraphs, are provided as follows:

- *Integrated offline and online services*: Online auction sites should allow people to bid online and complete transaction offline. Also they should form strategic alliances with Chinese postal services and local delivery firms to take advantage of low delivery cost as a result of cheap labour in China (CNNIC 2004; Anonymous 2005). The strategy of "order online and pay offline" is probably the most practical way for the current online trading status in China (Bin et al. 2003, p55).

- *Better customer services*: Such as provide more information search functions in the site (CNNIC 2004), 24/7 services (Tan & Wu 2002), among many others.
- *Effective marketing and promotion strategies*: Online auction businesses should create an image in the market that buying via online auction is a prestige or a fashion that everyone should follow. But their marketing activities should not focus too much on the idea of getting cheap products via online auction since Chinese consumers believe "Cheap products are never good" (Yang 2004, p. 135). Also strategic alliances with famous local and international firms will definitely boost Chinese consumers' trust towards auction sites.
- *Flexible and localised payment methods*: Payment systems such as wireless transfers via postal saving bank, payment via debit cards (even though the credit card penetration rate is low in China, there are more than 400 million debit cards in China), and payment via mobile phones (Bin et al. 2003; Ortolani 2005; Anonymous 2005), online payment systems (i.e., previously mentioned Paypal, tenpay, Alipay, Baifubao used in leading online auction sites in China), should be made available to more users. Given the large population of mobile phone users (more than 600 million by the end of 2008, Chinatechnews 2008), online action sites should also explore the opportunity of mobile auction.
- *Customised auction sites for Chinese consumers*: Online auction sites in China should not copy everything from their counterparts in the west. They have to customise and localise the sites. For example, Eachnet.com used China National Identification Card instead of credit card for confirmation (Fannin 2003). They also need to take into consideration of such factors as: language (in Chinese), proper content suitable for the Chinese & environment in China, and free training for participating in online auction (Tan & Wu 2002).

7. Conclusions

This research has developed and tested a model of online auction in China. This research has a number of limitations and thus a number of prospective research directions. The first limitation is the sample size. Our sample size for China, although adequate for the tool used, is not large enough. It is also not collected via a random sampling approach. The issues of reflective/formative measures also have not been addressed in this study. Our immediate plan is to do further analysis addressing the issues associated with formative/reflective measures and conduct larger scale research in China. Despite the above limitations our research unearths some interesting findings, which provide some valuable insights in the domain of online auction in China.

References

Agarwal, R. & Prasad, J. (1997) The role of innovation characteristics and perceived voluntariness in the acceptance of information technologies, Decision Sciences, vol. 28, no. 3, pp. 557-582.

Agarwal R. and J. Prasad (1998) The antecedents and consequences of user perceptions in information technology adoption, Decision Support Systems, vol. 22, no.1, pp. 15-29.

Agarwal, R. & Prased, J. (1999) Are individual differences germane to the acceptance of new information technologies, Decision Sciences, Vol. 30, No. 2, pp. 361-391.

Ajzen, I. & Fishbein, M. (1980) Understanding Attituder and Predicting Social Behavior, Prentice-Hall, Inc., Englewood Cliffs, New Jersey 07632.

Ajzen, I. (1991) The Theory of Planned Behaviour: Some Unresolved Issues, Organizational Behaviour & Human Decision Processes, Vol. 50, pp. 179 – 211.

Ajzen I. and Driver B. (1992) Application of theory of planned behavior to leisure choice, Journal of Leisure Research, vol. 24, no. 3, pp. 207-224.

Anonymous (2005) Chinese Ecommerce: Fortune Waits, New Media Age, Jan 27 2005, pp. 23.

Australian Competition & Consumer Commission (ACCC) (2009) Internet auctions, Online, Available at: http://www.accc.gov.au/content/index.phtml/itemId/85563 (accessed April 30, 2009).

Ba, S. and Pavlou, P. A. (2002) Evidence of the effect of Trust Building Technology in Electronic Markets: Price Premiums and Buyer Behavior, MIS Quarterly, Vol. 26, No. 3, pp. 243-268.

Ba, S., Whinston, A. B. and Zhang, H. (2003) Building Trust in Online Auction Markets through an Economic Incentive Mechanism, Decision Support Systems, Vol. 23, pp. 273-286.

Bakos, Y. (1998) The Emerging Role of Electronic Market Places on the Internet, Communications of the ACM, Vol. 41, No. 8, pp. 35-42.

Bapna, R., Goes, P. and Gupta, A. (2001) Comparative Analysis of Multi-item Online Auctions: Evidence from the Laboratory, Decision Support Systems, Vol. 32, pp. 135-153.

Bapna, R. Goes, P. and Gupta, A. (2003a) Analysis and Design of Business-to-Consumer Online Auction, Management Science, Vol. 49, No. 1, pp. 85-101.

Bapna, R. Goes, P. & Gupta, A. (2003b) Replcating Online Yankee Auctions to Analyze Auctioneers' and Bidders' Strategies, Information Systems Research, Vol. 14, No. 3, pp. 244-268.

Bapna, R., Goes, P., Gupta, A. and Karuga, G. (2002) Optimal Design of the Online Auction Channel: Analytical, Empirical, and Computational Insights, Decision Sciences, Vol. 33, No. 4 , pp. 557-577.

Barclay, D, Higgins, C and Thompson, R. (1995) The Partial Least Squares (PLS) Approach to Causal Modeling: Personal Computer Adoption and Use as an Illustration, Technology Studies, Vol. 2, No. 2, pp. 285-309.

Beam, C and Segev, A. (2004) Auctions on the Internet: A Field Study, Working Paper 98-WP-1032, 1998. Available at http://haas.berkeley.edu/cmit/wp-1032.pdf.

Beam, C., Segev, A., Bichler, M., and Krishnan, R. (1999) On Negotiation and Deal making in Electronic Markets, Information Systems Frontiers, Vol. 1, No., pp. 241-258.

Beedell, J D C and Rehman, T (1999) Explaining Farmers' Conservation Behaviour: Why do Farmers Behave the Way They Do?, Journal of Environmental Management, Vol 57, pp. 165-176.

Beedell, J and Rehman, T (2000) Using Social-Psychology Models to Understand farmers' Conservation Behaviour, Journal of Rural Studies, Vol 16, pp. 117-127.

Berger I. (1993), A framework for understanding the relationship between environmental attitudes and consumer behavior, in Marketing Theory and Application, eds. Varadarjan R. and Jaworski B., Chicago: American Marketing Association, vol. 4, pp. 157-163.

Bin, Q., Chen, S. J. & Sun, S. Q. (2003) Cultural Differences in E-Commerce: A Comparison between the U.S. and China, Journal of Global Information Management, Vol. 11, No. 2, pp. 48-55.

Budish, E.B. & Takeyama, L. N. (2001) Buy Prices in Online Auctions: Irrationality on the Internet?, Economics Letters, Vol. 72, pp. 325-333.

Chen, S. & Ning, J. (2002) Constraints on E-commerce in Less Developed Countries: The Case of China, Electronic Commerce Research, Vol. 2, No. 1-2, pp. 31-42.

Cheung S.F, Chan K.S, and Wong S.Y (1999), Re-examing the Theory of Planned Behaviour in Understanding Wastepaper Recycling, Environment and Behaviour, vol. 31, no. 5, pp. 587-612.

China Internet Network Information Center (CNNIC) 2009, 23rd Statistical Survey on the Internet Development in China, January 2009, Available at: http://www.cnnic.com/uploadfiles/pdf/2009/1/13/92458.pdf [Accessed on Feb 2 2009].

China Internet Network Information Center (CNNIC) 2008, 2008 Survey on Online Shopping in China, June 2008, Available at: http://www.cnnic.com/uploadfiles/pdf/2009/1/13/92458.pdf [Accessed on Feb 2 2009].

China Internet Network Information Center (CNNIC) 2004, China Statistical Report on Popular Internet Issues, November 16 2004, Available at: http://www.cnnic.net.cn/download/manual/2004111602.doc [Accessed on Feb 28 2005].

Chinatechnews (2008) Chinese Mobile Phone Users over 600 Million, Available at: http://www.chinatechnews.com/2008/07/25/7067/-chinese-mobile-phone-uesrs-over-600) (Accessed on Feb 8 2009).

Chin, W. (1998a) The Partial Least Squares Approach to Structural Equation Modeling, in Modern Methods for Business Research, G. A. Marcoulides, Ed. Mahwah – NJ: Lawrence Erlbaum Associates, Inc., pp. 295-336.

Chin, W (1998b), Issues and Opinion on Structural Equation Modelling, MIS Quarterly, March, pp. vii – xvi.

Chin, W and P. R. Newsted, (1999) Structural Equation Modeling Analysis with Small Sample Using Partial Least Squares, in Statistical Strategies for Small Sample Research, R. H. Hoyle, Ed. Thousand Oaks – California: Sage Publication, Inc., pp. 307-341.

Chinaview (2008) China's Top Auction Site Taobao Transactions to Surpass 100 bln yuan in 2008. Available at: http://news.xinhuanet.com/english/2008-04/10/content_7954707.htm (Accessed on Feb 8 2009).

Chow, I.H.S.(1994) An Opinion Survey of Performance Appraisal Practices in Hong Kong and the People's Republic of China, Asia Pacific Journal of Human Resource, Vol. 32, No.3, pp. 67-78.

Clark, D. (2000) China Reluctant to Buy in to E-commerce, Telecommunications International, Vol. 34, No. 11, pp. 141-144.

Efendioglu, A. M. & Yip, V. F. (2004) Chinese Culture and E-commerce: An Exploratory Study, Integrating with Computers, Vol. 16, pp. 45-62.

Davis, F. D., Bagozzi, R. P. & Warshaw, P. R. (1989) 'User acceptance of computer technology: a comparison of two theoretical models', Management Science, vol. 35, no. 8, pp. 982-1002.

Emiliani, M. L. and Stec, D. J. (2002) Realizing Savings from Online Reverse Auction, Supply Chain Management, Vol. 17, No.1, pp.12-23.

Falk, R F and Miller, N B (1992), A Primer for Soft Modelling, The University of Akron Press, Akron.

Fan, M., Stallaert, J. & Whinston, A. B. (2003) Decentralized Mechanism Design for Supply Chain Organizations Using an Auction Market, Information Systems Research, Vol. 14, No. 1, pp. 1-22.

Fannin, R. (2003) The eBay of China: Eachnet, Chief Executive, August/September 2003, pp. 31-32.

Fishbein, M and Ajzen, I (1975), Belief, Attitude and Behaviour: An Introduction to Theory and Research, Addison-Wesley, Reading, MA.

Fornell, C. and Larcker, D. F. (1981) Evaluating Structural Equation Models with Unobservable Variables and Measurement Error, Journal of Marketing Research, XVIII, (February 1981), pp. 39-50.

Gefen, D., Straub, D. W. and Boudreau, M. C. (2000) Structural Equation Modeling and Regression: Guidelines for Research Practice, Communications of the Association for Information Systems, Vol. 4, No. 7, pp.1-77.

Gefan, D, Karahanna, E and Straub, D W (2003) Trust and TAM in On-line Shopping: An Integrated Model, MIS Quarterly, Vol 27 (1), pp. 51-90.

Gilkeson, J H and Reynolds, K. (2003) Determinants of Internet Auction Success and Closing Price: An Exploratory Study, Psychology and Marketing, Vol. 20, No. 6, pp. 537-566.

Grover V. (1993) Empirically derived model for the adoption of customer-based inter-organisational systems, Decision Sciences, vol. 24, no. 3, pp. 603-639.

Hage, J. & Aiken, M. (1970) Social change in complex organizations, Random House, New York.

Hair, J. F., Anderson, R. E., Tatham, R. L. & Black, W.C. (1998) Multivariate Data Analysis, Fifth Edition, Prentice-Hall International: London.

Hartwick, J and Barki, H (1994) Measuring User Participation, User Involvement, and User Attitude, MIS Quarterly, Vol 18(1), pp. 59-82.

Heezen, J and Baets, W. (1996) The Impact of Electronic Markets: The Case of the Dutch Flower Auctions, Journal of Strategic Information Systems, Vol. 5, pp. 317 – 333.

Hofstede, G. (1993) Cultural Constraint in Management Theories, Academy of Management Executive, Vol. 7, No. 1, pp. 81-94.

Hu, P. J., Patrick Y. K., Liu, R. S. & Tam, K. Y. (1999) Examining the technology acceptance model using physician acceptance of telemedicine technology, Journal of Management Information Systems, Vol. 16, No. 2, pp. 91-112.

Igbaria, M., Guimares, T., and Davis, G.B. (1995) Testing the Determinants of Microcomputer Usage via a Structural Equation Model, Journal of Management information Systems, Vol 11, No 4, pp. 87-114.

Igbaria, M, Zinatelli, N, Cragg, P and Cavaye, A. L. M. (1997) Personal Computing Acceptance Factors in Small Firms: A Structural Equation Model, MIS Quarterly, September, pp. 279-302.

Jap, S. D. (2002) On-Line Reverse Auction: Issues, Themes, and Prospects for the future, Academy of Marketing Science Journal, Vol. 30, No. 4, pp. 506-525.

John, G., Wheeler, R., Coughlan, J., Bull, K., Armes, D., Jephcott, D., Bricknell, D. & Barling, B. (2002) The Price of Electronic Bids, Supply Management, September, pp.19-26.

Kamins, M. A., Dreze, X., and Folkes, V. S. (2004) Effects of Seller-Supplied Prices on Buyers' Product Evaluations: Reference Prices in an Internet Auction Context, Journal of Consumer Research, Vol. 30, No. 4, pp. 622-628.

Karahanna, E, Straub, D W and Chervany, N (1999), Information Technology Adoption Across Time: A Cross-sectional Comparison of Pre-Adoption and Post-Adoption Beliefs, MIS Quarterly, Vol 23, No.2, pp. 183-213.

Ku, G. and Malhotra, D. (2001) The On-line Auction Phenomenon: Growth, Strategies, Promise and Problems, Negotiation Journal, Vol. 17, No. 4, pp.349-361.

Lansing, P. & Hubbard, J. (2002) Online Auctions: The Need for Alternative Dispute Resolution, American Business Review, January, pp. 108-116.

Lee, H. G. (1997) AUCNET: Electronic Intermediary for Used Car Transactions, Electronic Markets, Vol. 7, No. 4, pp. 24 – 28.

Limayem, M., Khalifa, M. and Frini, A. (2000) What Makes Consumers Buy from Internet? A Longitudinal Study of Online Shopping, IEEE Transactions on Systems, Man and Cybernetics – Part A: Systems and Humans, Vol. 30, No. 4, pp. 421 – 432.

Liu, B. (2004) Online Auctions Attracts Netizens, China Daily, Feb 20 2004, pp. 9.

Lucking-Reiley, D. (2000) Auctions on the Internet: What's Being Auctioned, and How? The Journal of Industrial Economics, XLVIII, No. 3, pp. 227 – 252.

Madden T.J, Ellen P.S. and Ajzen I. (1992) A Comparison of the Theory of Planned Behaviour and the Theory of Reasoned Action, Personality and Social Psychology Bulletin, vol. 18, no. 1, pp. 3-9.

Mathieson, K. (1991) Predicting User Intentions: Comparing the Technology Acceptance Model with the Theory of Planned Bahavior, Information System Research, vol. 2, no. 3, pp. 173-191.

McDonald, C. G. & Slawson, V. C. (2002) Reputation in an Internet Auction Market, Economic Inquiry, Vol. 40, No. 4 , pp. 633-650.

Neo, B. S. (1992) The Implementation of an Electronic Market for Pig Trading in Singapore, Journal of Strategic Information Systems, Vol. 1, No. 5, pp. 278 – 288.

Ortolani, A. (2005) Chinese Begin Paying by Cellphone, Wall Street Journal, February 2 2005, pp. 1.

Pavlou, P A (2002) Institutional Trust in Interorganizational Exchange Relationships: The Role of Electronic B2B Marketplaces, Journal of Strategic Information Systems, Vol 11 (4), pp. 105-143.

Randall D. and Gibson A. (1991) Ethical decision making in the medical profession: An application of the theory of planned behavior, Journal of Business Ethics, vol. 10, no. 2, pp. 111 - 122.

Pavlou, P. A. & Gefan, D. (2004) Building Effective Online Marketplaces with Institution-Based Trust, Information Systems Research, Vol. 15, No. 1, pp. 37-59.

Rogers, E. M. (1995), Diffusion of Innovations, 4th ed., Free Press: New York.

Schneider, S.C. & Barsoux, J.L.(1997) Managing Across Cultures, Prentice Hall: Europe.

Segev, A. and Beam, C., (1998) Auctions as Negotiations, Available at http://www.haas.berkeley.edu/~citm/auction/curraauction.html.

Tan, Z. X. & Wu. O. Y. (2002) Globalization and E-commerce I: Factors Affecting E-commerce Diffusion in China, Communications of the Association for the Information Systems, Vol. 10, pp. 4-32.

Taylor S. and Todd P.A. (1995) Understanding Information Technology Usage: A Test of Competing Models, Information Systems Research, vol. 6, no. 2, pp 144-177.

Thong J. Y. L. (1999), An Integrated Model of Information Systems Adoption in Small Business, Journal of Management Information Systems, vol. 15, no. 4, pp. 187-214.

Triandis H.C. (1980), Values, Attitudes, and Interpersonal Behavior, in Beliefs, Attitudes and Values, ed. Page H. M., University of Nebraska Press, Lincoln, pp 125-143.

Tung, L L and Quaddus, M. A. (2002) Cultural Differences Explaining the Differences in Results in GSS: Implications for the Next Decade, Decision Support Systems, Vol. 33, pp. 177 – 199.

Turban, E. (1997) Auctions and Bidding on the Internet: An Assessment, Electronic Markets, Vol. 7, No. 4, pp. 7 – 11.

Vaculik, J. (2003) Bidding by the Bar: On-line Auction Sites for Legal Services, Texas Law Review, Vol. 82, No. 2, pp. 445-480.

Van Heck, E and Vervest, P. (1998) How should CIOs deal with web-based auctions? Communications of the ACM, Vol. 41, No. 7, pp. 99-100.

Wang, K., Wang, E. T. G. and Tai, C. F. (2002) A Study of Online Auction Sites in Taiwan: Product, Auction Rule, and Trading Type, International Journal of Information Management, Vol.22, pp. 127 – 142.

Yang, R. (2004) To Reach China's Consumers: Adapt to Guo Qing, in Harvard Business Review on Doing Business in China, Harvard Business School Publishing Corporation: USA, pp. 123-140.

Zhao, H. X. (2002) Rapid Internet Development in China: A Discussion of Opportunities and Constraints on Future Growth, Thunderbird International Business Review, Vol. 44, No. 1, pp. 119-138.

CHAPTER 4

FACTORS INFLUENCING ONLINE ADVERTISING: A NATIONAL SURVEY AMONG SMALL & MEDIUM ENTERPRISES IN AUSTRALIA

Jan Heiligtag & Jun Xu

Graduate College of Management, Southern Cross University, Australia

Mohammed Quaddus

Graduate School of Business, Curtin University of Technology, Australia

This study investigates the current status and factors influencing the adoption of online advertising in Australian small and medium enterprises (SMEs). A model of online advertising adoption arising from the literature was tested. Primary data were collected from a self-administered questionnaire through a mail survey of 1000 Australian SMEs, which eventually led to 249 valid questionnaires. The results of the survey uncover some important information on the current status and understanding of online advertising in Australian SMEs. It is observed that the current status of adoption of online advertising of Australian SMEs can be considered well advanced. Online advertising had been widely adopted by the surveyed organisations (67.9%). And it appeared that most of the surveyed marketing decision-makers were at least to a certain degree aware of online advertising's benefits and its opportunities. In the meantime, relative advantage, cost effectiveness, complexity, compatibility, top management support, organisation innovativeness and customer interaction were found to be significant in the adoption of online advertising of Australian SMEs. Overall, the empirical findings of this research were reasonably consistent with past empirical findings. However business size was not identified to be a critical variable in this research. A compact prediction model of online advertising, only consisting of three factors of relative advantage, cost effectiveness, compatibility, was further developed for forecasting and classifying category of adopter or non-adopter of online advertising. The results provide practical suggestions to those companies who are embarking on the adoption of online advertising in Australia or elsewhere.

1. Introduction

The Internet has been claimed as a truly new communication medium since the invention of television (Ducoffe 1996). It allows information to be accessed without geographical location constraints and offers the possibility of delivering messages enhanced by colour, sound and animation effects, as well as two-way interactions. The interactive nature of the Internet facilitates customer support and market activities to a greater degree than traditional media (Hoffman, Novak & Schlosser 2000).

This growth has created various opportunities for businesses to not only improve their current marketing strategies (e.g. Barnes & Cumby 2002; Lazer & Shaw 2000) but also to engage in new ones. Such a new marketing practice is advertising products and services on the Internet, usually referred to as online advertising. The Australian online advertising sector has increased steadily and is predicted to have the strongest growth of all advertising media along with TV in the coming years (PricewaterhouseCoopers 2005).

According to Commercial Economic Advisory Service of Australia (CEASA)'s figures for main media spend in 2005, advertising revenue for all print, television, radio, outdoor, online and cinema increased by 11% compared with 2004, to A$11.58 billion. Even though advertising is currently still dominated by traditional media like TV and print, the online advertising sector has grown an impressive 60 percent for the full calendar year to December 2005 to A$620 million (see Figure 4.1), clearly eclipsing its nearest rival, the outdoor advertisement industry (Audit Bureau of Verification Services 2006). Yahoo Australia and New Zealand sales director Jules Robinson explained the rapid growth of online advertising with traditional TV and print advertisers who are now incorporating online advertising into their advertising plans and using it as part of their basic advertising mix (Alarcon 2004). Prominent advertisers allocated 7% of their advertising spending on online advertising in 2004, up a substantial three percentage points from 4% in 2003, according to the latest emitch/Roy Morgan Internet Advertising Intentions and Attitudes Survey (2005) conducted in late January 2005. The survey forecasted this strong trend to continue, underlining the importance of online advertising as part of the overall media-mix.

According to Martin Hoffman, CEO of Australia's leading online publisher ninemsn, online advertising is now a mass media (ninemsn 2005). He states that there are almost 10 million Australians online and big name advertisers have followed them onto the web. Especially broadband is assumed to have been a big driver of growth over the last year. According to the PricewaterhouseCoopers' 'Australian Entertainment and Media Outlook: 2004-2008' (PricewaterhouseCoopers 2005) report, the growth in online advertising spending in Australia will continue in the coming years. It is also worthwhile to note that online advertising spending is increasing worldwide. For example, the most progressed nation with respect to online advertising, the United States (US), had a significant increase in their national online advertising spending in 2005 as well. According to IAB and PwC's Internet advertising revenue report (IAB/PwC 2006) online advertising spending has grown to US$12bn in the US, exceeding 2004 by 30%. Accordingly, Goldman Sachs defined 2005 as the potential 'breakout year' for online advertising (Mediapost 2005). The research firm eMarketer (2006) expects this trend to continue and predicts online advertising spending to grow to US$15.6bn for the year 2006. With respect to a long range forecast, Forrester (2006) predicts that online advertising spending in the US reaches US$26 billion by the year 2010, which will represent 8 percent of all advertising spending. They argue that almost half of all marketers plan to increase online advertising spending by decreasing spending in other channels.

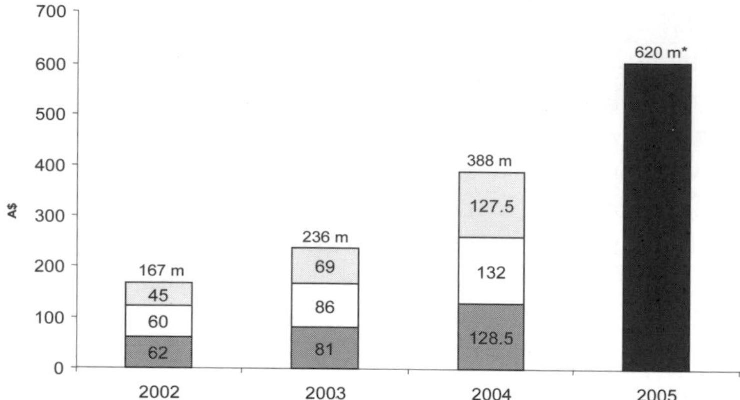

Search and directories advertising (defined as online directory or search engine listings)
Classifieds advertising (defined as advertisements placed to buy or sell an item or service)
General advertising (defined as display advertisements such as banner advertisements of many different sizes and formats, sponsorships, partnerships, affiliate marketing programs and emails)
* no further details available

Figure 4.1: Online advertising spending Australia 2002-2005
(Source: developed for this research based on Audit Bureau of Verification Services (2006))

Despite of the many advantages of online advertising (e.g. its cost effectiveness and flexible nature) and the increased spending on online advertising, the extent to which companies, particularly small and medium enterprises (SMEs), take advantage of online advertising is subject to debate. According to Australian Bureau of Statistics (2002), small businesses have less than 20 employees and medium businesses have less than 200 employees. According to the latest census data from the Australian Bureau of Statistics (ABS 2002) 97% of all private sector businesses are SMEs, who in total employ more than half of all private sector employment. It can be argued that the marketing needs of SMEs are sufficiently different from their larger counterparts, who might often engage in branding campaigns and have the necessary financial resources to advertise their products and services in a cross media mix. Since SMEs have a distinctive and unique need for certain advertising methods such as online advertising, there is a necessity to better understand the factors that affect the adoption of online advertising in SMEs. This need is also amplified when one considers the potential opportunities online advertising offers with respect to growth and profitability. Consequently, the issue of factors affecting the adoption of online advertising in Australian SMEs constitutes the focal point of this investigation. Acknowledging the fast growth of online advertising in Australia as well as the importance of SMEs to the Australian economy; the main goal of this research is to investigate the distinguishing factors of Australian SMEs that adopt online advertising. Where there exist some past studies on adoption of e-commerce of SMEs, there is a silence in the literature with respect to the adoption of online advertising of SMEs. Consequently, this study is aiming to close the gap via investigating the adoption of online advertising in Australian SMEs. In particular, this research will answer the following research questions: (1) What is the current status of online advertising in Australian SMEs?; (2) What factors are affecting the adoption of online advertising in Australian SMEs?; (3) What factors can be used to predict the adoption of online advertising in Australian SMEs?.

This chapter is organized as follows. The following section presents relevant background. The research model and hypotheses are presented next. This is followed by the demographic information of the national survey. The data analysis through t-test and logistic regression is also presented in this section. Conclusions regarding research questions and implications for theory and practice are discussed next. The chapter finishes with summary, limitations and future research directions.

2. Background

Online advertising is an information technology innovation that helps organisations to advertise their products and services to a large audience by using a variety of online advertisements. There are various definitions for online advertising available in the research community. For example, Dreze and Zufryden (2004) provided a broader definition by defining online advertising as a proactive form of visibility where companies pay to be visible in the Internet landscape. It is also worthwhile to note that online advertising is often referred to as Internet advertising or interactive advertising. In this study, online advertising is defined as banners, keywords, logos, text or text links on websites as well as emails containing information about retailers or service providers or their products or services (Dowling, Kuegler & Testerman 1996). Generally, the overall goal of online advertising is to influence buying habits and change consumption patterns towards the advertised products and services. Cartellieri et al. (1997) identified five potential objectives of online advertising in order to achieve this goal:

- Delivering content: A click-through on an online advertisement leads to the website of the advertiser and gives more detailed information about its products and services. A direct response is intended in this scenario.
- Enabling transaction: Assuming a click-through leads to a merchant with e-commerce functionality, it can lead directly to a sale. A direct response is also sought in this scenario.
- Shaping attitudes: An online advertisement that is consistent with the company brand can positively influence its brand awareness.
- Soliciting response: An online advertisement can help to establish new leads or to enable a two-way communication by email or other interactive communication tools.
- Encouraging retention: An online advertisement might be intended as a reminder about the product and services of the advertiser.

A wide range of online advertising types exists and is steadily growing. The following Table 4.1 gives an overview of the most common online advertising types.

The steadily increasing number of both consumers and businesses connecting to the Internet indicates a viable target audience for advertising messages for many firms. Businesses with an Internet presence spend on online advertisements in their effort to enhance site visibility and presence on the Internet, and thereby increase the traffic on their website. In the meantime, advertisers with a small online advertising budget are also able to reach a large target audience with online advertising. For example, a cost-per-click on Australia's leading search engine Google.com.au costs A$0.01 (Google-AdWords 2006). Internet users have nowadays to choose from a steadily increasing number of websites, which all compete for a fraction of the user's limited Internet surfing time. The broadband technology developments such as

Table 4.1: Profiles of common online advertising types

Medium	Definition	Advantages	Disadvantages
Website	The virtual location (domain) for an organisation's or individual's presence on the World Wide Web.	Communicate detailed information that users can navigate at will; can track users and customise site	Narrow reach
Banner ad (inkl. PopUp)	A graphic image displayed on a website usually linked to the advertiser's website.	Link direct buying opportunity; wide reach; effective targeting	Low attention; short life; fleeting exposure; clutter
Interstitial	Ad that appears between two content pages. Also known as transition ads, intermercial ads, splash pages and Flash pages.	Catch users' attention; link to buying opportunity	Can annoy users
Rich media	A method of communication that incorporates animation, sound, video, and interactivity.	Attention-getting; link to buying opportunity	Can annoy users with slow Internet-connection
Dynamic ad placement	The process by which an ad is inserted into a page in response to a user's request.	Serves up customised ads to users in real time	Difficult to execute well; can annoy users
Search engine	A program that helps Internet users to find information on the Internet.	Good credibility; good position available; significant audiences	High competition; information overload
Classifieds and listings	The presence on a heavily trafficked website in order to have great reach to potential customers.	Relatively inexpensive; good exposure; qualified audience	Clutter
Opt-in email	List of Internet users who have voluntarily signed up to receive commercial e-mail about topics of interest.	High demographic selectivity; inexpensive; high credibility	Requires substantial user base; clutter
Mass email	Unsolicited emails to a large number of Internet users; often unwanted (spam).	High reach; inexpensive; flexible	Low attention; significant resentment
Customer service	Assisting help seeking Internet users by interactive communication.	High target value; generates loyal customers	Expensive to provide comprehensive support

(Source: adapted from Mohammed et al. (2002) and IAB (2005))

DSL and cable have increased the availability of the Internet, and the diffusion of high-speed Internet connections has been instrumental in speeding up and greatly facilitating the navigation process through the Internet. Additionally, search engines with more sophisticated search algorithms (e.g. Google) have evolved. Thus, Internet users are further provided with more relevant search results helping them to better find the websites they seek. Over time, Internet users have also become more sophisticated in terms of their ability to use online resources, such as websites, search engines and directories, to more efficiently use the Internet. They also have become more focused on their own information needs and tend to increasingly avoid distractions from their information search goals (Dreze & Zufryden 2004).

Online advertising gives user access to information not immediately accessible to them. In this respect online advertising has a potential advantage over traditional media because companies offer consumer-relevant information on their websites at an increasingly rate without any time constraints. The interactivity of online advertisements is probably one of the most significant differences between online advertising and traditional media advertising. When customers are surfing the Internet for products and services, they generally are actively searching rather than passively receiving the message broadcast by advertisers, which is the case for TV commercials (Salam, Pegels & Rao 1997). Online advertising will be more relevant to consumers. Advertising on an interactive network such as the Internet can be considered as a form of direct marketing communication (Ducoffe 1996), which has the advantage of addressable media technology to communicate to the consumer with a greater efficiency than ever experienced before through traditional media channels. Online advertisements are flexible; they can be customised and altered quickly and easily in response to consumer profiles and changing market conditions. In comparison to online advertisements traditional advertisements such as print advertisements or TV spots are often subject to deadlines and have to be produced well in advance of the appearance of the advertisements. This limitation makes it difficult to revise advertisements in a timely fashion to respond to changing market conditions. Furthermore, online advertisements can be customised for and by users (Ducoffe 1996). Online advertising can initiate transactions on a business' website when users respond to advertisements. This process will increase the speed as well as the convenience of purchases or inquiries for consumers and businesses alike since the fulfilment process is accelerated electronically.

The future of online advertising looks very promising. Major Internet research firms (e.g. eMarketer 2006; Forrester 2006; Jupiter 2005) forecast increasing spending on this medium as companies realise the effectiveness of online advertising in reaching target audiences with measurable results – especially with the expected better targeting and reporting capabilities. Generally, the Internet is more and more seen as a mature business and online advertising becomes more comparable to the well established TV and print advertising (Patrick 2005). Accordingly, marketers are expected to further shift advertising spending from traditional media to digital media in the foreseeable future (e.g. Barwise & Farley 2005; Shields 2005).

With respect to the further development of online advertisements used, rich-media will become more important due to the rapid growth in broadband users and the continued progress in hardware and software technologies. The types of online advertisements have already expanded from banner advertisements to search-related advertisements, where the advertisement content appearing on the website is directly linked to a user's search request. Especially because the effectiveness of search-related advertisements are commonly seen as easy to measure, advertisers only pay for the advertisements' placement when people click on them, and can track when clicks translate into purchases. Accordingly, experts predict that search engine marketing will reinvent itself as a lead-generation channel while continuing to drive significant advertising revenue in the foreseeable future. Furthermore, it is expected that brand advertisers will drive the next wave of growth for the paid search market (24/7-Realmedia 2005). Publishers are also expected to further adapt their websites to IAB standards to make the website appearance less cluttered by too many online advertisements and more appealing to users. Advertisers already follow this path and address user's criticism by relying more on 'take-over' advertisements. This means one advertiser covers the entire page and thereby giving it a more consistent appearance (Maddox 2005a). Online video advertisements, which have slowly been gaining acceptance by advertisers as the technology improves, are expected to significantly grow in the next two years, according to a report by eMarketer (2006). Also expected to advance the growth of online video advertisements are new guidelines released in late November 2005 by the IAB (Maddox 2005b). However, it will still take some time until advertisers actually use the chance of producing interactive online video advertisements, engaging viewers' attention in ways that TV spots cannot. So far online video advertisements are just replaying TV spots, which do not make full use of the interactive element of the Internet (Lawton 2005).

Another promising invention is the 'Really Simple Syndication' (RSS) news feed that is targeted to specific media placements. These feeds open the possibility of turning advertising units into branded-content syndication services. For example, the BBC already booked an advertising campaign that streams BBC.com headlines in online advertisements. The campaign is a small example of a larger effort to make online advertising more inviting with useful bits of content tailored to specific interests, delivered wherever consumers are (Morrissey 2005). Furthermore all indicators point to consumer generated media (e.g. blogs) becoming a promising 'advertising spend' opportunity. Especially for advertisers looking to reach specific micro-communities as behavioural targeting becomes increasingly indispensable for delivering the right content to the most receptive audience (24/7-Realmedia 2005). The increased possibilities and actual use of video and animation technologies is causing advertisers to reconsider the purpose of online advertisements. Historically, online advertisements were used to simply draw users to the advertiser's websites. Nowadays and even more in future times online advertisements can be utilised for rich branding experiences and a way to collect valuable customer information. Advertisers are turning their online advertisements into mini-websites, allowing Internet users to watch video clips, take quizzes and request more information, all without going to the advertiser's website. This reinvigoration of online advertisements could lead to a creative renaissance on the Internet (Morrissey 2005).

Even though the benefits of online advertising appear to be very attractive to adopting organizations, there has not been much empirical research done to validate the potential benefits of online advertising. Furthermore, some existing studies that investigate information technology adoption decisions have concentrated more on large businesses (e.g. Agarwal, Higgins & Tanniru 1991; Leonard-Barton 1992; Leonard-Barton & Sinha 1993). For example, Agarwal et al. (1991) analysed technology innovation in large companies such as Hewlett Packard, Ford Motor Company and Chaparral Steel. However, these studies might not be applicable to SMEs because of the fundamental differences between large companies and their smaller counterparts (Blau, Heydebrand & Stauffer 1966; Blili & Raymond 1993; Dandridge 1979; Senn & Gibson 1981; Welsh & White 1981). There is a lack of empirical study of adoption of online advertising in SMEs. This study thus adds to the body of literature through the empirical study on the adoption of online advertising in Australian SMEs.

3. Hypotheses of the Study

Based on the literature review, the following hypotheses were proposed. The hypotheses have been grouped under innovation, environmental and organizational characteristics (see Figure 4.2). Due to space limitations the constructs are not described fully in the chapter.

Hypotheses related to the innovation characteristics:

- Hypothesis H1: The relative advantage of online advertising positively influences the adoption decision of online advertising.
- Hypothesis H2: The compatibility of online advertising positively influences the adoption decision of online advertising.
- Hypothesis H3: The cost effectiveness of online advertising positively influences the adoption decision of online advertising.
- Hypothesis H4: The complexity of online advertising negatively influences the adoption decision of online advertising.

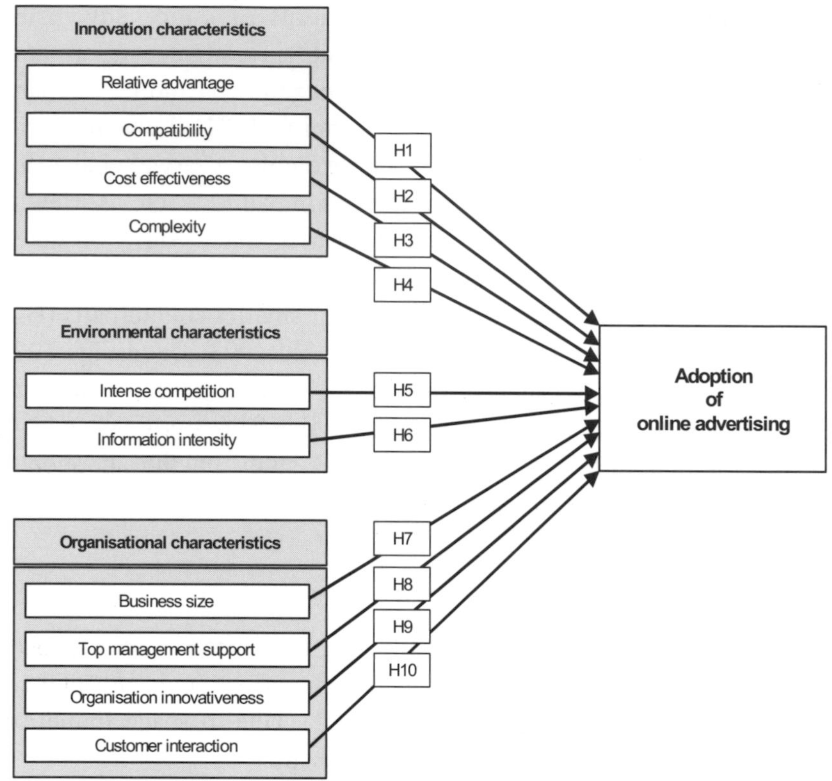

Figure 4.2: The Research Model

Hypotheses related to the environmental characteristics:

- Hypothesis H5: Intense competition positively influences the adoption decision of online advertising.
- Hypothesis H6: Information intensity positively influences the adoption decision of online advertising.

Hypotheses related to the organisational characteristics:

- Hypothesis H7: Business size positively influences the adoption decision of online advertising.

- Hypothesis H8: Top management support positively influences the adoption decision of online advertising.
- Hypothesis H9: Organisation innovativeness positively influences the adoption decision of online advertising.
- Hypothesis H10: Customer interaction positively influences the adoption decision of online advertising.

4. The National Survey

The national survey was conducted among 1,000 SMEs in Australia. The questionnaires were distributed to 1,000 marketing decision-makers in these companies, who appeared to be most relevant to our study. The mailing list of the top 1,000 companies was created from online database of Dun & Bradstreet's The Business Who's Who. In the end, 249 valid questionnaires were returned, which results in a response rate of 24.9%. A non-response error is regarded negligible in this research since the differences between early and late respondents are found statistically non-significant.

5. Results of the National Survey

5.1. Demographic Information

Respondent profile

The respondents' characteristics were classified in the seven categories of gender, age, education attained, academic specialisation, position, years in their current position and years in their current field.

Gender

Almost two-third (63.5%) of the respondents were male. This reflects the male dominance in senior marketing positions.

Age

The majority (57%) of the respondents were between 35 and 54 years old, with 35-44 years old being the largest group (29.3%) in the sample followed by 45-54 years old (27.7%).

Highest education attained

Almost two-third of the respondents (63.4%) has at least attained a bachelor's degree, with 12.4% having a graduate diploma, 13.7% a master's degree and only 0.4% a doctorate. The remaining respondents had either obtained a high school degree (15.3%) or a diploma (19.3%).

Academic background

Respondents were asked to nominate in what field their major academic training was. Majority (57.8%) of the respondents had an academic background in business, followed by Arts/literature/language (1.4%), Engineering (8.4%) and Social science (6%).

Position

Given that the survey was directed towards marketing decision-makers, it is not surprising that the majority of the respondents were either marketing managers (43.4 %) or sales & marketing manager (12.9%). The second largest group was owner/CEO/chairman (14.9%), which indicates the involvement of the top management of SMEs in marketing decisions to some extent.

Years in current position

The majority (54.6%) of the respondents had been in their current position for less than six years with 3-5 years being the overall largest group with 29.3%. Of the respondents with six or more years in their current position (45.4%) the group with 11-20 years in the current position was the largest group with 20.1%.

Years in current field

The respondents had significant work experience in their current field. Four out of five respondents (80.3%) had six or more years work experience in the current field, with 11-20 years being the largest group (28.1%). Given that marketing decision-makers were surveyed it is not surprising that only 6.4 percent had less than two years work experience in their current field.

Company profile

The respondents' company profile was analysed based on eight characteristics: number of employees, revenue, industry classification, years of company in business, location, population density at location, geographical market focus and economic development.

Number of employees

Almost half of the respondents (45.0%) worked for organisations with 50-199 employees. Organisations with 20-49 employees represent the second largest group with 27.7%. Approximately, one quarter (27.3%) of the organisation surveyed had less than 20 employees.

Revenue

At least 90% of the surveyed SMEs generated revenue in the amount of A$1M or more, with the largest group being in the range from A$1,000,000-4,999,999 (25.7%), followed by SMEs with an annual revenue between A$10M-25M at 25.3%.

Industry classification

The distribution of the respondents by industry reveals that most noticeable are the retail trade and manufacturing sector with 22.5% and 14.9% respectively. In contrast, government administration and defence as well as electricity, gas and water supply were each only represented by three organisations (1.2%).

Years of company in business

Most of the organisations surveyed can be considered as well established. More than four out of five organisations (86.3%) were at least 11 years in business, with organisations in business for more than 20 years being the largest group at 55.0%, followed by organisation whose foundation falls in the range of 11-20 years (31.3%). Organisations that were established within the last five years accounted only for 2.8 %.

Location

The surveyed organisation by their respective states reveal that Victoria, New South Wales and Queensland were represented the strongest with 24.1%, 20.1% and 16.9% respectively. All states were fairly well represented, with Northern Territory having the weakest representation (3.2%).

Population density at location

Almost three out of four organisations (72.7%) were settled in a high population area, followed by organisations from average population areas with 18.5%. Only 8.8% of the surveyed organisations were from low population areas.

Geographical main market focus

Majority of the organisations has a nationwide market focus (50.6%). 44.2% of the respondents primarily concentrate on local or regional customers. Only one out of five surveyed companies (19.7%) reports the international market as their main focus.

Economic development

In terms of growth and development the surveyed organizations reveal that overall the SMEs were in good condition. A high proportion of the SMEs (71.1%) were growing at least at a moderately rate if not strongly

(24.9%). Only 5.6% of the respondents found their organisations to be shrinking.

Website information

The respondents' website strategy was analysed with respect to its purpose and time of adoption. This information was collected since an existent of website can be seen as an essential requirement for meaningful online advertising.

Purpose of website

Respondents were asked to indicate the purpose of their organisation's website. Majority of the respondents (94.8%) used their website as a marketing tool to inform customers about their products and services, followed by the goal of informing business partners (35.3%). Almost one-third of the participating organisations (30.9%) used their website as an e-commerce platform for selling products and services through their online-shop. It is also worthwhile to note that 3.2% of the respondents used their website for hiring purposes by informing potential employees about jobs. Only 2% of the respondents had no website in place, which reflects how far the adoption of websites in the business sector has progressed.

Website adoption

Most of the surveyed organisations (45.8%) introduced their first business website between the year 1998 and 2000, with year 2000 having the highest adoption rate (20.5%), followed by 1998 (12.9%) and 1999 (12.4%). 11.2% of the respondents reported that their website was already established in 1995, which indicates that at least some Australian SMEs can be considered as very innovative in terms of adopting new information technologies. In 2005 the adoption rate was only 1.2%, which manifests that almost all participating organisations had a website in place.

Online advertising information

This section presents the participating organisations' current status of online advertising. The respondents' online advertising strategy was analysed with respect to its perceived advantages and disadvantages, adoption rate, types of online advertisements used, reasons for adopting, target audience, year of adoption, use of a media agency, spending on online advertising (absolute and relative to the total advertising budget) and revenue generated from online advertising.

Advantages and disadvantages of online advertising

Respondents were asked to indicate the advantages and disadvantages of online advertising in an open-ended question. Similar responses were grouped together to find a list of advantages of online advertising.

The biggest advantages of online advertising is its cost effectiveness (31.7%). Other major advantages of online advertising include its market reach, flexible nature and targeting potential with 18.1%, 14.4% and 12.9% respectively. Respondents also found that online advertising is advantageous with respect to having instant access to it (10.8%), its tracking abilities (6.8%) and its 365x24 availability (5.2%). Some respondents also used online advertising to collect data and feedback (4.4%). Lastly, 3.6 percent of the respondents suggested online advertising as a meaningful addition to other marketing channels.

The respondents also revealed a number of disadvantages of online advertising. Targeting problems (8%) as well as low awareness (7.6%) were perceived as most significant disadvantages. 6.4% of the participating organisations also found online advertising to be intrusive and/or annoying. Furthermore, the measurement of the effectiveness of online advertising was questioned by 4.4% of the respondents. Some respondents (4.0%) also reported technical problems with the creation and design of online advertisements as well as problems due to spam-blocking filters and corresponding regulations.

Adoption of online advertising

In terms of the adoption of online advertising in Australian SMEs our survey showed that two-thirds of the respondents (67.9%) reported that their organisations have already adopted online advertising.

The rest of the section only analyses data from the 169 respondents that adopted online advertising.

Use of online advertisements

Respondents were queried to indicate what types of online advertisements they use. It was found that the preferred types of online advertisements were email with 74.0%, followed by keywords on search-engines with 68.6% and listings on partner websites with 59.8%. The use of banners (37.9%), listings on portal websites (29.6%) as well as sponsorships (25.9%) was also frequently reported from the respondents. This finding shows that all types of online advertisements were part of the respondents' online advertising efforts.

Reasons for using online advertising

Respondents were asked to indicate the main reasons why they have adopted online advertising. It was found that more than three-quarter (76.3%) of the respondents used online advertising to increase the brand awareness of their products and services, closely followed by 70.4% of the respondents who advertised online to generate traffic towards their organisation's website. It is also worthwhile to notice that 3.5% of the respondents, which had chosen the 'other'-option, wrote that they utilise online advertising to collect data.

Target audience

The survey revealed that the participating organisations evenly targeted private customers (29%) and businesses (27.8%). Most respondents (43.2%) reported that their online advertising efforts are targeted towards both, private customers and businesses.

Online advertising adoption

Most of the surveyed organisations (46.2%) adopted online advertising between the year 2001 and 2003, with 2001 and 2002 having the highest adoption rates of 16.0%, followed by 2003 with 14.2%. Quite surprisingly, 10.1% of the respondents reported that they have already been using online advertising prior to 1996. This can be seen as another indicator for the innovative nature of at least some Australian SMEs. It was interesting to see that the online advertising adoption lags three years behind the adoption of websites (see earlier discussion).

Use of a media agency

In order to get a better understanding of the online advertising expertise and technical capabilities respondents were asked to indicate if they use an online media agency that administers their online advertising activities. It was found that one out of five respondents (20.1%) used a media agency. The remaining respondents (79.9%) administered their online advertising in-house, which can be seen as an indicator for their online advertising proficiency as well as for their technical knowledge in this regard.

Online advertising spending

Respondents were asked to specify how much financial resources they spent on online advertising and how much of their total advertising spending was allocated towards online advertising. It was found that the majority of the respondents (61.6%) spent at least A$2,000 on online advertising, with the largest group of respondents (24.9%) spent at least A$10,000 on online advertising, followed by 22.5 percent of the respondents who spent between A$2,000 - A$4,999 and 14.2% of the respondents who spent A$5,000-9,999. Approximately one out five respondents (20.2%) spent less than A$1,000 on online advertising.

On the other hand, the percentage of the total advertising budget allocated towards online advertising was fairly low. In most cases (57.4%) the respondents allocated five percent or less of their total advertising budget towards online advertising. One out of five respondents (20.1%) reported that they allocated 6-15% for online advertising. 5.9% of the respondents allocated more than 25% of their advertising budget towards online advertising efforts. It is also interesting to see that 10.1% of the respondents were not able to answer this question. This indicates that some SMEs do not allocate their advertising budget according to a predefined plan.

Revenue based on online advertising

The respondents were asked to indicate how much of their revenue is approximately generated from online advertising. The intention was to get a better understanding of the respondents' perception of the effectiveness of their online advertising efforts with regard to generating revenue. It was revealed that almost half of the respondents (45.6%) did not know how much of their revenue is based on online advertising efforts. 28.4% of the respondents reported that less than 6% of their revenue where generated from online advertising, followed by 14.8% of respondents who indicated that 6-15% of their revenue comes from online advertising and 8.9% of respondent who found 16-25% of their revenue are based on online advertising. Lastly, 11.3% of the respondents stated that more than 15% of their revenue has its origin in their online advertising activities.

Advertising channels

This last section presents an overview of the advertising channels used by the respondents. It was found that a broad variety of advertising channels was used by the participating SMEs. Interestingly, online advertising was reported as the most used advertising channels (67.9%), which reflects the fast diffusion of this new marketing tool in the market, especially if one considers that online advertising has just been introduced to the market in 1994. Besides online advertising the respondents made widely use of magazines (65.1%) and direct mail (62.7%), followed by promotions (52.2%) and newspaper (47.8%). Approximately one-third (35.7%) of the respondents used phone calls to advertise their product and services. Radio, TV and outdoor advertising were also quite frequently reported with 29.7%, 22.9% and 19.3% respectively. Some respondents also named yellow pages (12.0%) and tradeshows as advertising channels (4.0%). SMEs, which do not advertise at all, accounted for 3.2% of the sample. Lastly, it is worthwhile to emphasise that this data represents only the channels used in the advertising strategy. It does not reflect how much of the advertising budget was actually allocated on the various channels.

5.2. Independent t-tests

Independent t-tests have been commonly used to compare two groups (Munro 2005). Following the example of other innovation adoption researchers (e.g. McCole & Ramsey 2005; Thong & Yap 1995) the independent t-test was used to test each hypothesis that the mean scores on the proposed factor will be significantly different for adopters and non-adopters of online advertising. Table 4.2 presents results of independent t-tests.

Table 4.2: Results of Independent T-test

	Adopter (n = 169)		**Non-adopters (n = 80)**		**t-test**	
Variable	**Mean**	**SD**	**Mean**	**SD**	**t-value**	**1-tail sig**
Innovation characteristics						
H1: Relative advantage	5.11	0.79	3.45	1.16	13.31	0.000*
H2: Compatibility	5.16	0.97	3.42	0.92	13.40	0.000*
H3: Cost effectiveness	4.95	0.86	3.19	1.06	13.91	0.000*
H4: Complexity	3.44	1.06	4.34	0.97	6.47	0.000*
Environmental characteristics						
H5: Intense competition	4.55	1.23	4.34	1.30	1.21	0.113
H6: Information intensity	4.38	1.11	4.28	1.26	0.68	0.250
Organisational characteristics						
H7: Business size	4.08	1.03	4.04	1.04	0.28	0.390
H8: Top management support	4.02	0.96	3.11	0.99	6.92	0.000*
H9: Organisation innovativeness	4.60	1.12	3.97	1.22	4.02	0.000*
H10: Customer interaction	5.91	0.87	5.58	0.95	2.77	0.003 **

(* significant at $p < 0.0005$; ** significant at $p < 0.005$)

It can be seen from the table that the hypotheses H5, H6 and H7 were rejected by the analysis while support for the hypotheses H1, H2, H3, H4, H8, H9 and H10 was established. This means that intense competition, information intensity and business size were not found to significantly influence the adoption decision of online advertising. Whereas relative advantage, cost effectiveness, complexity, compatibility, top management support, organisation innovativeness and customer interaction were found to positively influence the adoption decision of online advertising in Australian SMEs with statistic significance.

5.3. Logistic Regression

In line with other innovation adoption studies (e.g. Cooper, R. B. & Zmud 1990; Dholakia & Kshetri 2004; Furst, Lang & Nolle 2002; Lassar, Manolis & Lassar 2005; Loh & Ong 1998; McCole & Ramsey 2005; Mollenkopf, White & Zwart 2001; Yao et al. 2002) this study utilised the direct logistic regression for the purpose of confirming the findings of the independent t-tests and the forward stepwise logistic regression to build a compact model for predicting group membership of adopters and nonadopters of online advertising.

Direct logistic regression

In this study direct logistic regression was used to confirm the findings of the independent t-test regarding the hypotheses. The following Table 4.3 shows the variables with their respective coefficients that built the logistic regression equation. The table also reports the significance levels of the variables based on the Wald test statistic. Relative advantage (Wald = 6.249, df = 1, $p < 0.05$), cost effectiveness (Wald = 16.606, df = 1, $p < 0.001$) and compatibility (Wald = 18.545, df = 1, $p < 0.001$) were found to be positively related to the adoption of online advertising with statistical significance. That is, the hypotheses H1, H2 and H3 were confirmed in this multivariate analysis. The table also gives an indication of the most important variables in the model. The best predictor for the adoption of online advertising was cost effectiveness (Exp(B) = 6.441), followed by compatibility (Exp(B) = 4.836) and relative advantage

(Exp(B) = 2.265). This finding is in line with the results from the independent t-tests where the same variables had the highest t-values.

Table 4.3: Variables in the equation (direct logistic regression: step 1)

	B	S.E.	Wald	df	Sig.	Exp(B)
Reladv	0.818	0.327	6.249	1	0.012	2.265
Cost	1.863	0.457	16.606	1	0.000	6.441
Compa	1.576	0.366	18.545	1	0.000	4.836
Info	-0.428	0.251	2.896	1	0.089	0.652
Custint	-0.220	0.289	0.580	1	0.446	0.802
inno_pm	-0.101	0.248	0.165	1	0.685	0.904
Complex	-0.501	0.376	1.775	1	0.183	0.606
Topmgt	-0.392	0.306	1.637	1	0.201	0.676
Compt	0.036	0.286	0.016	1	0.900	1.037
Size	0.294	0.244	1.450	1	0.228	1.342
Constant	-11.7	2.978	15.436	1	0.000	0.000

(reladv=Relative advantage; compa=Compatibility; cost=Cost effectiveness; info=Information intensity; custint=Customer interaction; inno_pm= Organisation innovativeness in introducing new products/services; complex=Complexity; topmgt=Top management support; compt=Competition; size=Business size)

After the logistic regression model had been calculated, its goodness-of-fit was assessed. The Omnibus tests of model coefficients as shown in Table 4.4 gives an overall indication of how well the model performed. This 'goodness of fit' test utilises the log-likelihood technique for comparing a constant-only model (containing no predictor variables) with the full model (containing all predictor variables). It basically tests the null hypothesis that the coefficients for the independent variables equal 0 (Munro 2005). The result of this test implied that the overall model is significant according to the model chi-square (chi-square = 201.396, df = 10, $p < 0.001$).

Table 4.4: Omnibus tests of model coefficients (direct logistic regression)

Step		Chi-square	df	Sig.
Step 1	**Step**	201.396	10	0.000
	Block	201.396	10	0.000
	Model	201.396	10	0.000

Table 4.5 displays the model summary. This summary provides an indication of the amount of variation in the dependent variable, adoption of online advertising, that is explained by the model (Munro 2005). The Cox & Snell R square is somewhat limited since it cannot reach 1.

Nagelkerke modified the Cox & Snell R square in order to overcome this limitation with his R square measure that ranges from 0 to 1 (Nagelkerke 1991). This also explains why the Nagelkerke R square is usually higher than the Cox & Snell R square. In this analysis the two measures suggested that between 55.5 percent and 77.6 percent of the variability of the dependent variable was explained by the proposed set of variables, which can be considered a good result.

Table 4.5: Model summary (direct logistic regression)

Step	-2 Log likelihood	Cox & Snell R square	Nagelkerke R square
1	111.265	0.555	0.776

In order to determine how well the model actually predicts group membership of adopters and non-adopters of online advertising, Table 4.6 compares the model-predicted classification with the observed classification. Generally, a classification table summarises the fit between the observed and predicted group memberships (Grimm & Yarnold 1995). It can be seen that the model predicts 85.0 percent of the nonadopters of online advertising and 94.7 percent of the adopters of online advertising correctly. Overall, 91.6 percent of the cases were classified correctly.

Table 4.6: Classification table (direct logistic regression)

	PREDICTED		
	Online advertising		Percentage correct
OBSERVED	No	Yes	
Step 1 Online advertising No	68	12	85.0
Yes	9	160	94.7
Overall Percentage			91.6

In summary, the results of direct logistic regression suggested a good model fit. All commonly used tests to assess the proposed model were found to be significant. The classification results of the equation were impressive. In line with the findings from the independent t-test cost effectiveness, compatibility and relative advantage were found to be significant and the most important variables in the equation. That is, the hypotheses H1, H2 and H3 were accepted in this analysis. The other factors that showed significance in the independent t-test were not significant in this direct logistic regression. The reason for this is the dominance of the three strong significant predictors that has most likely paled the influence of the other variables. One has to keep in mind that direct logistic regression has the usual differences with interpretation when predictors are correlated. Furthermore, a predictor that is highly correlated with the outcome by itself might show limited predictive capability in the presence of other predictors (Tabachnick & Fidell 2001).

Forward stepwise logistic regression

In this study the forward stepwise logistic regression was used to build a practical model for predicting group membership of adopters and non-adopters of online advertising, which is based on a few significant variables. The computed model of the stepwise logistic regression is not intended to test hypothesis. It is only meant to be used for predictive purposes since it is based on a limited number of significant factors, which eases the model use in practice.

The following Table 4.7 shows the variables with their respective coefficients that built the logistic regression equation after step 3 of the stepwise procedure, where the algorithm stopped its computation. Relative advantage (Wald = 5.906, df = 1, $p < 0.05$), cost effectiveness (Wald = 15.487, df = 1, $p < 0.0005$) and compatibility (Wald = 18.725, df = 1, $p < 0.0005$) were found to be positively related to the adoption of online advertising with statistical significance. The best predictor for the adoption of online advertising was cost effectiveness (Exp(B) = 4.988), followed by compatibility (Exp(B) = 3.722) and relative advantage (Exp(B) = 2.097). Again, this finding is in line with the results from the both tests underlining the importance of these factors in the adoption of online advertising context.

Table 4.7: Variables in the equation (forward stepwise logistic regression)

		B	**S.E.**	**Wald**	**df**	**Sig.**	**Exp(B)**
Step 3	**reladv**	0.741	0.305	5.906	1	0.015	2.097
	cost	1.607	0.408	15.487	1	0.000	4.988
	compa	1.314	0.304	18.725	1	0.000	3.722
		-14.6	2.102	48.766	1	0.000	0.000

After the logistic regression model had been calculated, its goodness-of-fit was assessed. Table 4.8 gives an overall indication of how well the model performed with respect to the Omnibus tests of model coefficients. The result of this test implied that the overall model is significant according to the model chi-square (chi-square = 192.156, df = 3, $p < 0.001$).

Table 4.8: Omnibus tests of model coefficients (forward stepwise logistic regression)

Step	**Chi-square**	**Df**	**Sig.**
Step 3 Step	6.327	1	0.012
Block	192.156	3	0.000
Model	192.156	3	0.000

Table 4.9 shows the model summary. In this analysis the Cox & Snell R square and the Nagelkerke R square suggested that between 53.8 percent and 75.2 percent of the variability of the dependent variable was explained by the proposed set of variables, which can be considered a good result.

Table 4.9: Model summary (forward stepwise logistic regression)

Step	**-2 Log likelihood**	**Cox & Snell R square**	**Nagelkerke R square**
3	120.506	0.538	0.752

Since the forward stepwise logistic regression was performed to generate a compact prediction model of the adoption of online advertising the following Table 4.10 is of major importance. Hereby, one should keep in mind that the assessment of the success of the model is based on its ability to correctly predict the outcome category for cases for whom outcome is known (Tabachnick & Fidell 2001). It can be seen from Table 4.10 that the model predicted 83.8 percent of the non-adopters of online advertising and 94.1 percent of the adopters of online advertising correctly. Overall, 90.8 percent of the cases were classified correctly.

Table 4.10: Classification table (forward stepwise logistic regression)

	PREDICTED		
	Online advertising		**Percentage correct**
OBSERVED	No	Yes	
Step 3 Online Advertising No	67	13	83.8
Yes	10	159	94.1
Overall Percentage			90.8

This classification result can be considered as good. Again the result is far superior compared to the 70.4 percent of the modified proportional chance criterion (as recommended by Hair et al. (2006)).

In summary, the results for the generated model suggest that there was a good model fit. All commonly used tests to assess the generated model were applied and found to be significant. Even though the model had consisted only of three predictor variables (relative advantage, cost effectiveness and compatibility) the classification results of the model were good. This can be seen as another indication of the importance of these factors in the adoption of online advertising context.

5.4. Conclusions Regarding the Research Issues

This section presents the conclusions of this research in accordance with the underlying research issues. The results of the data analysis are discussed under the heading of each research issue and compared with previous findings in the literature relevant to the issue at hand.

5.4.1. Conclusions regarding the current status of online advertising in Australian SMEs

What is the extent of popularity of online advertising in Australian SMEs?

The extent of online advertising adoption within Australian SMEs was impressive with almost 70 percent of the SMEs surveyed utilising online advertising. This finding is consistent with the notion of Riquelme (2002) who found that benefits from online advertising were the third most important factor to establish a connection with the Internet. It should also be noted the wide spread use of websites, which are an integral part of a meaningful online advertising, was even more impressive with almost all SMEs having one. The most commonly reported reason for maintaining a website was to inform customers about product and services, which reflects the importance of a website with respect to respondents' marketing strategy. This finding is consistent with the results of the study by McCole and Ramsey (2005) who analysed New Zealand's SMEs in a similar context. Overall, it can be concluded that the majority of Australian SMEs have recognised the benefits of advertising online and therefore adopted online advertising.

In recent years a respectable number of the surveys dealing with SMEs has engaged in online advertising for the first time. Thus, it appears to be likely that this trend will continue and even more SMEs will adopt online advertising in coming years. Thereby, the ongoing exposure to online advertising, which almost every Internet user frequently experiences, might enhance the adoption of online advertising. More and more companies of all sizes will embark on online advertising. Businesses, who are yet unwilling to adopt online advertising, cannot escape this phenomenon in the long run. With the steady growth of more sophisticated and appealing online advertisements it is likely that negative mindsets towards online advertising are about to change. Online advertising is likely to become an integral part of almost every advertising campaign.

Why do Australian SMEs adopt online advertising?

Generally, Australian SMEs use online advertising to increase the brand awareness of their products and services and to generate traffic towards their organisations' website.

In detail, Australian SMEs mostly value the cost effectiveness of online advertising. No other advertising medium offers the same wide market reach at comparable cost. This is especially important for the SMEs of this study who reported that their main market focus is on the national level. Furthermore, it might very well be that online advertising is the only way for SMEs, who have a limited advertising budget to advertise to the national audience. Especially the performance-based payment methods of online advertising appears to be of interest in this respect.

The flexible nature of online advertising was also appreciated by the respondents, which again underlines the unique characteristics of online advertising. Online advertising enables advertisers to quickly advertise to their target audience and to alter their advertisements in a timely fashion. For example, an SME might want to inform potential customers about a new product, which just had become available to the market. If email marketing is applied in this scenario, the target audience can be addressed almost in real time. Accordingly, the targeting possibilities and the instant accessibility of the Internet were also frequently reported as advantages of online advertising. Other advertising media, such as TV or print, cannot compete with online advertising in this regard.

Lastly, respondents recognised the tracking abilities of online advertising. Online advertisers usually receive a detailed 'advertising-reporting', which shows when and where a user clicked on an advertisement. This detailed feedback enables SMEs to efficiently optimise their online advertising efforts in terms of websites used, advertisements used and time of advertising and it should be used accordingly.

Why Australian SMEs do not adopt online advertising?

Interestingly, targeting was also perceived as the main disadvantage of online advertising by nonadopting respondents. This different perception of online advertising can be seen as an indication for a lack of education regarding online advertising and its possibilities. It is highly likely that some SMEs will change their attitude towards online advertising if they are informed about its abilities in detail. For example, keyword advertising on search-engines offers excellent and cost effective opportunities for targeting potential customers.

Some respondents also criticised online advertising for its low awareness and its intrusive and annoying nature. This perception might be a result from the personal experience of the marketing decision-maker, which he/she translated into his/her professional life. However, it can be argued that this perception might change over time since online advertisements are getting more appealing. Furthermore, regulations for conducting online advertising in a user-friendly way are being introduced (e.g. reducing of spam mails).

What kind of online advertisements do Australian SMEs use?

All types of online advertisements were used by the participating SMEs. This should be seen as an indicator for the advanced online advertising knowledge that Australian SMEs have. Interestingly, the clear majority of respondents administered their online advertising in-house. This can be interpreted as a sign for the online advertising proficiency in Australian SMEs as well as for their technical knowledge in this regard. This finding suggested that computer self-efficacy is important to the adoption of online advertising. SMEs should become comfortable with the technical side of online advertising. SMEs that lack knowledge in this context might not be able to adopt online advertising or are not aware of the opportunities of online advertising. It might also indicate that online advertising has become simple enough to be used by fairly non-sophisticated users.

What role does online advertising play in the advertising mix of Australian SMEs?

Generally, Australian SMEs use all common advertising channels. Interestingly, online advertising was most often reported in this regard. Nonetheless, the actual spending on online advertising is rather limited. Thus, it can be concluded that online advertising only plays a minor role in the advertising mix of Australian SMEs. It might be that Australian SMEs only use online advertising as an additional channel to their existing and proven advertising mix. Given the forecasted growth of online advertising it is likely that this allocation will change in the future in favour of online advertising. A recent study by Outsell (2006) confirms that smaller businesses are shifting their advertising budget away from traditional media to online advertising. Generally, the overall advances in online advertising might lead SMEs to reconsider their entire advertising mix.

In summary, the current status of the adoption of online advertising in Australian SMEs can be considered well advanced. Online advertising has been widely adopted by the surveyed organisations. It appears that most of the marketing decision-makers were at least to a certain degree aware of online advertising's benefits and its opportunities. Given the relatively low spending on this advertising channel it appears that online advertising was not the dominating channel for their marketing campaigns but rather a meaningful addition to their offline advertising efforts. Nonetheless, it can also be concluded that a smaller proportion of the surveyed organisations were either not aware of the benefits of online advertising or felt that it did not fit in their existing advertising strategy. It has yet to be determined if the rate of nonadopting SMEs will further decrease and to what extent this will happen in future times. Based on the qualitative feedback the respondents provided, it is likely that more SMEs will adopt online advertising when they are more educated about this relatively new advertising tool while technical barriers are further diminishing; especially if one takes the steady growth and acceptance of the Internet into account.

5.4.2. Conclusions regarding factors affecting the adoption of online advertising in Australian SMEs

This study has examined potential determinants of online advertising adoption in Australian SMEs. To this end ten hypothesis identified from the innovation adoption literature were tested. Seven of the ten hypotheses, namely relative advantage (H1), compatibility (H2), cost effectiveness (H3), complexity (H4), top management support (H8), organisation innovativeness (H9) and customer interaction (H10) were found to be significant in the adoption of online advertising in Australian SMEs. In contrast with some previous adoption research, no significant relationships were observed with respect to intense competition (H5), information intensity (H6) and business size (H7) and the decision to adopt online advertising. A discussion and comparison of each hypothesis with respect to findings from the literature are discussed next.

Innovation characteristics:

Relative advantage (H1)

Relative advantage is a strong significant factor contributing to the adoption of online advertising in Australian SMEs. This means that adopters who utilise online advertising perceive their organisation as having a relative advantage, brought by their perceived benefits of online advertising. This findings is consistent with the results of prior studies that have found relative advantage to be a significant variable in many innovation adoption contexts. Generally, SMEs adopt online advertising if they perceive a gap in their current performance or want to exploit new opportunities. The findings of this study suggested that online advertising adopting SMEs believe that online advertising increases the profitability and effectiveness of their company. It was seen as a meaningful extension of their market reach. Furthermore, respondents believed that online advertising has a positive effect on their e-commerce activities.

Compatibility (H2)

The compatibility of online advertising was found to be a strongly significant factor affecting the adoption of online advertising. Adopting respondents reported that online advertising was compatible with their existing values, needs and past experiences. This finding is in line with the innovation adoption literature, which often emphasises the importance of fit between the innovation and the organisation (e.g. Cooper & Zmud 1990; Ettlie 1986; Lai 1997) . The findings of this study suggested that adopting organisations generally had a positive attitude towards online advertising. It is worthwhile to note that the reported compatibility with the company's infrastructure has to be seen in relation with the existence of a company website. A website is usually in place when companies do advertise online because online advertisements direct users to the advertiser's website. Since almost all participants of the survey (98 percent) reported they had a website in place, the conclusion on this hypothesis appears to be appropriate.

Cost effectiveness (H3)

In line with prior studies (e.g. Ching & Ellis 2004; Fink, 1998; Premkumar, Ramamurthy & Nilakanta 1994) that reported cost effectiveness as a significant variable for initiating many innovations, this study also found SMEs to be cost-sensitive. That is, the cost effectiveness of online advertising was found to be strongly significant in discriminating adopters from nonadopters of online advertising. This finding is not surprising given the financial budget limitations of most

SMEs (Thong 1999; Welsh & White 1981). SMEs carefully compare the perceived costs and benefits of an innovation before they adopt it. If online advertising is not perceived as beneficial in terms of its cost effectiveness, there is no meaningful reason to adopt it. Accordingly, it can also be argued that some surveyed SMEs did not adopt online advertising because they might not be aware of its benefits or did not perceive the benefits as greater than its costs. Generally, the adopting SMEs in this study felt that the benefits of online advertising outweigh its costs. Furthermore, the costs of online advertising were not perceived as high. However, this finding has to be seen in relation with the reported low proportion of the advertising budget allocated to online advertising. Online advertising was also perceived as a cost effective way to marketing the companies' products and services, thereby reducing the cost of acquiring new customers. Overall, the perception of cost effectiveness was the strongest reason for the online advertising adoption decision.

Complexity (H4)

Complexity was also found to be a significant predictor of the adoption of online advertising in Australian SMEs. This outcome validates findings of previous studies, which suggested that less complex innovations are more often adopted (e.g. Bedell et al. 1985; Premkumar & Roberts 1999; Thong 1999). Participants of this study reported that the integration and implementation of online advertising in their current business operations were fairly easy and they did not experience many problems in this regard. Generally, the complexity of an innovation appears to be of critical importance. If the organisation is lacking the necessary experience to implement and use online advertising, it is unlikely to adopt it. This view is supported by Moch and Morse (1977) who suggested that the existence of experts being able to identify the innovation as desirable within organisations positively influences the adoption of innovations.

In this study only four out of five online advertising adopting SMEs reported they did not utilise the services of a media-agency for administering their online advertising campaign, which indicates their advanced in-house knowledge with respect to online advertising and related Internet technologies. This also points to a trend within SMEs towards accepting more responsibility themselves for the acquisition of new Internet technologies. This suggestion is supported by Fink (1998) who found an increased experience and awareness for information technologies among SMEs in his study. Companies who lack this knowledge are likely to be more hesitant regarding the use of online advertising.

In brief, the findings on innovation characteristics are consistent with other studies that have found relative advantage, compatibility, cost effectiveness and complexity to be key variables in the adoption decision of innovations.

It is worthwhile to note that cost effectiveness, compatibility and relative advantage respectively, emerged as the overall most significant factors with respect to discriminating adopters and nonadopters of online advertising in Australian SMEs. These innovation characteristics showed the most significant differences in the independent t tests and were the strongest predictors for the adoption of online advertising in the direct logistic regression as well as in the forward stepwise logistic regression. This finding is also in line with the qualitative feedback of the survey respondents who nominated these factors as main advantages of online advertising and therefore particularly important in explaining their adoption decision. All proposed innovation characteristics considered, a SME's decision to adopt online advertising is mainly based on its perception whether online advertising can:

- help to target potential customers in a cost effective way;
- easily be integrated and implemented in existing structures;
- help to sell products and services (online);
- increase profitability; and
- complement the existing advertising mix.

Environmental characteristics:

Intense competition (H5)

Intense competition was not found to be a significant factor with respect to the adoption of online advertising in this study. Thus, it cannot be concluded that it is a strategic necessity to use online advertising in a competitive environment as other innovation adoption studies have reported. This result is contrary to the postulated hypothesis and prior studies (e.g. DeLone 1988; DosSantos & Peffers 1998; Globerman 1975), which reported that competition positively influenced the adoption decision of innovations.

Generally, the adopters and nonadopters of online advertising perceived their industry as moderately competitive, as evidenced by the mean scores of both groups of their responses. Adopters reported an insignificantly higher rivalry among the companies in their industry.

Even though the finding on this hypothesis was unexpected, the results of this study are in line with the findings of Thong and Yap (1995), Ching and Ellis (2004) and Lee (2004), who also found that competition was not significant in their innovation adoption study. In response to his nonsignificant result on competition, Lee (2004) suggested that competitive pressure as a driver of adoption is different in the SME context. He argued that SMEs might believe that they can compete best by focusing on their internal factors, which they can control rather than adopting strategies of larger competitors. In line with that suggestion Ching and Ellis (2004), who studied the adoption of e-commerce with a qualitative methodology, proposed it may very well be that competitive factors are outweighed by more firm-specific considerations in the final adoption decision. Nonetheless, the role of competition in the adoption of innovation context remains in question. It can only be concluded that the effect of competition on the adoption decision appears to be contingent on the specific nature of the innovation under investigation as Chau and Tam (1997) argued. In this study no significant relationship could be revealed. However, industry specific investigations may reveal deeper insights on this issue. It appears reasonable that in some industries, e.g. some sectors of retail trade, it might very well be a strategic necessity to use online advertising. More research is required to address this suggestion.

Information intensity (H6)

Information intensity was also dismissed as a significant factor in the adoption of online advertising. This finding is again at odds with the expectations reported in the innovation adoption literature (e.g. Malone,

Yates & Benjamin 1987; Teo, Tan & Buk 1997; Yap 1990), which basically argued that businesses in different sectors have different information-processing needs and those in more information-intensive sectors were more likely to adopt innovations than those in less information-intensive sectors. However, the generally limited research findings on this factor were not univocal. For example, Grover (1993) found information intensity in direction opposite from his predicted positive relationship with the adoption decision. Again this suggests that the relevance of information intensity with respect to the adoption decision context is specific to the innovation under investigation. Certainly more research is required to shed more light on the influence of this factor. These mixed research findings support Fichman and Kemerer's (1992) view that a unifying theory might be inappropriate with respect to the fundamental differences of innovations. They argued that the variations in innovations and the adoption context in which the theory is supposed to be applied to vary too much.

Overall, it appeared that SME's adoption decision of online advertising is not related to how much information is needed to sell their products and services, how long their cycle times are or how complicated it is to specify or order their specific products.

In conclusion, contrary to the postulated hypotheses the environmental factors of intense competition and information intensity were not found significant in predicting adopters and nonadopters of online advertising in this study. However, managers learn from their interaction with the environment as Lee and Runge (2001) pointed out. They do not learn about the benefits of online advertising solely as individuals but rather from the trade press, friends, family members, colleagues and business competitors. Thus, some other environmental characteristics more related to social interaction might turn out to be of importance with the decision to adopt. Further research is recommended in this regard.

Organisational characteristics:

Business size (H7)

Although it was expected that smaller SMEs take less advantage of online advertising, business size was not found to be of significance with respect to the adoption decision. This finding is inconsistent with previously held notions in the literature (e.g. Dewar & Dutton 1986; Ettlie 1983; Grover 1993), which have found it being a critical variable in adoption decision within the small business category, that is, the larger ones of the smaller businesses were more likely to adopt. This finding can be explained with the initial cost of adopting online advertising, which are fairly reasonable. Some other innovation studies investigated information technologies that were more costly to set up. Thus, SMEs can adopt online advertising regardless of their size and their potential financial limitations to some extent.

Generally, the findings on business size in the literature were inconclusive. The link between business size and business strategy is not yet clearly defined in the literature. In the investigated online advertising context it appears that various other organisational factors (e.g. organisational slack, degree of centralisation), which are likely to be related to the size of an organisation, were more important in the adoption decision. Therefore, more research into other internal organisational factors with respect to the adoption of online advertising is recommended.

Top management support (H8)

Top management support was found to be a significant determinant in the adoption of online advertising. This finding concurs with findings from other researchers (e.g. Baldridge & Burnham 1975; Ettlie 1983; Grover 1993), who stress the importance of top management support in the adoption decision.

Interestingly, the scores on top management support were only moderate for adopting SMEs. Moreover, the differences between adopters and non-adopters on this factor were not as big as expected. It was also found that top management of both adopting and non-adopting SMEs is not fully aware of the benefits of online advertising and was only somewhat interested in the adoption of online advertising, which again reveals the need for educational training in this regard.

Overall, it appears that top management support is required to adopt online advertising, but the relative moderate scores on that construct can be seen as an indication that some reservations are still pertinent to this new advertising medium. Thus, top management does not appear to be the main driving force behind the adoption. Instead the vision and commitment of the marketing decision-makers pushes the adoption. In this environment with only moderate top management support, top management may approve or make the final adoption decision but is not likely to be involved in other aspects of the adoption process. According to the detailed qualitative feedback of the survey, the marketing decision-makers (who were not part of the top management to a large extent) convince top management of the benefits of online advertising to get adequate resources and support for the implementation of it.

Organisation innovativeness (H9)

Organisation innovativeness with respect to the introduction of new products and services as well as the targeting of new markets was found to be a significant variable in the adoption of online advertising. This finding is in line with previous research (e.g. Damanpour 1988; Lee & Runge 2001), which suggested that firms who have successfully introduced new products and services in new markets are more likely to adopt innovation.

As expected Australian SMEs that have a need to market their new products and services at the marketplace and/or target new markets are more comfortable with online advertising adoption. It can be argued that these innovative companies are more likely to adopt online advertising than companies who are operating in a less dynamic environment and are more likely to rely on their existing proven advertising strategy.

This construct has not received much attention in the innovation adoption literature. Thus, more research is recommended in this regard.

Customer interaction (H10)

Customer interaction was also found to be a significant facilitator of the adoption of online advertising. This finding is supported by the literature (e.g. Ettlie 1983; Grover 1993; Utterback 1974), which had reported customer interaction as a significant variable in the adoption of innovation context.

Generally, all of the surveyed marketing decision-makers reported they were actively involved in building and maintaining direct customer contact and that they consider customers as an important source of ideas. However, online advertising adopting SMEs scored significantly higher on this construct. It can be argued that there is a link between customer interaction and advertising itself. Companies, which are aware of the needs and interests of their customers, are more likely to make use of this information in a customised advertising campaign. This approach appears to be an excellent way of targeting the right customers with the right advertising message. Email-advertising campaigns might be effectively utilised in this regard.

In summary, most of the proposed hypotheses regarding organisational characteristics were supported. While top management support, organisation innovativeness and customer interaction were found to be of significance in the adoption decision of online advertising, business size was not identified to be a critical variable in this research.

Of the three relevant categories identified in the adoption innovation literature, two proved to be of importance in predicting the adoption of online advertising. While organisational characteristics do provide discriminating power, the innovation characteristics clearly stand out as the best predictors. The environmental factors were proved to be the least effective in predicting adoption of online advertising. Thus, it can be concluded that environmental characteristics were not an important factor in making decisions to adopt online advertising in the Australian SME context. Overall, the empirical findings of this research were reasonably consistent with past empirical findings.

6. Implications of the Results

6.1. Implications for theory

The proposed study and its rich findings expand the existing literature on online advertising by focusing on factors affecting the adoption of online advertising in Australian SMEs. The presented research findings have the following implications for theory about the adoption of online advertising and related issues:

- significant factors of the adoption of online advertising;

- literature review;
- use of prediction model;
- marketing decision-maker information;
- national focus; and
- need for future research.

Significant factors of the adoption of online advertising

The first implication of this research derives from the testing of the proposed hypotheses in respect to the adoption of online advertising in Australian SMEs. The study found support for the influence of both innovation and organisational characteristics but not for environmental characteristics in the adoption of online advertising in Australian SMEs. Seven factors were found to be significant in influencing the adoption of the Internet, namely cost effectiveness, compatibility, relative advantage, complexity, top management support, organisation innovativeness and customer interaction. The hypotheses testing model also indicated the most influential variables in predicting the adoption of online advertising in Australian SMEs. Especially, cost effectiveness, compatibility and relative advantage are recognised as the most significant predictors of the adoption of online advertising. These findings are considered to be the most significant and important contribution of this research.

Literature review

The proposed hypotheses were based on an extensive literature review that provides a comprehensive overview of current as well as past innovation adoption studies (mainly from the US). This detailed overview might be useful to other researchers investigating adoption of innovations. An instrument for measuring the adoption of online advertising consisting of various constructs was derived from the literature and customised for the research context at hand. This instrument can be used in future studies and can also be adapted for other fields of interest. Moreover, the extensive literature review in this study also revealed inconsistencies in the literature, which confirmed the importance of studying innovation adoption in different contexts. It is also worthwhile to note that the results of this study generally confirm the generalisability of research findings obtained primarily in the US to the Australian context. Accordingly, the research findings of this study are likely to be applicable to comparable Western nations.

Use of prediction model

Another important implication for theory is the empirical support for the development of prediction models that explain the adoption of online advertising in Australian SMEs. Despite the extensive innovation adoption literature and the continuing research in this area, no study has yet proposed a research model for predicting the adoption of online advertising and applied it empirically. The conceptual framework developed could also be applied in comparable research settings.

Marketing decision-maker information

The extensive descriptive information collected in this study revealed numerous interesting findings. For example, this research gave a first insight of who the marketing decision-makers are, what companies they represent, how they allocate their advertising budget, how they perceive online advertising and to what extent they make use of it. Therefore, the descriptive findings of this study expanded the literature of online advertising for the Australian market.

National focus

Another implication of this study is derived from the fact that the study investigated a national sample of SMEs. To the best of the author's knowledge this is the first rigorous academic study that investigated the adoption of online advertising in Australian SMEs from a theoretical as well as empirical perspective. Prior studies are more basic in nature, lack a strong theoretical foundation and usually only offer broad information on online advertising spending. Moreover, these studies commonly do not focus their investigation on SMEs. In contrast, this study applied a rigorous research methodology and successfully filled the research gap concerning the lack of knowledge about the adoption of online advertising in Australian SMEs.

Need for future research

Based on the descriptive information collected with the mail survey and secondary data presented in this research it can be concluded that online advertising is an impressively dynamic and growing phenomenon in the Australian marketplace. This finding underlines the necessity of further research in this area. Thereby, this study can serve the research community as a meaningful starting point for future research studies and debates. The empirically investigated factors that affect the adoption decision of online advertising and the descriptive information about the participating marketing decision-makers, their respective organisations and their Internet strategies are useful in a broad variety of research settings of future studies.

6.2. Implications for Practice

Besides having several implications for theory the research findings also have contributed to a deeper understanding of online advertising in Australia SMEs in a practical way. The following managerial practices should be considered:

- the need for online advertising;
- cost of online advertising;
- approaches to adopt online advertising;
- approaches to promote online advertising;
- competitive overview; and
- suggestions for the successful use of online advertising.

The need for online advertising

Online advertising is of strong importance in coming years. SMEs should consider adopting online advertising to advertise their products and services in the Internet landscape. The use of the Internet is steadily growing and it has already become an integral part of most people's life. Understanding that the Internet is increasingly becoming the marketplace for Internet users, advertisers in general will continue shifting traditional advertising spending to the Internet due to increased Internet consumption and better targeting as well as reporting capabilities. SMEs, which do not follow this trend, run the risk of falling behind their competitors. Overall, it is important for SMEs to understand the importance of online advertising. Online advertising can make the following contributions to SMEs:

- generate traffic towards SME's website;
- increase brand awareness of products and services;
- provide in-depth information about products and services;
- reduce marketing costs due to increased media efficiency; and
- reach new customers (especially those missed by other advertising channels).

Cost of online advertising

The cost of online advertising can vary strongly. In this study, respondents reported that their annual spending on online advertising ranged from less than A$500 to more than A$10,000; with the majority spending more than A$2,000 on online advertising. SMEs should customise the extent of their online advertising efforts in relation to their available advertising budget. Financial limitations should not hinder SMEs from adopting online advertising. Especially, performance-based payment methods should be considered when financial restrictions are present. Search-engines are of particular interest in this regard. They are usually open to cost-per-click methods and enable SMEs to advertise online in a cost efficient way. For example, a cost-per-click on Australia's leading search engine Google.com.au costs A$0.01 (Google-AdWords 2006). On the other hand SMEs might want to engage in a branding campaign using banners. All things considered, all SMEs (even those with a small online advertising budget) are able to reach a large, targeted audience with online advertising.

Approaches to adopt online advertising

Before online advertising can be used in a meaningful way, a company website should be in place. This website should be frequently updated and present current information about the SME's products and services. Next, an online advertising strategy should be developed. The first important step in developing an online advertising strategy is to define the target group. This target group might differ from existing customers since online advertising can reach out to new demographics. Once the SME has profiled its potential online target group, it should research how this group can be accessed online. Thereby, the SME should ask the following questions:

- What websites might potential customers frequently visit?
- At what time do they visit these websites?
- What advertising options are available for these websites?
- What keywords appear to be relevant in the search-engine context?
- How can I obtain the email addresses of potential customers?

Finding answers for these questions can be challenging. SMEs, who are not able to answer these questions, should consider using an online advertising agency. These agencies gather detailed information on a broad variety of websites with its visitor profiles and are specialised in planning online advertising campaigns. Moreover, online advertising agencies create all kinds of online advertisements. When a SME has an understanding of the Internet use of its potential customers, it can start planning its online advertising campaign. Using online advertising for the first time, it is recommended to use different online advertisements on a broad variety of websites. Based on the subsequent ad reporting on the effectiveness of this campaign, the SME is able to adjust its online advertising efforts accordingly.

In this approach it might be advantageous to turn one employee into an online advertising specialist. This might actually be the case in some of the surveyed SMEs as indicated by the reported unpopular practice of using an advertising agency, which shows the respondents' online advertising proficiency and technical knowledge. An in-house online advertising specialist enables SMEs to administer online advertising campaigns in a more flexible and independent way.

Approaches to promote online advertising

The results of this study point to several issues online advertising agencies should consider in their advertising strategy. The findings of this study provide marketing practitioners with suggestions on how to tackle the problem of nonadoption of online advertising in Australian SMEs. It is reasonable to believe that the nonadoption of an innovation in the marketplace may be attributed to the supplier promoting it, instead of the decision making-unit considering adoption of the innovation not important as some researchers argue (Frambach 1993; Stevens, Warren & Martin 1989). In this case, a need for formulating a marketing strategy aimed specifically at nonadopters of online advertising appears to be appropriate. The results of this study offer the practitioner audience valuable insights into how to tailor their communication strategy to SMEs who have not yet adopted online advertising. The practical prediction model developed in this research appears to be most useful for marketing managers in predicting the adoption of online advertising in Australian SMEs. Especially the finding of the strong significance of relative advantage, cost effectiveness and compatibility in the prediction of online advertising adoption could be translated into such an advertising strategy. These drivers of the adoption enable proactive intervention with respect to targeting organisations, which may be less inclined to adopt online advertising. If online advertising agencies stress these factors when addressing new potential clients it might increase their success rate in acquiring new customers. For example, online advertising agencies should emphasise that online advertising can be easily implemented and used to target potential customer in a cost effective way. They should also stress the importance of online advertising in a cross media advertising mix, that is, an advertising campaign, which utilises a variety of media channels in a balanced way, is more likely to increase the brand awareness of products and services. The importance of a cross media advertising mix including online advertising was proven in various studies (Marketing-Evolution 2006).

Besides targeting companies that already advertise, online advertising agencies should also target companies who have not yet engaged in advertising at all. For these companies, who potentially have limited financial resources, online advertising might be the only option to advertise to a broader audience. Thereby, a full service approach is recommended. Offering ongoing advice and support for the implementation of online advertising might help to overcome the perceived barriers for adopting online advertising. The less cumbersome it is to use online advertising, the more likely a SME is to use it.

Online advertising agencies should target the marketing decision-makers of SMEs in their promotion efforts. The findings of this study showed that usually not the top management but the marketing decision-maker is the main driving force behind the adoption. This marketing manager has to be convinced of the benefits of online advertising because he or she subsequently convinces top management of the benefits of online advertising to get adequate resources and support for the use of it. Thereby, the marketing decision-makers may need some educational training about online advertising in general. Some respondents of this study mentioned that they are not really aware of the benefits of online advertising, what possibilities online advertising offers and how it actually works. Moreover, it appears that some misperceptions about online advertising were present in the sample. For example, some respondents mentioned the high costs of online advertising as a disadvantage. These respondents might be not aware of cost-per-click models with which they only pay for users that are actually transferred to their websites. Accordingly, a well-defined educational program would most likely have a positive effect on the adoption of online advertising.

Competitive overview

This research gives marketing decision-managers a valuable insight in the current practices of online advertising in their market. This study was a large scale, cross-industry analysis of the adoption of online advertising in Australian SMEs. Given the provided extensive descriptive information of Australian SMEs about their online advertising strategy, this research provides a base from which marketing decision-makers are able to compare their online advertising activities as well as their general advertising efforts against other Australian SMEs and to obtain a general overview about their market. Accordingly, most of the marketing decision-makers (83 percent) requested a summary of the research findings as offered by the authors. Based on the findings of this study some respondents might rethink their advertising strategy because they were not aware of the current trends of online advertising in the Australian marketplace.

Suggestions for the successful use of online advertising

This study showed that online advertising is a dynamic phenomenon that will constantly evolve. Therefore, the following suggestions should be generally considered when a SME wants to use online advertising in a meaningful way:

- allocate a budget for online advertising;
- plan online advertising efforts in balance with other advertising efforts;
- appoint an online advertising specialist;
- target the right kind of users;
- communicate the right message to users;
- frequently try different websites for online advertising;
- frequently try different types of online advertisements;
- critically determine the effectiveness of online advertising campaigns;
- give online advertising time to make an impact on sales;
- constantly update your website;
- monitor the online advertising strategies of competitors; and
- stay informed about new trends in online advertising.

The practical aspects of this research strengthened not only the foundation of this research but also were highly appreciated by the participating SMEs as reflected in their high interest in the research findings.

7. Summary, Limitations and Future Research Directions

7.1. Summary

This research has developed and tested a model of online advertising adoption model for Australian SMEs. And it has also studied the current status of online advertising among Australian SMEs. The results of this research have both practical and theoretical implications.

7.2. Limitations of this Study

Inherent within any study are limitations that affect the overall validity and reliability of the research findings and therefore need to be recognised. In this study, limitations could arise from the research methods applied.

This study was cross-sectional in nature. Thus, the direction of causality can only be inferred. It was not possible to directly determine the perceptions of marketing decision-makers at the time of the adoption of online advertising. It is possible, though less likely, that the surveyed marketing decision-makers were influenced by the experiences they made with online advertising after it was adopted. It might be that respondents have changed their attitude towards online advertising since they have adopted it and therefore their answers might not reflect their perceptions of online advertising at the time of its adoption. However, the relative newness of online advertising might reduce such effects. Nonetheless, the retrospective nature of this study has to be considered a limitation. The only way to resolve this issue is to study the adoption decision over an extended period of time. Therefore, a longitudinal study would be useful to validate the conclusions of this study.

Some care should be taken when interpreting the research findings due to the sampling method. A truly random sample was not possible to achieve in this study because no complete list of all Australian SMEs was available. Thus, this research was per definition only a convenience sample. Thereby, another limitation of this study derives from the use of an electronic database (Dun & Bradstreet's The Business Who's Who of Australia) as a source of sampling. The database cannot be considered complete as some records had not been updated recently, e.g. missing addresses changes (indicated by non deliverable letters). The use of such a database may lead to an element of self-selection since it did not include all Australian SMEs. Furthermore, it might well be that SMEs who use online advertising are overrepresented in the sample since they could be more interested in the research topic. Almost 70 percent of the firms that were contacted did not respond to the request. This may have produced some non-response bias. Accordingly, the observation drawn from this study may render the study's findings non-generalisable for the entire population of Australian SMEs.

Like previous research, the authors have to acknowledge that there may be other potential determinants of online advertising adoption in Australian SMEs that this study did not include. Limitations might also result from the variable measurement of the proposed variables, which was primarily perceptual and therefore leads to the classic problems of Likert scales, namely bias and anchoring as pointed out by Grover (1993). However, validity and reliability tests were performed using standard methods advocated in the literature. Also the study utilised the responses of marketing decision-makers as representative of these constructs. Thereby, this study assumed that the decision to adopt online advertising is of rational nature. This approach assumes that these respondents are eligible to make accurate judgments regarding the innovation adoption decision and the company's business strategy. However, in this context it cannot be ruled out that an overreporting or underreporting of certain phenomenon might have occurred as a result of the respondent's job satisfaction or personal and role characteristics (Bagozzi, Yi & Phillips 1991).

Lastly, the geographical focus on Australia can be seen as a limitation. Conducting this research in different countries that are economically comparable to Australia will most likely strengthen and validate the findings of this study. It would also be interesting to see this study being conducted in developing countries to further understand the adoption process. Thereby, it has to be pointed out that the way in which organisations develop their strategies and utilise technology in their marketing efforts may vary across cultural boundaries (Geiger & Martin

1999). Nonetheless, the findings of this study are likely to be applicable to other Western nations that have similar Internet adoption pattern.

Notwithstanding these limitations, this research has proposed and tested a number of important factors, which affect the adoption of online advertising in Australian SMEs. Thereby, a predictive model of online advertising adoption was developed. In conclusion, this study was successful in advancing the understanding of the adoption of online advertising in Australian SMEs.

The limitations of this study offer many opportunities for future research since addressing the above mentioned limitations is likely to be of interest to both researchers and practitioners.

7.3. Recommendations for Future Research

This study provides the impetus for future studies on many related issues. Firstly, this research has investigated factors that affect the adoption decision of online advertising in Australian SMEs. Even though the authors argue that they included all important factors this cannot be proved. Future research should build on the findings of this study and should always try to identify additional factors associated with the adoption of online advertising. Thereby, the refinement of the survey instrument applied in this study is also recommended. For example, the environmental characteristics investigated in this study were not significant; however, it might be that other environmental characteristics may be of significance in the adoption decision of online advertising.

In this research SMEs, defined as businesses with less than 200 employees, were under investigation. It would be interesting to see if further differences between adopters and nonadopters may be noted if larger firms were the focus of the investigation. Accordingly, future research should also apply the proposed research model to a sample including large firms as well as small firms. This would help to determine if the results postulated here are general in nature or only applicable to SMEs.

Studies could also be conducted across nations and include culture specific measures to determine how online advertising adoption is determined by culture variables. Differences based on technology infrastructure, common business practices, governments regulations might be of interest in this context as well.

Future research with different methodologies than the one applied in this study is also recommended to shed more light on the issue of online advertising adoption. An alternative approach to investigate the adoption decision of online advertising would be to focus on qualitative research methods instead of using quantitative methods as this study has done. That might generate some new interesting insights into this relatively young phenomenon. The investigation of factors affecting online advertising can also be facilitated by multiple participants within each surveyed organisation. It would be interesting to see which organisation members are actually involved in the adoption decision and to what extent their perceptions differ regarding the proposed factors.

This study used a cross sectional data collection method. To fully understand the dynamic processes that are involved in the adoption decision of online advertising, conducting a longitudinal study may be fruitful. Longitudinal research could also reveal valuable insights into different evolution stages of online advertising as it is steadily evolving.

Although the generalisability of the findings of this study is enhanced through the analysis of several industries, industry-specific research is recommended to further the understanding of the processes at work with respect to the adoption of online advertising. Thereby, it would be interesting to see if industry-specific variables have a significant affect on the adoption decision.

Lastly, future research can also examine the organisations' decision to choose from various online advertisement types in their advertising campaigns. Online advertising is still evolving and there is less certainty about its effectiveness in terms of branding, targeting, and its impact on generating revenue. Generally, it would be interesting to see how marketing managers choose among different advertising channels and to what extent they allocate their advertising budget among the different channels.

References

24/7-Realmedia (2005) 24/7 Real Media's interactive marketing experts reveal their online advertising predictions for 2006, viewed 20 December 2005, <http://www.247realmedia.com/about/press_2005/2005-11-08.html>.

ABS (2005) ABoS 2002, 1321.0 Small businesses in Australia, viewed 10 April 2005, <http://www.abs.gov.au/Ausstats/abs@.nsf/e8ae5488b598839cca25682000131612/97452f3932f44031ca256c5b00027f19!OpenDocument>.

Alarcon, C. (2004) Online fodder for advertisers, viewed 14 May 2005, <http://www.bandt.com.au/news/67/0c026967.asp>.

Agarwal, R., Higgins, C.A. & Tanniru, M. (1991) Technology diffusion in a centralized MIS environment', Information and Management, Vol. 20, No. 1, pp. 61-70.

Audit Bureau of Verification Services (2006) Online advertising expenditure report for calendar 2005, viewed 29 April 2006, <www.hotkey.net.au/~ceasa/>.

Bagozzi, R.P, Yi, Y. & Phillips, L.W. (1991) Assessing construct validity in organisational research, Administrative Science Quarterly, Vol. 36, pp. 421-58.

Baldridge, J.V. & Burnham, R.A. (1975) Organisational innovation: individual, organisational and environmental impacts, Administrative Science Quarterly, Vol. 20, No. 2, pp. 165-76.

Barnes, J.G. & Cumby, J.A. (2002) Establishing customer relationships on the Internet requires more than technology, Australasian Marketing Journal, Vol. 10, No. 1, pp. 36-46.

Barwise, P. & Farley, J.U. (2005) The state of interactive marketing in seven countries: interactive marketing comes of age, Journal of Interactive Marketing, Vol. 19, No. 3, pp. 67-80.

Bedell, J.R., Ward, J.C., Archer, R.P. & Stokes, M.K. (1985) An empirical evaluation of knowledge utilisation, Evaluation Review, Vol. 9, No. 2, pp. 109-26.

Black, N.F., Lockett, A., Winklhoffer, H. & Ennew, C. (2001) The adoption of Internet financial services: a qualitative study, International Journal of Retail and Distribution Management, Vol. 29, No. 8, pp. 390-8.

Blau, P.M., Heydebrand, W.V. & Stauffer, R.W. (1966) The structure of small bureaucracies, American Sociological Review, Vol. 31, No. 2, pp. 179-91.

Blili, S. & Raymond, L. (1993) Information technology: threats and opportunities for small and medium-sized enterprises, International Journal of Information Management, Vol. 13, No. 6, pp. 439-48.

Cartellieri, C., Parsons, A., Rao, V. & Zeisser, M. (1997) The real impact of Internet advertising, McKinsey Quarterly, Vol. 3, pp. 44-63.

Chau, P.Y.K. & Tam, K.Y. (1997) Factors affecting the adoption of open systems: an exploratory study, MIS Quarterly, Vol. 23, No. 1, pp. 1-24.

Ching, H.L. & Ellis, P. (2004) Marketing in cyberspace: what factors drive e-commerce adoption?, Journal of Marketing Management, Vol. 20, pp. 409-20.

Cooper, R.B. & Zmud, R.W. (1990) Information technology implementation research: a technological diffusion approach, Management Science, Vol. 36, No. 2, pp. 123-39.

Damanpour, F. (1988) Innovation type, radicalness, and the adoption process, Communication Research, Vol. 15, pp. 545-67.

Dandridge, T.C. (1979) Children are not 'little grown ups': small business needs its own organizational theory, Journal of Small Business Management, Vol. 17, No. 2, pp. 53-7.

Delone, W. H. 1988, 'Determinants of success for computer usage in small business', MIS Quarterly, vol. 12, no. 1, pp. 51-61.

Dewar, RD & Dutton, JE 1986, 'The adoption of radical and incremental innovations: an empirical analysis', Management Science, vol. 32, no. 11, pp. 1422-33.

DosSantos, B. & Peffers, K. (1998) Competitor and vendor influence on the adoption of innovative applications in electronic commerce, Information and Management, Vol. 34, No. 3, pp. 175-84.

Dholakia, R.R. & Kshetri, N. (2004) Factors impacting the adoption of the Internet among SMEs, Small Business Economics, Vol. 23, pp. 311-22.

Dowling, P.J., Kuegler, T.J. & Testerman, J.O. (1996) Web advertising and marketing, Prima Publishing, Rocklin, CA.

Dreze, X. & Zufryden, F. (2004) Measurement of online visibility and its impact on Internet traffic', Journal of Interactive Marketing, Vol. 18, No. 1, pp. 20-37.

Ducoffe, R.H. (1996) Advertising value and advertising on the Web, Journal of Advertising Research, September/October issue, pp. 21-35.

eMarketer (2006) Ad spending trends: the Internet and other media, viewed 20 February 2006, <http://www.emarketer.com/Report.aspx?ad_spend_oct05>.

emitch/Roy-Morgan (2005) Internet advertising intentions and attitudes survey, viewed 22 November 2005, <http://www.roymorgan.com/news/polls/2005/371/>.

Ettlie, J.E. (1983) Organisational policy and innovation among suppliers to the food processing industry, Academy of Management Journal, Vol. 26, No. 1, pp. 27-44.

Ettlie, J.E. (1986) Implementing, manufacturing technologies: Lessons from experience.' in DDa Associates (ed.), Managing technological innovation, Jossey-Bass Publishers, San Francisco, CA, pp. 72-104.

Fichman, R.G. & Kemerer, C.F. (1992) Toward a theory of the adoption and diffusion of software process innovations, paper presented to IFIP Conference on Diffusion, Transfer, and Implementation of Information Technology, New York.

Fink, D. (1998) Guidelines for the successful adoption of information technology in small and medium enterprises, International Journal of Information Management, Vol. 18, No. 4, pp. 243-53.

Forrester (2006) US online marketing forecast: 2005 to 2010, viewed 19 January 2006, <http://www.forrester.com/Research/Document/Excerpt/0,7211,36546,00.html>.

Frambach, R.T. (1993) An integrated model of organisational adoption and diffusion of innovations', European Journal of Marketing, Vol. 27, No. 5, pp. 22-41.

Furst, K., Lang, W.W. & Nolle, D.E. (2002) Internet banking, Journal of Financial Services Research, Vol. 22, No. 1, pp. 95-117.

Geiger, S. & Martin, S. (1999) The Internet as relationship marketing tool - some evidence from Irish companies, Irish Marketing Review, Vol. 12, No. 2, pp. 25-36.

Globerman, S. (1975) Technological diffusion in the Canadian tool and die industry, Review of Economics and Statistics, Vol. 57, No. 4, pp. 428-34.

Google-AdWords (2006) Account fees and payment options, viewed 20 January 2006, <https://adwords.google.co.uk/select/AfpoFinder?currency=AUD&country=AU&targetCountry=AU>.

Grimm, L.G. & Yarnold, P.R. (1995) Reading and understanding multivariate statistics, American Psychological Association, Washington.

Grover, V. (1993) An empirically derived model for the adoption of customer-based interorganizational systems', Decision Sciences, Vol. 24, No. 3, pp. 603-40.

Hair, J.F., Black, W.C., Babin, B.J., Anderson, R.E. & Tatham, R.L. (2006) Multivariate data analysis, 6th edn, Prentice-Hall, Upper Saddle River, NJ.

Grover, V. (1993) An empirically derived model for the adoption of customer-based interorganizational systems', Decision Sciences, Vol. 24, No. 3, pp. 603-40.

Harrison, D., Mykytyn, P.P. & Riemenschneider, C.K. (1997) Executive decisions about adoption of information technology in small businesses: theory and empirical tests, Information Systems Research, Vol. 8, No. 2, pp. 171-95.

Hoffman, D.L., Novak, T.P. & Schlosser, A.E. (2000) The evolution of the digital divide: how gaps in Internet access may impact electronic commerce', Journal of Computer-Mediated Communications, Vol. 5, No. 3, pp. 233-45.

IAB (2005) IAB resources and research - glossary of interactive advertising terms, viewed 18 June 2005, <http://www.iab.net/resources/glossary.asp>.

IAB/PwC (2006) Internet advertising revenue report 2005, viewed 26 April 2006, <http://www.iab.net/resources/adrevenue/pdf/IAB_PwC_2005.pdf>.

Jupiter (2005) U.S. online advertising forecast, 2005 to 2010, viewed 24 January 2006, <http://www.jupiterresearch.com/bin/item.pl/home>.

Lai, V.S. (1997) Critical factors of ISDN implementation', Information and Management, Vol. 33, pp. 87-97.

Lassar, W.M., Manolis, C. & Lassar, S.S. (2005) The relationship between consumer-innovativeness, personal characteristics, and online banking adoption, International Journal of Bank Marketing, Vol. 23, No. 2, pp. 176-99.

Lazer, W. & Shaw, E. (2000) Executive insights: global marketing management: at the dawn of a new millennium, Journal of International Marketing, Vol. 8, No. 1, pp. 65-77.

Lawton, C. (2005) Interactive web ads begin to click; marketers start to realize that Internet's potential can go beyond TV spots, Wall Street Journal, 12.07, p. 10.

Lee, J. (2004) Discriminant analysis of technology adoption behavior: a case of Internet technologies in small business, Journal of Computer Information Systems, Vol. 44, No. 4, pp. 57-66.

Lee, J. & Runge, J. (2001) Adoption of information technology in small business: testing drivers of adoption for entrepreneurs, Journal of Computer Information Systems, Vol. 42, No. 1, pp. 44-57.

Leonard-Barton, D . (1992) Core capabilities and core rigidities: a paradox in managing new product development, Strategic Management Journal, Vol. 13, pp. 111-25.

Leonard-Barton, D. & Sinha, D.K. (1993) Developer-user interaction and user satisfaction in internal technology transfer, Academy of Management Journal, Vol. 36, No. 5, pp. 1125-39.

Loh, L. & Ong, Y. (1998) The adoption of Internet-based stock trading: aconceptual framework and empirical results, Journal of Information Technology, Vol. 13, pp. 81-94.

Maddox, K. (2005a) Marketers anticipate online spending rise, B to B, Vol. 90, No. 16, p. 28.

Maddox, K (2005b) Online video ads see big growth, B to B, Vol. 90, No. 16, p. 14.

Malone, T.W., Yates, J. & Benjamin, R.I. (1987) Electronic markets and electronic hierarchies, Communications of the ACM, Vol. 30, No. 6, pp. 484-97.

Marketing-Evolution (2006) Cross media optimisation study (XMOS) - creative imperatives, sales impact, viewed 10 February 2006, <http://www.iab.net/xmos/case.asp>.

McCole, P. & Ramsey, E. (2005) A profile of adopters and non-adopters of e-commerce in SME professional service firms, Australasian Marketing Journal, Vol. 13, No. 1, pp. 36-48.

Mediapost (2005) Goldman Sachs predicts $12.3 billion online ad market in '05, viewed 20 November 2005, <http://publications.mediapost.com/index.cfm?fuseaction=Articles.showArticle&art_aid=30631&art_search>.

Moch, M.K. & Morse, E.V. (1977) Size, centralization, and organizational adoption of an innovation, American Sociological Review, Vol. 42, No. 5, pp. 716-25.

Mollenkopf, D., White, M. & Zwart, A. (2001) EDI adoption in New Zealand firms: understanding proactive versus reactive adoption behaviour, Journal of Marketing Channels, Vol. 8, No. 1/2, pp. 33-63.

Mohammed, R.A., Fisher, R.J., Jaworski, B.J. & Paddison, G.J. (2002) Internet marketing: building advantage in a networked economy, McGraw-Hill, New York, NY.

Moore, G.C. & Benbasat, I. (1991) Development of an instrument to measure the perceptions of adopting an information technology innovation, Information System Research, Vol. 2, No. 3, pp. 192-222.

Morrissey, B. (2005) Advertisers fight banner blindness with news feeds', Adweek, Vol. 46, No. 36, p. 10.

Munro, B.H. (2005) Statistical methods for health care research, 5th edn, Lippincott Williams & Wilkins, Philadelphia.

Nagelkerke, N.J.D. (1991) A note on a general definition of the coefficient of determination, Biometrika, Vol. 78, No. 3, pp. 691-2.

ninemsn (2005) ABVS reports online growth – comments from ninemsn, viewed 19 May 2005, <http://mediacentre.ninemsn.com.au/mediacentre/pressreleases/145.aspx>.

Outsell (2006) Outsell's annual ad spending study: where and why advertisers are moving online, viewed 20 March 2006, <http://www.outsellinc.com/adstudy/>.

Patrick, A.O. (2005) Yahoo to track impact of Internet ads', Wall Street Journal, 16.12.2005, p. 4.

Premkumar, G., Ramamurthy, K. & Nilakanta, S. (1994) Implementation of electronic data interchange: an innovation diffusion perspective', Journal of Management Information Systems, Vol. 11, No. 2, pp. 157-86.

Premkumar, G & Roberts, M 1999, 'Adoption of new information technologies in rural small businesses', Omega, International Journal of Management, vol. 27, pp. 467-84.

PricewaterhouseCoopers (2005) Australian entertainment & media outlook 2004-2008: key findings, viewed 10 October 2005, <http://www.pwc.com/extweb/ncpressrelease.nsf/DocID/0BF393874D90DC2ACA256EFB0023ECD6>.

Riquelme, H. (2002) Commercial Internet adoption in China: comparing the experience of small, medium and large businesses, Internet Research: Electronic Networking Applications and Policy, Vol. 12, No. 3, pp. 276-86.

Salam, A.F., Pegels, C.C. & Rao, H.R. (1997) An exploratory investigation of the Internet involvement: instrument development, measurement and implications for electronic commerce', paper presented to 3rd Americas Conference on Information Systems, Indianapolis, 15-17 August 1997.

Senn, J.A. & Gibson, V.R. (1981) Risks of investment in microcomputers for small business management, Journal of Small Business Management, Vol. 19, No. 3, pp. 24-32.

Shields, M. (2005) Forecast 2006: interactive media', Mediaweek, Vol. 16, No. 1, p. 12.

Tabachnick, B.G. & Fidell, L.S. (2001) Using multivariate statistics, 4th edn, Pearson, Needham Heights, MA.

Stevens, R.E., Warren, W.E. & Martin, R.T. (1989) Nonadopters of automatic teller machines', Akron Business and Economic Review, Vol. 3, No. 2, pp. 55-63.

Teo, T.S.H., Tan, M. & Buk, W.K. (1997) A contingency model of Internet adoption in Singapore, International Journal of Electronic Commerce, Vol. 2, No. 2, pp. 95-118.

Thong, J.Y.L. (1999) An integrated model of information systems adoption in small businesses, Journal of Management Information Systems, Vol. 15, No. 4, pp. 187-214.

Thong, J.Y.L. & Yap, C.S. (1995) CEO characteristics, organizational characteristics and information technology adoption in small businesses, Omega, International Journal of Management, Vol. 23, No. 4, pp. 429-42.

Utterback, J.M. (1974) Innovation in industry and the diffusion of technology, Science, Vol. 183, pp. 620-6.

VMS (2006) BannerStream, viewed 21 January 2006, <http://www.vmsolutions.com.au/banner.index.htm>.

Welsh, J. & White, J. (1981) A small business is not a little big business', Harvard Business Review, Vol. 59, No. 4, pp. 18-32.

Yao, J.E., Xu, X., Liu, C. & Lu, J. (2002) Organisational size: a significant predictor of IT innovation adoption, The Journal of Computer Information Systems, Vol. 43, No. 2, pp. 76-82.

Yap, C.S. (1990) Distinguishing characteristics of organizations using computers, Information and Management, Vol. 18, pp. 97-107.

CHAPTER 5

E-LEARNING IN EMERGING COUNTRIES: CASE STUDIES OF REPUBLIC OF TUNISIA, THE KINGDOM OF SAUDI ARABIA, AND PEOPLE'S DEMOCRATIC REPUBLIC OF ALGERIA

Imed Ben Dhaou & Foudil Abdessemed

College of Engineering, University of Al Jouf, Sakaka, Saudi Arabia

E-learning and e-training have enabled the inclusion of all members of society into the development scheme. Higher education and IT skills are believed to be the corner stone for wealthy society and sustainable development. This chapter surveys e-learning services and the use of ICT to improve education quality for citizens in Tunisia, Saudi Arabia, and Algeria. It also analyses the bottlenecks that faces e-learning and e-training. Finally, it reports guidelines and recommendations to overcome those obstacles.

1. Introduction

The wide spread use of ICTs (Information Communication Technology), Internet and the world wide web has enabled the proliferation of electronic services (e-services) that span daily lives of citizens in industrialized countries. E-services aim at, among other things, (i) reducing production costs, (ii) improving quality of life, (iii) interconnecting people at low-cost, (iv) improving the democratization of information, and (v) reducing culture barrier between nations (Richard 1997; United Nations 2005).

While citizens of developed countries, referred to as ICT-developed countries, are enjoying the benefits of digital revolution, citizen of developing and emerging countries referred to as ICT-emerging countries, are left behind which resulted in a huge gap between those two categories. This is widely referred to as the digital gap or the digital divide. In 2008, it is reported that among the 955 millions inhabitants of Africa only 51 millions are Internet users. In contrast, in Northern America, among the 337 millions inhabitants 108 millions are Internet users. The estimated Internet users worldwide are 1 billion in which Africans Internet users represent 3.5% only (Internet World Stats 2008).

International communities have become cognized of the threats posed by the digital divide for ICT-emerging societies to achieve Millennium Declaration Goals (MDGs).The Millennium Declaration Goals (MDG) is the followings (United Nations 2008):

- Eradicate extreme poverty and hunger
- Achieve universal primary education
- Promote gender equality and empower women
- Reduce child mortality
- Improve maternal health
- Combat HIV/AIDS, malaria and other diseases
- Ensure environmental sustainability
- Develop a global partnership for development

To address the digital gap, many initiatives and projects have been recognized and proposed in recent years. In this vein we cite the 50x15 initiative proposed by AMD that aims to achieve 50 percent digital inclusion for human kind by 2015 (50x15 2009), the Global Digital Solidarity Fund (DSF) and the Global eSchools and Communities Initiatives (GeSCI) (Global eSchools 2008).

In the last decade, many scholars have analyzed the causes of the digital gap. It is believed that the digital gap had resulted from discrepancy in the following performances: (a) Income and GDP, (b) telecommunication infrastructure, (c) education and IT literacy, (d) web-content, (e) gender, (f) technological levels, (g) social inequality between different segments of the society, and finally, (h) political views and regulations (United Nations 2005).

In its 2005 global e-government readiness report the United Nations has ranked member states and countries using the following indices, (a) web measurement, (b) telecommunication infrastructure, (c) human capital, and (d) e-government readiness (Unite Nations 2005).

The web measure index is used to assess the quality of e-government services provided to citizens at various levels, which is Government-to-Business (G2B), Business-to-Government (B2G), Government-to-Government (G2G), Government-to-Citizen (G2C), and Citizen-to-Government (C2G). The sophistication of e-government websites has been measured using the following five stages: (1) Emerging presence in which the site presents limited and basic information, (2) enhanced presence whereby public policy and governance sources of current and archived information are provided, (3) interactive presence where the website provides interactive online services such as multimedia documents, downloadable official documents and contact information for government officials, (4) transactional presence that allows bidirectional interaction between citizens and government officials, and (5) networked presence in which the website integrates G2C, G2G and C2G interactions.

The telecommunication infrastructure index is the measure of available assets for data, voice and video communications. These assets include cellular phone, internet, landline phone, radio, and television. Radio was excluded from the calculation of the telecommunication index albeit its contribution in, among others, public debates and informing the society of government regulations

In the United Nations 2005 report (Unite Nations 2005), human capital index is also referred to as education index and it is obtained firstly by statistically computing the percentage of people aged 15 and above who can read and write simple statement. The obtained index is called Adult literacy index. Secondly, the Gross enrolment index is estimated using the number of student enrolled at the primary, secondary and tertiary level regardless of age as a percentage of the population of school age for that level. Finally, education index is computed using the following rule: Education Index=2/3 (Adult Literacy Index) +1/3(Gross Enrolment Index).

E-readiness index measures the ability of a given country to use ICT in the development process and wellbeing of its citizens. In the 2005 United Nations survey this index has been obtained as weighted average of web assessment index, telecommunication infrastructure index and human capital index.

Universities are government institutions that provide services for citizens at various levels of education and trainings. Traditionally the relationship between different entities within the university is done using paper-and-pen, face-to-face communication and in some rare cases through phone conversation. In this context, communications between teachers and students are done within the boundary of the classroom. These traditional ways of services delivery have started to be inadequate due to the following grounds: (i) Increasing numbers of services, students and staff, (ii) increasing demands on quality of services and quality of education, (iii) the need to shorten the administrative work, and (iv) the ever increasing number of disciplines and departments. In recent years universities have started to deploy the web for service access and delivery. University e-services have profoundly changed the concept of education and training and helped the migration of the university into the Cyber University known as virtual university.

This chapter aims to analyze the key factors for successful implementation of the ICTs in higher education through three case studies, namely: Tunisia, Saudi Arabia and Algeria. It also reports some guidelines to consolidate e-services and e-learning in these countries.

2. E-learning and ICT in Tunisia

2.1. ICT and E-services in Tunisia

Tunisia is an emerging country situated on the Mediterranean cost of North Africa with estimated 2008 population of 10 million inhabitants. The area occupied by Tunisia is 133,945.8 square kilometers (Internet World Stats 2008).

The gross national income per capita in 2008 is 3.200 U.S. dollars (World Bank 2008). In Tunisia, Internet users are estimated to be one million seven hundred users. They represent 17% of the total population. Tunisia has the most advanced telecommunication infrastructure in Africa. The 2005 survey conducted by the United Nations (United Nations 2005), had found the Tunisian's telecommunication index to be 0.0993.

To obtain the telecommunication infrastructure index, the United Nations proceeded firstly by selecting six indicators which are: PCs/1000; Internet users/1000 persons; Telephone lines/1000 persons; On-line population; Mobile phone/1000 persons; TVs/1000 persons. Each member state was profiled based on these indicators as shown in the Table 5.1 below where we take Tunisia as an example for 2005. The index for each indicator is computed using the following formula: Index= (Actual value –Minimum value)/ (Maximum value - Minimum value).

Table 5.1: Indicators for Tunisian's telecommunication infrastructure in 2005

Indicators (per 1000 persons)	Actual Value	Maximum Value	Minimum Value	Index
PCs	40	818 (San Marino)	0	0.049
Internet Users	64	675 (Iceland)	0	0.095
Telephone Lines	11.77	104 (Monaco)	0	0.1132
On-line Population	4.08	69.8 (Iceland)	0	0.058
Mobile Subscribers	19.69	119.38 (Luxembourg)	0	0.1649
TVs	19	96.5 (Sweden)	0	0.197

(Source: developed from United Nations 2005)

Hence, the telecommunication infrastructure index is computed as follows: Telecommunication index=1/5(PC index + Internet user index + Telephone line index + On-line population index) + 1/10(Mobile user index +TV index). For example the telecommunication index for Tunisia is: 1/5(0.049 + 0.095 + 0.1132 + 0.058) + 1/10(0.1649 + 0.197) = 0.0993.

Tunisian's telecommunication index is higher than the African's average index (reported to be 0.0366). However, this index is far less than the world average index which is equals 0.1898. The telecommunication index enabled Tunisian to be 4th in rank in Africa. Therefore, has a tremendous opportunity for promoting e-government and e-services in both public and private sectors. This is due to the fact that there is a strong political will within the United Nations and international communities to eradicate poverty in Africa in accordance with MDGs.

In 2005, the education index (human capital index) for Tunisia has been reported to be 0.74 (United Nations 2005). The benchmarking of digital services and ICT penetration in Tunisian society carried out by the

United Nations has shown that Tunisia suffers from the digital gap. The 2005 indices for e-government readiness and web quality are respectively 0.3310 and 0.1538 (United Nations 2005). Those facts call for drastic measures to bring Tunisian society into a mature level of deploying ICTs to achieve MDGs. To address these issues, the Tunisian government has launched ambitious national programs for promoting ICTs in various disciplines. In higher education Tunisia has adopted program for education quality improvement (Global eSchools 2008).

2.2. Higher Education in Tunisia

In Tunisia, universities and higher education institutions are government institutions, though in recent years private universities have started to gain wide acceptance within the society due to their contribution and innovation in improving quality of education and training for Tunisian and foreign students alike. Private and public universities work within the scope of the Tunisian ministry of higher education, scientific research and technology. Figure 5.1 depicts communication scheme between different organizations, groups and individual within a typical Tunisian university.

The 2008 statistics (Tunisian Ministry of Higher Education 2008) show that in Tunisia there are 35 thousand students; 18 thousand teachers spread over 190 institutions for higher education and research. Those institutions are grouped into 12 universities and a virtual university. Students and university's teachers represent 3.55% of the total population. In 2007, Tunisian government has spent 5.33% of its budget for financing higher education (Tunisian Ministry of Higher Education 2008). Each university and higher education institute has a website where students, academic and non-academic staff can download documents and reports. The websites provide latest news regulations, and announcements such as exam calendar, course modules, and vacancies. Each university and higher education institute has a link for on-line registration service. Based on all these e-services these sites can be ranked as web sites with enhanced presence (United Nations 2005).

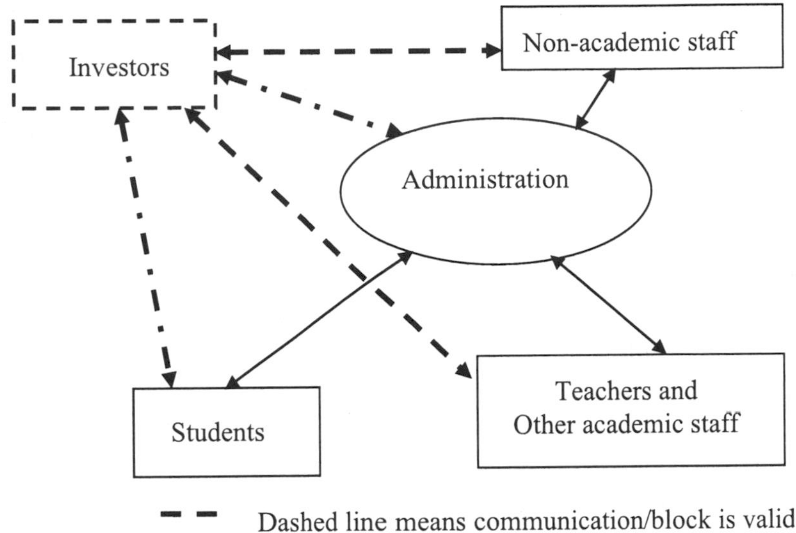

Figure 5.1: Structure of a typical Tunisian university
(Source: developed from Tunisian Ministry of Higher Education 2008)

2.3. E-learning in Tunisia

Tunisia has a virtual university (VUT) that was established in 2002. The objectives of this university are: (1) To ensure and generalize remote teaching, (2) to federate initiatives related to educational technologies, (3) to work towards the emergence of a numerical pedagogy, (4) to support a culture of permanent training in an environment centered on knowledge and innovation, (5) to reconsider the articulation between work and training, (6) to answer the challenges of the growing number of students in higher education, (7) to promote equal opportunity in higher education, and to fight against exclusion from education by widening the spectrum of the public targeted beyond the traditional students, and (8) to take part in the widening of access to higher education in a prospective vision and to work with the improvement of quality and level of higher education studies (Virtual University 2008).

The courses offered by the university are prepared using multimedia technologies. To widen the spectrum of e-learning program the VUT has installed 10 access centers and over 35 centers are planned. Those centers are connected through cable or satellite Internet. E-learning services and courses are also accessed using video conference centers. Among the 190 higher institutions for education and research in Tunisia, only four have video conference centers.

To gain momentum in distant learning and to gain full benefit of ICT the VUT is actively participating in various international projects such as the EURO-MED project AVICENNA. The objectives of the AVICENNA project are: (1) To accelerate the adoption and setting-up of e-learning centers in each partner country, (2) to equip the Avicenna Knowledge Centers (AKCs) and networking them via Internet, (3) to train the staff of the centers (directors, technical experts and tutors), (4) to train teachers to produce e-learning multimedia courses which shall be used in Internet network and Intranet satellite, (5) to develop courses in scientific and engineering disciplines and select norms and quality evaluation procedures, (6) to set up an Open Virtual Library of multimedia e-learning courses in English, Arabic, French and other languages, and finally, (7) to provide e-learning sessions for students (Avicenna Virtual Campus 2008).

3. ICT and E-Learning in the Kingdom of Saudi Arabia

3.1. ICT and E-services in Saudi Arabia

Saudi Arabia is an emerging country situated in the Middle East with estimated 2008 population of 28 million inhabitants. The gross national income per capita in 2008 is 15.440 U.S. dollars (World Bank 2008). Saudi Arabia is the largest country in Arabian Peninsula with an estimated area of 2,240,000 square kilometers. In Saudi Arabia, there are 6 million Internet users that represent 22% of the total population (Internet World Stats 2008).

Saudi Arabia has a very modern telecommunication infrastructure in the Middle East and is rapidly becoming more competitive. The telecommunication index in the 2005 United Nations survey is 0.1445. This value is less than the world average index which is 0.1898. The indices for web quality, education quality and e-government readiness are, respectively 0.37, 0.71 and 0.4105 (United Nations 2005).

E-services indices (United Nations 2005) show that Saudi Arabia suffers from the digital gap. To reduce the gap and to get full benefits from ICT the government of Saudi Arabia has setup ambitious projects with the aim to benefit from the digital revolution. In this vein, we site the Yesser project which has been launched to implement e-government services G2C, C2G, G2B, B2G and G2G. The project has the following four objectives: (a) raising the productivity and efficiency of the public sector, (b) providing better and more easy-to-use services for individual and business customers, (c) increasing return on investment (ROI), and finally (d) providing the required information in a timely and highly accurate fashion (Saudi E-government program 2008).

3.2. Higher Education in Saudi Arabia

In Saudi Arabia there are 21 universities owned by the government. Similar to Tunisia, private higher education in Saudi Arabia is gaining new momentum. The structure and communications between different entities within each university is akin to that in Tunisia as depicted in Figure 5.1.

The 2007 estimates show that there are 400 thousand registered Saudi students (Elaph newspaper 2007). In 2008 over four thousand Saudi students have been admitted to study in Europe, United States of America, and Asia. In 2005, the government of Saudi Arabia has spent 1% of its GDP for education and research (Middle East Online 2008). Students at the various Saudi's universities use e-services, named EduGate (Adaptive Tech soft Company, 2009), for, among other operations, (1) online registration, (2) monitoring the academic progress, (3) viewing transcripts and grades. Teachers also use EduGate to, among others, (a) monitor academic progress of the prospective student, (b) insert marks and absences for students and (c) edit their profiles. The web-site for the Saudi ministry of higher education has many electronic services for (d) equivalence of foreign diplomas, (e) government funded Saudi students studying abroad, (c) self-funded Saudi students studying abroad, (f) statistical division of the ministry for higher education, and

(g) common Saudi comities (Ministry of Education, Kingdom of Saudi Arabia 2008). All Saudi universities have websites that present an easy access to EduGate.

3.3. E-learning in Saudi Arabia

To increase the efficiency of higher education, the government of Saudi Arabia has adopted distant and e-learning technologies. Recently, the government has established a center for e-learning and distant learning. This center has the following missions: (a) Deliver higher education to all in an effective way through e-learning, (b) deliver quality higher education through e-learning, (c) promote education via technology, (d) ensure quality standards for e-learning, and finally, (e) bridge the gap of education and technology (Saudi National Center for E-learning and Distance Learning 2008). The center provides all needed infrastructure, technical assistance and training programs for e-learning and distant learning. Currently the center has five national projects: Jusur, Tajseer, Portal, Excellence Award, National Repository, and Taiseer. The detailed description of each project is available on line (Saudi National Center for E-learning and Distance Learning 2008).

Jusur is a Saudi Learning Management System (LMS) designed to manage the E-learning process in the kingdom of Saudi Arabia. *Tajseer* aims at improving teaching at Saudi's universities through the use of ICTs and e-learning technologies. This project has the following objectives: (a) Supporting and implementing Jusur system, (b) providing training program for universities staff and teachers for effective use of Jusur, (c) update existing LMS tools and provide effective solutions to controversial problems and (d) spread awareness among universities on new horizons offered by new LMS tools. *Portal* provides the following services to spread knowledge and share experience of e-learning and distant learning: (a) access to Jusur LMS, (b) track the latest developments in e-learning and distant learning, (c) inform general public and Saudi's universities on the activities of the national center, ministry of higher education and universities(d) access digital courses, (d) share knowledge and experience among users through the establishment of digital forum, (e) create a glossary for e-learning terms and (f) advertise the center to the general public. *Excellent award* is a project created at the center with the aim to encourage universities to effectively use e-learning and distant learning. The national repository offers mechanism to create and mange learning objects that can help universities for easy course development. Taiseer helps to share Jusur among faculty members and students. It offers on-line registration and use with no conditions.

4. ICT and E-Learning in People's Republic of Algeria

4.1. ICT and E-services in Algeria

Algeria is a North African country. With an area of 2 381 741 square kilometers, Algeria is the largest country bordering the Mediterranean, and the second largest in Africa after Sudan. Algeria is an emerging country with 33,769,669 populations for 2008, according to US census Bureau (US Census 2009). There should be no doubt that the instability due to the civil war more than a decade caused the worst economic disaster for the country. Its effect has been spread out over all different areas. The economy as well as the growth not only stagnate at a low level but have registered a net decrease. According to the World Bank, the Gross National Income is 3.62 U.S. dollars. The statistics of 2008 (Internet World Stats 2008) show that 3500,000 are internet users, which only represent 10.4% of the population.

Algeria has a moderate telecommunication infrastructure. The telecommunication index in the 2005 United Nations survey is 0.0365 which is less than the world average index. The indices for web quality, education quality and e-government readiness are, respectively 0.2462, 0.69 and 0.3242 (United Nations 2005).

The above indices clearly show that Algeria is suffering from the digital gap and motivate further the Algerian government to take precise steps to escape digital gap and to gain full benefits from the digital technology. Recently the Algerian government has launched several IT projects such as cyberparc which is dedicated to information technology and communication (ICT) in the new town of Sidi Abdallah near Algiers. Furthermore, many initiatives have been taken as a part of the e-commission chaired by the head of government that aims at creating a government Intranet Network (RIN), and many electronic applications within the framework of e-commerce, e-learning, e-justice e-health, e-services, and e-culture (El Watan 2007). Four pilot projects under the cooperation of the European Union MEDA II which concern e-school, e-commune were conducted in consultation with relevant ministries. Moreover, the project "OUSRATIC", initiated by the government that aims to provide each house with a computer has succeeded to sell 700 000 computers. A draft space program with a cost of 82 billion Dinars has been developed further. The plan covers the period 2006-2020.

4.2. Higher Education in Algeria

Currently, the Algerian university is built around a university network consisting of sixty institutions covering forty one regions and distributed as follows: 29 Universities, 16 Academic colleges, 11 Schools and National Institutes and 4 Teacher training colleges. These academic institutions are organized in schools and institutes to support educational activities, scientific and research with an academic staff estimated at 30,510. On the other hand the network research institutions include 3 national agencies, 40 research centers, 5 research units. There are also 639 research laboratories located at the national level including 4 outside higher education sector (Statistical report 2008). The number of new students for the year 2007/2008 is estimated at 270,285 and the estimate of graduates in the same year was about 120,000. Taking into account the statistical data which have already been transmitted, the number enrolled in post-graduation is estimated at 47,588 students.

4.3. E-learning in Algeria

The project of the University of Tomorrow is ongoing. The Algerian authorities want to outsource congested higher education and universities and to reduce social problems as majority of the universities are located in coastal cities.

To gain experience from e-learning and distance learning Algerian universities are taking part in various international projects such as the

EUMEDGRID and AVICENNA project. The EUMEDGRID project (EUMEDGRID 2009), aims to set up in the Mediterranean a grid infrastructure for research, which can become part of EGEE (Enabling Grid for e-science). Its objective is to raise grid awareness and competences among the researchers operating in the Mediterranean area, to make them able to profit of this new powerful tool, to foster collaboration with European and worldwide projects and to promote scientific and industrial development in the area.

5. Summary and Recommendations

Higher education in Republic of Tunisia, the Kingdom of Saudi Arabia and Republic of Algeria has experienced huge transitions towards openness and quality. In the last decade tremendous efforts have been put in by the three governments to further enhance quality of education through the effective use of ICTs, e-learning and e-training. While lots of progress has been made as compared to the beginning of this millennium, ICT and e-learning in those countries remain at inadequate levels of exploration and deployment.

Firstly, University web-services in these countries are not fully automated. Moreover, the number of e-services does not cover all the university needs. Till today exams are supervised and checked using traditional way of identification. In industrialized countries, exams are supervised using ICTs. During exam session, the ID of each student is checked using RF-ID technology to prevent, among other things, cheating, plagiarism, and falsifying grade reports (Ma et al. 2005).

Secondly, E-learning in these countries is at the infancy stage. This is due to many issues such as (i) lack of awareness among students, teachers and parents, (ii) reduced availability of e-learning services, (iii) lack of adequate number of sufficiently trained staff, (iv) inadequate telecommunication infrastructure, (v) unacceptable level of e-government readiness, and (vi) lack of availability of e-services and e-training programs in Arabic language.

To address these issues the following steps can be considered: (a) Increasing awareness among students, parents and teachers on the potential of e-learning in various disciplines, (b) slowly moving to cyber domain to deliver asynchronous e-courses such as the open courseware from Massachusetts Institute of Technology, (c) equipping university campuses and student accommodations with ICTs, (d) constantly improving quality of university website, (e) increase the number of e-services provided by universities for students, teachers and other staff members, (f) improving LMS (Learning Management System) tools to get full benefits of the latest technologies in e-learning such as smart board and smart document camera, (g) cross-border cooperation particularly with Arabic states to promote Arabic language in the IT domain, and (h) interconnecting campuses and higher education institutes with high-speed Internet.

References

Adaptive Tech soft Company (2009) Online, Available at: http://www.ats-ware.com [accessed on December 18, 2009].

Avicenna Virtual Campus (2008) Online, Available at: http://pleiad.unesco.org/ [accessed on November, 15, 2008].

El Watan newspaper Online (2007) Online, Available at: http://www.elwatan.com/ [accessed on November 29, 2008].

Elaph newspaper (2007) article published on 3'd of August 2007, Online, Available at: http://www.elaph.com [accessed on February 20,.2009].

EUMEDGRID project (2009) Online, Available at: hhtp://www.eumedgrid.org [accessed on February 18, 2009].

Global eSchools and Communities Initiatives (2008) Online, Available at: http://www.gesci.org [accessed on August 23, 2008].

Internet World Stats (2008) Online, Available at: http://www.internetworldstats.com/ [accessed on August 23, 2008].

Ma, J. H., Nakamura, A. & Huang, R.H. (2005) A Random ID Update Scheme to Protect Location Privacy in RFID-Based Student Administration Systems. Proceedings of 16th International Workshop on Database and Expert Systems Applications, pp. 67-71.

Middle East (2008) Online, Available at: http://middle-east-oline.com/education/?id=67773, first published 26-09-2008 last updated 27-09-2008 [accessed on November 15, 2008].

Ministry of Education, Kingdom of Saudi Arabia (2008) Online, Available at: http://www.moe.gov.sa/ [accessed on December, 12.2008].

Richard S. R. (1997) The Social impact of computers, 2nd Ed., Academic Press.

Statistical report (2008) The Algerian Ministry of higher education.

Saudi E-government Program (2008) Online, Available at: http://www.yesser.gov.sa/english/default.asp [accessed on November 12, 2008]

Saudi Ministry of High Education (2008) Online, Available at: http://www.mohe.gov.sa [accessed on November 11, 2008].

Saudi National Center for E-learning and Distance Learning (2008) Online, Available at: http://www.elc.edu.sa/portal/ [accessed on November 12,2008].

The World Bank (2008) Online, Available at: http://web.worldbank.org [accessed on August 23, 2008].

Tunisian Ministry of Higher Education (2008) Scientific Research and Technology, Online, Available at: http://www.mes.tn [accessed on August 23, 2008].

United Nations (2005) UN Global E-government Readiness Report 2005: From E-government to e-inclusion, Department of Economic and Social Affairs, Division for Public Administration and Development Management..

United Nations (2008) Online, Available at: http://www.un.org/millenniumgoals/ [accessed on November 30, 2008].

US Census Bureau, (2009), Online, Available at: http://www.census.gov [accessed on February 29,.2009].

Virtual University of Tunisia (2008) Online, Available at: http://www.uvt.rnu.tn [accessed on September 3, 2008].

CHAPTER 6

CONSUMERS' ADOPTION OF ELECTRONIC TICKETING: AN APPLICATION IN THE AIR TRAVEL INDUSTRY IN TUNISIA

Anis Allagui

Institut Supérieur de Gestion, Gabes University, Tunisia

Mohamed Slim Ben Mimoun

Institut Supérieur de Gestion, Sousse University, Tunisia

This chapter aims to identify the factors in decision making for accepting e-ticketing by Tunisian individuals. Based on constructs from the technology acceptance model, a model is developed for studying consumers' acceptance towards e-ticketing system of a national air travel company. The travelers' intention to purchase e-tickets is chosen as dependent variable in the model. The several variables in the model are then identified and operationalized according to previous research. Data were collected among air travel potential customers in Tunisia through survey, and are analyzed using regression analysis. The findings are discussed with regard to limitations of the study and managerial insights are addressed.

1. Introduction

Lately, Electronic ticketing (E-ticketing) has been one of the major innovations in air travelling industry. It has changed the overall market structure as most of airline companies have already, or are on the point, to adopt e-ticketing systems worldwide. The International Air Transport Association (IATA) announced that by May 31, 2008, airline tickets will be 100% electronically delivered, which will save the industry up to US$ 3 billion annually.

As using e-tickets, paper based tickets will disappear and travellers do not have to indicate tangible proof of their reservation. It was predicted that, in US, E-ticketing would be widely adopted by the corporate customers as well as the knowledgeable business leisure travellers (McCuhbrey 1999). Indeed, in 2000, over 70% of the U.S. domestic travelers have used E-tickets, while only 11% e-tickets were used to travel within or around Asia (Coleman 2000). E-ticketing usage in Africa is even lower. In fact, a survey of African airlines carried out by GBCS - Air Transport Consulting showed that very few in the African airline industry are currently using e-ticketing (Southwood 2007). However CEOs interviewed expected to implement e-ticketing by the deadline but there is little sign of any project implementation in many airlines. Sales and Marketing personnel interviewed were particularly keen on being able to offer their customers airline ticket sales using the Internet.

Nevertheless the pace of E-ticketing in developing countries is accelerating, awareness and acceptance level of the travellers towards E-ticketing appears to be low at the moment (Wan and Che 2004). This might be caused by emergent problems due to lack of infrastructure standardisation between airline industry operators. Actually, even though electronic tickets are perceived easy to use and convenient by individuals and organizations, their essential disadvantage up to now is that computer settings do not recognize E-tickets issued by other transporters: "When a passenger's flight has been cancelled or delayed, the passenger might spend hours trying to swap electronic tickets for paper tickets so as to book a new flight on another carrier" (Bennett 2002). Or worse, "if an airline folds, it could take months or even a year to sort out the electronic paper trail" (Stringer 2002).

From the users' point of view, another important issue in E-ticketing is the uncertainty and insecurity that buyers might feel at the time of online booking, especially at flight cancellation and delay circumstances (Bennett 2002). These obstacles would relate E-ticketing acceptance and adoption by individuals to their perception of this system. The aim of this study is to expose the principal factors that may influence air travelers' acceptance, especially, their intention toward using E-ticketing in Tunisia. Research results would be useful to Tunisian's aviation industry, particularly to the airlines in understanding their customers' attitude towards electronic ticketing and formulating their market strategies for E-ticketing services.

2. Background

2.1. Operation and Spread of Electronic Ticketing

An e-ticketing system permits to concerned travel operators to send out ticketing information straight to the airline's database, enabling passengers to check-in and board the flight without showing a paper ticket. Mc Cuhbrey (1999) define e-ticket as "*a record of a reservation made using a valid credit card number stored in the computer database of the airline company*". E-ticketing by definition combines the issue and delivery of ticket into a single operation and remains arguably the most critical commercial tool aimed at cutting rising costs in the airline industry (Ainin et al. 2008).

Thus, e-tickets substitute for the paper-based flight coupons by an electronic ticket image that is stored in the airline's information database. With an e-ticket, details of the passengers' journey are stored and retrieved using a unique lookup code (Ainin et al. 2008). Consequently, travel agents do not need any more to issue a physical ticket to passengers as the code can be transmitted throughout any communication tool (email, PDA, phone, etc).

As a novel mean of editing tickets, this model is becoming more and more prevalent in a way of downsizing the costs that goes to printing tickets. Ultimately, the aim of an e-ticket-based airline industry is to get rid of the heavy process which exists, through bilateral arrangements and cost up to US$150,000 for implementation and administration annually (Abeyratne 2005).

The first airline to start experimenting with e-ticketing, in 1984, was United Airlines but it took six years before the procedure was actually implemented. Since then, e-tickets have been widely accepted in US. with a usage rate over 70% for domestic flights. Many other airlines in the world such as Delta, KLM, Northwest airline, Icelander airline have the experience of providing e-tickets. Electronic ticketing delivering had become universal in North America and consumers' orders for airline tickets are widely realized virtually.

Following the trends of Internet usage and high speed connexions adoption, African ICT infrastructure for airline industry are at present poor thus costly to operate and maintain (Malanga 2006). It resulted that out of 200 African airlines, 10 only issue e-tickets at the moment, and only 18 airlines have contracts signed for ET. It is only 6 African airlines that have issued E-tickets so far. Among these, Tunisair, the national public airline transporter, launched e-ticketing since March 2005 by establishing a merchant website and intended to generalize electronic sales in 2007. In 2006, Tunisair announced that 32% of tickets were delivered electronically on eligible markets.

2.2. E-ticketing Acceptance by Consumers

E-ticketing advantages concern both companies and consumers. In fact, while it creates charge savings for the air travel corporations, voyagers get their benefits in terms of convenience and a more secure way of travelling. There is no need for travelers to hold a tangible ticket anymore, which implies that the fear of losing or misplacing their travel proof disappears. All the passenger needs to do is to carry the ubiquitous "photo identification". Moreover, the passengers are able to check-in on the internet and choose their seats, meals or order specific requests, in addition to the greater flexibility to the passenger and the travel agent to make changes to the itinerary. It was expected that "technology savvy" consumers would be the better prepared to adopt this new booking method.

The use of the internet is not the unique way to buy a travelling e-ticket. If online transactions (sale and distribution) occur mainly on this channel, the e-ticket purchase can be done either by phone or at a ticket office. Further, the document scan be mailed, sent by fax or email, or picked up at a ticketing location. Customers who perceive benefits of general use of the internet will be given many opportunities such as 24 hours available service in any geographical location which liberates customers and airlines branches from being restricted in special place. Also, the ability of comparison between different airlines' services and prices and reducing time loss in queues to receive paper-based ticket would significantly affect the intention to use and adopt this booking method.

McIvor et al. (2003) list a bundle of important factors which affect on customers in order to use airlines' website for buying e-ticket. These factors can be clustered as bellow:

- Real-time decision-making mechanisms: reduction of information asymmetry helps customer to make a decision
- Up-to-date information for customers: all the websites evaluated contained up-to date information on flights, schedules, promotions and complementary services. This will help the customer to make a best decision by comparison different website. Also this way is better than old brochure which airlines provide in order to provide information for their customers
- Reductions in customers' search and transaction costs: on-line buyers benefit from better selection in terms of choice (of airlines, flights, schedules, destinations, levels of service and complementary services); speed (time, convenience of access capabilities on the Internet); and reduced transaction costs (monetary, effort, mistakes) (McIvor et al. 2003)
- Bundling products and services
- Offering additional services not directly related to the core travel offering
- Receiving low(er) prices/discounted fares
- Customizing offerings to suit individual customer needs
- New transaction structures play integral role in lowering transaction costs for customers

2.3. Technology Acceptance Model

Introduced by Davis et al. (1989), the technology acceptance model (TAM) became a widely used model in IS research. It was adapted from the Theory of Reasoned Action (TRA) (Fishbein & Ajzen 1975) and identified the relationships between perceived ease of use (PEOU), perceived usefulness (PU), attitudes, and behavioral intentions towards a target system.

TAM suggests that that usage of Information Systems is determined by user behavioral intentions, which themselves are jointly determined by user perceived usefulness and attitudes toward using the IS, the last of which are jointly determined by user perceived usefulness and perceived ease of use. This also has a positive but indirect effect on attitude through perceived usefulness (Shih, 2004).

Recently had identified a number of studies that have successfully adopted TAM to examine the acceptance of new technologies such as personal computers (Igbaria et al. 1997), word processors and spreadsheets (Chau 1996) Web browsers (Morris & Dillon 1997), the use of Websites (Lederer et al. 2002; Lin & Lu 2002), Web retailing (Chen et al. 2002; O'cass and Fenech 2003), online purchase intentions (van der Heijden 2003) and Internet banking (Chau and Lai 2003).

O'Cass and Fenech (2003) use key consumer characteristics such as opinion leadership, impulsiveness, Web shopping compatibility, Internet self-efficacy, perceived Web security, satisfaction with Web sites, and shopping orientation to understand the adoption of Web retailing by Internet users. They found that Internet users' perceived usefulness and perceived ease of use are affected in various degrees by opinion leadership, Web shopping compatibility, Internet self-efficacy, perceived Web security, impulsiveness, satisfaction with Web sites, and shopping orientation. Zhang and Prybutok's (2003) work further confirms the validity of the TAM in an online context. By extending and applying TAM to consumer Web shopping experience, they find that TAM is a generic model and can be used to predict consumer behavior. Legris et al. (2003) conclude that TAM is a useful model, but that still other important factors need to be identified and added into the model. They cite in particular variables related to social and human changes.

However, few studies explaining the acceptance of e-ticketing using the TAM. Based on the belief–attitude–intention–behaviour relationship in the TRA, this study proposes a model extending TAM to predict consumer e-ticketing adoption. The model not only includes PEOU, PU, attitudes toward e-ticketing and user acceptance, but also adopts the trust toward the site as additional variable influencing e-ticketing adoption (Wan & Che 2004).

3. Conceptual Framework and Research Propositions

Based on theory findings, the research framework is developed to study individual's acceptance of E-ticketing usage by including constructs from the technology acceptance models (TAM).

The model focuses on two salient beliefs that impact the attitude toward using the technology, in this case the electronic ticketing system, which are perceived usefulness and its perceived ease of use. This model is based on a cost-benefit paradigm, where users, facing the introduction of a new technology in a working context, build their attitude toward using it by balancing the perceived cost of using it in term of time and cognitive costs in one hand and the perceived benefits of using it in the other hand (Hallegatte and Nantel 2006). Besides, trust was included in the model as an antecedent of attitude and the behavioral intention to use electronic ticketing system. Trust was successfully introduced within the TAM framework, in previous online shopping context, either as a direct antecedent of purchase intention (Gefen et al. 2003) or as an antecedent of intention to transact (Pavlou 2003).

Seven research propositions were then developed to study the underlying factors and their impacts on the usage intention toward E-ticketing. The research framework is shown in Figure 6.1. The components of the model are discussed as follows.

3.1. Intention to Use E-ticketing

Intention is defined as the "*strength of conscious plan to perform the targeted behaviour*" (Harrison et al. 1997), and was presented as a predictor of behaviour in the case of non environmental changes will occur. The choice of "intention to use" to study customers' acceptance toward E-ticketing was driven by two reasons. First, according to Gattiker (1990), technology acceptance is viewed as an individual's psychological state with regard to his or her voluntary or intended use of a particular technology. Considerable studies report a strong and significant causal link between behavioural intention and targeted behaviour (Sheppard et al. 1988; Venkatesh & Davis 2000). Therefore, using behavioural intention as a dependent variable to study individual technology acceptance is theoretically justifiable. Second, E-ticketing has not been widely adopted by most travellers since its introduction in Tunisia in 2005. As a result, measuring intention instead of actual usage as a dependent variable is more appropriate due to the lack of having any database with former real users of such system.

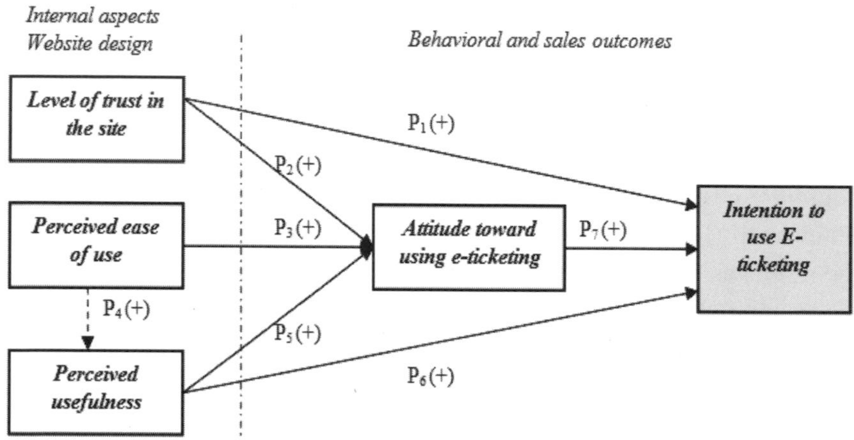

Figure 6.1: Conceptual framework of ticketing system usage in an e-commerce context (Source: developed for this study)

3.2. Trust

Many different definitions of trust have been proposed, and various studies have found that it is strongly associated with attitude towards products and services and towards online behaviours. Loiacono and al. (2002) presented trust of one of the major dimensions of Web site quality.

Recent models of consumer e-commerce behavior, including the Internet consumer trust model (ICTM; Grazioli & Jarvenpaa 2000; Jarvenpaa, Tractinsky, & Vitale 2000) and the electronic exchange model (EEM; Swaminathan, Lepkowska-White, & Rao 1999), suggest that *trust* is an important factor in electronic exchange.

Gefen (2000) indicated that trust in an e-commerce vendor increased a user's intention to use the vendor's web site and was the most efficient factor for reducing uncertainty. Gefen and Straub (2003) demonstrate empirically that higher trust in a site leads to higher intention to use and bay from this site. We propose then the following:

- **P1:** Higher levels of trust towards the site will result in decreased levels of intention to use e-ticketing.
- **P2:** Higher levels of trust towards the site will result in a positive attitude toward using e-ticketing.

3.3. Perceived Ease of Use

Perceived ease of use can be described as the degree to which a person believes that using a particular system is free of effort (Davis 1989). In e-ticketing context, we define ease of use as the extent to which a consumer believes that use of e-ticket is free of effort.

Previous research has demonstrated that individuals are more likely to have a positive attitude toward a new technology if they perceive that it is easy to use (Davis 1989; Saade and Bahli 2005; Shang et al. 2005). Studies using TAM have suggested also that perceived ease of use influences perceived usefulness, the easier a technology is to use, the more useful it is perceived to be (Davis 1989; Shih 2004; Shang et al. 2005). Therefore, we propose that:

- **P3:** Perceived ease of use will have a positive direct impact on attitude toward using e-ticketing.
- **P4:** The greater perceived ease of use, the more usefully visitors perceive the site.

3.4. Perceived Usefulness

Perceived usefulness was defined as the degree to which a person believes that using a particular system could enhance his or her job performance: it is the extent to which an individual believes that using the system enhances his/her performance (Davis et al. 1989).

In the context of E-ticketing, we define 'usefulness as the extent to which a consumer believes that the adoption of e-ticketing will provide gain of time, facilitate reservation process and enable quicker check-in.

Studies that have incorporated TAM have consistently found support for the relationship between perceived usefulness and attitude and/or behavioural intention (Karahanna et al. 1999; Venkatesh & Davis 1996) In fact, TAM incorporates both an indirect link (through the mediating variable of attitude) as well as a direct link between usefulness and intention (Vijayasarathy 2004; Shang et al. 2005). Consequently, we propose:

- **P5:** Perceived usefulness (PU) of the website will positively influence the visitors' intention to use e-ticketing.
- **P6:** PU is positively related to website visitors' attitude toward using e-ticketing.

3.5. Attitude Toward Using E-ticketing

Attitude towards use is the user's evaluation of the desirability of employing a particular information systems application (Lederer et al. 2000).

According to TAM, attitude towards technology affects use of the technology (Koufaris 2002). Attitude mediates the effect of perceived usefulness and ease of use on actual behaviour (adoption versus non-adoption) of technology (O'Cass and Fenech 2003). This suggests the following research proposition:

- **P7:** Attitude toward using e-ticketing relates positively to intention to use e-ticketing.

4. Methodology

4.1. Data Collection and Measurements

Data for the study were collected through a survey among a sample of Tunisian consumers. A database containing a large number of valid email addresses was used to target respondents. After removing incomplete responses, 160 valid questionnaires provided the final data of the study.

The sample is biased towards female respondents (62.5%). The age of the greater part of questioned individuals is ranged between 20 and 30 years (82.5%) as they are essentially graduate and undergraduate students (69.4%).

A questionnaire was then designed to address the issues relating to intention to use the website of the major carrier in the country (Tunisair) for e-ticketing related services. The measurement instrument was developed using a combination of existing scales from an I.S./Marketing literature. Model constructs were assessed with a 5 point Likert-type scale ranged from 1 (strongly disagree) to 5 (strongly agree).

4.2. Validity and Reliability of Constructs

Constructs' validity was examined through exploratory factor analysis (EFA). Principal components extraction showed that all variables were unidimensional and all items were highly correlated to the respective factor (loadings >.63). Furthermore, eigenvalues and total explained variance were examined for all model variables and showed excellent levels (correspondingly >2.2 and >59.2%).

An inspection of the correlation matrix revealed that the majority of the inter-item correlations were significant (greater than 0.3) at the 0.01 level and more highly related to each other than with items associated with other measures in the model.

The reliability of the constructs was assessed using Cronbach's α. The alpha values for the constructs were 0.779 to 0.855. All of them are then above the recommended acceptance level of 0.7 which indicates that the instrument can be considered reliable and internally consistent.

5. Findings and Discussion

A series of multiple-regression analyses was performed to determine whether the propositions developed in this study received empirical support. Multicolinearity does not appear to be a major concern, as the maximum variance inflation factor among the independent variables is approximately 1.8. Study results, which are shown in Table 6.1, are now reported.

5.1. Statistical Analyses

5.1.1. Perceived Ease of Use and Perceived Usefulness

Consistent with findings from previous work, the regression result shows a highly significant relationship between Perceived ease of use (PEOU) and perceived usefulness (PU) ($p < .0001$), thus providing support for proposition 4. With only one predictor and an R square of 0.35, the model further supports the important role of PEOU in determining its PU in an online setting.

5.1.2. Antecedents of Consumers' Attitude Towards E-ticketing

As anticipated, level of trust ($b = 0.429$) and perceived usefulness ($b = 0.436$) are significantly, positively related to consumers' attitude towards electronic ticketing usage ($p < .001$). Thus, propositions 2 and 5 receive empirical support. However, a non significant relationship between perceived ease of use and attitude was found ($b = -.037$; $p > .6$), which runs counter to proposition 3. Among the three predictors of consumers' attitude towards e-ticketing, perceived usefulness had the highest regression coefficient, and as such, seemingly the greatest impact. The regression equation explains 50.8% of the variance in the attitude variable.

5.1.3. Antecedents of Intention to Use E-ticketing

Trust and perceived usefulness are positively associated with intention to use e-ticketing. Furthermore, attitude towards e-ticketing is related to its usage intention by consumers. Both of these findings were expected. Consequently, propositions 1, 7 and 6 are supported. Trust seems to be the most important variable in determining intention to adopt the e-ticketing system by individuals ($b = .625$; $p = .000$ versus $b = .282$ and $b = .179$; $p < .05$ respectively for attitude and perceived usefulness). The overall R square for this equation is 0.495.

Table 6.1: Results of regression analysis of E-ticketing usage intention

Dependent variable	*Independent variable*	*Coefficients*		
		Std error	*β*	*t*
Perceived usefulness	Perceived ease of use	.064	.591	9.2
ANOVA $F_{full\ model} = 84.636$ ($p<.05$)				
Attitude towards e-ticketing	Trust	.063	.429	6.82
	Perceived ease of use	.070	-.037	-.523
	Perceived usefulness	.073	.436	5.95
ANOVA $F_{full\ model} = 53.688$ ($p<.05$)				
Intention to use e-ticketing	Trust	.073	.386	5.30
	Perceived usefulness	.082	.179	2.16
	Attitude towards using e-ticketing	.081	.282	3.46
ANOVA $F_{fiill\ model} = 37.91$ ($p<.05$)				

5.2. Results Discussion

This article attempts to address the call for work on the consumer intention of using e-ticketing system. The model described in this article identified key antecedents that are likely to influence intent of purchasing air travel tickets through the Internet and explored the relationships among these constructs.

Theoretically, the article contributes to the body of literature on technology adoption in two ways. First, it broadens the technology acceptance model by synthesizing findings from previous studies and by integrating a key relational marketing variable which is trust towards the website. Second, the framework presented in the present research is specifically designed for a B-to-C Tunisian e-commerce setting and is among the first to explore the e-ticketing system acceptance by consumers in such a context.

The survey results showed initially that, as most of the former studies found, the link between ease of use and usefulness is confirmed. It means that users of air travel e-ticketing systems perceive that the effectiveness of the website will be greater when its usage is perceived as easy as it can be.

Additionally, among a set of predictors of consumers' attitude towards e-ticketing, trust and perceived usefulness figure as key precursors. As if individuals develop a favorable attitude will likely be adopters, it is important to them that the product/service is trusted and useful. Hence, to improve the usage of e-ticketing, the relevant parties need to conduct an informational-oriented promotion, providing helpful instruction on how to use the technology easily and in a secure manner. That will increase the users' level of trust towards the e-ticketing and consequently their attitude would be positive.

The unanticipated result was the absence of a significant relationship between perceived ease of use and attitude toward e-ticketing. It might be explained by the fact that some participants did not use e-ticketing before and were not sure about how easy is it. Indeed, the perceived novelty of this relatively new booking system in Tunisia and its unrecognizing by a majority of travelers might be a research limit.

It was also found that the intention to use e-ticketing reflect an interesting aspect of consumers' behavior. Actually, trust and attitude, and at a lower level perceived usefulness, are significant explaining factors of e-ticketing usage intention. Subsequently, the consumers questioned declared that they will be using e-ticketing to book or buy online air plane tickets once if it is trustworthy and display a certain number of benefits to them.

The related practical implications to these findings would concern mainly the communication campaigns for the e-ticketing system. Companies have to ensure a good positioning in the consumers' mind and definitely base their ads on values like transparency and excellent customer oriented service, in order to be able to develop solid relationships with the consumers that are the potential users and online shoppers through electronic ticketing. An e-ticket website will require not only a browsing facility to view different goods but also provision within the site to enable the potential buyer to review available products and services and also pay for them online. This may require the initial measure of simply using an online e-commerce hosting service. An airline company or online air travel agency might consider adding more features to distinguish its web site from those of the competitors, and enhance the user-friendliness for air travel ticketing interfaces' design, thereby possibly gaining in popularity.

6. Conclusions and Future Research Recommendation

This chapter aimed to determine important factors leading to e-ticketing adoption by Tunisian consumers and permit to study the technology acceptance model (TAM) applied to the case of Tunisair, the biggest airline company in the country. Main results led in favor of the TAM variables explaining consumers' attitude and intention to use and adopt e-ticketing system for booking or buying air transportation online.

Some limitations are associated to the present work. The exploratory nature of the research is a limit in itself, thus generating only preliminary findings. Consequently, much additional research is necessary to ascertain whether the posited model would receive further empirical support. Due to the fact that there may be response prejudice in our study caused by a part of respondents who didn't even hear about the existence of e-ticketing, future undertakings can expand this work first on a larger sample that would be directly concerned by booking or buying e-tickets within the next days (weeks). Research that will study other companies in the travel industry will allow generalizing our results and increasing extern validity.

Theory extension on the subject might study the impact of web design issues on consumer behaviors while shopping for e-tickets on the Internet. Usability and other aspects of interface components (color scheme, interactivity, layout, etc) could have an impact on decision making, satisfaction or loyalty towards the vendor website.

References

Abeyratne, R. (2005) Electronic Ticketing in Air Transport-Commercial: Strategies and Consequences, Journal of World Trade, Vol. 39, No. 6, pp. 1095 -1119.

Ainin, S., Ng, J. & Mohezar, S. (2008) E-Ticketing as a New Way of Buying Tickets: Malaysian Perceptions. Journal of Social Sciences, Vol. 17, No. 2, pp. 149-157

Bennett, M. (2002) E' doesn't mean easy, Block Enterprise, Vol. 32, No. 6, p. 87.

Chau, P.Y.K., (1996) An empirical assessment of a modified technology model, Journal of Management Information Systems, Vol. 13, No. 2, pp. 185–204.

Chau, P. Y.K., & Lai, V. S. K. (2003) An empirical investigation of the determinants of user acceptance of Internet banking, Journal of Organizational Computing & Electronic Commerce, Vol. 13, No. 2, pp. 123-146.

Chen, M. L., Gillenson, D.L. & Sherrell (2002) Enticing on-line consumers: an extended technology acceptance perspective, Information & Management, Vol. 39, No. 8, pp. 705–719.

Coleman, Z. (2000) Asian travel Steering clear: Web surfing can leave business travelers wiped out, Asian Wall Street Journal, p. 7, April 17.

Davis, F. D. (1989) Perceived usefulness, perceived ease of use, and user acceptance of information technology, MIS Quarterly, Vol. 13, No. 3, pp. 319-337.

Davis, F. D., Bagozzi, R. P. & Warshaw, P. R., (1989) User acceptance of computer technology: a comparison of two theoretical models, Management Science, Vol. 35, No. 8, pp. 982-1003.

Fishbein. M. & Ajzen. I. (1975) Belief, altitude, intention and behavior: An introduction to theory and research, Reading. MA: Addison-Wesley.

Gattiter, U. E. (1990) Technology management in organizations, Newbury Park, CA Sage.

Gefen, D., & Straub, D. (2003) Managing User Trust in B2C e-Services, e-Service Journal, Vol. 2, No. 2, pp. 7–24.

Gefen, D. (2000) E-commerce: The role of familiarity and trust, Omega: The International Journal of Management Science, Vol. 28, pp. 725-737.

Gefen, D., Karahanna, E., & Straub, D. W. (2003) Inexperience and experience with online stores: The importance of tam and trust, IEEE Transactions on Engineering Management, Vol. 50, No. 3, pp. 307-321.

Grazioli, S., & Jarvenpaa, S. L. (2000) Perils of Internet fraud: An empirical investigation of deception and trust with experienced Internet consumers, IEEE Transactions on Systems, Man, and Cybernetics—Part A: Systems and Humans, 30, pp. 395-410.

Hallegatte, D. & Nantel, J. (2006) The Intertwined Effect of Perceived Usefulness, Perceived Ease of Use and Trust in a Website on the Intention to Return, The E-Business Review, Volume 6, pp. 1-6.

Harrison, D. A., Mykytyn Jr., P. P. & Riemenschneider, C. K. (1997) Executive decisions about adoption of information technology in small business: Theory and empirical tests, Information Systems Research, Vol. X, No. 2, pp. 171-195.

Igbaria, M., Zinatelli, N., Cragg, P., & Cavaye, A.L.M., (1997) Personal computing acceptance factors: a structural equation model, MIS Quarterly, Vol. 21, No. 3, pp. 279–302.

Jarvenpaa, S. L., Tractinsky, N., & Vitale, M., (2000) Consumer trust in an Internet store, Information Technology and Management, Vol. 1, pp. 45-71.

Karahanna, E., Straub, D. W. & Chervany, N. L. (1999) Information technology adoption across time: a cross-sectional comparison of pre-adoption and post-adoption beliefs, MIS Quarterly, Vol. 23, No. 2, pp. 183–213.

Koufaris, M. (2002) Applying the Technology Acceptance Model and Flow Theory to Online Consumer Behavior, Information Systems Research, Vol. 13, No. 2, pp. 205-223.

Lederer, A. L., Maupin, D. J., Sena, M. P., & Zhuang, Y. (2000) The technology acceptance and the World Wide Web, Decision Support Systems, Vol. 29, pp. 269–282.

Legris, P., Ingham, J., & Collerette, P. (2003) Why do people use information technology? A critical review of the technology acceptance model, Information & Management, Vol. 40, No. 3, pp. 191-205.

Loiacono, E. T., Watson, R. T., & Goodhue, D. L. (2002) WebQual: A measure of website quality, AMA Winter·Proceedings, pp. 432– 438.

Malanga, D. N. (2006) E-Ticketing implementation in Africa, NOVATECH Conference, 07 – 09 November, Bamako, Mali.

McCuhbrey, D. I., (1999) Disintermediation and reintermediation in the U.S. Air travel distribution indurrry: A Delphi study, Communications of the AIS, Vol. 1, Article 18, Online, Available at: Available at: http://aisel.aisnet.org/cais/vol1/iss1/18 (accessed 11 December 2008).

McIvor, R., O'Reilly, D. & Ponsonby, S. (2003) The impact of Internet technologies on the airline industry: Current strategies and future developments, Strategic Change, Vol. 12, pp. 31–47.

Morris M. G. & Dillon A. (1997) How User Perceptions Influence Software Use, IEEE Software, Vol. 14, No. 4, pp. 58-65.

O'Cass A. & Fenech T. (2003) Web retailing adoption: exploring the nature of internet users Webretailing behaviour, Journal of Retailing and Consumer Services, Vol. 10, pp. 81–94.

Pavlou, P. A. (2003) Consumer acceptance of elcctronic commerce: Integrating trust and risk with the technology acceptance model, International Journal of Electronic Commerce, Vol. 7, No. 3, pp. 101-131.

Saade, R. & Bahli, B. (2005) The impact of cognitive absorption on perceived usefulness and perceived ease of use in on-line learning: an extension of the technology acceptance model, Information & Management, Vol. 42, pp. 317–327.

Shang R., Chen Y. & Shen L. (2005) Extrinsic versus intrinsic motivations for consumers to shop on-line, Information and Management, Vol. 42, pp. 401–413.

Sheppard, B., Hanvick, J. & Warshaw, P. R. (1988) The theory of reasoned anion: A meta-analysis of past research with recommendation for modifications and future research, Journal of Consumer Research, Vol. 15, pp. 325-343.

Shih, H.P. (2004) An empirical study on predicting user acceptance of e-shopping on the Web, Information and Management, Vol. 41, No. 3, pp. 351–368.

Southwood, R. (2007) Africa: IATA E-Ticketing Deadline Creeping Up Fast On continent's Unprepared Airlines, Balancing Act (London), Online, Available, http://allafrica.com/stories/200705240993.html (accessed 11 December 2008).

Stringer, K. (2002) Travelers can find problems with electronic tickets, Wall Street Journal (Earrrm ed.), p. 5, July 30.

Swaminathan, V., E. Lepkowska-White & Rao B.P. (1999) Browsers or Buyers in Cyberspace? An Investigation of Factors Influencing Electronic Exchange, Journal of Computer-Mediated Communication, Vol. 5, No. 2, Online, Available at: www.ascusc.org/jcmc/vol5/issue2/swaminathan.htm (accessed 11 December 2008).

Van der Heijden H. (2003), Factors influencing the usage of websites: the case of a generic portal in The Netherlands, Information and Management, Vol. 40, No. 6, pp. 541–549.

Venkatesh, V. & Davis, F.D. (1996) A model of the antecedents of perceived ease of use: development and test, Decision Sciences, Vol. 27, No. 3, pp. 451–481.

Venkatesh, V. & Davis, F. D. (2000) A theoretical extension of the technology acceptance model: Four longitudinal studies, Management Science, Vol. 46, No. 2, pp. 186-204.

Vijayasarathy, L. R. (2004) Predicting Consumer Intentions to Use On-Line Shopping: The Case for an Augmented Technology Acceptance Model, Information and Management, Vol. 41, No. 6, pp. 747–762.

Wan, G. H. & Che P. (2004) Chinese Air Travelers' Acceptance towards Electronic Ticketing, Engineering Management Conference, 2004, IEEE International Proceedings, pp. 269- 275

Yu, J. Ha, I., Choi, M. & Rho, J. (2005) Extending the TAM for a t-commerce, Information & Management, Vol. 42, No. 7, pp. 965-976.

Zhang, X., & Prybutok, V. (2003) Online shopping intentions, Journal of Internet Commerce, Vol. 2, No. 1, pp. 3-18.

CHAPTER 7

SUCCESS FACTORS OF E-TAILING: A CHINA STUDY

Weibing Xuan & Jun Xu

Graduate College of Management, Southegfrn Cross University, Australia

Mohammed Quaddus

Graduate School of Business, Curtin University of Technology, Australia

This chapter reports a study aiming at investigating the factors of successful e-tailing in China's retail industry. A single case study was undertaken in one of the top retailers in China. Both qualitative and quantitative data were collected, including in-depth interviews and focus group interviews with key personnel in the case organization, and questionnaire survey with randomly selected customers of the retailer. A comprehensive combined model of success factors of e-tailing was developed and is presented in detail. Some unique and interesting factors associated Chinese e-tailing have been identified; and some useful practicable suggestions are also provided for Chinese retailers or any businesses who are embarking on e-tailing in China or/and planning to enter the China's retail market.

1. Introduction

As one of the market trends, e-tailing has been widely used in retail industry (Samiee et al. 2004). More and more retailers are starting to realize the benefits of e-tailing (Agrawal 2001; Sullivan 2004), and believe that the knowledge about how to achieve successful e-tailing may be the key to survive the competition in the 21st century (Ogden 2005).

In the last decade, the Internet had a great development in China. In 2006, the number of internet users in China had reached 123 million, rising from only 1.17 million in 1998 (CNNIC 1998, 2006). On the other hand the development of e-commerce in China has been slow. The market size of e-commerce in China is still small in terms of the transaction volume, especially business to consumer (B2C) e-commerce. For example, the transaction volume of B2C in China went up to RMB5.6 billion (US$700 million) in 2005. However, compared to the global B2C e-commerce market, US$700 million is a very small percentage and is not in proportion with China's large internet population (IResearch 2005). Moreover, as a result of its entry to the World Trade Organization (WTO), China's retail industry, which plays an important role in China (Data shows that retailing sales will represent almost 50% of total GDP in 2010 (ATKEARNEY 2005)), is becoming more competitive than ever before. More and more foreign retailers are entering China to compete for its huge market (1.3 billion population and a booming middle class) and explore opportunities arising from its strong economic growth (Ernst & Young 2005; ONDA 2004). China's retailers therefore need more tools and strategies to compete with their giant competitors. They have been finding ways (i.e., via mergers and acquisitions) in enhancing their competitiveness. Given the benefits of e-tailing (e.g. global reach and reduced costs), it could help retailers establish competitive advantages in both the short and long terms. However in contrast to the rapid development of internet and increasing volume of internet usage, e-tailing is still in the preliminary stages in China (CNNIC 2006; IResearch 2005), and there are no successful e-tailing marketers in China's retail industry at present.

Furthermore, there is a silence in the literature on e-commerce development in China. Especially there is a lack of empirical studies of e-commerce in China. Therefore, there is very much a need for empirical studies on the implementation of E-commerce in China, especially in its retail industry. Additionally, there are few studies related to B2C e-commerce in China's retail industry. A number of studies have been done to investigate the success of e-commerce, with most of them conducted in western countries (i.e., Delone & McLean 2003; Seddon 1997; Teo & Wong 1998; Wixom & Watson 2001). While some research (such as Dedrik & Kraemer 2001; Efendioglu et al. 2004; Ernst & He 2000) has been done to investigate e-commerce in China, the success of

B2C e-commerce in China has not yet been studied adequately, especially in China's retail industry.

This research aims to address the gap by investigating the implementation of e-tailing in China's retail industry, and by examining the success factors associated with that implementation. We studied e-tailing success factors through case study approach in China by comprehensively examining a top Chinese retail group, which was formed by the merger of four state-owned retailers, and currently holds the primary position in China's retail industry. As far as the authors are aware this research is the first comprehensive and empirical study focusing on e-tailing in China. The research issues undertaken in this study include: (1) how is e-tailing being used in the case organization?; (2) What are the barriers to the implementation of e-tailing in the case organization?; (3) What are the factors for achieving successful e-tailing in the case organisation?

This chapter is organized as follows. Next section presents relevant background. Case study approach is then discussed followed by data analysis, discussions of results addressing research questions and implications for theory and practice. This paper concludes with summary, limitations and future research directions.

2. Background

2.1. E-tailing

E-tailing is "retailing conducted online, over the Internet" (Turban et al. 2006, p. 83); it is also called B2C e-commerce which refers to retail transactions of products or services from businesses to individual customers. In this study e-tailing and B2C e-commerce are viewed as equivalent, and these two terms are used interchangeably. Even though the most common use of e-tailing is the sale of products or services online, but online retailing businesses do not only undertake simple sales, they also include other applications, as do physical retailing outlets. Some of those applications include:

(i) Selling goods and testing new products: Many giant retailers use the internet as a tool to test new products and services. This strategy is useful to reduce risks in the early stages of new product marketing and sales (Mullaney 2004).

(ii) Market research: Retailers can use their online presence to gain valuable customer information for predication of future customer demand. In the offline environment, such data are difficult and expensive to collect and analyze (Rao 1999). Online market research has some powerful advantages, such as monitoring real-time buying decisions, more accurate and reliable data (Baker 2005)

(iii) Promotional tool: Following on from market research, valuable customer data can be used to conduct pricing and promotional experiments. A website can be used as a tool to conduct promotional experiments, due to the wide reach of the internet and its cost-effectiveness (Rao 1999).

(iv) Marketing tool: A website can also be an effective channel to communicate with customers (Peterson et al. 1997). The internet has made businesses' dreams of interactivity, personalization, customization and 24/7 availability a reality.

(v) Online customer services: Many new services (i.e., delivery status information and personalized products) can be available uninterruptedly online, which is almost impossible or too expensive to have in the physical world.

2.2. Retail industry in China

History of the Chinese retail industry

As China continues to make great achievements in economic reform and enters the WTO, China's retail industry is becoming the largest emerging retail opportunity in the world, in terms of the population and the boom in the middle class. Figure 7.1 shows the development of GDP and retail sales in China from 2001 to 2010. It is estimated that retail sales will reach US$754 billion in China in 2006, and will further increase to an enormous US$2.4 trillion by 2020 (ATKEARNEY 2005; The Economist 2006).

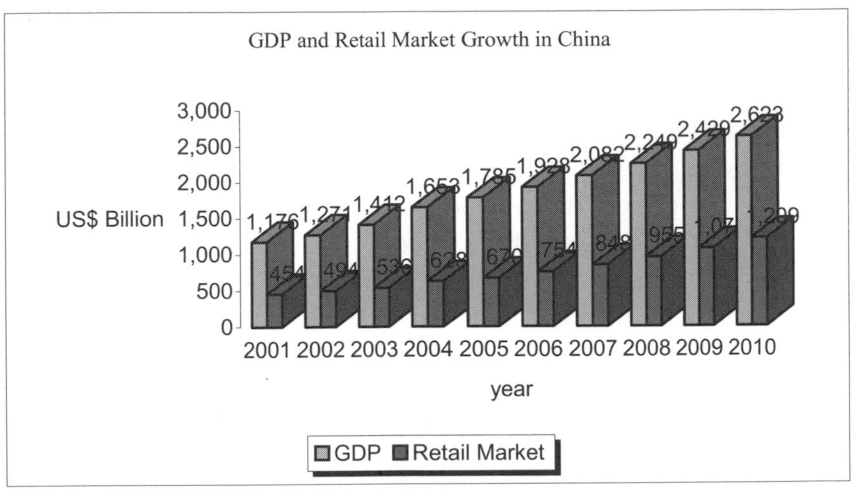

Figure 7.1: GDP and retail market growth in China
(Source: Developed from ATKEARNEY 2005)

According to Figure 7.1, China's GDP shows an impressive growth rate but the growth of the retail market is even faster. In 2010, retail sales will account for almost 50% of total GDP in China. The story was very different before China began its economic reform.

Under the planned economy, China's retail industry grew slowly from 1949 to the 1970s. According to East Asian Executive Reports (Anonymous 1995), at that time distributors in China existed only as extensions of the manufactures. All goods had to be submitted to the government. In other words, all goods could only be purchased with special coupons and/or ration cards issued by the government. Until the late 1970s, there were only three government approved kinds of retail: bai huo (multi-story department store), za huo (neighbourhood general store), and zao wan menshi bu (convenience store). Prices were also set by the government, and product lines were cobbled together based on availability, not on consumer demand. Also, there was no competition as a result of the lack of stand-alone distribution.

At the start of the economic reform in the late 1970s and early 1980s, retail sales in China changed dramatically and increased by approximately 13.9% per year. State-owned retailers had the right to purchase goods at their own discretion, and more food items and consumer goods were available in those stores. In the same period, department stores developed rapidly. By 1985, there were 10.7 million retailing stores (CIA World Factbook 1987) and most new retail stores were privately owned, whereas privately owned stores had been totally forbidden in China before the economic reform. State-owned retailers started to either lease or turn their businesses over to privately owned retailers, and more and more private retailers rented counters inside state-owned retail outlets, such as department stores. The market share of state-owned retailers dropped from 90.3% in 1976 to 40.5% in 1985, due to the boom in private retailing (CIA World Factbook 1987), and those market shares were dispersed to many small retailers. This historical process produced a different retailing system to that in western countries. For example, no national retailing brand such as Wal-Mart in the United States, was built in China. Most of China's retailing brands are localized, such as Wang Fujing in Beijing, and Shanghai No.1 Department Store in Shanghai (The Economist 2006). And they mainly focus on their local markets and would not open subsidiaries in other cities, and the majority of Shanghai residents would not recognize retailers from other cities, such as Wang Fujing from Beijing.

From 1987, more and more retailing establishments were located in both downtown commercial districts and in residential areas (including state, collective, and private businesses or vendors) (CIA World Factbook 1987). In residential areas, retailing stores are able to provide for almost all the daily needs of their customers, but department stores in the Central Business Districts (CBDs) offer a wider range of products as well as numerous specialty shops that may not be available in retail stores in residential areas (i.e., sports products, cameras and musical instruments shops).

Since the mid-1990s, the revenue of department stores started to drop due to excessive supply. New retail formats appeared (such as supermarkets, franchises, convenience stores, and warehouses). According to the National Statistics Bureau (2003), by 2001, there were 399 thousand registered retailers in China; 16.5% of them were department stores, 2.1% supermarkets, and 33% speciality stores.

With the growth of the middle class, many more modern retail formats emerged in China. One of them is the shopping centre. In the 20th century, this retail model made the most successful use of land, real estate, and the retail business concept (Beyard & O'Mara 1999) and was launched in the United States and Canadian cities over a peiod of 40 years, from the 1950s to the late 1980s. The shopping centre does not only serve as a shopping destination, but also offers a wide range of dining, entertainment and recreational experiences (Wang et al. 2006). China did not have real shopping centres until the mid-1990s. Since then, more and more shopping centres were developed, especially in large cities such as Beijing, Shanghai, Guanzhou and Shenzhen (Li 2004). Most of the new shopping centres were invested in by foreign investors, particularly from south-east Asia.

However, due to the government's protection-oriented policy, many international retailers have limited operations in China. Until 2001, 99.6% of retailers in China were locally owned and only 0.4% were foreign retailers. This balance has changed since China became a formal member of the WTO. According to the contract between the WTO and the People's Republic of China, all restrictions in China's retail distribution system (including wholesaling, retailing, franchising, and commissions for agency services) had to be eliminated by the end of 2004. This means that since 2004, foreign retailers have been able to operate their businesses in China with more freedom (ONDA 2004). This change forced the stakeholders in China's distribution industry, including all local retailers, to improve their capability and competence, in order to compete with giant global retailers.

Foreign retailers in China

The National Retail Federation (cited in ONDA 2004) suggested that the Chinese market will be the next global retailing trend because of the country's huge growth and the elimination of regulations (ONDA 2004). China is now the seventh-largest economy in the world, has the largest population in the world and a booming middle class (Ernst & Young 2005; The Economist 2006). More international retailers are entering China. Samiee et al. (2004) outlined three motivational forces for the entry of international retailers into the Chinese market. Firstly, income has been increasing rapidly in China, especially since the country has virtually recovered from the economic crisis of 1997. Therefore the discretionary spending of the Chinese has increased.

Secondly, retail market shares in China are largely fragmented. Fortune (cited by Samiee 2004) noted that the total sales of the top four retailers in China were just over US$2057 million in 2000. According to Xinhua Net (2003), China's National Bureau also reports that the revenue of 76.1% of the retailers in China is less than RMB 1 million and only 1.9% of retailers had more than RMB 10 million sales revenue in 2003. A recent study by Ernst & Young (2005) concludes that the top six retailers account for only one-fifth of national consumption. These figures demonstrate that the majority of the retailing market share is divided amongst many small retailers and that there are very few large retailers. Therefore international retailers face less competition from local Chinese retailers, and it is easier for them to achieve market expansion.

Another vital reason for the increased foreign retail presence in China is the rapid penetration and growth of the internet and the resulting development of e-commerce in China, as discussed previously. China has the second largest number of internet users in the world, with potential for further growth.

As indicated by the China National Statistics Bureau (Xinhua Net 2003), most foreign retailers entered the Chinese market after 1997. By 2001, 5234 stores had been established in China by foreign retailers. The formats of the retail industry focused on the hypermarket, warehouse and membership store. Most of these retail stores were concentrated in big cities, such as Shanghai, Beijing, Guangzhou and Shenzheng.

While foreign retailers enjoyed the huge potential market in China, for a long period they suffered from Chinese industry policies. To protect local enterprises, especially state-owned enterprises, the Chinese government issued a series of regulations and tightened the rules to restrict the development of international retailers in China. Therefore, access to the Chinese market is restricted for foreign investors (Buckman 2003). At the present time, international retailers rely heavily on one of seven models to enter the Chinese market (Samiee et al. 2004). These seven models are: (1) manufacturer-run shops; (2) retail shops as part of hotels or foreign residential facilities; (3) retail stores in shopping complexes; (4) management companies; (5) joint construction projects; (6) joint operations and licensing agreements; (7) single licenses, as well as other miscellaneous methods. These models are depicted in Table 7.1.

Table 7.1: Entry models for foreign retailers in China

Entry model	Explanation
Manufacturer-run shops	Foreign manufacturers who establish joint ventures in China and sell in department stores or direct retail stores. Example: Baleno.
Retail shops as part of hotels or foreign residential facilities	Small shops in hotels or residential facilities for foreigners. Example: First Store of Isetan
Retail stores as tenants of a shopping complex	Leasing an area inside a shopping mall or department store. Example: Second department store of Isetan
Management companies	Establishing joint venture management companies with Chinese partners by using their own name. Example: Carrefour
Joint construction projects	Access by international retailers to China's market through this model requires senior staff member from the local developer to join the management board of the retail establishment.
Joint operations and licensing agreements	YaoHan adopted this strategy to set its outlet with Shanghai No.1 Department Store in China.
Single licenses	Foreign retailers such as Wal-Mart obtained approval either from the state government or from local government which was in principle valid for the opening of only one retail outlet.
Miscellaneous	Some foreign retailers, particularly those from Hong Kong, took advantage of loopholes in the existing regulations on retail joint ventures, established retail outlets in China through special arrangements. Strictly speaking, these joint ventures are considered to be illegal.

(Source: developed from Samiee et al. 2004)

As indicated above, those models were the only options for foreign retailers to enter the Chinese market prior to 2004. However, this situation has changed since China entered the WTO. According to the agreement between China and the WTO, China had to lift all restrictions by the end of 2004. Table 7.2 summarises the important milestones for the Chinese retail industry after China's entry to the WTO. Many new regulations have been established, and allow international retailers to have more freedom to operate their businesses than ever before. For example, from December 2004, wholly foreign-owned enterprises are permitted in retail, wholesale and trade, and international retailers can select the location independently. The capital limit for both wholesale and retail has also been dropped, and the actual application procedure for set-up has been simplified (The Economist 2006). The following table provides a timetable of the WTO influences.

Table 7.2: Major milestones in the retail industry after China's entry to the WTO

		Retail industry
Dec 2001	Immediately after joining the WTO	• Enabling provision of related services such as follow-up service after sale
Dec 2003	Within two years of joining the WTO	• Opening all provincial cities • Allowing majority investment by foreign-capital companies • Relaxing volume restrictions
Dec 2004	Within three years of joining the WTO	• Planning to abolish 'volume restrictions', 'regional restrictions' and 'investment restrictions' • Planning to abolish all restrictions within three years concerning wholesale and retail businesses that are not related to franchises and outlets • Planning to grant trading rights to companies meeting prescribed conditions

(Source: adapted from ONDA 2004)

The year 2005 was the first year in which China fully opened its retail market to foreign businesses. China's Ministry of Commerce approved 1027 investments by foreign retailers and wholesalers to 2005, and these investments injected US$1.9 billion direct foreign investment into China in 2005 (Xu 2006). This number, 1027, is equivalent to the total number of approved foreign retailers' and wholesalers' investments of the previous 12 years from 1993 to 2004; and 61% of new investments were for wholly foreign-owned enterprises. Besides opening new wholly foreign-owned stores, foreign retailers are trying to expand their retail network through a series of mergers and acquisitions. Such merger and acquisition activities allow foreign retailers to have a head-start over local competitors, or allow them to catch up after a late entry. By the end of 2005, 80% of the world biggest retailers had entered China; causing more intense competition in China's retail industry (Anonymous 2006 (b)).

China's local retailers

After the opening of the Chinese retail market in 2004 and without protective government regulations, international retailers can easily defeat local Chinese retailers, due to their size and capability. There are only two choices left to retailers in China: grow or die (Brilliance Group 2005).

In order to face the huge competition from foreign retailers, major local retailers are trying to match their competitors in terms of size and capacity (Xu 2006). A shortcut to this end is through mergers and acquisitions, which could improve the position of local retailers in the following respects (Anonymous 2006(a); The Economist 2006):

- Building scale and market share outside their regional strongholds: Acquisition and consolidation will allow retailers to expand their businesses beyond the domestic markets.
- Snapping up prime locations: Excellent business locations are the basis of development and are critical to the survival of retailers. However primary locations are limited. Mergers and acquisitions are effective methods to obtain such locations, even though the merger price is sometimes much higher than the real value.
- Increasing income through leasing space to suppliers for in-store displays: In China, suppliers have to pay Jing chang fei (participation fees) to put their products on retailers' shelves. Retailers also lease space for in-store displays and help pay for promotions. This means that if the retailers can attract more suppliers, their monthly fixed income would increase, with very low risk.
- Boosting their bargaining power with suppliers.

Merger and acquisition activities strengthen retailers and place them in better bargaining positions in their negotiations with suppliers. The government also plays a very important role in merger and acquisition activities (ONDA 2004). Since the end of 2004, when the Chinese government has no longer been able to limit foreign retailers because of WTO contracts, the government has been working to enhance the competence of local Chinese retailers. Government-planned mergers and acquisitions have been enacted among major domestic distribution companies, especially in the big cities such as Shanghai (Anonymous 2006(a)). According to the Ministry of Commerce (Xu 2006), 20 of China's retail companies were selected to form domestic giants to face the competition from foreign retailers and most of them are state-owned or ex-state-owned companies.

Table 7.3: Top 10 retailers in China

Retailers	**Headquarters**	**Sales (yuan, bn)**	**Number of Stores**
Brilliance Group	China	72.1	6,345
Gome	China	49.8	537
Suning	China	39.7	363
Vanguard	Hong Kong	23.0	2,133
Wumart	China	19.1	659
Carrefour China	France	17.4	73
Shanghai Yongle Electrical	China	15.2	255
Trust-Mart	Taiwan	13.2	96
Parkson China	Malaysia	11	36
Lotus	Thailand	10.1	61
Wal-Mart China	US	9.9	60
B&Q China	UK	5.2	48

(Source: developed from The Economist 2006)

Table 7.3 presents the top 10 retailers in China in 2005. Recently, Hong Kong-listed Gome, the second largest retailer in China, offered US$680 million to buy Shanghai Yongle, which is the seventh biggest retailer in China, making Gome's market share rise more than 10%. In May 2006, Gome also bought Jiangsu Five Star appliances, China's fourth biggest appliance chain (The Economist 2006). These merger and acquisition activities strengthened Gome's position and enlarged its market share, enhancing its capabilities to compete with foreign rivals, such as America's Best Buy, one of the most famous American appliance chains.

Merger and acquisition activities give Chinese retailers a quick way to put themselves into a position to compete with foreign retail giants. However, researchers and some internal studies (Brilliance Group 2005; Xu 2006) warn that without a well-integrated process, simply developing large retail operations could be very risky. For example, the Shanghai Brilliance Group failed to merge with Dalian Dashang Group Co. Ltd due to a poor integration process. One important reason for the failure was that the subsidiaries of the Brilliance Group are a very diverse group of businesses, with different histories, business models, suppliers, cultures, management styles, information systems, and so forth. Integration with such a diversified company is a very difficult task.

In addition to mergers and acquisitions, information technology is a strategy taken into consideration by China's retailers. Some reports (Anonymous 2006(a); Xinhua Net 2003) have stated that the development of information technologies will change the business model and management style of China's retail industry. As an application of IT, e-commerce will develop quickly in the future. For example, Fourteen out of twenty three middle and senior level managers in the Brilliance Group indicated that e-commerce should be the development trend in the Shanghai Brilliance Group (Brilliance Group 2005). As senior analyst, Ms Tong (IDC 2006) indicated that due to huge competition in the retail industry, more retailers are starting to realize the importance of the internet and are creating their own websites. However, few of these websites have been implemented properly.

Currently, most of the top retailers in China are state-owned enterprises or have a government background, and since the 1990s these firms have been investing heavily in upgrading their computer systems. However, most firms have not started to build their e-commerce platform (Tan & Ouyang 2004). This indicates that IT is still developing slowly in China's retail industry. Statistics (Anonymous 2005(b)) show that in 2003 the total IT investment in China's retail industry was US$0.8 billion, while Japanese retailers invested US$5.187 billion in IT, which is six times more than China. The IT investment in China's retail industry is less than 0.2% of total sales revenue, while the ratio in most international giant retailers is over 2% of total sales revenue. Some reasons for this have been mentioned by past studies (i.e., Frank 2004;

Gunasekaran & Ngai 2005), include the senior management's short-term focus on return on investment, and insufficient capital.

2.3. Development of the internet and e-commerce in China

This section summarizes and reviews the development of e-commerce in China, beginning with the development of the internet in China, followed by a discussion of the development of e-commerce. Following these discussions, some important barriers and obstacles to the development of e-commerce in China are analyzed.

2.3.1. Internet development in China

The number of Internet users in China has grown markedly since 1998. This growth reached a 20% rate of increase in 2006 and has made China the world's second largest Internet market. In July 2006, the number of Internet users in China had reached 123 million, rising from only 1.17 million in 1998. As the current number of users accounts for only 9.46% of the country's total population, it shows the huge potential for Internet usage in China, which has a total current population of 1.3 billion. In the meantime, over the last seven years broadband has become the major Internet access method in China. In July 2006, broadband was used by 77 million Internet users, increasing from only 9.8 million in 2003. Therefore it has become the most popular internet access method in China. Dial-up was the most popular access method from 1999 to 2005. However, the number of dial-up users has dropped rapidly, from 55 million to 47.5 million from July 2005 to July 2006. Also since 1999, leased-line access has been another fast-growing method, however, this method has shown a slight decrease, from 29.7 million in July 2005 to 26.8 million in July 2006 (CNNIC 1999-2006).

Average weekly internet usage time has shown a similar increase to that of the numbers of Internet and broadband users. The average weekly Internet usage time has increased from 8.7 hours in July 2001 to 16.5 hours in July 2006. But surprisingly, within these 16.5 hours of weekly Internet usage time, 11 hours were spent on online gaming, which accounts for almost 67% of total weekly Internet usage time. This may be because of the age and educational level of the majority of Internet users. The statistics conducted by CNNIC (2006) show that over 50% of Internet users are under 25 years old and a total of 90% are under 40. Almost 50% of Internet users have a high school or under high school educational level. Accordingly, most Internet users are young people with a lower educational level.

2.3.2. Development of e-commerce in China

Since 2002, China has become the second largest internet market and the biggest mobile phone market in the world, with 123 million internet users (CNNIC 2006) and 426 million mobile phone users (Burns 2006). However, the development of e-commerce in China has been slow.

Both B2B and B2C e-commerce in China are still in the preliminary stages despite their rapid growth in recent years. According to Hong (2003), the total of China's e-commerce transaction volume was RMB9.33 billion in 2000; and B2B accounted for more than 90% of the total e-commerce transaction volume. Figure 7.2 presents the total volume of China's B2C e-commerce from 2003 to 2010, showing that the transaction volume of B2C in China went up to RMB5.6 billion (US$700 million) in 2005, and is estimated to reach RMB8.2 billion in 2006. However, compared to the global B2C e-commerce market, US$700 million is a very small percentage and is not in proportion with China's large Internet population, even though the growth rate is impressive.

iResearch also summarised the number of China's B2C users and the percentage of the total of China's netizens (Internet users) from 2003-2010, as shown in Figure 7.3. The iResearch report (2005) showed that there were only 16 million B2C users in 2005, while the total number of internet users had already reached 111 million by the end of that year. The report also predicted that there will be 20 million B2C users at the end of 2006 and that this number will finally reach 65 million in 2010. A recent report published in July 2006 by CNNIC (2006) shows that the number of B2C users had already reached 30 million in mid-2006, which is higher than the prediction made by iResearch, suggesting that the speed of B2C user growth is faster than predicted. In addition, one-quarter of the B2C users shop online very frequently.

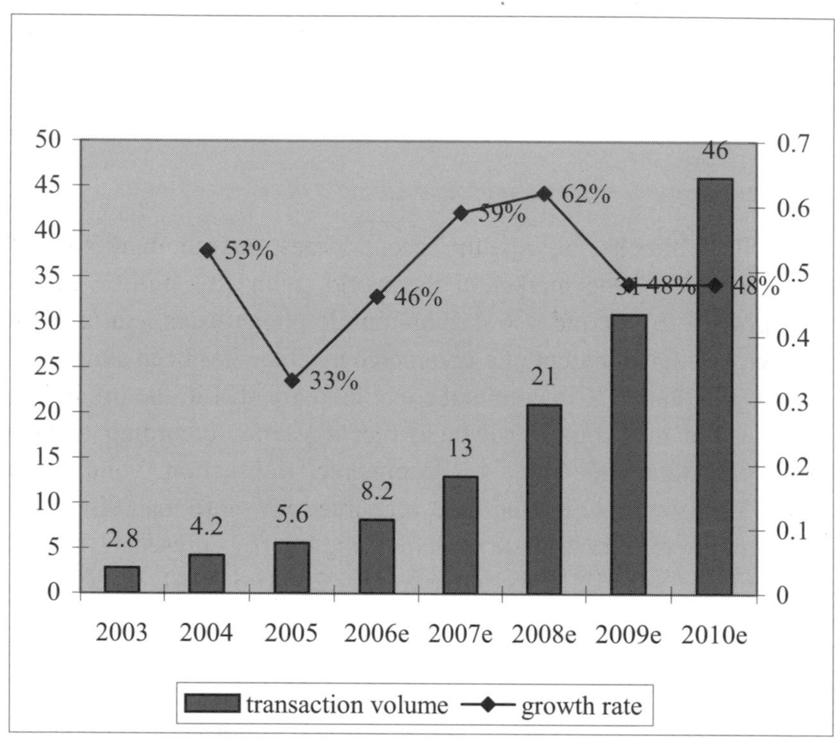

Figure 7.2: Transaction volume of China's B2C e-commerce 2003-2010
(Source: Developed from iResearch 2005)

In summary, on the one hand, the Internet has enjoyed rapid development in China in the last decade. On the other hand, the development of e-commerce in China has been slow compared to the strong growth of the internet in China. The follow section investigates the success factors of the development of e-commerce in China.

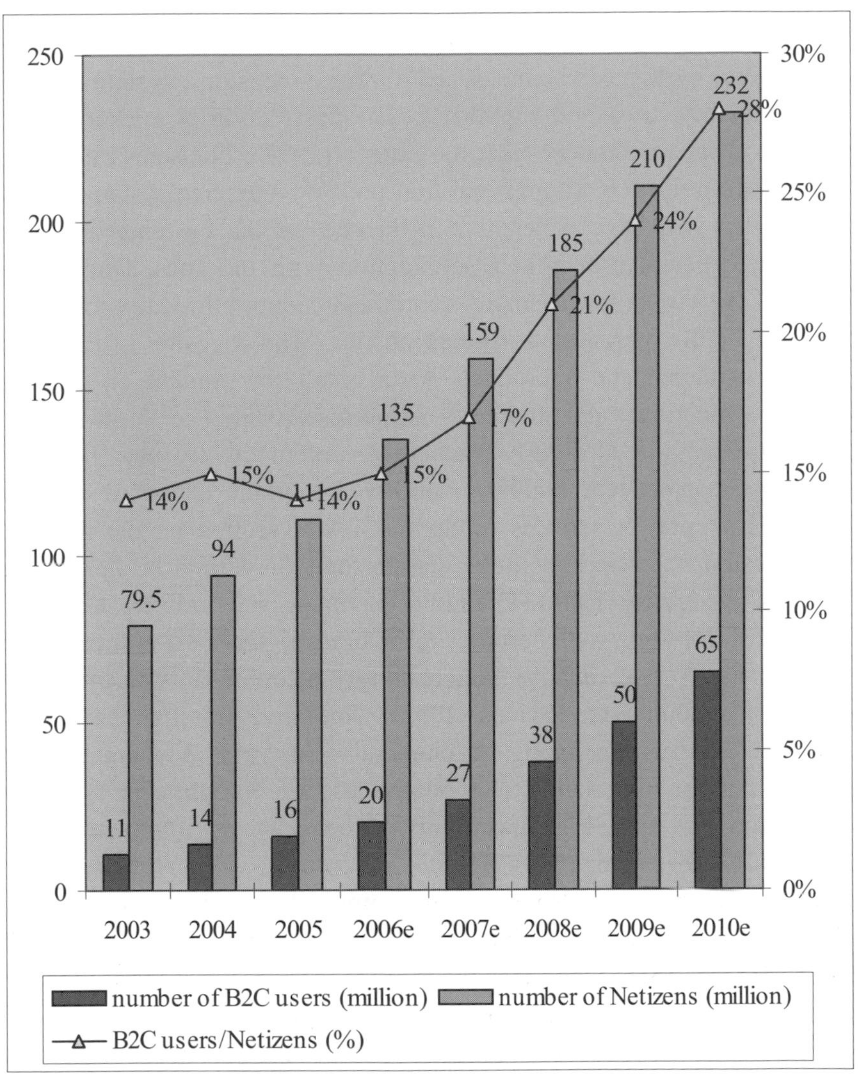

Figure 7.3: Percentage of China's B2C e-commerce users of the total of China's netizens, 2003-2010
(Source: Developed from iResearch (2005)

2.5. E-tailing Success Factors

E-commerce system can be measured in four dimensions: system quality, content quality, trust and support & services (Molla & Licker 2001). Findings from researchers such as Chiger (1997), Nielsen (1998) and Lohse and Spiller (1998) point out that poor e-commerce system quality of websites will have a negative influence on the customers' online shopping experience and their satisfaction with the sites. Due to the nature of the virtual environment, customers cannot physically touch the products before purchasing from websites. The website is the only channel to understand a product. As a result the content on the site should be functional and attractive. Some researchers (i.e., Von Dran et al. 1999; Zhang et al. 2000) argue that content quality may be more important than system quality. Another important factor of website quality is support & services (including FAQs section on the website, online customer services facilities, search function within the site, online feedback & review facilities, online payment and delivery services, online customization tools, escrow & insurance services, etc) provided by a website. Service quality is increasingly recognized as an important aspect of e-commerce (Santos 2003). Research findings have also suggested that trust (including attributes of security, privacy, and product quality) has an important effect on the use of e-commerce and user satisfaction, due to the high uncertainty of the online environment (Gefen et al. 2003; Urban et al. 2000).

Past research have also identified some other factors affecting the adoption of e-commerce, such as organizational factor (i.e., Molla 2004, Teo and Ang 1999, Wade and Nevo 2005, Ba & Lee 2003), external factor (Gibbs et al. 2002, Molla 2004), consumer factor (i.e., Dillon and Reif 2005, Gibbs et al. 2002, Ratchford et al. 2001; Teo 2001), senior management factor (Stylianou et al. 2003, Molla 2004); and e-commerce strategies (Barnes et al. 2004, Gunasekaran and Ngai 2005).

According to the discussion above, a theoretical framework (see Figure 7.4) was developed from the literature review, and served as theoretical foundation of the following empirical case study research. Six factors are included in the framework, namely, (1) organisational factor;

(2) senior management factor; (3) e-commerce strategies; (4) external factor; (5) consumer factor; and (6) e-commerce system measurement.

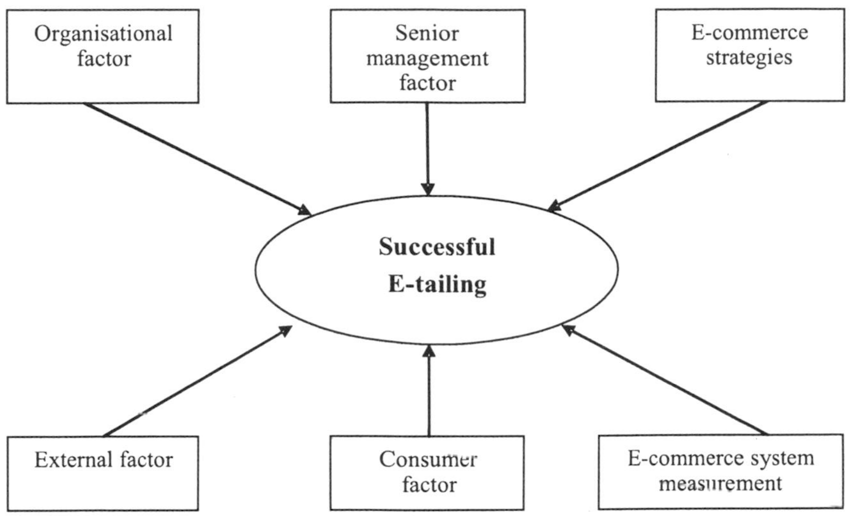

Figure 7.4: The Theoretical model
(Source: developed for this research)

3. Research design

3.1. Case Study Method

Case study was examined and selected as the suitable method, due to the following reasons. Firstly, the case study method was widely used in the IS field (Markus 1983; Orlikowska & Robey 1991; Walshan 1993, 1995), and it is the most popular qualitative research method for research on information systems (Darke et al. 1998). Secondly, the case study method can be used to answer the questions 'how' and 'why'. This research intends to explore and build a new model of e-commerce success through answering the research question, 'How can successful e-tailing in case organization can be achieved?, and thus a survey or an examination of archival records is less likely to produce an answer to the question, whereas a history or case study is more likely to produce an answer to the research question. The third reason for using the case study is that this method focuses on contemporary, as opposed to historical, events (Yin 1989). E-commerce is a new area of commerce in China, especially e-tailing, and there are no widely-accepted theories or models to measure the success of e-tailing in the Chinese context. The purpose of this study is to investigate the current practices of e-commerce in China's retail industry and explore specific factors and models to measure the success of e-commerce in China's retail industry. Therefore, this is a contemporary, not an historical, event. Finally, the researcher has no control over the contemporary set of events. The case study is preferred in examining contemporary events, but only when the relevant behaviors cannot be manipulated. According to Bonoma (1985), the case study is best suited for research when the researcher is interested in understanding dynamic contemporary events in an environment over which the researcher has no control. Therefore, the case study method should be used when a 'how' or 'why' question is being asked about a contemporary set of events, over which the investigator has little or no control. This research intends to investigate the contemporary issues of e-tailing operations in China's retail industry, and this context is definitely not under the control of the researcher.

3.2. Selection of Case

To select the case(s) for this case study research, criteria were developed for case selection. Those criteria included: (1) multiple retail format; (2) state-owned enterprise; (3) have or have had an e-commerce system: (4) if there is only one case suitable for this research, then the case also needed to meet the single case requirements indicated by Yin (2002). A selection pool was established, based on the ranking of the top ten retailers in China. The appropriate case(s) were then selected, based on the criteria. At the end there is only one case meeting all the selection criteria. The chosen case organization is state-owned, has active e-commerce arms in its subsidiaries, and is the only retailer in the top ten to have a multiple retail format. Therefore, this retail group was the only one suitable for this case study, and is importantly a very unique and representative case in China's retail industry.

3.3. Data Collection

Due to the advantages provided by the combined method (Gable 1994; Jick 1979; Kaplan & Duchon 1988; Trend 1989), both qualitative and quantitative data were collected in this research. The qualitative data included in-depth interviews and focus interviews, and the quantitative data included survey questionnaires. Qualitative methods were used to investigate the factors relating to the organisation, while survey questionnaires were distributed to randomly selected customers of the case retail group. Permission was gained from the Human Resources Department of the case organization to allow the researcher to personally select the employees for both the in-depth interviews and focus group studies. Table 7.5 shows how six factors arising from literature were addressed by the research methods. The in-depth interviews and focus group studies addressed all six factors, namely senior management factor, organisational factor, e-commerce factor, contextual factor, consumer factor, and e e-commerce system measurement. The survey questionnaires were used to address the consumer factors and customers' views on e-commerce system. Both internal document and external publications were used as secondary sources to triangulate the results.

Table 7.5: Data collection by different methods

Factor	Data source
Senior management factor	Interview, Focus group
Organisational factor	Interview, Focus group
E-commerce strategy	Interview, Focus group
Contextual factor	Interview, Focus group
E-commerce system measurement	Interview, Focus group, Questionnaire
Consumer factor	Interview, Focus group, Questionnaire

(Source: developed for this research)

This research has adopted the criterion of 'information richness" as suggested by Patton (1990) to identify the number of research subjects. Data collection is finished with diminishing returns from the cases or interviews, or the researcher has enough cases and data to satisfactorily address the research question (Voss et al. 2002). An application letter for permission for the research to be conducted was sent to the Human Resources Department of the retail Group, prior to data collection. As soon as permission was attained from the company, the potential participants for the in-depth interviews and focus group studies were selected, based on the selection criteria and discussions with the Human Resource Department of the retail Group. An information letter and a consent letter were sent to the potential participants prior to the interviews, to provide them with information on this research. The in-depth interviews focused on the middle-to-high level managers in the subsidiaries of the retail Group, while the focus group interviews focused on the low-to-middle level employees in the subsidiaries of the Group. Each interview lasted around approximately one hour. In total, sixteen in-depth interviews with middle-to-high level managers and three focus group studies with low-to-middle level managers were conducted. Interview and focus group participants were selected from eight main sub-organizations of the retail group (see Table 7.6). All the interviews and focus group studies are tape-recorded with permission. The qualitative data collection process was completed when the data reached saturation level (Dick 2005).

Table 7.6: Information of Participants of In-depth Interviews and Focus Group Studies

Name of Subsidiaries	Business of Sub-organizations	Number of Field Studies
Company 1	Department store	3 in-depth interviews and 1 focus group
Company 2	Department store	5 in-depth interviews and 1 focus group
Company 3	Department store	1 in-depth interviews
Company 4	Department store	1 in-depth interviews and 1 focus group
Company 5	Department store	1 in-depth interview
Company 6	Administration organisation	2 in-depth interview
Company 7	Supermarket	1 in-depth interview
Company 8	Supermarket	2 in-depth interview

(Source: developed for this study)

Since e-tailing involves both retailing businesses and their customers. Studying customers of the case retail group is an essential part of this research. Furthermore data on customers could complement findings of qualitative studies and used for triangulation purposes. Taking into consideration of the size of the retail group's customers and the resources implications, questionnaire survey was used to collect customer data. Due to the lack of a customer database, the requirement of reasonable size for survey method (between 100 and 200) (Hoeleter 1983), and average 15-20% survey response rates (Zikmund 2003), survey questionnaires were distributed to 1,000 randomly selected customers in the shopping areas of the retail group. 200 valid questionnaires were received.

3.4. Data Analysis

Following suggestions by Dube & Pare 2003; Eisenhardt 1989; Kaplan & Duchon 1988; Miles & Huberman 1994; Kelliher 2005; Taylor-Powell & Renner 2003; and Voss et al. 2002, qualitative data collected from in-depth interviews and focus group studies were analysed as per the following steps:

(vi) Within-case analysis: Manually review the transcripts, line-by-line and sentence-by-sentence, to discover the key patterns/themes and produce key words/phrases.

(vii) Produce labels/categories of these key words/phrases: Identify high-level factors and corresponding variables. Match these factors and variables with those from the literature. Revise and update accordingly without sacrificing any factors and variables obtained from the interview.

(viii) Organize the data as per the factors and variables identified at step 2: As the data is being categorised, other themes that can serve as subcategories may be identified. Continue to categorise until all relevant themes have been identified and labeled.

(ix) Describe the meaning of categories including key characteristics, scope and limitations. Examples of text were coded into categories that illustrate meanings, associations and perspectives associated with the category.

(x) Cross-case analysis: Identify the similarities and differences in the factors and variables under each factor.

(xi) Use the concept of 'union' in integrating the factors and variables, i.e. combine similar factors and variables and give them a common name. Retain the unique factors and variable(s).

(xii) Develop a final table including all the factors and variables identified through steps 1-6.

(xiii) Develop the combined model of successful e-tailing in China's retail industry.

For data collected from questionnaire survey, frequency statistics were conducted for responses to e-commerce system measurement.

4. Results and Implications

4.1. Factors and Variables of E-tailing success

Altogether 6 factors and 64 variables were identified from in-depth interviews, focus group studies and questionnaire survey. The six factors are in line with the six factors identified in the literature review. Of the 64 variables, seven new variables are not explicitly expressed in the literature of information systems and e-commerce success. They are (1) membership (i.e., currently e-commerce is mainly focused on VIP members who bring very impressive profits to the business) ; (2) organisational mission (i.e., stated-owned-enterprises (SOEs) VS private firms); (3) profit objectives (i.e., as a result of being a SOE, need to balance both financial objectives and social responsibility); (4) e-commerce campaigns (i.e., successful e-commerce needs effective marketing and promotion targeting Chinese consumers); (5) business size (i.e., implementing in the whole group via centralization approach VS de-centralizing implementation in each sub-organization); (6) first mover advantage (i.e., impress and attack customers before other retailers embark on e-tailing), and (7) credit system (i.e., the need for a credit system to take care of business and individual reputations). Where possible, the factors and variables have been labeled in line with the literature. However, the variables within each factor and their meanings are different from earlier studies and are more specific to e-tailing in China.

Other interesting results are also found. For example, out of 64 variables, only two variables (investment and return on investment) were mentioned by all 16 interview participants, and one variable (product categories and prices) was mentioned by fifteen interview participants. Sufficient investment in e-tailing (i.e., in information system/information technology expertise, information system infrastructure') was identified as critical determinant in e-tailing. In the same time, like any other business operations and projects, return on investment is an important benchmark for performance evaluation of e-tailing (Frank 2004; Gunasekaran & Ngai 2005). Most participants of the research do not have much confidence in the profitability of e-commerce as a result of the case organization's current emphasis on the tangible short-term financial gains. The variable of product categories and prices is one of the most significant variables affecting successful e-tailing. Literature, such as Smith 2000; Steinfield 2004; Turban et al. 2006, has suggested that suitable products and cheaper prices are critical in the e-tailing success. This research also found that while customers believe all dimensions of e-commerce system performance (measuring by service quality, content quality, trust, support & service) is important for an e-commerce system, their views are not supported by the participants of in-depth interviews and focus group studies. It indicates the retail group has no clear idea of how to meet its customers' expectations in the virtual environment.

4.2. Demographic Information of Survey Participants

Among 200 respondents, 57% were female, showing that there were more females in the shopping centre areas. 32.5% of the respondents have had online shopping experiences. One hundred and ninety-nine respondents indicated their age, with only one respondent withholding age information. Overall, the majority of the respondents were 21-29 years old (43.7%), followed by those 15-20 years old (23.6%). Twenty-one point six percent of respondents were between 30 and 39 years old. Only 7.5% of the respondents were 40-49 years old, and only 2.5% were 50-59 years old. In total, 199 respondents supplied their education level, and over half had Bachelor degrees (27.6%) and graduate diplomas (31.2%). Another majority group was respondents with high school education, with 19.6% having attended high school and 17.1% having completed high school. Only 3% of respondents had a Master's degree, and 1.5% had obtained a diploma. Moreover, 66% of the respondents had a business academic background. Other academic training was represented, in smaller percentages. Only 8% of the respondents were arts/literature/language graduates and 4% had a computer academic background. Social sciences were the fourth-largest group, with only 2% of respondents. Three further academic fields were represented, but only occupied 0.5% of respondents, meaning that there was only one respondent for each of these three academic backgrounds. One hundred and ninety-four respondents indicated their income level. The majority household income before tax annual was less than RMB 60,000. The largest group was in the range RMB 15,000 to RMB 30,000 (31.4%). The second largest group was in the range RMB 30,001 to RMB 60,000, with 25.8%, followed by the group with a household income of less than RMB 15,000, at 24.7%. Nine point eight percent of the respondents were in the range RMB 60,000 to RMB 90,000, and only 8.2% of respondents earned more than RMB 90,000 annual household income before tax. All of these percentages were calculated in exclusion of the missing data. Some popular items purchased online (by these 65 respondents who have done online shopping) are presented in Table 7.7 (in the order from most popular to least popular).

Table 7.7: Popular Online Products

Product category	Percentage
Cloth and accessories	35.4%
Books and magazines	33.8%
Consumer electronics	33.8%
Others	24.6%
Computer & IT	18.5%
Movies	18.5%
Home, lifestyle and baby	16.9%
Music	15.4%
Sporting goods	15.4%
Computer games	12.3%
Antiques and art	10.8%
Business (office and industrial)	10.8%
Cameras and accessories	10.8%
Toys, hobbies and crafts	9.2%
Jewellery, gems and watches	4.6%
Cars, bikes and boats	1.5%
Phones	1.5%

4.3. Final Combined Model

Figure 7.5 presents a combined model of e-tailing success. This is a comprehensive model which includes all the factors and variables identified in both interviews (16 in-depth interviews and 3 focus group interviews) and 200 surveyed questionnaires. In total, six components and 64 sub-factors were found to have an impact on the success of e-tailing. Among these 64 variables, 57 factors were confirmed by the literature, and 7 new variables were extended for e-tailing success in China. This model can be used in further investigations to test the model in new contexts.

5. Discussions of Results

5.1. Discussion of research issues

5.1.1. Research issue 1

This section discusses research issue 1: 'How is e-tailing being used in the case organization?

In-depth and focus group interviews were conducted in seven subsidiaries (five department stores and two supermarkets) and one administrative unit of the case organization. Six out of seven of these subsidiaries have their own websites (four department stores and two supermarkets). Both supermarket subsidiaries have been operating their websites for at least three years, while the operation of websites in the department store subsidiaries began less than two years prior to this research. In terms of the function of those six websites, three provide a B2B service to their suppliers, and all six websites offer various activities for customers, such as promotional information, membership services, and online shopping. Interestingly, only one website, that of a department store, offers online sales, while both supermarket websites have been conducting online sales for several years. Overall, the supermarket subsidiaries have launched e-commerce, including online shopping, earlier than the department store subsidiaries. This is probably because of the products they sell, and because of the fact that they fall under different industry departments, with different leaders.

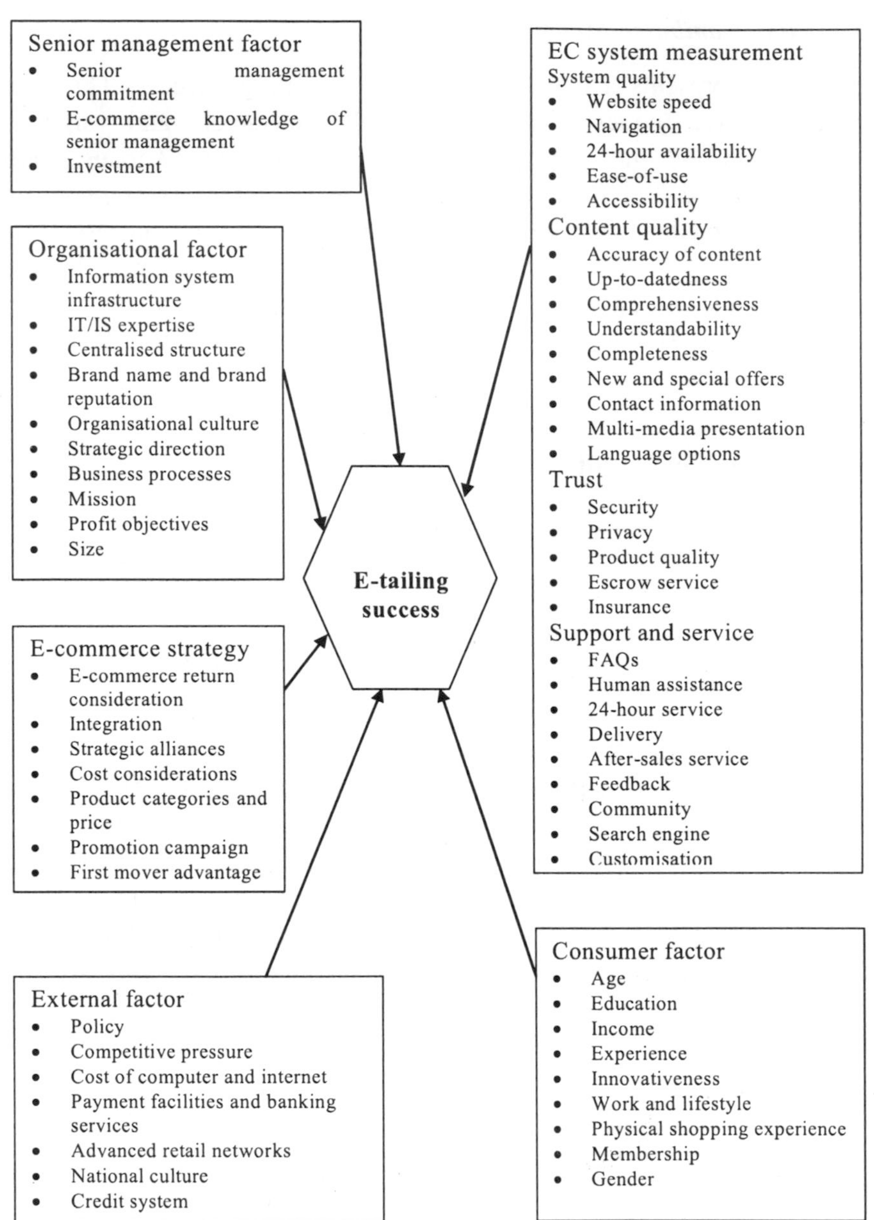

Figure 7.5: Final combined model

5.1.2. Research issue 2

This section discusses research issue 2: What are the barriers to the implementation of e-tailing in the case organization?

The data from all three sources (in-depth and focus group interviews and survey questionnaires) indicated that there are some barriers to the implementation of successful e-tailing in the case organization. Table 7.8 depicts these barriers in the categories of external and internal barriers.

Table 7.8: Barriers to implementing e-tailing in the case organization

External	**Internal**
1. high cost of internet access	1. business processes
2. lack of payment facilities and effective banking services	2. senior management commitment
	3. investment
3. advanced retail networks	4. senior management knowledge of e-commerce
4. lack of cultural trust	
5. poor delivery network, lack of legal and policy frameworks	5. IT/IS expertise
	6. organisationl mission
6. education in e-commerce	7. profit objectives
7. need for the physical shopping experience	8. information system infrastructure
	9. integration
	10. organisational culture
	11. product issues
	12. strategic direction

(Source: developed for this research)

5.1.3. Research issue 3

This section discusses research issue 3: What are the factors for achieving successful e-tailing in the case organization?

Firstly, the surveyed customers were mainly concerned with e-commerce system measurements. As the end-users of an e-commerce system, they indicated what they considered to be the important functions of online shopping sites. Effective e-commerce systems need to have reliable systems with careful content design, and moreover, online trustworthiness and qualified support and service would enhance the effectiveness and efficiency of an e-commerce system. However, this research found that some e-commerce system measurements mentioned by the customers were not mentioned by the interviewees from the case organization, indicating that the organisation dose not understand what their customers concerns and desires are in relation to online systems. Therefore, a mismatch is indicated between customers and the case organisation, in terms of e-commerce systems.

Secondly, three out of the four senior management factors were mentioned by the organisational interviewees: senior management commitment, investment, and the e-commerce knowledge of senior management. Among those factors, some inter-relationships were indicated at the interviews, indicating that investment in e-commerce is the result of senior management commitment, and the commitment of senior management derives from their knowledge of e-commerce.

Thirdly, almost all of the organisational variables extracted from the literature were mentioned by the interviewees except task coordination, this is probably because the group never has a systematic E-commerce approach and lacks of E-commerce knowledge and experience. This suggests that organisational factors have some effect on the quality of an e-commerce system. For example, the e-commerce system is the web-front store, and the organisation provides the backup support for that system. Without effective support and strong internal systems, the e-commerce system cannot be a success. Furthermore, some new factors were identified in the organisational categories, some being typically Chinese, due to the Chinese market economy, such as organisational missions and profit objectives.

Fourthly, seven e-commerce strategy success factors arose from this research, including five confirmed variables and two new, extended variables. This suggests that the organisation is concerned with e-commerce returns and cost considerations, and that they believe that effective strategies are important to the success of e-tailing, such as promotional campaigns and strategic alliances. This finding shows that the organization is currently considering strategy initiation and assessment, but there is a lack of strategy formulation and implementation.

Fifthly, external factors are an aspect of the E-tailing success which cannot be controlled by the organisation. This category consists of a number of barriers, such as the PC and internet access costs, payment facilities and banking services, and advanced retail networks. One new factor was identified in the interviews conducted for this research, namely the credit history system, suggesting that currently there is a lack of an effective credit history system throughout Chinese society. A well-operating credit history system would be useful to build reputation and enhance customer trust.

Sixthly, consumer factors describe the characteristics of the online customer. Most of the variables were confirmed by both the interviews and surveys, however, the customer surveys indicated that age and gender are less significant to online shopping activities. The new factor arising from the interviews is membership: participants believed that e-commerce activities should be more focused on the customers who have current membership.

The aim of this research was to investigate the factors and variables of successful e-tailing in China. According to the literature, six factors and 59 variables have been identified. The findings of this research confirm that most of those variables are important to the success of e-tailing in China, and some new variables have been explored. However, the organisational interviewees seem less concerned with the quality of their e-commerce systems than the customer, rather, the organisational interviewees were more concerned with the organisational factors, senior management factors, e-commerce strategies, and external factors.

6. Implications of the Research

The findings of this study have made contributions to the body of knowledge of e-tailing and to the real-world practices. A new e-tailing success model, consisting of 6 factors and 64 variables, has been generated in this research. Retailers who are embarking on e-tailing or have adopted e-tailing could use factors and variables of the model to examine or guide their e-tailing implementation activities.

This research found that e-commerce, especially e-tailing, is under-utilised in China's retail industry due to a lack of investment (financial and human resources), inappropriate business processes, lack of integration, product categories and prices, and so forth. Interestingly, supermarkets have more advanced e-commerce systems than department stores. However, all the interviewees from both the department stores and supermarkets realised the benefits of e-tailing. As they indicated, they have more advantages in the implementation of e-commerce than pure-players, in terms of brand name and brand reputation, customer service and customer trust. In addition, such findings will provide assistance to retailers who are interested in entering the Chinese market.

This research confirms the differences between a company which operates an effective web-front store and a company which does not have an effective web-front store, in the case organization. For example, one of its supermarkets generates RMB5.2 billion in sales revenue from their online membership and the number of members reached 7.5 million in 2005. The positive performance of e-commerce in this supermarket has boosted management's confidence in e-commerce even though its other subsidiaries are less advanced in adopting e-commerce.

In addition, the Chinese government could build up better e-tailing (or in e-commerce in general) environment and infrastructure by investing in internet networks and national platform of financial services, establishing & effectively implement pro-e-commerce regulations and polices, equipping e-commerce knowledge and skills to both consumers and businesses, and providing assistance to businesses regarding setting up and running e-commerce applications.

Lastly, in line with the findings of this research, we present the success factors of e-tailing and the strategies to address those factors and variables e-tailing (see Figure 7.6 to Figure 11 (a-d)).

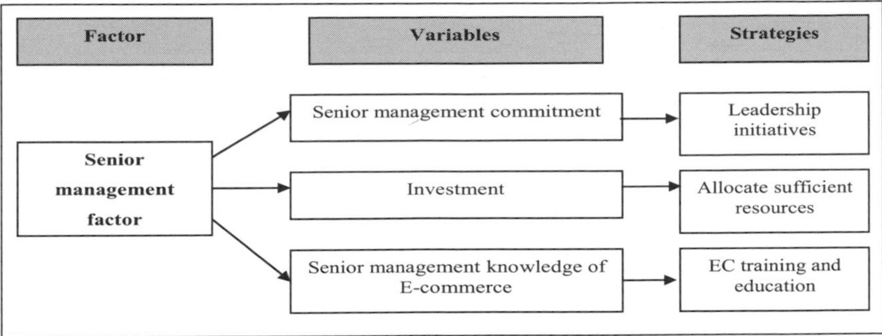

Figure 7.6: senior management factor of e-tailing and its relevant strategies

Factor	Variables	Strategies
Organisational factor	Information system infrastructure	Integration and investment
	IT/IS expertise	Investment; More professional staff
	Centralisation	Form a dedicated EC team
	Brand name and reputation	Use existing famous brands
	Organisational culture	Motivation & reward policy
	Strategic direction	Strategic planning & alignment
	Business processes	Adjust the business process
	Mission	Include E-tailing in the mission
	Profit objectives	A balanced set of profit objectives
	Size of organisation	Initiatives from the top; Integration within the group

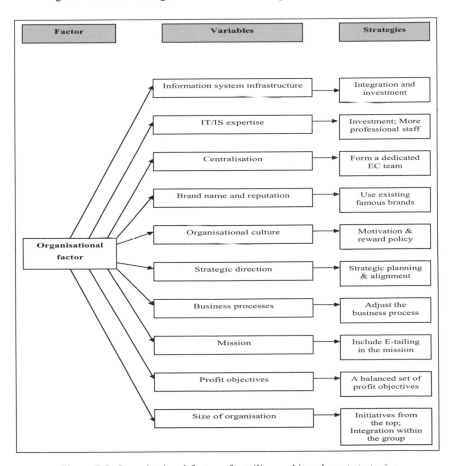

Figure 7.7: Organisational factor of e-tailing and its relevant strategies

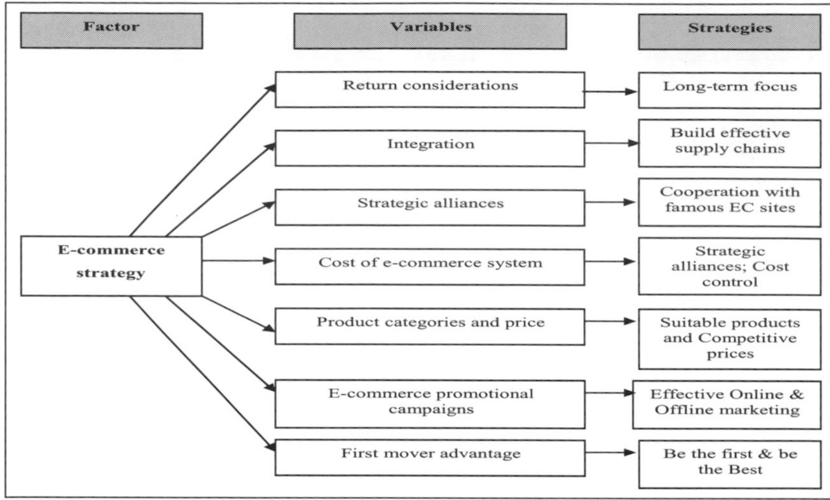

Figure 7.8: E-commerce strategies of e-tailing and its relevant strategies

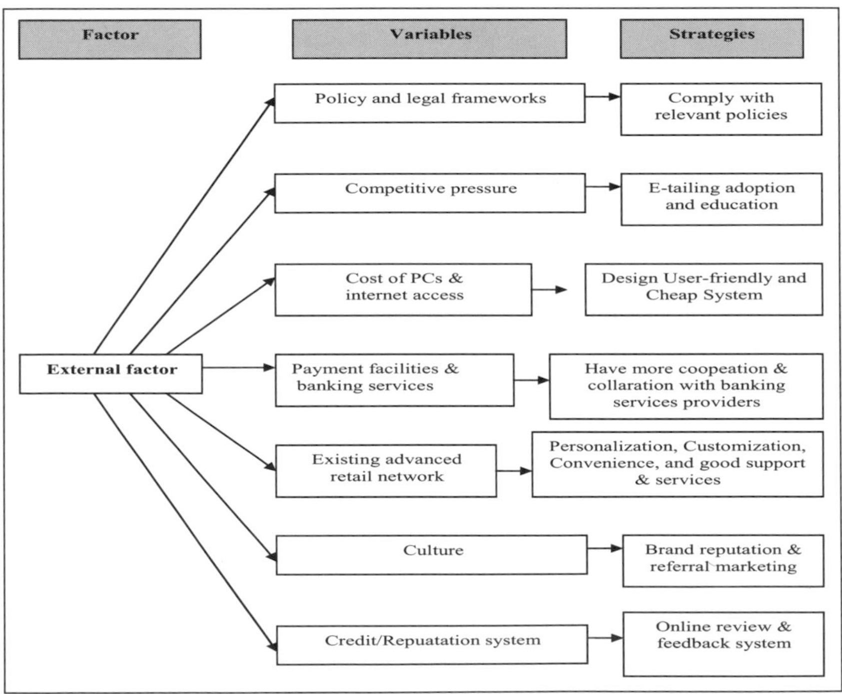

Figure 7.9: External factor of e-tailing and its relevant strategies

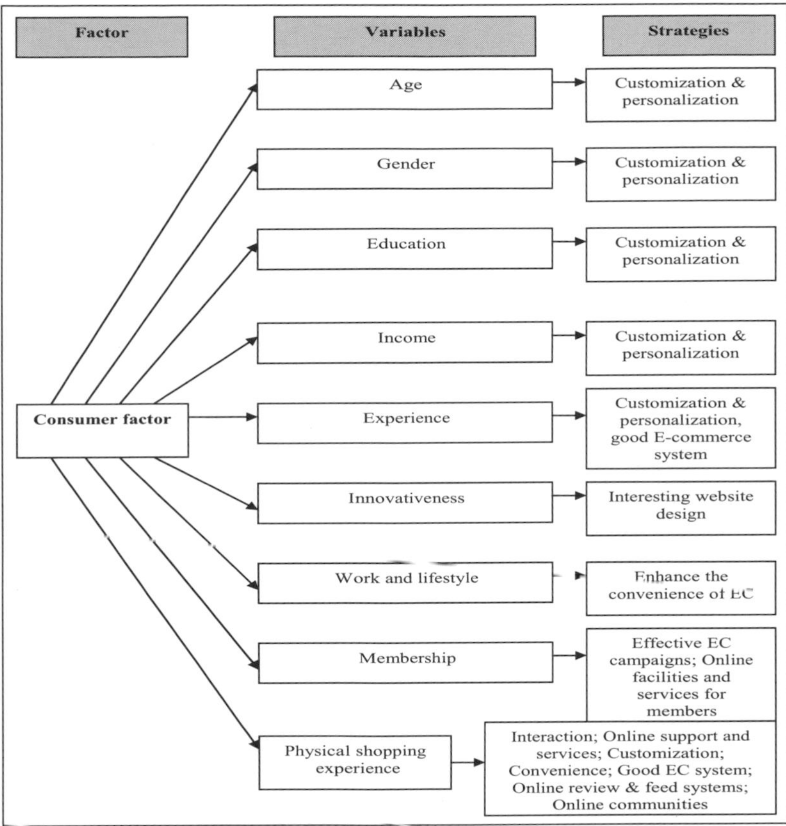

Figure 7.10: consumer factor of e-tailing and its relevant strategies

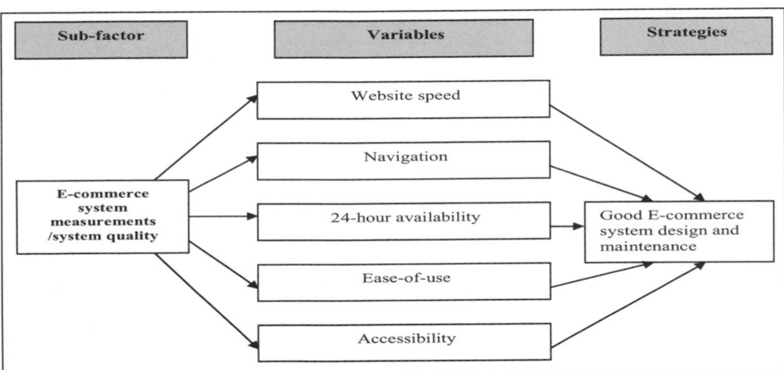

Figure 7.11 (a): system quality of system measurements and its relevant strategies

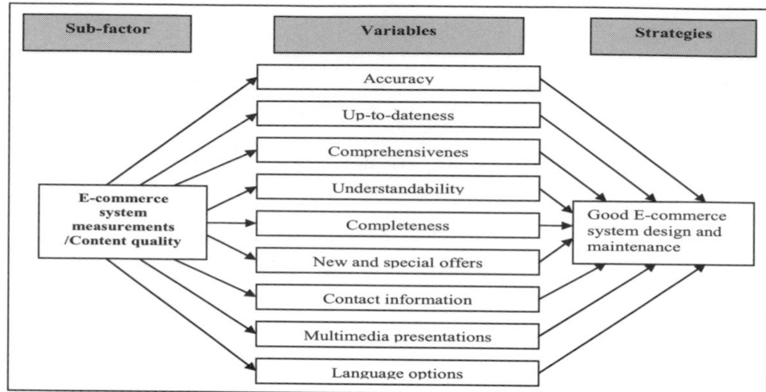

Figure 7.11 (b): Content of system measurements and its relevant strategies

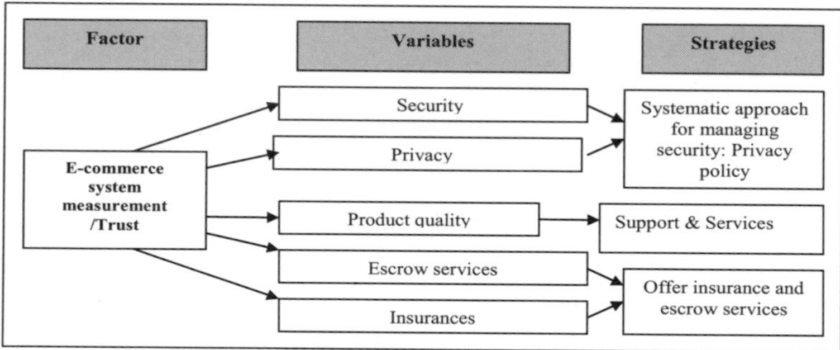

Figure 7.11 (c): Trust of system measurements and its relevant strategies

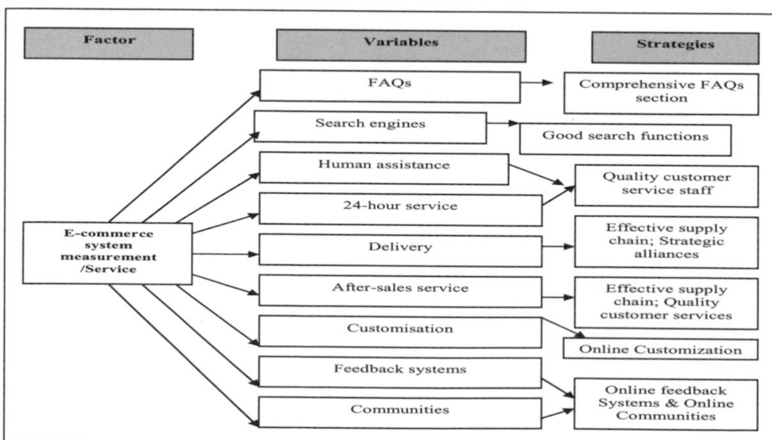

Figure 7.11 (d): Support services of system measurements and its relevant strategies

7. Summary, Limitations and Future Research Directions

7.1. Summary

This research studied e-tailing in a case retail organization in China. By collecting data from various sources (i.e., interviews, focus groups, surveys, documents, observations), a comprehensive model of e-tailing success was developed, and some e-commerce strategies were generated. The developed model and those generated e-commerce strategies could be adapted for guiding e-tailing implementations or enhancing e-tailing operations for various retail organizations in different countries.

7.2. Limitations of the Research

Firstly, the research investigated the factors affecting the achievement of success in e-tailing in China's retail industry. Thus, the research findings are more suited to the Chinese e-commerce market than to that of other countries in terms of economy, culture and technological issues. As these fundamentals may differ between countries, the barriers and e-tailing success factors may also differ between countries. Secondly, click-and-mortar B2C e-commerce was the type of e-commerce investigated in this research, and includes many specific variables and barriers which do not exist for the pure-player e-commerce enterprise, such as existing business processes. Therefore, the research findings may need to be adapted for application to the pure-player environment.

The primary limitation in this research may be the use of a single case study, due to the fact that the research findings from a single case may not generalisable to other cases. This limitation can be overcome by selecting the case(s) based on the criteria suggest by Yin (2002). Moreover, the new theory or model needs to be tested in further research and other cases, to measure its replicability. The final limitation to this research is that the content of the interviews could be seen as business secrets. Therefore, the interviewees may have concealed some information from the interviewers, especially during the focus group interviews, as the group members may have been reticent to share their comments and understandings with colleagues from other subsidiaries.

This research overcame this limitation by carefully organising the interviews and triangulating the data from different sources.

7.3. Recommendations for Further Research

This research has three major implications for further research. Firstly, a single case study method was used to investigate e-tailing in China. Thus, the research was primarily qualitative. Future research could be conducted using a purely quantitative method, as it would be useful to test the developed model and achieve generalisability of the findings of this research by using other research methods and investigating other Chinese retail firms. Furthermore, this research focused on click-and-mortar firms and future research could investigate successful e-tailing in pure-player based e-commerce. Secondly, this research focused on the case retail group including different retail formats, whereas future research could focus more directly on one specific retail format, such as the supermarket or the shopping centre. As different retail formats have specific product categories and prices and business processes, the contributions made by this research may be expanded by exploring specific retail formats in more detail. Thirdly, this research was undertaken in the specific context of China's retail industry. Future similar research could be conducted in other developing countries, such as Vietnam, India or Thailand, as different macro-environments and customer behaviours may influence the success of e-tailing.

Overall, the findings of this research can be seen as a starting point in the development of the body of knowledge in the field of e-tailing. Further related research can be developed with both more general and more specific focus, such as cross-national research, specific retail formats, other retail firms and alternative e-commerce structures.

References

Agrawal, D.P., Singh, D., Kabiraj, S. and Andrews, A. (2001) Strategies and models for E-retailing: attempted retrospection in the Indian context. Indian Institute of Technology and Management, India.

Anonymous (1995) East Asian Executive Report, Jan 15, pp. 10-15.

Anonymous (2005a) Industry-at-a-Glance Report, Small Business Research & Information center, viewed on Oct 2, 2005, from www.udel.edu/alex/online/market5.html

Anonymous (2006a) Research report of M&A activities in China retailing industry in 2006-2007 [in Chinese], p. 204.

Anonymous (2006b) The analysis of competition in China retailing industry in 2005 [in Chinese], viewed on Oct 2, 2005, from www.likshop.com.cn

ATKEARNEY (2005) The 2005 global retail development index. Destination: China. A.T.Kearney. Inc.

Bai, R.J. and Lee, G.G. (2003) Organizational factors influencing the quality of the IS/IT strategic planning process, Industrial management & data systems, Vol. 103, No 8, pp. 622-632.

Baker, C. (2005) Weighing online marketing's benefits, Multichannel News, Vol. 26, No. 21; p.91.

Barnes, D., Hinton, M. and Mieczkowska, S. (2004) Managing the transition from bricks-and-Mortar to click-and-Mortar: A business process perspective, Knowledge and Process Management, Vol. 11, No 3, pp. 199-209.

Beyard, M., O'Mara, W. (1999) Shopping centrc development handbook (3rd ed.) , Washington DC: Urban Land Institute

Bonoma, T.V. (1985) Case research in marketing: opportunities problems and a process, Journal of Marketing Research, Vol. 22, No.2, pp. 199-208.

Brilliance Group (2005) New Insight, Brilliance Group.

Buckman, R. (2003) China may tighten retail rules, Wall Street Journal, December 11, pp B-7.

Burns, S. (2006) Chinese mobile users hit 426m, viewed on Oct 4, 2006, from http://www.itweek.co.uk/vnunet/news/2162843/china-mobile-users-hit-426m

CCID Consulting (2002) 2001-2002 Annual Report of e-commerce in China.

Chiger, S. (1997) List shopping, online, Catalog Age, Vol. 14, No. 7, pp. 95-97.

CIA World Factbook (1987) China retail sales, The Library of Congress Country Studies.

CNNIC (1998a) 1st statistics report on the internet development in China, China Internet Network Information Center.

CNNIC (1998b) 2nd statistics report on the internet development in China, China Internet Network Information Center.

CNNIC (1999a) 3rd statistics report on the internet development in China, China Internet Network Information Center.

CNNIC (1999b) 4th statistics report on the internet development in China, China Internet Network Information Center.

CNNIC (2000a) 5th statistics report on the internet development in China, China Internet Network Information Center.

CNNIC (2000b) 6th statistics report on the internet development in China, China Internet Network Information Center.

CNNIC (2001a) 7th statistics report on the internet development in China, China Internet Network Information Center.

CNNIC (2001b) 8th statistics report on the internet development in China, China Internet Network Information Center.

CNNIC (2002a) 9th statistics report on the internet development in China, China Internet Network Information Center.

CNNIC (2002b) 10th statistics report on the internet development in China, China Internet Network Information Center.

CNNIC (2003a) 11th statistics report on the internet development in China, China Internet Network Information Center.

CNNIC (2003b) 12th statistics report on the internet development in China, China Internet Network Information Center.

CNNIC (2004a) 13th statistics report on the internet development in China, China Internet Network Information Center.

CNNIC (2004b) 14th statistics report on the internet development in China, China Internet Network Information Center.

CNNIC (2005a) 15th statistics report on the internet development in China, China Internet Network Information Center.

CNNIC (2005b) 16th statistics report on the internet development in China, China Internet Network Information Center.

CNNIC 2006a 17th statistics report on the internet development in China, China internet Network Information Center.

CNNIC (2006b) 18th statistics report on the internet development in China, China Internet Network Information Center.

Darke, P., Shanks, G. and Broadbent, M. (1998) Successfully completing case study research: combining rigour, relevance and pragmatism, Information Systems Journal. Vol. 8, pp. 273-289.

Delone, W.H. and McLean, E.R. (2003) The Delone and McLean model of information system success: A ten-year update, Journal of Management Information Systems, Vol. 19, No. 4, pp. 9-30.

Dedrick, J. and Kraemer, K.L. (2001) China IT report, The Electronic Journal on Information Systems in Developing Countries, Vol. 6, No. 2, pp. 1-10.

Dillon, T.W. & Reif, H.L. (2004) Factors influencing consumers' e-commerce commodity purchases, Information Technology, Learning and Performance Journal, Vol. 22, No. 2, pp. 1-12.

Dick B. (2005) Ground theory: a thumbnail sketch, viewed on Oct 7, 2006, from: http://www.scu.edu.au/schools/gcm/ar/arp/grounded.html

Dube, L. and Pare, G. (2003) Rigor in information systems positivist case research: current practices, trends, and recommendations, MIS Quarterly, Vol. 27, No. 4, pp. 597-635.

Efendioglu, A.M., Yip, V.F. and Murray, W.L. (2004) e-commerce in developing countries: issues and influences, University of San Francisco.

Eisenhardt, K.M. (1989) Building theories from case study research, Academy of Management Review, Vol. 14, No. 4, pp. 532-550.

Enrst, D. and He, J.C. (2000) Asia Pacific issues: The future of e-commerce in China, East-West Center.

Ernst & Young (2005) The path to success for retailers and consumer brands in China, Global retail and consumer products & Ernst & Young China.

Frank, D. (2004) Buying into enterprise architrave, Federal Computer Week, Vol. 18, No. 2, p. 46.

Gable, G. (1994) Integrating case study and survey research methods: an example in information system. European Journal of Information Systems, Vol. 3, No. 2, pp. 112-126.

Gefen, D., Karahanna, E. and Straub, D.W. (2003) Trust and TAM in online shopping: An integrated model, MIS Quarterly, Vol. 27, No. 1, pp. 51-90.

Gibbs, J., Kraemer, K.L. and Dedrik, J. (2002) Environment and policy factors shaping e-commerce diffusion: A cross-country comparison, Centre for Research on Information Technology and Organisation, University of California.

Gunasekaran, A. and Ngai, E.W.T. (2005) e-commerce in Hong Kong: an empirical perspective and analysis, Internet Research, Vol. 15, No. 2, pp. 141-159.

Hoelter, J.W. (1983) The Effects of Role Evaluation and Commitment on Identity Salience, Social Psychology Quarterly, Vol. 46, pp. 140-147.

Hong, X (2003) Online Dispute Resolution in China- Present Practices & Future Developments, Proceedings of the UNECE Forum on ODR 2003, viewed on Oct 13, 2005, from http://www.e-works.net.cn/ewkArticles/Category76/Article10619.htm.

IDC (2006) IT solution should be improved while foreign investment enter China retailing industry [in Chinese], IDC CHINA.

IResearch (2005) China B2C e-commerce Research Report 2005, iResearch Consulting Group.

Jick, T.D. (1979) Mixing qualitative and quantitative methods: triangulation in action, Administrative Science Quarterly, Vol. 24, pp. 602-611.

Kaplan, B. and Duchon, D. (1988) Combining qualitative and quantitative methods in information systems research: a case study, MIS Quarterly, Vol. 12, No. 4, pp. 571-586.

Kelliher, F. (2005) Interpretivism and the Pursuit of Research Legitimisation: An Integrated Approach to Single case Design, Electronic Journal of Business Research Methods, Vol. 3, No. 2, pp. 123-132.

Li, Y. (2004) Shopping mall: the new retail giant in China, People's Daily, p. 2.

Leonard, L.N.K. and Cronan, T.P. (2003) Website Retailing: Electronic Supply Chain replenishment, Journal of End User Computing, Vol.15, No.3, pp. 45-55.

Lohse, G.L. and Spiller, P. (1998) Electronic shopping. Communications of the ACM, Vol. 41, No. 7, pp. 81-87.

Markus M.L. (1983) Power, politics, and MIS implementation, Communications of the ACM, Vol. 26, No. 6, pp. 430-445.

Miles, M.B., & Humberman, A.M. (1994) Qualitative data analysis: An expanded source book, Thousand Oaks, CA: Sage.

Molla, A. (2004) The impact of eReadiness on eCommerce Success in Developing Countries: firm-level evidence, Institute for Development Policy and Management.

Molla, A., & Licker, P.S. (2001) E-commerce systems success: an attempt to extend and respecify the Delone and MacLean model IS success', Journal of Electronic Commerce Research, Vol. 2, No. 4, pp. 131-141.

Mullaney, T.J (2004) e-tailing finally hits its stride, Business Week, December 20, Iss. 3913; p. 36

Nielsen, J. (1998) Seven deadly sins for web design, Technology Review, viewed on July 7, 2005, from http://www.techreview.com/articles/oct98/nielsen-sidebar.htm.

Ogden, J.R. (2005) Retail: Integrated retail management. Boston: Houghton Mifflin

ONDA, T. (2004) China's Distribution Service Market Entering Phase of Full-Scale Opening, NRI Papers, Nomura Research Institute.

Orlikowski, W.J. and Robey, D. (1991) Information technology and the structuring of organisations, Information Systems Research, Vol. 2, No. 2, pp. 143-169.

Patton, M.Q. (1990) Qualitative Evaluation and Research methods, Sage Publications.

Peterson, R., Balasubramanian, S. and Bronneaberg, B.J. (1997) Exploring the implications of the internet for consumer marketing, Journal of the Academy of Marketing Science, Vol. 25, No. 4, pp. 329-346

Ratchford, B.T., Talukdar, D. and Lee, M.S. (2001) A model of consumer choice of the The internet as an information source, International Journal of Electronic Commerce, Vol. 5, No. 3, pp. 7-21.

Rao, B. (1999) Developing an effective e-tailing strategy, Electronic markets, Vol. 9, No. 1/2, pp. 89-92

Samiee, S., Yip, L.S.C. & Luk, S.T.K. (2004) International marketing in Southeast Asia-retailing trends and opportunities in China, International Marketing Review, Vol. 21, No. 3, pp. 247-254.

Sabherwal, R., Jeyaraj, A., & Chowa, C. (2004) Information system success: Dimensions and Determinants, College of business administration, University of Missouri.

Santos, J. (2003) E-service quality: a model of virtual service quality dimensions, Managing Service Quality, Vol. 13, No. 3, pp. 233-246.

Seddon, P.B. & Kiew, M.Y. (1994) A partial test and development of the Delone and McLean model of IS success. In J.I. Degross, S.L. Huff, and M.C. Munro (eds.), Proceedings of the International Conference on Information System, Atlanta, GA: Association for Information Systems, pp. 99-110

Smith, P. (2000) Hi tail to E-tail, New Zealand Management, Vol. 47, No 6, pp. 22-25.

Steinfield, C. (2004) Does online and offline channel integration work in practice? Department of Telecommunication, Michigan State University.

Stylianou, A.C, Robbins, S.S. & Jackson, P. (2003) Perceptions and attitudes about e-commerce development in China: an exploratory study, Journal of Global Information Management, Vol. 11, No. 2, pp. 31-47.

Sullivan, L. (2004) E-commerce: promise fulfilled, Information week, Nov 8, 1013, pp. 70-73.

Tan, Z.X. and OuYang, W. (2004) Globalization of e-commerce: Diffusion and Impacts of the internet and e-commerce in China, Centre for research on information technology and organisations, University of California.

Taylor-Powell, E. & Renner, M. (2003) Analysing Qualitative data, Program development and evaluation, University of Wisconsin-Extension.

Teo, T.S.H. (2001) Demographic and Motivation Variables Associated with The internet Usage Activities, The internet research: electronic network applications and policy, Vol. 11, No. 2, pp. 125-137.

Teo, T.S. and Ang, J.S. (1999) Critical success factors in the alignment of IS plans with business plans, International Journal of Information Management, Vol. 19, No. 2, pp. 173-185.

Teo, T.S.H. & Wong, P.K. (1998) An empirical study of the performance impact of computerization in the retail industry, Omega-The International Journal of Management Science, Vol. 26, No. 5, pp. 611-621.

The Economist (2006) Ready for warfare in aisles- retailing in China, The Economist, London, Vol. 380, No. 8489, p. 60.

Trend, M.G. (1989) On the reconciliation of qualitative and Quantitative methods in Evaluation research, Sage Publications, Beverly Hills.

Turban, E., King, D., Lee, J. & Viehland, D. (2006) Electronic Commerce A managerial perspective, International Edition, Prentice Hall.

United Nations (2003) e-commerce and development report 2003, The internet edition prepared by the UNCTAD secretariat, United Nations Conference on Trade and Development.

Urban, G., Sultan, F. and Qualls, W. (2000) Placing trust at the center of your The internet strategy, Sloan Management Review, Vol. 42, pp. 1-13.

Von Dran, G.M., Zhang, P. and Small, R. (1999) Quality Websites, An application of the Kano model of Website Desing. In: Haseman W.D. and Nazareth D.L. eds. Proceedings of the fifth AMCIS. 13-15: Association for information system, pp. 898-901.

Voss, C., Tsikriktsis, N. & Frohlich, M. (2002) Case research in operations management, International Journal of Operation & Production Management, Vol. 22 No. 2, pp. 195-219

Wade, R.M. and Nevo, S. (2005) Development and Validation of a Perceptual Instrument to Measure E-Commerce Performance, International Journal of Electronic Commerce, Vol. 10, No. 2, pp. 123-148.

Walsham, G. (1993) Interpreting Information system in organization, Wiley, Chichester.

Walsham, G. (1995) Interpretive case studies in IS research: nature and method, The Management School, Lancaster University.

Wang, S.G., Zhang, Y.C. and Zhang, Y.F. (2006) Opportunities and Challenges of Shopping Centre Development in China: A case study of Shanghai, Journal of Shopping Center Research, Vol. 13, No. 1, pp. 19-55.

Wong, X.D., Yen, D.C. and Fang, X. (2004) e-commerce development in China and its implication for business, Asia Pacific journal of Marketing and Logistics, Vol. 16, No. 3, pp. 68-83.

Wixom, B.H. and Watson, H.J. (2001) An empirical investigation of the factors affecting data warehousing success, MIS Quarterly, Vol. 25, No. 1, pp. 17-41.

Xinhua Net (2003) National Statistics Bureau: the five unignoreable problem in China retailing industry [in Chinese], Xinhua Net, viewed on Jun 22, 2005, from http://news.xinhuanet.com/zhengfu/2003-07/14/content_972699.htm

Xu, W. (2006) Retail therapy, China daily, Updated: 2006-09-11.

Yin, R.K. (1989) Case study Research: Design and methods, Sage publications.

Yin, R.K. (2002) Case study research: design and methods, 3rd edition, Sage publication. Thousand Oaks.

Zhang, X.F., Li, Q., Lin, Z.X. (2005) e-commerce Education in China: Driving forces, status, and strategies, Journal of Electronic Commerce in Organizations, Vol. 3, No. 3, pp. 1-17.

Zikmund, W.G. (2003) Business Research Methods, 7th ed, Thomson South-Western.

CHAPTER 8

A FRAMEWORK FOR BUSINESS-TO-BUSINESS E-COMMERCE EVALUATION CHALLENGES AND CRITICAL SUCCESS FACTORS

Chad Lin

Curtin University of Technology, Australia

Yu-An Huang

National Chi Nan University, Taiwan

Business-to-business e-commerce (B2BEC) which deals with Internet-supported commercial activities between two or more different companies is becoming increasingly imperative for companies aiming at improving their competitiveness and this has led to much of research and new IT investments. Its growth outpaced all of other forms of electronic commerce. However, the potential for realizing significant benefits for implementation of B2BEC does not appear to have been enough to provide impetus for extensive adoption by organizations. Although B2BEC provides the organizations a wealth of new opportunities and ways of doing business, it also presents them with a series of challenges. Therefore, the case study approach was utilized to investigate the process of B2BEC investment evaluation in nine Australian organizations within the hospitality sector. The key objectives of this exploratory research are: (1) to establish current practices and norms in managing B2BEC evaluation in Australian organizations; and (2) to development a framework of challenges and critical success factors in B2BEC evaluation. A key contribution of the book chapter is to identify and examine challenges and critical success factors faced by Australian organizations undertaking B2BEC evaluation. Moreover, a framework was proposed for Australian organizations to measure their B2BEC investments.

1. Introduction

B2BEC trade represents the largest growth sector - that is, 80% of revenues - in e-commerce (Pires and Aisbett 2003). Forecasts for the value of B2BEC in the US alone range between US$600 billion and US$2.8 trillion for 2003 (Fensel et al. 2002). It is estimated that B2BEC can increase the level of output in the developed economies by an average of 5% cent over time (McIvor and Humphreys 2004). Currently, the most popular electronic commerce applications used by organizations in their B2B relationships are EDI, web-forms, XML, and other varieties of Internet initiatives such as electronic marketplace and B2B portals (Chan and Swatman 2003; Hsaio 2003). Depending on the characteristics of the products, market variability, market volatility, and continuity of the business relationship between the channel partners the B2BEC markets can take different forms, such as electronic hierarchies, cooperative arrangements, and spot markets (Kim and Umanath 2005). Specifically, the main characteristics of B2BEC include: externalities and exponential growth; critical mass; customer cohesion; content and category depth; broadening and deepening hub services; and disintermediation (Zeng et al. 2003). In the competition of the global marketplace, it is no longer organizations that compete. It is networks such as B2BEC that compete and the competitive advantage depends on the ability of organizations to forge relationships with external partners across the globe (Kandampully 2003).

Teo and Ranganathan (2004) have defined it as the "use of the Internet and Web-technologies for conducting inter-organizational business transactions." IT investments in B2BEC are used to assist in the inter-organization acquisition of goods into the value chain and to provide interfaces between customers, vendors, suppliers and sellers (Kleist 2003). It is facilitated by internets, intranets, extranets, private exchanges, and even neutral electronic market exchange mechanisms through linking suppliers, partners and customers across the public networks of the web, using servers, routers and facilities belonging to a variety of owners and investors (Kleist 2003; Turban et al. 2004). It is not a new phenomenon as it has existed in the form of EDI for more than thirty years (Laudon and Laudon 2004). B2BEC allows organizations' business partners to access their internal business systems via the Internet. The major benefits of B2BEC are as follows:

- It increases competitiveness in the marketplace (du Plessis and Boon 2004; Kandampully 2003; Laudon and Laudon 2004);
- It can reduce an organization's costs such as procurement costs and search costs (Kandampully 2003; McGaughey 2002; McIvor and Humphreys 2004);
- It provides a wide-coverage, high-functionality, low-cost tool for venturing into new markets (Domaracki 2001; Lee et al. 1999);
- It provides an efficient and effective channel for information exchange and sharing (Kleist 2003; Raisinghani et al 2005);
- It enables organizations to trade on a 24x7x365 basis, and enhances coordination and collaboration among them (Domaracki 2001; Laudon and Laudon 2004);
- It increases productivity of employees dealing with buying and/or selling (Kandampully 2003; McGaughey 2002; Turban et al. 2004);
- It reduces errors and improves quality of services (McGaughey 2002);
- It reduces inventory levels and costs and increases production flexibility, permitting just-in-time delivery (Raisinghani et al. 2005);
- It provides a means of achieving the desired degree of interconnectivity without huge investment and greater technical complexity (Chau and Jim 2002);
- It facilitates mass customization (Kandampully 2003; Turban et al. 2004);
- It helps to build global relationship with partners, suppliers and customers (du Plessis and Boon 2004; McGaughey 2002; Steinmueller 2002); and
- With its non-proprietary standards, low entry and switching costs and the openness of the Internet, organizations in the SME sector are attracted to conducting B2BEC transactions with larger trading partners (McGaughey 2002).

However, the potential for realizing significant benefits for implementation of B2BEC does not appear to have been enough to provide impetus for extensive adoption by organizations (Power 2004). Although B2BEC provides the organizations a wealth of new opportunities and ways of doing business, it also presents them with a series of challenges (Laudon and Laudon 2004): (1) many new B2BEC business models are difficult to evaluate and therefore, have yet to prove enduring sources of profit; (2) Web-enabling business processes for B2BEC requires far-reaching organizational change; (3) the legal environment for B2BEC has not yet solidified and organizations must be vigilant about establishing trust, security and consumer privacy. In particular, organizations often take the short-term view of evaluating their electronic commerce success by only looking at the potential advantages of IT use while at the same time are unaware of the factors that may hinder the benefits attainment in the long term (Quaddus and Achjari 2003) such as managing the relationship between the justification of the B2BEC initiatives to stakeholders and the level of commitment towards project success (Irani 2002).

As mentioned earlier, spending on B2BEC in the coming years will grow rapidly and it will figure as a significantly large vehicle for electronic transactions. Tremendous growth well into the foreseeable future is expected for B2BEC, with the main driving force being the commercialization of Internet organizations. Electronic commerce researchers and consultants all share an interest in maximizing the business value of B2BEC, while academics and practitioners are keen to know how organizations can exploit that value (Lee et al. 1999). To keep abreast of changing requirements, organizations require new metrics to measure whether their web efforts are paying off (Cutler and Sterne, 2000) and what conditions are optimal when engaging in B2BEC activities (Kaefer and Bendoly 2004).

Organizations must look at B2BEC from a strategic perspective and measure its contribution because it can assist organizations in developing and controlling strategic, tactical, and operational plans that define the appropriate role of B2BEC in the enterprise (McGaughey 2002). However, the difficulty of measuring benefits is one of the major problems in B2BEC adoption (Teo and Ranganathan 2004). Senior managers not only wish to evaluate their B2BEC investments in terms of business measures and productivity gains but also want to find out where value has arisen in many areas of the organization as well as how to measure the electronic commerce initiatives (Zhu and Kraemer 2002).

Therefore, the main objectives of this exploratory research are: (1) to establish current practices and norms in managing B2BEC evaluation in Australian organizations; and (2) to develop a framework of challenges and critical success factors in B2BEC evaluation. In-depth case studies were conducted in nine Australian organizations within the hospitality sector. A key contribution of the book chapter is to identify and examine challenges and critical success factors faced by Australian organizations undertaking B2BEC evaluation. Moreover, a framework was proposed for Australian organizations to measure their B2BEC investments.

2. Literature Review

IDC forecasts that B2B worldwide along will hit US$7.6 trillion in 2009, a significant increase on the US$6.8 trillion of 2004 (this included both B2B and B2C) (Greenberg 2000; IDC 2005). An earlier IDC report indicated that Australian B2BEC spending reached A$11.83 billion in 2001 (Pearce, 2002). In the Asia-Pacific region, it will be worth US$270 billion a year by 2003, about 20 percent of the world total (webMethods 2001). IDC predicts that it will grow at compound annual growth rate of 22% (IDC 2005).

2.1. Business-to-Business Electronic Commerce and Evaluation

As indicated earlier, the growth of B2B has outpaced all other forms of electronic commerce, thus it represents the largest growth sector, in terms of revenues, in electronic commerce. B2BEC is an initiative which requires the participation of multiple firms making some sort of complementary investment to enable one another's EC strategy (Burn and Ash 2005; Lin et al. 2007a). Fahey et al. (2001) state that EC "embodies the most pervasive, disruptive, and disconcerting form of change: it leaves no aspect of managing organizations untouched, it challenges long-accepted business models, and organization leaders have little to draw on from their past experience to manage its effects" (p. 890).

Although the effective leverage and evaluation of IT investments in B2B can result in improved organizational performance (Lin et al. 2005b; Melville et al. 2004), there is little doubt that the less precisely bounded environment of B2B technology adds more complexity to the IT measurement problem as this type of investment is physically distributed between suppliers and vendors, making the evaluation process even more difficult (Zhuang 2005). The problem becomes more evident as IT is used to link the supply chain or to change the structure of industries, since costs and benefits have to be tracked across functional and organizational boundaries (Barua et al. 2004; Liu and Lin 2008). Existing business models are unequal to this task and planning for such systems has to encompass capabilities for managing and evaluating organizational capabilities to create value across the network of alliances and hence requires evolutionary approaches which can be tailored to business needs at different stages of organizational maturity (Lin et al. 2007a). Needless to say, many organizations find these issues challenging (Love et al. 2005; Tsao et al. 2004). They need methodologies to measure and monitor the performance of the specific contribution of inputs in generating outputs (Lin and Pervan, 2003) as well as their associated Internet channels such as B2B (Kim and Umanath 2005).

2.2. Constraints and Challenges to B2BEC Evaluation

Therefore, it appears that our current understanding of B2BEC evaluation has little impact on organizational practice, and factors such as power and politics which greatly affect the evaluation process are extremely difficult to identify and measure (Howcroft and McDonald 2004; Lin et al. 2007f). Failure to plan for and, derive the benefits from an IT investment such as B2BEC can have detrimental consequences on organizational performance (Lin et al. 2005a). Some of the major problems associated with B2BEC evaluation are:

- Organizations often fail to measure their B2BEC investments and identify relevant risks, costs, and benefits (Lin and Pervan 2003; Lin et al. 2008);
- Traditional financially oriented evaluation methods (e.g. ROI, NPV) can be problematic in measuring B2BEC investments and quantifying relevant benefits and costs (Lin and Huang, 2007a; Sugumaran and Arogyaswamy 2004);

- Organizations often have neglected to devote appropriate evaluation time and effort to IT investments such as B2BEC as well as to deal with the extended investment time frame. Organizations have failed to understand that B2BEC investments require richer evaluation approaches than mono-dimensional cost-benefit analysis (Stamoulis et al. 2002);
- The nature of electronic commerce technology makes it harder for organizations to allocate and assign costs and benefits to B2BEC projects, further blurring the lines of capital investment and return from IT spending in the B2B channel (Subramani 2004); and
- It is very difficult to evaluate intangibles and make relationship between B2BEC and profitability explicit (Lin et al. 2007b; Straub et al. 2002).

Indeed, many organizations have found that costs and benefits for B2BEC can be difficult to estimate and control (Giaglis et al. 1999; Lin et al. 2007c; Standing and Lin 2007). For instance, many organizations face a challenge of measuring and monitoring the performance of the specific contribution of inputs in generating outputs as well as its associated Internet channels (Kim and Umanath 2005). Moreover, other less quantifiable items such as loyalty, trust, knowledge, brand awareness, relationships, the boundaries of inter-organizational networks, value creation and customer satisfaction all makes the evaluation even more difficult (Lin et al. 2007d; Subramani 2004). Some new and old measures need to be differentially applied for evaluating phenomena such as electronic commerce and the Internet (Lin and Huang 2007a; Straub et al. 2002).

2.3. Limits-to-Value Model

The Limits-to-Value Model proposed by Chircu and Kauffman (2000) showed that possible IT investment constraints/challenges included valuation barriers (i.e. industry and organizational barriers) and conversion barriers (i.e. resource, knowledge, and usage barriers) to realize B2BEC benefits (see Figure 8.1). Many of the elements discussed in the model relate to the organization's ability to use IT effectively and this can potentially be one important constraint or challenge to B2BEC investments (e.g. Chircu and Kauffman 2000; Teece 1987). This is one issue that we seek to examine here. For example, the shortage of IT infrastructures remains to be one of the most critical constraints or challenges to IT investments (Chircu and Kauffman 2000). Organizations need to overcome these constraints or challenges to obtain as much realized B2BEC value from B2BEC investments as possible (Standing and Lin 2007). In addition, organizations need to have sufficient IT infrastructures such as complementary assets to overcome these constraints or challenges to realize the benefits of B2BEC investments (Chircu and Kauffman 2000; Lin et al. 2007a). Organizations are often unsuccessful in obtaining full value from their IT investments because they fail to invest sufficient complementary assets (Teece 1987). The complementary assets include new organizational processes, work routines, organizational knowledge, and responsibility structures. B2BEC investment constraints or challenges appear when organizations fail to invest in the requisite complementary assets.

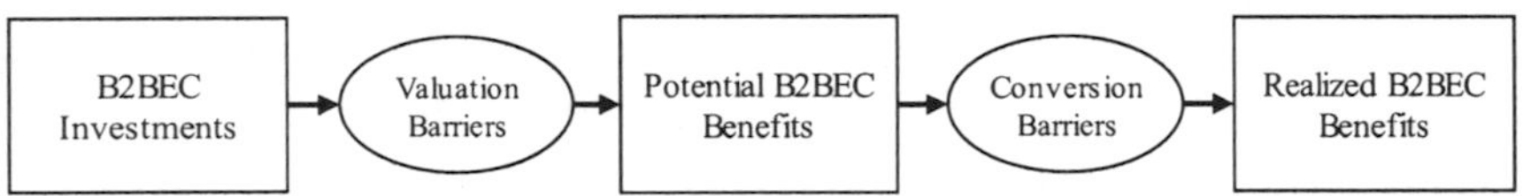

Figure 8.1: The limits-to-value model for B2BEC
(Source: adapted from Chircu and Kauffman (2000))

This research focuses on how the organizational valuation barrier (i.e. lack of integration with other IT systems) and conversion barrier (i.e. knowledge, resource, and usage barriers) affect the realization of B2BEC benefits in IT investments (Lin et al. 2007e).

2.4. Critical Success Factors for IT and B2BEC Adoption

According to Butler and Fitzgerald (1999), critical success factors (CSF) are the functions or areas where things must go right to ensure successful competitive performance for an organization. Several ways of identifying such factors are in use, including analysis of industrial structure, scanning of environments, industrial expert opinion, best practice analysis, analysis of competitors, assessing the internal feeling or judgment of companies, and data gathering about profit impact on market strategy (Leidecker and Bruno 1984; Lin et al. 2006). The literature furnishes many attempts at critical factor identification for the successful adoption of IT and/or B2BEC initiatives. For example, Eid et al. (2002) list twenty-one and classify them into five categories: marketing strategy, web site, global, internal, and external. Wirtz and Kam (2001) and Paulson (1993) identify fifteen and classify them into four categories: marketing strategy, internal, information technology, and governmental support. Hope et al. (2001) and Thatcher and Foster (2003) identify several critical factors related to B2BEC adoption such as organizational readiness, enterprise culture, marketing strategy, internal factors, information technology, and governmental support. Lin and Huang (2007b), Lin et al. (2007a), Standing and Lin (2007), and Tsao et al. (2004) have identified other factors such as IT investment evaluation methodologies, user involvement, organizational goals which are critical to the successful adoption of B2BEC.

3. Research Objective and Methodologies

Despite the growing popularity of B2BEC and its numerous benefits, there is very limited research on the effects of organizational benefits, critical success factors, and constraints or challenges on evaluation in Australia. There is much evidence to suggest that the integration of B2BEC evaluation rarely exists in organizations (Lin and Pervan 2003; Lin et al. 2007a; Murphy and Simon 2002). Therefore, the case study approach was utilized to investigate the process of B2BEC investment evaluation in Australian organizations. The key objectives of this exploratory research are: (1) to establish current practices and norms in managing B2BEC evaluation in Australian organizations; and (2) to development a framework of challenges and critical success factors in B2BEC evaluation.

Case studies were conducted with participants from nine Australian organizations within hospitality industry and their major IT contractors (see Table 8.1 below). The questions asked related to their major IT contracts, contractual relationship between these organizations and contractors, and IT investment evaluation methodology or technique deployed. Other data collected included contract documents, planning documents and minutes of relevant meetings. Transcripts were coded and analyzed. Semi-structured interviews were used to gain a deeper understanding of issues. Qualitative content analysis by Miles and Huberman (1994) was used to analyze the data from the case study. The analysis of the case study results was conducted in a cyclical manner and the results were checked by other experts in the field. Finally, the guidelines set out by Klein and Myers (1999) for conducting and evaluating interpretive field studies in information systems were also followed in an attempt to improve the quality of this research by minimizing some of the case study's main weaknesses mentioned above (e.g. human subjectivity and inexperienced researcher).

Table 8.1: Demographics of participating organizations

Participating organization	Position of interviewees	Use of formal/informal evaluation methods/processes	Number of IT projects examined in this research
1	IT & External contract managers	Yes	3
2	IT & External contract managers	No	5
3	IT Director & External contract manager	No	2
4	IT & External contract managers	Yes	3
5	IT & External contract managers	No	4
6	IT & External contract managers	Yes	2
7	IT & External contract managers	No	5
8	IT & External contract managers	No	3
9	CIO & External contract manager	Yes	4

4. Research Findings

A number of issues arose from the analysis of case study data and the key issues are presented below.

4.1. Organizational Barriers and Motivation Factors

Lack of clearly defined strategy and business objectives

There appeared to be a lack of obvious linkage between the expected outcomes of the e-commerce projects adoption and organizational goals. According to Mirani and Lederer (1993), alignment with stated organizational goals has a key bearing on how investment is organized and conducted, and the priorities that are assigned to different IT investment proposals. Objectives for adopting the B2BEC systems by organizations varied greatly. The objectives mentioned by most organizations were basically those benefits that were expected to be delivered by the e-commerce systems. They were all related to the improved custom services, cost savings and time savings. As previously suggested by studies conducted in other countries (e.g. Enterprise Ireland, 2004 in Ireland; Levy et al. 2001 in UK; Locke and Cave 2002 in New Zealand), many organizations simply failed to establish a linkage between the reasons for adopting an e-commerce system and their organizational goals. These systems were often installed without linking the benefits to their organizational goals.

Lack of interest in B2BEC from supplier or buyers

Case studies also revealed that there was a lack of interest in B2B-EC from supplier or buyers in relation to B2BEC. Good B2BEC system integration with other organizational systems is critical. However, according to Clay and Strauss (2002), lack of B2BEC system integration is one of the most cited reasons for B2BEC failure. Most participating organizations had great difficulties or simply failed to integrate their B2BEC system with other functions. Most did not have an IT strategy to integrate their B2BEC with other systems. They implemented B2BEC just to obtain gains promised by the vendors but did not believe that B2BEC could be integrated with other functions within their organizations. Proper integration of B2BEC and other functions of organizations clearly required a lot of managerial, financial, and technical resources as well as organizational capabilities. Organizational benefits arising from these B2BEC systems were often been hampered by the lack of integration with other functions. Furthermore, only organizations with higher level of IT maturity which had more sophisticated B2BEC and had been using it for a while had seen the integration of various functions as a main benefit. In fact, only those few organizations with high level of IT maturity had its B2BEC extensively integrated with other functions within the organization.

Lack of sponsorship by business

Results indicated that problems arising from the lack of sponsorship by business such as lack of internal management sponsorship & desire as well as management time and focus can have negative impact on organizational capabilities and benefits. Obtaining top management commitment throughout the implementation stage was found to be critical to the success of the IT investments in e-commerce (Power, 2004). Most organizations interviewed indicated that their senior executives had provided sufficient management leadership as well as obtained necessary organizational commitment towards the implementation of IT investments in e-commerce. Most senior executives were very enthusiastic about their IT investments in e-commerce during the implementation stage.

4.2. Conversion Barriers and User Factors

Low employee motivation/interest in B2BEC implementation & use

It appeared that most organizations' top management was not aware that there was some dissatisfaction and resistance among their employees or users regarding the implementation of some of their IT investments in e-commerce. No obvious user resistance management plan was put in place by most organizations interviewed. Therefore, it was not surprising that to find that employees' reaction about adopting these systems was not taken into account by these organizations. Although most senior managers knew good user resistance management was a critical part of successful adoption of any IT investments in B2BEC, it appeared that there was significant resistance by users during the implementation of these systems. Very few organizations had taken steps to alleviate user resistance during the implementation stage by, for example, involving users in the planning stage, as mentioned by Lin and Shao (2000). Many users and even customers complained about not being consulted and informed about the B2BEC investments during the adoption and implementation stages.

Lack of understanding of B2BEC evaluation

The confusion among case study participants about what constitutes a formal B2BEC investment evaluation methodology demonstrated a lack of understanding of such methodologies. This may be due to the fact that these Australian organizations were unable to introduce a formal B2BEC investment evaluation methodology due to constraints in time, expertise and costs. In addition, many organizations stated that there was a lack of understanding of the impact of the proper B2BEC investments evaluation and benefits realization processes (Lin and Pervan 2003; Lin et al. 2007a).

Lack of user involvement/participation in B2BEC adoption

The relevant literature has stressed that there is a direct relationship between user involvement and system success (Lin and Shao 2000). However, the adoption and use of the B2BEC systems by the Australian organizations interviewed were generally forced upon the employees by the senior management. Many stakeholders and users within the organizations interviewed said they were not extensively consulted beforehand and were not involved in the designing and adoption of these systems. Those organizations which kept the users and customers in the dark would tend to have low usage for their systems. Furthermore, many benefits expected from the adoption of these systems were mainly tailored for the senior managers.

4.3. Conversion Barriers and Resource Factors

Lack of B2BEC resources (technical, human capital and financial)

Responses from the participants revealed that there was a lack of B2BEC-related resources: lack of financial resources, lack of B2B technical expertise, and lack of managerial expertise. All of the organizations interviewed had Internet access and agreed that the further adoption of IT will be an important factor for the future success of the organization. The participating organizations indicated that they had used email to communicate with their customers and suppliers and to increase internal efficiencies. All but one of the organizations interviewed had a website. However, half of these organizations failed to utilize their websites to conduct business effectively with their customers and suppliers. Many organizations indicated that they had insufficient technical, human capital, and financial resources to implement and maintain the sort of websites that they required to effectively conduct their business online. Most users were not satisfied with the B2BEC projects that had been adopted by their organizations.

Evaluation for any electronic commerce initiatives is difficult and requires much more rigorous evaluation process (Straub et al., 2004). However, only a handful of organizations interviewed had carried out some sort of evaluation processes (i.e., KPI analysis, qualitative analysis). The other organizations were simply relied on their senior management's impressions or gut feeling/intuition. For example, when asked about the evaluation process, one senior manager from the travel industry admitted that there was no formal evaluation process and said: "We didn't use any evaluation process for our B2BEC projects" Most organizations indicated that either they did not have the capability and resources to do so or they did not know they had no evaluation process. While almost all of the senior managers interviewed thought it would be worthwhile to do it, most of them simply did not do it or relied on their intuition. In addition, many respondents simply said they did not know who was responsible for evaluation or said it was others who should be doing it.

4.4. The B2BEC Evaluation Challenges and Critical Success Factors Framework

As mentioned earlier, one key objective of this exploratory research is to develop a framework of challenges and critical success factors for B2BEC evaluation that can help senior managers to better manage their B2BEC initiatives as well as to ensure that the benefits expected are actually realized in order to improve their organisation's long term profitability. This framework has been developed from the extensive literature review and case study results (Figure 8.2). The following paragraph briefly describes the framework.

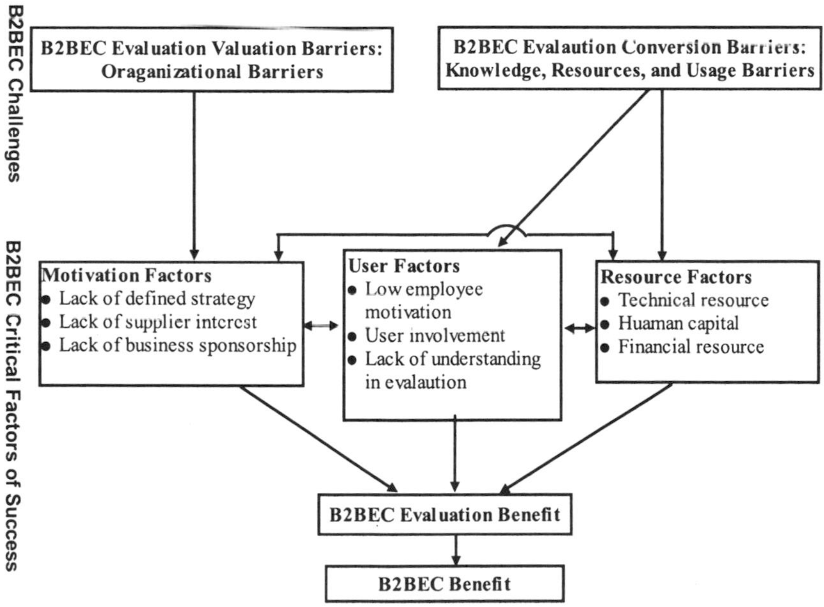

Figure 8.2: The B2BEC Evaluation Challenges and Critical Success Factors Framework

The framework is consist of two major barriers or challenges that need to be overcome in order to realize evaluation benefits which in turn assist in producing organizational B2BEC benefits. The three main factors (motivation, user and resource) are the key critical success factors which organizations should pay attention in order to overcome the B2BEC evaluation valuation (organizational) and conversion (knowledge, resources, and usage) barriers. Motivation critical success factors include lack of clearly defined strategy and business objectives, lack of interest in B2BEC from suppliers or buyers, and lack of sponsorship by business. User critical success factors are made up of low employee motivation/interest in B2BEC implementation and use, and lack of understanding in B2BEC evaluation whereas resources critical success factors include technical resources, human capital, and financial resources.

5. Conclusions

Case studies were conducted in nine Australian organizations which sought B2BEC services and expertise from external contractors. While these organizations appear to operate without any major problem, the mostly negative issues shown above indicate weaknesses in the way it deals with the motivation, user, and resource factors in relation to overcoming valuation and conversion barriers or challenges. The problems mentioned in the above issues were caused by the lack of attention to B2BEC evaluation with respect to the above-mentioned critical success factors.

So why didn't these organizations formally evaluate its B2BEC? One possible explanation was that none of the IT staff was familiar with the formal B2BEC evaluation process. Seddon et al. (2002) suggest that under some circumstances cost of formal B2BEC evaluations may seem likely to exceed benefits. However, the results from the case studies indicate that the use of a evaluation methodology enabled greater control and better management of B2BEC contracts.

One key contribution of the research is the development of the B2BEC Evaluation Challenges and Critical Success Factors Framework. The framework suggests that the three main factors (motivation, user and resource) can assist organizations in overcoming their valuation and conversion challenges and constraints. Paying close attention to these critical success factors will enable organizations to reap benefits from their B2BEC investments.

Despite large investments in B2BEC over many years, it has been difficult for organizations to determine where benefits have occurred, if indeed there have been any. B2BEC evaluation practice remains a hotly debated topic in the IS literature. Little published work has been conducted in Australia and there is still a lot to be learned in the area of processes and practices of B2BEC evaluation and benefits management. We hope that more studies of the practice of B2BEC evaluation will benefit other researchers in this field. Through the case study results presented in this chapter it is hoped that better approaches may be developed for Australian organizations.

References

Barua, A., Konana, P. and Whinston, A. B. (2004) An Empirical Investigation of Net-Enabled Business Value, MIS Quarterly, Vol. 28, No. 4, pp. 585-620.

Burn, J M. and Ash, C. G. (2005) A Dynamic Model of e-Business Strategies for ERP Enabled Organisations, Industrial Management and Data Systems, Vol. 105, No. 8, pp. 1084-1095.

Butler, T. and Fitzgerald, B. (1999) Unpacking the Systems Development Process: An Empirical Application of the CSF Concept in a Research Context, Journal of Strategic Information Systems, Vol. 8, No. 4, pp. 351-71.

Chan, C. and Swatman, P. M. C. (2003) International Examples of Large-Scale Systems – Theory and Practice IV: B2B E-Commerce Implementation in the Australian Context, Communications of the Association for Information Systems, Vol. 11, pp. 394-412.

Chau, P.Y.K. and Jim, C.C.F. (2002) Adoption of Electronic Data Interchange in Small and Medium Sized Enterprises, Journal of Global Information Management, Vol. 10, No. 4, pp. 61-85.

Chircu, A.M. and Kauffman, R.J. (2000) Limits to value in electronic commerce-related IT investments, Journal of Management Information Systems, Vol. 17, No. 2, pp. 59-80.

Clay, K. and Strauss, R. P. (2002) Institutional Barriers to Electronic Commerce: An Historical Perspective, Advances in Strategic Management, Vol. 19, pp. 247-273.

Cutler, M. and Sterne, J. (2000) E-Metrics: Business Metrics for the New Economy, NetGenesis, Source: [On-Line]: http://www.netgen.com/emetrics/.

Domaracki, G. S. (2001) The Dynamics of B2B E-Commerce. AFP Exchange, July/August, pp. 50-57.

du Plessis, M. and Boon, J. A. (2004) Knowledge Management in eBusiness and Customer Relationship Management: South African Case Study Findings, International Journal of Information Management, Vol. 24, pp. 73-86.

Eid, R., Trueman, M. and Ahmed, A. M. (2002) A Cross-Industry Review of B2B Critical Success Factors, Internet Research: Electronic Networking Applications and Policy. Vol. 12, No. 2, pp. 110-123.

Enterprise Ireland (2004) IT/eBusiness Status and Issues of Small and Medium Sized Irish SMEs, BSM Ltd Report, available on-line at: http://www.enterprise-ireland.com/ebusiness/eBIT_ICTissues.htm.

Fahey, L., Srivastava, R. Sharon, J. S. and Smith, D. E. (2001) Linking e-Business and Operating Processes: The Role of Knowledge Management. IBM Systems Journal, Vol. 40, No. 4, pp. 889-908.

Fensel, D. Omelayenko, B. Ding, Y., Klein, M., Schulten, E., Botquin, G., Brown, M., Flett, A., and Dabiri, G. (2002) Intelligent Information Integration in B2B Electronic Commerce, Kluwer Academics Publishers, Boston.

Giaglis, G. M., Paul, R. J. and Doukidis, G. I. (1999) Dynamic Modelling to Assess the Business Value of Electronic Commerce, International Journal of Electronic Commerce, Vol. 3, No. 3, pp. 35 – 51.

Greenberg, P. A. (2000) B2B E-Commerce: The Quiet Giant, E-Commerce Times, Source: [On-Line] http://ecommercetimes.com.

Hope, B. G., Hermanek, M., Schlemmer, C. and Huff, S. L. (2001) Critical Success Factors in the Development of Business-to-business Electronic Commerce, Journal of Information Technology – Case and Applications, Vol. 3, pp. 7-33.

Howcroft, D. and McDonald, R. (2004) An Ethnographic Study of IS Investment Appraisal, The 12th European Conference on Information Systems (ECIS2004), Turku, Finland, June 14-16.

Hsiao, R. (2003) Technology Fears: Distrust and Cultural Persistence in Electronic Marketplace Adoption, Journal of Strategic Information Systems, Vol. 12, pp. 169-199.

IDC (2005) Worldwide Internet Usage and Commerce 2005-2009 Forecast update, IDC, USA.

Irani, Z. (2002) Information Systems Evaluation: Navigating Through the Problem Domain, Information and Management, Vol. 40, pp. 11-24.

Kaefer, F. and Bendoly, E. (2004) Measuring the Impact of Organizational Constraints on the Success of Business-to-business E-commerce Efforts: A Transactional Focus, Information and Management, Vol. 41, pp. 529-541.

Kandampully, J. (2003) B2B Relationships and Networks in the Internet Age, Management Decision, Vol. 41, No. 5, pp. 443-451.

Kim, K. K. and Umanath, N. S. (2005) Information Transfer in B2B Procurement: An Empirical Analysis and Measurement, Information and Management, Vol. 42, No. 6, pp. 813-828.

Klein, H. K. and Myers, M. D. (1999) A Set of Principles for Conducting and Evaluating Interpretive Field Studies in Information Systems, MIS Quarterly, Vol. 23, No. 1, pp. 67-94.

Kleist, V. F. (2003) An Approach to Evaluating E-Business Information Systems Projects, Information Systems Frontiers, Vol. 5, No. 3, pp. 249-263.

Laudon, K. and Laudon, J. (2004) Management Information Systems: Managing the Digital Firm, Pearson Education, Inc., New Jersey, USA.

Lee, C. Y., Seddon, P., and Corbitt, B. (1999) Evaluating the Business Value of Internet-based Business-to-Business Electronic Commerce, Proceedings of 10th Australasian Conference on Information Systems (ACIS 1999), Wellington, New Zealand, 1 - 3 December.

Leidecker, J.K. and Bruno, A.V. (1984). Identifying and Using Critical Success Factors. Long-Range Planning, Vol. 17, No. 1, pp. 23-32.

Levy, M., Powell, P., and Yetton, P. (2001) SMEs: Aligning IS and the Strategic Context, Journal of Information Technology, Vol. 16, pp. 133-144.

Lin, C. and Huang, Y. (2007a) A Model of IT Evaluation Management: Organizational Characteristics, IT Evaluation Methodologies, and B2BEC Benefits, Lecture Notes in Computer Science, September, pp. 149-158.

Lin, C. and Huang, Y. (2007b) An Integrated Framework for Managing eCRM Evaluation Process, International Journal of Electronic Business, Vol. 5, No. 4, pp. 340-359.

Lin, C. and Pervan, G. (2003) The Practice of IS/IT Benefits Management in Large Australian Organizations, Information and Management, Vol. 41, No. 1. pp. 13-24.

Lin, C., Huang, Y. and Burn, J. (2007a) Realising B2B e-Commerce Benefits: The Link with IT Maturity, Evaluation Practices, and B2B e-Commerce Adoption Readiness, European Journal of Information Systems, Vol. 16, No. 6, pp. 806-819.

Lin, C., Huang, Y. and Tseng, S. (2007f) A Study of Planning and Implementation Stages in Electronic Commerce Adoption and Evaluation: The Case of Australian SMEs. Contemporary Management Research, Vol. 3, No. 1, pp. 83-100.

Lin, C., Huang, Y., and Cheng, M. (2007c) The Adoption of IS/IT Investment Evaluation and Benefits Realization Methodologies in Service Organizations: IT Maturity Paths and Framework, Contemporary Management Research, Vol. 3, No.. 2, pp. 173-194.

Lin, C., Huang, Y., Cheng, M., and Lin, W. (2007b) Effects of Information Technology Maturity on the Adoption of Investment Evaluation Methodologies: A Survey of Large Australian Organizations, International Journal of Management, Vol. 24, No. 4, pp. 697-711.

Lin, C., Lin, K., Huang, Y., and Kuo, W. (2006) Evaluation of Electronic Customer Relationship Management: The Critical Success Factors, The Business Review, Cambridge, Vol. 6, No. 2, pp. 206-212.

Lin, C., Pervan, G. and McDermid, D. (2007d) Issues and Recommendations in Evaluating and Managing the Benefits of Public Sector IS/IT Outsourcing, Information Technology and People, Vol. 20, No. 2, pp. 161-183.

Lin, C., Pervan, G., and McDermid, D. (2005b) IS/IT Investment Evaluation and Benefits Realization Issues in Australia, Journal of Research and Practices in Information Technology, Vol. 37, No. 3, pp. 235-251.

Lin, C., Pervan, G., Lin, H-C, and Tsao, H. (2008) An Investigation into Business-to-Business Electronic Commerce Organizations, Journal of Research and Practices in Information Technology, Vol. 40, No. 1, pp. 3-18.

Lin, K., Lin, C. and Tsao, H. (2005a) IS/IT Investment Evaluation and Benefit Realization Practices in Taiwanese SMEs, Journal of Information Science and Technology, Vol. 2, No. 4, pp. 44-71.

Lin, W., Huang, Y., and Lin, C. (2007e) Information Technology Executives' View on the Factors that Influence the Success of Information Technology Investments, The Journal of Human Resource and Adult Learning, Vol. 3, No. 1, pp. 41-52.

Lin, W.T., and Shao, B.B.M. (2000) The Relationship Between User Participation and System Success: A Simultaneous Contingency Approach, Information and Management, Vol. 37, pp. 283-295.

Liu, Y. and Lin, C. (2008) How Are Public Sector Organizations Assessing their IT Investments and Benefits - An Understanding of Issues For Benchmarking, International Journal of Advanced Information Technologies, Vol. 2, No.2, pp. 86-100.

Locke, S., Cave, J. (2002) Information Communication Technology in New Zealand SMEs, Journal of American Academy of Business, Vol. 2, No. 1, pp. 235-240.

Love, P.E.D., Irani, Z., Standing, C., Lin, C. and Burn, J. (2005) The Enigma of Evaluation: Benefits, Costs and Risks of IT in Small-Medium Sized Enterprises, Information and Management, Vol. 42, No. 87, pp. 947-964.

McGaughey, R. E. (2002) Benchmarking Business-to-business Electronic Commerce, Benchmarking: An International Journal, Vol. 9, No. 5, pp. 471-484.

McIvor, R. and Humphreys, P. (2004) The Implications of Electronic B2B Intermediaries for the Buyer-Supplier Interface, International Journal of Operations & Production Management, Vol. 24, No. 3, pp. 241-269.

Melville, N., Kraemer, K. and Gurbaxani, V. (2004) Review: Information Technology and Organizational Performance: An integrative Model of IT Business Value, MIS Quarterly, Vol. 28, No. 2, pp. 283-322.

Miles, M.B. and Huberman, A.M. (1994) Qualitative Data Analysis: An Expanded Sourcebook, Sage Publications, California.

Mirani, R. and Lederer, A.L. (1993) Making Promises: The Key Benefits of Proposed IS Systems, Journal of Systems Management, Vol. 44, No. 10, pp. 10-15.

Murphy, K. E. and Simon, S. J. (2002) Intangible Benefits Valuation in ERP Projects, Information Systems Journal, Vol. 12, pp. 301-320.

Ngai, E. W. T. and Wat, F. K. T. (2002) A Literature Review and Classification of Electronic Commerce Research, Information and Management, Vol. 39, pp. 415-429.

Paulson, J. (1993) EDI - An Implementation Review. Production and Inventory Management Journal, Vol. 34, No. 2, pp. 77-81.

Pearce, J. (2002) Australia's Rosy Outlook for B2B E-Commerce, ZDNet Australia, Source: [On-Line] http://www.zdnet.com.au/newstech/ebusiness/story/0,2000048590,20263951,00.htm

Pires, G. D. and Aisbett, J. (2003) The Relationship between Technology Adoption and Strategy in Business-to-Business Markets: The Case of E-Commerce, Industrial Marketing Management, Vol. 32, pp. 291-300.

Power, D. (2004) The Comparative Importance of Human Resource Management Practices in the Context of Business to Business (B2B) Electronic Commerce, Information Technology & People, Vol. 17, No. 4, pp. 380-406.

Quaddus, M. and Achjari, D. (2003) Electronic Commerce Success Model: An Empirical Study, 4th International We-B Conference, 24-25 November, Perth, Western Australia.

Raisinghani, M. S., Melemez, T., Zhou, L., Paslowski, C., Kikvidze, I., Taha, S., and Simons, K. (2005) E-Business Models in B2B: Process Based Categorization and Analysis of B2B Models, International Journal of E-Business Research, Vol. 1, No. 1, pp. 16-36.

Seddon, P., Graeser, V., and Willcocks, L. (2002): Measuring Organizational IS Effectiveness: An Overview and Update of Senior Management Perspectives, The DATA BASE for Advances in Information Systems, Vol. 33, No. 2, pp. 11-28.

Stamoulis, D., Kanellis, P., and Martakos, D. (2002) An Approach and Model for Assessing the Business Value of e-Banking Distribution Channels: Evaluation as Communication, International Journal of Information Management, Vol. 22, pp. 247-261.

Standing, C. and Lin, C. (2007) Organizational Evaluation of the Benefits, Constraints and Satisfaction with Business-To-Business Electronic Commerce, International Journal of Electronic Commerce, Vol. 11, No.3, pp. 107-153.

Steinmueller, W.E. (2002) 'Settling the e-CRM frontier: the experience of innovating European firms', Socio-Economic Trends Assessment for the Digital Resolution (STAR), Issue Report No. 23, September, pp.1-34.

Straub, D. Rai, A. and Klein, R. (2004) Measuring Firm Performance at the Network Level: A Nomology of the Business Impact of Digital Supply Networks, Journal of Management Information Systems, Vol. 21, No. 1, pp. 83-114.

Subramani, M. (2004) How Do Suppliers Benefit From Information Technology Use in Supply Chain Relationships, MIS Quarterly, Vol. 28, No.1, pp. 45-73.

Sugumaran, V. and Arogyaswamy, B. (2004) Measuring IT Performance: "Contingency" Variables and Value Modes, The Journal of Computer Information Systems, Vol. 44, No. 2, pp. 79-86.

Teece, D. J. (1987) Profiting from Technological Innovation: Implications for Integration, Collaboration, Licensing and Public Policy, In Teece D. J. (ed.) The Competitive Challenge, Harper and Row, New York, pp. 185-219.

Teo, T. S. H. and Ranganathan, C. (2004) Adopters and Non-adopters of Business-to-business Electronic Commerce in Singapore, Information and Management, Vol. 42, pp. 89-102.

Thatcher, S. M. B. and Foster, W. (2002) B2B E-Commerce Adoption Decision in Taiwan: The Interaction of Organizational, Industrial, Governmental and Cultural Factors, Proceedings of the 36th Hawaii International Conference on System Sciences (HICSS2003).

Tsao, H., Lin, K. H., and Lin, C. (2004) An Investigation of Critical Success Factors in the Adoption of B2BEC by Taiwanese Companies, The Journal of American Academy of Business, Cambridge, Vol. 5, No. 1/2, pp. 198-202.

Turban, E., King, D., Lee, J. and Viehland, D. (2004) Electronic Commerce 2004: A Managerial Perspective, Pearson Education International, New Jersey, USA.

webMethods (2001) Webmethods Aggresively Expands Presence In Asia Pacific, WebMethods Press Release, Source: [On-Line] http://www.webmethods.com.

Wirtz, J. and Kam, W. P. (2001) An Empirical Study on Internet-Based Business to Business E-Commerce in Singapore. Singapore Management Review, Vol. 23, No. 1, pp. 87-112.

Zeng, Y. E., Wen, H. J., and Yen, D. C. (2003) Customer Relationship Management (CRM) in Business-to-business (B2B) E-commerce, Information Management & Computer Security, Vol. 11, No. 1, pp. 39-44.

Zhu, K. and Kraemer, K. L. (2002) e-Commerce Metrics for Net-Enhanced Organizations: Assessing the Value of e-Commerce to Firm Performance in the Manufacturing Sector, Information Systems Research, Vol. 13, No. 3, pp. 275-295.

Zhuang, Y. (2005) Does Electronic Business Create Value For Firms? An Organizational Innovation Perspective, Journal of Electronic Commerce Research, Vol. 6, No. 2, pp. 146-159.

CHAPTER 9

THE DIFFUSION OF WEB 2.0 PLATFORMS: THE PROBLEM OF OSCILLATING DEGREES OF UTILIZATION

Tobias Kollmann, Christoph Stöckmann & Carsten Schröer

E-Business & E-Entrepreneurship Research Group, University of Duisburg-Essen, Germany

Following assumptions from the literature, in e-business scenarios, critical mass winners are destined for lasting progress and firm success. But the real life teaches another lesson. Apparently successful market leaders are frequently challenged by various inconveniences with the potential to jeopardize their market position. Due to occurring quantitative, qualitative and legal problems, a market is never settled. The chapter shows how a successful management can deal with the issue of oscillating degrees of utilization, in particular how to avoid ending up in a vicious circle and how to enhance the probability of initiating a virtuous circle to superior market success.

1. Critical Mass as a Success Factor

The extension of electronic networks and the use of information and telecommunication technologies for the digitalization of value creation lead to a new economic dimension (Lumpkin & Dess 2004). This newly established level of value creation, the so-called Net Economy, provides room for innovative business models and successful start-up firms (Kollmann 2006). An increasing number of companies participate in the economic potential of the internet which leads to a rising level of competition. Competing players either win a market and participate in a stable and sustainable business development or fail with their idea within a short period of time (Shapiro & Varian 1999). The roots of this phenomenon are derived from economies of scale effect that keeps aggravating itself instead of declining. Every new user of an offered web 2.0 platform helps to raise the value of a network and makes it even more attractive for further participants. A higher number of communication and transaction activities are the possible outcome. A rising quantity of community members also increases the perceived attractiveness (site stickiness) of a platform. This can be illustrated by the following two examples: A rising number of members subscribing to an E-Community (Kollmann 2006) raises the chance to meet likeminded individuals or to receive answers to posted questions. Also a rising number of users to an E-Marketplace (Kollmann 2006) rises the probability to find interested counterparts for offered products of a supplier.

According to the presented scenarios, a special focus has to be put on the critical mass phenomenon, because the subjectively perceived attractiveness of a system (e.g. community) is highly correlated with the already registered number of users. A certain number of users within a network are necessary to create value among the participants at a sophisticated level. Reaching this level is essential for a network, because the enrolled participants will be reinforced to use the system on an ongoing basis, and it will become easier to convince new users to join in (Kollmann, 1998). The minimum number of participants to maintain a sufficient utility on a long-term basis is referred to as the critical mass (Weiber 1992).

Especially in a Net Economy setting young companies experience a very competitive environment to reach the critical mass (Kollmann, 1998). Usually, the winners of this race oftentimes drive smaller competitors or copycats off the market. This conception reinforces itself in a Web 2.0 setting (O'Reilly 2005), where customers or members leave the status of pure information consumers. Their status changes to an active information provider and editor role (O'Reilly 2005). Therefore, growth at a fast pace in regards to the number of users becomes the critical success factor to leave the zone of competition as a winner. Actually, the winner of this battle is able to establish a close too monopolistic market position (Shapiro & Varian 1999). The attractiveness for new users to join a network is even higher, if everyone else already joined in.

Following the stated assumptions Web 2.0 critical mass winners are destined for lasting company performance and profits. But the real life teaches another lesson. Apparently successful market leaders are frequently challenged by various inconveniences with the potential to jeopardize their market position. In accordance with the theoretical model eBay for example, market leader for internet auctions, announced a growing number of membership accounts alongside with rising revenues and profits (eBay 2006). The unmentioned downside of this success story was a flood of insolvencies among professional eBay dealers. The International E-Business Association (IEBA), an association for power sellers, sees the roots for many discontinued businesses closely connected with an increasing number of sellers and a resulting higher level of competition. Both factors lower profits and force sellers to predatory pricing strategies. In this context insolvency reasons for most of the dealers are not on an individual, entrepreneurial level. They are based on the market characteristics of electronic marketplaces, and a substantial number of insolvencies by professional dealers of a platform will sooner or later hit the marketplace vendors. Other critical mass winners within the Web 2.0 environment like the online community MySpace or the video platform YouTube are not only the centre of interest because of their enormous growth rates and success stories. Critical notes about security issues, copyright violations, or identity theft and fraud affairs are also on the spot of public interest. Web 2.0 companies might face severe challenges, if the offered content on their platforms violates ethical or legal standards. Insufficient qualities of the offered content, as well as a mismatch between information supply and demand in the case of eBay, gain the potential for adverse effects for a market position.

Therefore, this chapter aims to show how quantitative, qualitative, as well as ethical and legal matters correspond with the market success of Web 2.0 platforms. In addition implications for the competition of platforms and the concept of critical mass as a foundation for success in the Net Economy will be discussed.

2. Web 2.0 Platforms in the Net Economy

In the past the internet used to be recognized as a technology to publish and distribute data, information and media content. This view was based on split-up roles: Private and commercial publishers of web content with an active role on the one hand, and passive consumers on the other hand. This golden rule changed in 2005, when Web 2.0 saw the light of day. A new category of website concepts was born. The established differentiation between active content providers and passive consumers diluted. Now users were able to generate and affect contents. User generated content became the slogan for the new internet. The active role of users built the basis for innovative business ideas, which were unthinkable some months ago. Many Web 2.0 business models, like the online community MySpace or the video platform YouTube, are centered around community structures. According to Kollmann (2006a) an E-Community facilitates contact and interaction between individuals or institutions via a digital network. Therefore, the integration of innovative ICT supports data- and knowledge transfer. These two features characterize the core activity for most of the Web 2.0 business models. Besides arranging and exchanging contacts and information, bringing together supply and demand for economic transactions, e.g. on an E-Marketplace (Kollmann 2006), is an integral feature of numerous platforms.

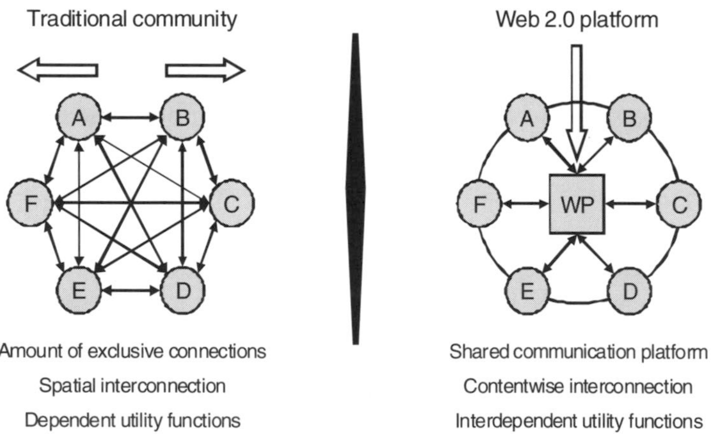

Figure 9.1: Illustration of traditional communities and Web 2.0 platforms

The common goal of Web 2.0 platforms is to win suppliers and consumers of information for their business model in order to match them (Kollmann 2006). Users of a Web 2.0 platform act alternating and parallel as information suppliers and consumers. Both activities have to be considered separately, because supplying and requesting information differ in regards to motivation and acceptance. This leads to a tripolar structure. The platform operator provides a matching service to perform an exchange of information or a business transaction at lower transaction costs (Lee & Clark 1996). The value of a platform not only depends on the operators' service capability and willingness to perform, but also on the contributions of the suppliers and consumers of information (derivative capability aspect). Platforms depend on queries. A higher number of queries provide a broader scope for matching activities (Kollmann 2001). Consequently a Web 2.0 platform is solely dependent on the participation willingness (acceptance) of its users. Therefore business development efforts concentrate on the so-called matching as a target parameter (Kollmann 2000, 2005).

When starting a platform, operators have to get awareness for their services. They are challenged by the question, which points are of interest to turn internet surfers into members or subscribers for a community, or respectively customers for a marketplace. This goal can only be reached by offering a matching platform that delivers an acceptable service. Therefore the scientific construct of acceptance obtained growing relevance in the marketing of ICT products and services over time (Kollmann 2001). The reason for this is that ICT technologies and applications (e.g. interactive TV, internet, cellular phones) need a specific pattern of utilization. The pure purchase is not an indicator for further activities of a user and therefore not a sufficient indicator for the economic success of a platform operator. Augmenting this idea, a full acceptance of a Web 2.0 platform is closely linked to three conditions:

(i) *Connecting* (Access to the platform): The customers have to get access to a platform via security code (e.g. log-in) or provided access software. A first time registration process reflects the purchase.

(ii) *Acting* (Demand and contribution of information): The customers have to use the services of the electronic platform. Information has to be requested and provided. This opens up the potential for matching.
(iii) *Interacting* (Clearing and matching): The customers have to interact on the platform; otherwise a matching of requested and provided information cannot be executed.

Coordination of the participants is proceeded over the electronic platform (n information suppliers, m information consumers, and the platform operator without time and local limitations, see Figure 1). Information and data between two or more counterparts is solely shared on the platform. The active placement and intervention into the matching process leads to a new responsibility for the platform operator, because the result of each matching affects all participants.

The attractiveness of traditional communities and marketplaces is primarily determined by the numbers of participants as a quantitative measure for their availability (see Figure 9.1). The center of those system architectures is the exclusive connection between two counterparts (e.g. trade show or farmers market). The interaction between A and B usually has no direct qualitative effect for the utility of C. Technological external effects are conceivable under certain conditions, e.g. if all participants benefit from a network effect associated with the extension of a telephone network, or other monetary effects. However, this interpretation of a quantitative point of view is insufficient to explain attractiveness of progressive internet platforms.

In a Web 2.0 system the interconnection of participants does not consist of exclusive one-on-one data links. An E-Community or E-Marketplace as a commonly shared platform represents the center of the system architecture (see Figure 1). Information of a database is available for every user on the network. Options to alter, comment, or expand the provided content are inherent to the system. A transparent provision of information leads to direct effects on the qualitative utility function of C (economies of scope), if A and B exchange information. An agreeing or derogative comment of B to a contribution from A, may lead to a valuation of C regarding the statement. Further, as Pavlou and Gefen

(2005) state, a psychological contract violation with an individual seller is proposed to prompt a generalized perception of contract violation with the entire community of sellers in a marketplace. Internet auctions for a specific item are open to several participants. The bid of A has a direct impact on the utility function of all other bidders. The following paragraph will deal with the resulting implications for the diffusion of Web 2.0 platforms.

3. The Diffusion of Web 2.0 Platforms

Research on diffusion provides answers to the question how an innovation will spread on a market (Rogers 2003; Pavlou & Fygenson 2006). Services of a Web 2.0 platform, which are offered as a commercial product, could be part of a study on diffusion, too. Research in this field is based on the presumption of a recurring use (acceptance) of a product or service, not on a onc-time purchase (adoption). In regards to the diffusion of Web 2.0 platforms the following three questions are of interest:

- Which factors have an impact on the diffusion of a Web 2.0 platform on a market?
- How fast does a Web 2.0 platform spread on a market?
- What are the growth characteristics of a network?

The successful diffusion of a Web 2.0 platform is completed, if all interactions of a defined market are handled by this platform. For the evaluation of diffusion the aforementioned quantitative alignment of the network effect (higher number of participants = higher probability to find appropriate counterparts for interaction) appears with an economies of scope effect (nature, size and trend of an executed transaction, including its impact on the overall system). The following paragraphs will analyze the main problem areas of diffusion and oscillating degrees of utilization in the light of both effects.

3.1. Problem Areas of Diffusion

The diffusion of a Web 2.0 platform is associated with quantitative, qualitative, ethical and legal challenges. Those issues will be discussed in the following.

3.1.1. Quantitative Problem Areas

Attractiveness of a web platform is significantly linked to the number of participants. A higher participation level raises the chance to reach other individuals. Every information supply (e.g. a provided video) as well as every information demand (e.g. on a personal level) need at least one counterpart to enable a platform provider to match requests. The service of the platform provider creates an indirect utility that is derived from the usage of an interactive relationship within the communication system, the so-called derivative capability aspect (Katz & Shapiro 1985; Farrell & Saloner 1985). The derivative utility following the usage increases with the number of participants and the intensity of use by the other participants (Weiber 1992). The result is a network effect. Common examples for goods with direct network effects are all types of ICT-systems. The utility of each participant is advanced with every new customer, who helps to grow the network. In connection with the bilateral customer orientation (information supply and demand) of the platform provider, specific characteristics within the diffusion of a platform can be derived for different development stages (Kollmann 2001).

1) *Chicken-and-Egg-Problem*: One reason for matching problems on a Web 2.0 platform is derived from the so-called Chicken-and-Egg-Problem (Durand 1983; Earston 1980). The following two examples aim to illustrate this circumstance. An insufficient number of suppliers or offers lead to an absence of customers on the platform. An insufficient number of customers or requests lead to a lack of suppliers. The dilemma situation, which counterpart (supplier or consumer) at first has to get involved with the platform, is deemed as an obstacle for the development of a business.

2) *Collateral-Critical-Mass-Problem:* The installed basis, i.e. the number of users already present in a platform, determines the utility of the platform for new users since a greater number of users also increases the number of potential interactions (Farrell & Saloner 1986). The larger the installed basis, the larger is the derivative utility for the participants (Kollmann 2001). Web 2.0-platform providers are confronted with a collateral critical mass, because of the bilateral orientation (Kollmann 1998). Suppliers need a certain level of counterparts or requests, in order to commit to or use a marketplace. Simultaneously, a certain level of suppliers or offers has to be provided, in order to persuade a customer to facilitate a marketplace. This problem supersedes itself, if the customer base on both sides grows to a sufficient point, where the derivative utility exceeds a certain level.
3) *Equilibrium-Problem*: Bilateral matching results in a mutual state of dependence regarding the number of suppliers and consumers, and respectively their offers and requests. Consequently the platform provider has to take into consideration that offers and requests almost equate themselves. Bilateral marketing activities support this endeavor (Kollmann 1998) and help maintaining a high matching level (one offer = one request).

3.1.2. Qualitative Problem Areas

Contrary to the established belief in an exclusive utilization act between supplier and consumer interaction, the critical phase of a matching includes an additional economies of scope effect associated with the quality of interaction. The decision to subscribe to and use a platform has to be expanded. Besides complying with quantitative issues, meeting the qualitative requirements of the suppliers and consumers with information is of equal importance. If they realize that the web platform complies with their demand and interaction needs, they are willing to utilize the platform's services. The following issues with regard to qualitative problems have to be solved (Kollmann 2001).

(a) *Matching-Performance-Problem*: An exclusive focus on the number of suppliers and consumers is insufficient to measure the quality of the interacting counterparts, as well as their level of satisfaction with regard to the exchange of information. The demanded level of interaction has to correspond with the expectations of the participants. The degree of satisfaction is closely linked to three core areas of need, which are information, relationships, and business (Hagel & Amstrong 1997), as well as the related concept of the heterogeneity-dependent level of commitment. Participants look for like-minded individuals on a platform and relevant content to fulfill their information needs. New discussion threads have to be established to acquire additional members, which cover further fields of interest. Platform operators are exposed to a dilemma situation, because of the diametrical impact of the heterogeneity of discussion threads with regard to a growing member base and the persistent commitment of current participants.

(b) *Reality-Check-Problem*: The structural conditions of virtual platforms disallow to validate provided information with reality. Anonymous publishing options among some platforms aggravate this issue. Information and reality fall apart frequently. Some of those discrepancies occur inadvertently, e.g. if a change of address is not entered into a database or an information is provided on a non-current standard of knowledge. More frequently intentional misrepresenting takes place by sugar-coating one's profile on the web, or even worse with criminal intention. Because the roots of a reality gap are unknown to the participants, misrepresentations might reduce the commitment or ongoing patronage of a user.

3.1.3. Ethical and Legal Issues

The addressed willful misrepresentation is an example for the multitude of ethical and legal issues associated with user generated content, among other legal problems of internet platforms and their foundation. Current lawsuits on those topics will give answers to important questions and provide future guidance on duties of Web 2.0 platform operators. Liabilities for provided content on a company's website and linked content from external sources, as well as infringements of users (e.g. announcement of a criminal offense) and related duties of care have to be clarified. The results of those decisions will inevitably have a major impact on the further diffusion and development of Web 2.0 platforms. In the following section two problems will be discussed.

- *Freedom-of-Expression-Problem*: Despite the fact that every human being possesses the right to express an opinion, legal and ethical standards have to be obeyed. Sometimes those standards are violated on anonymous web-based communication platforms. Comments with an extremist, offending, or sexually harassing content cannot be tolerated by any platform operator. Other categories, like advertising and promotion activities, can be classified as unwanted too. Guidance for communication on the internet is given by the so-called netiquette, derived from internet and etiquette. The recommended behavior of the netiquette is not legally binding, but helps to maintain and develop a positive net culture. The voluntary agreed upon rules are frequently incorporated in codes of conduct of platform operators. A breach of the rules leads to a closing of discussion threads, cancelation of comments, or dismissal of accounts, because a negative communication culture bears the lasting potential to lower the acceptance of a platform.
- *Adoption-of-External-Content-Problem*: Particularly on video platforms users provide, intentionally or unintentionally, copyrighted material from other websites or real sources. By now, copyright holders mandate agencies to retrieve their protected material. The platform operator is responsible for inflicting penalties of participants and to remove copyrighted materials. Preventing an upload of protected material is virtually impossible, because the violation of a copyright just becomes apparent after a user has posted illegal content. Even reactive behavior leaves a legal stain on the platform operator's vest, as despite the fact of a fast content removal a breach of law already happened. Since there is no appropriate method available on the market to avoid the upload of copyrighted material, all prominent platform operators strive towards general licensing agreements with bailees. Those arrangements would allow

them to leave copyrighted material on their websites and protect them from costly lawsuits and negative impacts on their market penetration.

3.2. Oscillating Effects of Web 2.0 Platforms

The classical theory of diffusion was developed for so-called singular goods. Their diffusion proceeds with the act of buying. In a critical mass system the scope has to be extended by the variables of connecting and acting (see chapter Web 2.0 Platforms in the Net Economy) as constitutive determinates for diffusion (Weiber 1992). With traditional consumer and producer goods the act of buying creates a positive and irreversible impact for diffusion. However, ICT service contracts bear the risk of being cancelled (e.g. mobile phone contract, website account), which limits the chance to realize demand synergies. As an extreme example reversible utility could cause a declining diffusion (see Figure 2; Weiber 1992). The characteristics of a diffusion curve in a critical mass system generally do not reflect a monotonically increasing function; in fact a considerable drop is also possible.

3.2.1. Diffusion Characteristics

The traditional model needs an expansion within a Web 2.0 setting, because the connecting act is an insufficient parameter to evaluate diffusion. It is just a necessary requirement for adoption. The market success of a Web 2.0 platform depends directly on the participants' constant utilization and interaction as a reliable measure for adoption, and therefore acceptance (Kollmann 2001). An adequate utilization and interaction discipline supports a premium quality of information and knowledge transfer among the participants of a platform with positive effects for the whole market system. Also the recurring utilization and interaction is a prerequisite to realize constant cash flows for the platform operators. Accordingly the concept of diffusion has to be extended beyond the purchase dependent quantitative measure of participants to the utilization and interaction dependent quantitative interaction measure. The reversibility of utilization and interaction has to be considered in this context. Due to the planning interval the sequence of the three adoption and acceptance acts is interpreted as a discontinued multiple event. This process is characterized by permanent oscillations making diffusion a permanent companion. The reach of market saturation is not only linked with negative adoption and acceptance ratios, but also with alternating positive and negative ratios. The direct consequence is an oscillating development at market saturation level.

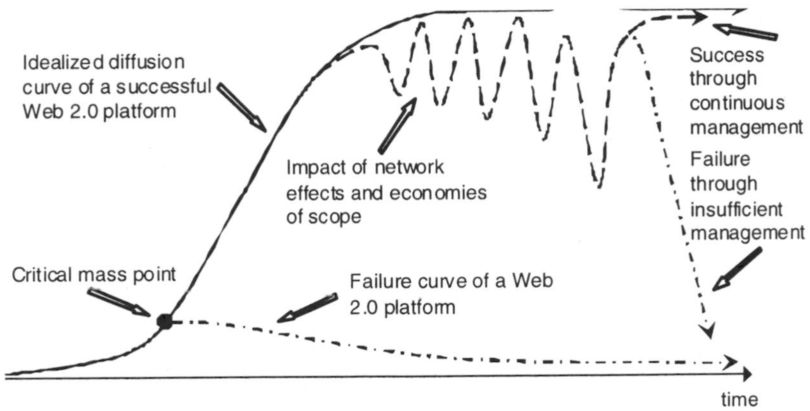

Figure 9.2: Diffusion of Web 2.0 platforms

This effect is caused by the circumstance of negative utilization and interaction levels, which lead to a renouncing or deregistration by the participants. The original decision of adoption is withdrawn. Potential reasons to resign are caused by effects from quantitative, qualitative, ethical and legal issues. Suppliers and consumers of information feel uncomfortable about these aspects. The interconnection of participants has a negative impact on their individual utility function and the whole market system. An oscillating diffusion is the result (see Figure 9.2). In this context special attention has to be paid to the proportion of information supply and demand. As postulated, both factors should create an equilibrium to meet all matching requests and create a high level of satisfaction among the community members. The ever-changing level of participants leads to an alternating level of supply and demand. Web 2.0 platforms with a transaction oriented business model (e.g. eBay) use the price of goods as an instrument to regulate the proportions of supply and demand. Even though the control mechanism does not converge, due to continuously changing prices and numbers as well as suppliers and consumers, an indifferent dynamic equilibrium is the possible outcome (see figure 3). Communication oriented platforms are faced with different challenges. A price based self-regulating mechanism does not exist in their business environment. Monitoring each market situation is important to perform intervening actions. From a platform operator's point of view the dynamic participation of suppliers and consumers is not necessarily associated with challenges. The dynamics reveal a harmful potential, if a critical supply surplus or excess demand is detected. Both scenarios cause the same effect (see Figure 9.3).

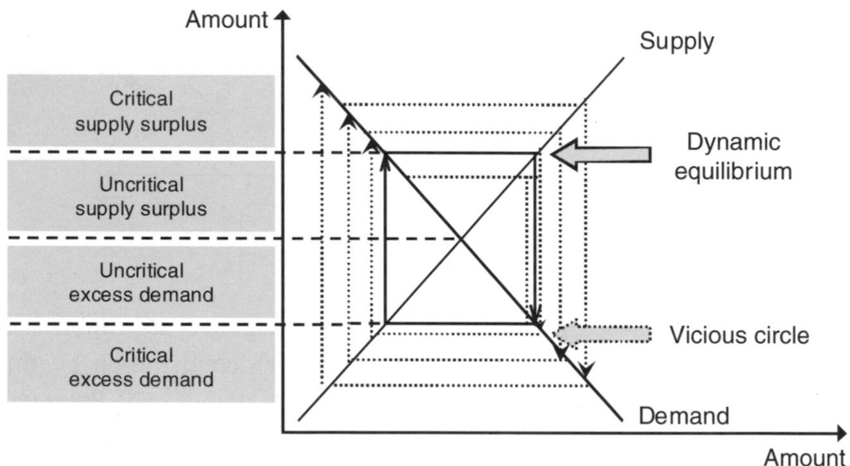

Figure 9.3: Adoption process of information supply and demand

The reduction of supply side participants will most likely lead to a decreasing information supply. Hence there is not enough potential to match all information requests. This causes a permanent loss of attractiveness on the demand side, as the offered information does not meet expectations. A lack of quantity and quality causes consumers to leave the platform. Likewise the lower number of requests makes it even more unattractive for suppliers to provide information. In this case the development of a platform does not induce an oscillation, but moreover a creeping and declining growth. Neither suppliers nor consumers of information are stimulated to return to the platform and utilize the services again (see Figure 3).

In conclusion, the control mechanism of supply and demand generates a self-aggravating effect with a positive (virtuous circle) and negative (vicious circle) development potential (Kollmann 1999). This control mechanism makes the management of a Web 2.0 platform complex, because the operator as an independent facilitator faces a bipolar user group simultaneously. Matching efforts should consider individual as well as general interaction requests to fulfill the expectation of opposed groups of interest.

The positive scenario (virtuous circle) in accordance with the critical mass effect leads to a continuous growth of power, achievement potential, and attractiveness of the platform. A significant gain of information suppliers typically shows an increase of requests with positive effects on the choice of the selected set of matching opportunities. In turn, the positive impact raises consumer satisfaction and the number of information requests. The flourishing demand for information lifts up the platform attractiveness for the suppliers and so forth (positive loop).

As stated before in this paragraph, changed market conditions may possibly restart a negative control mechanism. Within this vicious circle a significant loss of information suppliers leads to a clear reduction of requested information. Negative impacts on the number of choices for a matching lead to a high number of unmatched interaction demands. This has a negative impact on consumer satisfaction and consequently on the amount of information request. A declining demand reduces the attractiveness of the platform for suppliers, which leads to an ongoing downturn of supply and so forth (negative loop). The Web 2.0 platform could suffer from those effects by a continuous loss of power and achievement potential. At the bottom line the existence of the platform might be at stake.

The oscillating characteristics of the diffusion curve lead to serious implications regarding the management of a Web 2.0 platform and the competition between web-based communication platforms in general.

Those aspects along with the illustration of the critical mass effect as a success guarantee will be explained in the following paragraph.

3.2.2. Competition on diffusion

Competition in the Net Economy is characterized by an oscillating utilization of platforms. Therefore reaching a critical mass does not automatically assure a promising and stable development (see Figure 9.4). Even on saturated or apparently settled markets threats for critical mass winners occur on a frequent basis. Alleged losers or innovative start-up companies occasionally create surprisingly good chances to grow against reputable competition.

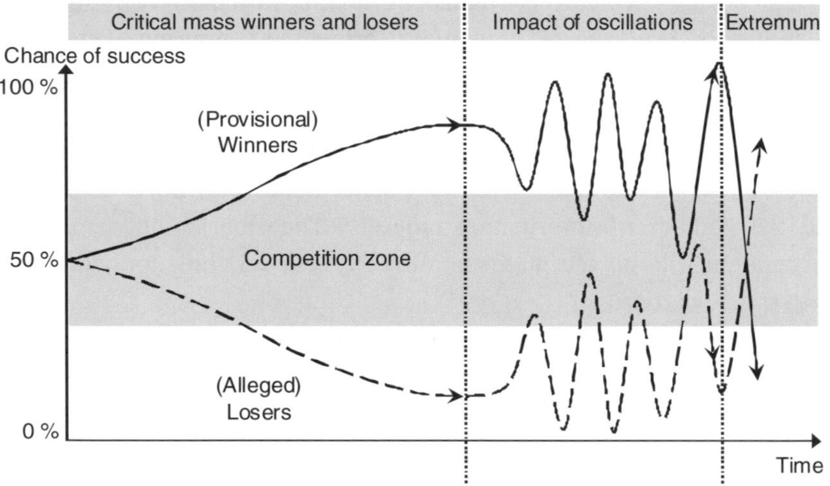

Figure 9.4: Competition in oscillating areas of conflict

As demonstrated, established Web 2.0 platforms are endangered to lose participants. In a worst case scenario they start a vicious circle with the potential to bring their company down. The goal of successful platforms is therefore to maintain equilibrium between the bipolar groups as well as safeguarding compliance with qualitative, legal, and ethical standards. Lasting survival is closely connected with a high level of commitment among the participants and protection against competition.

The continued management of a web platform becomes the critical factor of success. Provisional critical mass winners have to be on permanent alert, instead of relaxing in their accomplished position. Ongoing market evaluations and proactive influence on current developments on the respective network through bilateral marketing are inevitable.

Weak phases of critical mass winners provide opportunities for start-ups and established competitors to attack the supremacy of market leaders. The existence of financial strength and survivability supports the gain of market shares (see figure 4). It is unrealistic to turn around a market completely or drive a leader in a certain field off the market, but addressing special target groups with innovative niche products receives growing popularity. Current examples are university and high school student communities, which recently started their services. Starting a positive control mechanism (positive loop) is the beginning to overcome the critical mass sustainably. Especially young start-ups are confronted with the challenge to reach critical mass. Their brand name is usually unknown to the broad public and the network attractiveness of their platform is limited. But the value of a network product is not solely based on the number of participants. Future development expectations also play an influential role (Hagel & Armstrong 1997). Well timed and promising announcements to the market in advance (vapor marketing) and the management of expectations combined with additional online and offline marketing activities bear the potential to occupy a niche by the massive acquisition of new customers.

4. Conclusion

As described, the critical mass concept is of crucial importance in the age of Web 2.0. However, current developments show further challenges besides this success factor. Those challenges have to be taken into account with the management of a Web 2.0 platform, because they could have a severe impact on company development and performance. Finally competitors and founders of (new) ventures should keep in mind that a market is never settled, because of the ever changing and oscillating degrees of utilization. Therefore there is always a probability to loose or capture a market or at least to shrink or grow against competition.

Successful management can deal with the issue of oscillating degrees of utilization, in particular how to avoid ending up in a vicious circle and how to enhance the probability of initiating a virtuous circle to superior market success. Especially the permanent supervision of a platform regarding the compliance with quantitative, qualitative, as well as ethical and legal standards is of great importance. Adjustments to external market conditions, proactive management of the platform, and a bilateral marketing approach are keys for enduring success within the Net Economy.

References

Durand, P. (1983) The public service potential of videotext and teletext, Telecommunications Policy, Vol. 7, No. 6, pp. 149–162.

Earston, A. (1980) Viewpoint. Telecommunications Policy, Vol. 4, No. 9, pp. 220–225.

eBay (2006) eBay Inc. Announces fourth quarter and full year 2005 financial results. Retrieved March 31, 2007, from http://investor.ebay.com/news/Q405/EBAY0118-123321.pdf.

Farrell, J. and Saloner, G. (1985) Standardisation, compatibility and innovation. Rand Journal of Economics, Vol. 16, No. 1, pp. 70–83.

Farrell, J. and Saloner, G. (1986) Installed base and compatibility: Innovation, product, preannouncement and predation. American Economic Review, Vol. 76, No. 5, pp. 940–955.

Hagel, J. and Armstrong, A. G. (1997) Net gain. Boston, MA: Harvard Business School Press.

Katz, M. L. and Shapiro, C. (1985) Network externalities, competition, and compatibility, American Economic Review, Vol. 75, No. 3, pp. 424–440.

Kollmann, T. (1998) Marketing for electronic market places– the relevance of two critical points of success, Electronic Markets, Vol. 8, No. 4, pp. 36–39.

Kollmann, T. (1999) Virtual marketplaces: Building management information systems for internet brokerage. Virtual Reality, 4(4), pp. 275–290.

Kollmann, T. (2000) Competitive strategies for electronic marketplaces, Electronic Markets, Vol. 10, No. 2, pp. 102–109.

Kollmann, T. (2001) Measuring the acceptance of electronic marketplaces. Journal of Computer Mediated Communication, Vol. 2, No. 6, n.p.

Kollmann, T. (2005) The matching function for electronic market places – determining the probability of coordinating of supply and demand, International Journal of Electronic Business, Vol. 5, No. 3, pp. 461–472.

Kollmann, T. (2006) What is e-entrepreneurship? – Fundamentals of company founding in the net economy, International Journal of Technology Management, Vol. 33, No. 4, pp. 322–340.

Lee, H. G. and Clark, T. H. (1996) Impacts of the electronic marketplace on transaction cost and market Structure, International Journal of Electronic Commerce, Vol. 1, No. 1, pp. 127–149.

Lumpkin, G. and Dess, G. (2004) E-business strategies and internet business models: how the internet adds value, Organizational Dynamics, Vol. 33, pp. 161–173.

O'Reilly, T. (2005) What Is Web 2.0. Design patterns and business models for the next generation of software. Retrieved March 31, 2007, from http://www.oreillynet.com/pub/a/oreilly/tim/news/2005/09/30/what-is-web-20.html.

Pavlou, P. A. and Fygenson, M. (2006) Understanding and predicting electronic commerce adoption: An extension of the theory of planned behavior, MIS Quarterly, Vol. 30, No. 1, pp. 115–143.

Pavlou, P. A. and Gefen, D. (2005) Psychological contract violation in online marketplaces: Antecedents, consequences, and moderating role, Information Systems Research, Vol. 16, No. 4, pp. 372–399.

Rogers, E. M. (2003) Diffusion of Innovations (5th ed.). New York: Free Press.

Shapiro, C. and Varian, H. R. (1999) Information rules: A strategic guide to the network economy (Reprint), Boston: Harvard Business School.

Weiber, R. (1992) Diffusion von Telekommunikation, Wiesbaden: Gabler.

CHAPTER 10

APPLICATION OF WIRELESS TECHNOLOGIES IN MOBILE BUSINESS

Xiangzhu Gao

School of Commerce & Management, Southern Cross University, Australia

A generic definition of electronic business (e-business) is the utilisation of information and communication technologies (ICT) in support of all business activities. The e-business evolves with the advancement of ICT, especially the World Wide Web (Web). At its early stage, the Web was accessed basically by means of wired connection, which restrained its functionality and application. Sir Tim Berners-Lee, the inventor of the Web, described the access feature of a more powerful Web: "I would like to see more people reaching the Web from devices big and small, fixed and mobile." The development of wireless technologies and mobile devices makes it possible that people reach the Web from any place and at any time. The business activities supported by wireless technologies and mobile devices are known as mobile business (m-business). The m-business extends the e-business and creates additional opportunities in business process. In this chapter, the evolution of the Web, wireless technologies and mobile technologies are described, and their effect on and application in m-business are discussed. The scenarios in the discussion show practical applications of the technologies and their driving forces leading to possible futures in business perspectives. Readers do not need to have detailed knowledge of the wireless technologies.

1. Web Evolution

The Web has been evolving. People try to use version numbers to mark different stages of the Web in the evolution. However, definitions of the stages are debatable. In this chapter, the characteristics of the stages are described and explained in regard to e-commerce.

1.1. Web 1.0

Traditionally, the Web is a system of interlinked hypertext documents accessed via the Internet. Web sites provide static and read-only documents or Web pages including text and images. One can search and read Web pages with a Web browser. Widespread computer illiteracy and slow Internet connections added to the restrictions of Web 1.0. Dial-up Internet access is the main connection method, and average bandwidth is 50 Kb per second (50 Kbps). One-way flow of information from Web sites to browsers is the major feature of Web 1.0.

At this stage, an e-commerce Web site is an online presence of the brick-and-mortar business. The purpose of the Web site is to make the business available at any time and remove the geographical restrictions associated with a brick-and-mortar business. Features of e-commerce Web sites include dissemination of information in forms of simple text and images to partners, buyers and employees, catalogue display to present products to potential customers, shopping cart application to keep track of selected items, and transaction process to complete payments (Getting, 2007; Schneider, 2007). Customers read information and do shopping with computers physically connected to the Web.

1.2. Web 2.0

The shift from Web 1.0 to Web 2.0 is a result of technological refinements, which include such adoptions as broadband connection (averagely 1Mbps), improved browsers and multimedia contents of Web sites. Web 2.0 extends Web 1.0 with the functionality of interactivity and personalisation of Web-delivered contents. Web 2.0 Web sites allow users to do more than just retrieving information. Users can write to the Web sites, own the data on the Web sites and exercise control over the data. Web pages can be dynamically generated at runtime, and therefore personalised user-friendly interfaces are possible. Web 2.0 not only changes what is on the Web, but also how it works (Turban et al, 2008).

It allows users to run software applications entirely through a browser. The concept of Web-as-participation-platform captures many of these characteristics, contrasting with the Web-as-information-source of Web 1.0.

A this stage, personal computers are still the major devices to access the Web. The multimedia presentation of products and others is delivered to customers at a quicker speed, making easy and convenient shopping and resulting in better shopping experience. Dynamically generating Web pages allows customised product configuration and personalised shopping environment. Web blogs and social networking profiles allow consumers to share experience, make reviews and be informed of new products or services. This will create branding opportunities, customer interactivity and loyalty, as well as attract new buyers. Businesses use the Web as a platform to run software applications (for example audio or video players) to make Web sites more appealing and the sale or service more intuitive. Web 2.0 greatly improves e-commerce in regard to both business activities and customer shopping experience.

1.3. Web 3.0

There is already an abundance of definitions of Web 3.0, since the phrase was coined by New York Times journalist John Markoff in 2006 (Molloy, 2008). However, the definitions are not consistent. The followings are the basic features of Web 3.0:

- Machine understandability – The semantics of data and services on the Web is defined in a language, such as Extensible Markup Language (XML), so that computers can understand the Web contents and services. The Web with this feature is referred to as semantic Web.
- Intelligibility – Intelligent applications, as autonomous agents, can learn and reason to help users make best use of Web resources.
- Virtual reality – Web applications allow users to interact with computer-simulated environments, where the users can see, hear, speak, smell and/or feel.
- Mobility – The Web is wireless-accessible by means of mobile devices to achieve ubiquitous connectivity.

Semantic Web will improve accuracy of searching information so that the information can be shared easily and widely. For example, semantic advertising applies a meta language to a Web advertisement. Reading the meta language, a search engine can understand the meaning of the advertisement so that it can index the advertisement correctly. A good index can help searchers find their interesting Web pages accurately. When a consumer searches the Web for a product, the search engine matches the searching terms with the index to retrieve advertisements that are relevant to the search topic.

Figure 10.1: VR

In e-business, common intelligent agents include buyer agents and seller agents. A buyer agent can be sent out by buyers to help locate stores, brands, products and services, and desired prices. It can also make comparisons between similar products as well. A sell agent can help the seller track demand and market share changes, engage in competitive knowledge mining, and even learn through collaboration from buyer agents (Smith et al, 2000).

Shopping is by nature an unorganised process: customers look, touch, compare and move in what seems to be random walk (Walsh, 2002). In a virtual reality (VR) environment, customers can talk with businesses, see and even feel or smell products, as if they were in a physical store. Technically, vision systems are now in common usage, but research on feeling capabilities is still in the laboratory (Long and Long, 2005). Figure 10.1[*] demonstrates that a user wearing stereo goggles, headset and sensory gloves interacts with a VR environment.

The central concept of mobility in Web evolution is that Web information and communication service are available anywhere and anytime. Pervasive availability of the Web provides new opportunities for e-business, and business activities that relate to the new opportunities are collectively referred to as m-business. Implementation of m-business requires the Web evolution and wireless communication technologies.

[*] All figures used in this chapter are from Wikipedia.

2. Wireless Communication Technologies

Wireless communication is data transmission over a distance without using electrical conductors or wires. Wireless communication technologies have been developing rapidly. Instead of giving a comprehensive introduction of the technologies, this section describes some typical technologies, with which the application of wireless communication technologies in business can be discussed in Section X.3.

2.1. Wireless Networks

Wireless networking technologies have been developing fast since ten years ago. The new technologies have greatly expanded the channels in which businesses reach consumers, and require that businesses adopt new business models for marketing purpose, competitive advantage and internal efficiency. It is essential that businesses are familiar with basic wireless networks so that they can make best use of them for their business models according to the features of the networks. Following is a brief description and comparison of four major wireless networking technologies.

2.1.1. Bluetooth

Bluetooth is a wireless networking standard for exchanging data over short-distances (about 10 meters) with very fast data transmission rates of up to 480 Mbps. It can create personal area network (PAN) to connect electrical devices such as desktop computers, laptops, mobile phones, personal data assistants (PDA), global positioning system (GPS) receivers, digital cameras, etc. Data is transmitted via small radio transmitter/receivers installed in each electronic device in the PAN.

2.1.2. Wi-Fi

Wi-Fi (wireless fidelity) is a wireless technology that can support a wireless local area network (WLAN) and provide high-speed access to the Internet with data transmission rates up to 54 Mbps. Wi-Fi networks can comprise an area as small as a single room with wireless-opaque walls or as large as a few square kilometers in the open. Most new personal computers and their peripherals, laptops, smartphones come with built-in wireless transmitters. Wireless adapters can be plugged into devices that do not support Wi-Fi to make them ready for network connection.

2.1.3. 3G

3G is the third generation of mobile phone network standards and technologies. It can support a wide area mobile phone network, which can be flexibly accessed in a very broad area. The 3G networks can offer users a wide range of advanced services including: wireless voice telephony, video calls, and broadband data transmission. Also, the 3G networks evolved to incorporate high-speed Internet access. Transmission rate of 3G is variable. It is suggested that the transmission speed is 384 Kbps at or below pedestrian speeds, 128 Kbps in a moving car and 2 Mbps in fixed application.

2.1.4. WiMAX

WiMAX (worldwide interoperability for microwave access) is the emerging wireless technology designed to enable high-throughput broadband mobile Internet access to the widest array of devices including laptops, handsets, smartphones, and consumer electronics such as gaming devices, cameras, camcorders, music players, etc. Compared with Wi-Fi, WiMAX provides improved performance and usage over much greater distances. WiMAX supports peak data transmission speed of about 70 Mbps, with an average between 1 Mbps and 10 Mbps. Moreover, WiMAX needs spectrum license, while Wi-Fi does not. Table 10.1 is the comparison among the four wireless networking technologies in regard to their application features and accessing devices.

Table 10.1: Comparison of four wireless networking technologies

	Accessing devices	Peak speed	Basic coverage	Cost	License
Bluetooth	desktop computer, laptop, mobile phone, PDA, GPS receiver, digital camera	480 Mbps	10 m	Low	No
Wi-Fi	personal computers & peripherals, laptops, smartphones	54 Mbps	32 m indoors; 95 m outdoors	Low	No
3G	mobile phones	2 Mbps	5 km	High	Yes
WiMAX	laptops, handsets, smartphones, gaming devices, cameras, camcorders, music players	70 Mbps	3.5 km	High	Yes

2.2. Global Positioning System

Beside wireless networking systems, mobile devices also use global positioning system (GPS), which is a satellite-based system that tracks objects anywhere worldwide. The user segment of the system is a receiver, which is known as a locator. The GPS determines the location of the locator in terms of latitude and longitude at an instant point of time. Initially developed by the United States Department of Defense for military use, the technology has been used for civilian purpose with limits restricting the altitude and speed of the receiver. With specific software, GPS works for specific tasks. For example, the GPS navigation device used in cars is supported by navigation software of digital map manipulated by geographic information system (GIS). The essential work of a GPS application is the development of the application software.

2.3. Mobile and Wireless Devices

A mobile device is an electronic device that has a display screen with touch input or a miniature keypad and can be easily carried or worn by a person. Typical examples of mobile devices are laptops, mobile phones, digital cameras, PDAs and GPS navigation devices. A mobile device may not have wireless communication functionality. Embedding some type of microchip of sensor, a mobile device can be used for wireless data transmission. For example, Broadcom Corporation introduced ultra-low power Wi-Fi chips optimised for mobile phones, portable media players, handheld gaming systems and digital cameras. Figure 10.2 is the demonstration of chips.

Figure 10.2: Chips

A mobile device can be designed to integrate multiple technologies for some specific usage. For example, a GPS locator embedded into a mobile phone adds value to the phone to make it also perform as a navigation device. BlackBerry, which is also known as smartphone, integrates push e-mail, mobile telephone, text messaging, Internet faxing, Web browsing and other wireless information services. Microchips of sensors can be embedded in any device or appliance in homes, offices, classrooms, personal automobiles, etc. With the evolution of wireless networking technologies, what was considered as imaginations is now becoming a reality.

3. Application of Wireless Technologies in Business

The most significant development for the Internet and the Web in the last five years has been the emergence of mobile wireless Internet access (Laudon and Traver, 2009). Many business activities that are completed by using a desktop computer can now be performed via wireless mobile devices, for example, email correspondence and access to the Web. However, wireless technologies also offer additional new opportunities that are unique to the wireless world and cannot be performed via fixed network (Okhrin and Richter, 2005). Turban et al (2009) introduced many examples of application of mobile technologies in business for improvement of productivity and convenience. In this section, focus is made on the application of wireless technologies for new business opportunities.

3.1. Products and Services

3.1.1. Product Design

In offices or homes, the number of computing, telecommunication, security, and entertainment devices has increased. Connection wires have become increasingly numerous and complex. One solution is to connect the devices with a cable to make signal transfer and synchronisation possible. For example, the high-definition multimedia interface (HDMI) uses a single cable to replace multiple connection wires for television, personal computer and associated devices. Another solution is infrared connection, which avoids using physical wires or cables but requires line-of-sight. Examples of infrared connection include remote control for entertainment devices and data transfer between computers. A common disadvantage of cable and infrared connections is that they are not suitable for rooms with walls.

Bluetooth, which uses radio technology, is a cheap and simple solution for short distance wireless connection. Currently, wireless computer keyboard and mouse are used in many offices and homes. These are the examples of application of Bluetooth technology within a single computer system. There is a great potential of application of Bluetooth technology in the design of home or office devices for wireless control and monitoring.

Most Wi-Fi access points are run privately within homes or businesses, but there are also numerous public Wi-Fi access points or "hotspots" available for larger areas. According to JiWire, Wi-Fi is currently available at more than 220,000 public hotspots and tens of millions of homes, corporations, and university campuses throughout the world (Business Technology, 2008). With Wi-Fi technology, it is possible to design products with a feature of long distance wireless control. On a hot day, for example, someone can turn on an air conditioner in the house on his/her way back home.

3.1.2. Mobile Services

Technical support is an integral part of a company's customer value proposition. It is closely related to customer satisfaction and trust on the company. Customers often leave the company if they have unsatisfactory experience in the process of technical support. Technical support may be delivered over the telephone or online by e-mail or a Web site. Product users may not understand the terms or instructions and cannot describe the problems correctly or properly during the phone call and in the email or Web page message. There are many funny dialogues between users and technical supporters posted on the Web, blaming that the users are ignorant. However, customers believe that they have paid for the service without a condition that they must have the knowledge for effective communication.

For some electronic products, such as a set top box, this problem can be solved by embedding a self-diagnose chip in the products. By means of a PAN, for example Bluetooth, the diagnose data are transmitted to a telecommunication device, such as a mobile phone or a computer, which in turn transmits the data to the technical service department of the company. Obviously field service also benefits from this product design.

The feature of short-range reach of Bluetooth makes the technology possible for local navigation and interest alert in a large shopping centre or shopping mall. At a location, a customer with a mobile device, for example a mobile phone with Bluetooth, can only receive the signal from a device that covers limited area including the location. Thus, the customer can know the location on the map showed on the phone display. When the customer inputs his/her interests such as products or stores, the display shows an optimised route to a set of interesting or relevant stores. Along the route, the customer gets an alert before a relevant store, possibly with a message of special advertisements of the store. Within a store, the customer can get the same type of guidance and alert.

If the customer has a child with him/her, a radio-frequency identification (RFID) passive tag, which is for the purpose of identification and tracking, can be worn by the child. If the child wanders outside a preset range while the customer is choosing or viewing products, the customer gets an alert. The customer can do shopping relaxed in peace of mind. The RFID technology becomes widely used in recent years. For example, in October 2005, the Department of Foreign Affairs and Trade of Australian Government introduced a new generation of passport – epassport, where an RFDI chip embedded in the centre page stores the holder's digitised photograph, name, gender, date of birth, nationality, passport number and expiry date. In 2007, Samsung announced the development of an RFID reader chip for mobile devices. The embedded RFID reader chips can provide consumers with product or service information retrieved from RFID tags incorporated in items such as movie posters, clothing, and museums or tourist exhibits (EDA Geek News Staff, 2007). Figure 10.3 shows square book tag, round CD/DVD tag and rectangular VHS tag used in libraries.

Figure 10.3: Tags

A context-aware pervasive system can be implemented by means of Bluetooth technology in a building such as a museum. The important aspects of the context are the information of a specific object, the location where this object is and the resources that are near the object. Entering a location in the building, a visitor's mobile device gets a signal, which is unique in the location. According to the signal, the mobile device plays audio description about the exhibits in the location, possibly in the visitor's native language if the user has let the device know this information. With this system, any visitor who enters any location at any time can hear the description that is specific to the location in a pre-selected language.

Similar service can be provided in larger areas such as a city by using GPS technology. The location of a city tour bus can be determined by GPS satellite, which transmits the data to the remote device on the bus. With the location information, the remote device plays audio description about the location in regard to its history, events, scenery, buildings, etc.

GPS can be integrated with other systems to make a context-aware system to provide specific services. Many large cities have transportation information systems to solve traffic problems. For example, Beijing has a

Web-based intelligent transportation system for real time traffic control. Drivers can make queries using a personal computer, a PDA or a mobile phone for information of traffic conditions of some relevant roads. A travel guidance system can be developed by integrating GPS and the intelligent transportation system. A mobile phone with GPS navigation function can be used to determine a route to the destination. On the way, an intelligent agent on the mobile phone accesses the transportation information system periodically. If traffic congestion occurs in a location on the route, the intelligent agent will determine an alternative route.

The wireless networking technologies can be applied flexibly to obtain various products or services. A student of Southern Cross University of Australia is doing a student project, in which he develops a software system for recording actual working time of an employee. A building company provides on-site service for local residents. The company charges its clients by employee working hours on the site. Some clients questioned the validity of the traditional time-logging method. So the company needs an objective method to record the working time. The student proposed a GPS/GIS based software system for a solution. An employee carries a GPS receiver, which gets data of location points in terms of latitude and longitude at 5-minute intervals. On completion of each day's work, the points data are transmitted to a computer in the company's office. The computer access local government's GIS, which stores data of local residents' lands, including boundaries in terms of latitude and longitude. Based on the boundary information, the points within a resident's land can be counted. The counting multiplied by 5 is the actual working time in minutes of the employee on the day.

Location-based services (LBS) work by knowing the location of a mobile device. Location-based transactions, roadside assistance, road pricing, and location-based products are some of possible LBS (Barnes, 2003).

3.2. Marketing

There are basically two methods of mobile marketing: pull method and push method. In m-business, the pull method uses mobile Web sites to attract mobile device users, while push method sends messages to them. Mobile Web is not accessible by browsers for personal computers, such as Internet Explorer. There are also many limitations to using mobile devices to access mobile Web. Major limitations include small screen size, limited input mechanism of keypad, slow access speed and high access cost. Two types of messages can be sent to mobile devices: text message and multimedia message, which can contain images, audio and even video contents. Short messaging service (SMS), which sends text message up to 160 characters, is available to all mobile phone users, while multimedia messaging service (MMS) is only available to mobile phones sold in the last few years.

In whichever method, mobile marketing is effective when appropriately targeted. User information collected for marketing purposes should be used to tailor such marketing to the interests of the user (Mobile Marketing Association, 2009a).

3.2.1. Pull Technology

Personalisation is the key to the marketing on mobile Web sites. With the personal information, the user interface of a mobile device is customised to reduce functionality and contents so that it just fits the user. A user profile can be created for personality. According to Germanakos et al (2005), a user profile generally includes three types of information:

- user characteristics, which contains knowledge, goals, background, experience, preferences, activities, demographic information (age, gender), socio-economic information (income, class, sector etc.), etc.
- device / channel characteristics, which contains bandwidth, displays, text-writing, connectivity, size, power processing, interface and data entry, memory and storage space, latency (high / low), battery lifetime, etc.
- user perceptual preference characteristics, which contains all the visual attention and cognitive psychology processes (cognitive and emotional processing parameters).

Depending on the practical marketing purposes, the above information or part of the information can be obtained by inquiring the user, accessing user's mobile device and learning from processes of interaction, observation or transaction.

The personal use of a mobile device makes consumer personalisation easier. Customers prefer personalised services. However, they are reluctant to disclose their personal information because of privacy concerns. Unlike desktop computers, which can be used or accessed by a number of people, a mobile device is normally owned and operated by one unique person (Mobile Marketing Association, 2009b). Customers using a mobile device feel that the interaction with the business is more private. Also, the business can be sure that it is always learning from a single individual, instead of a number of people, who may be different in user characteristics and user perceptual preference characteristics. Many technical characteristics are not known to users, but can be easily obtained in the process of accessing users' mobile devices.

For business, the central objective of personalisation is to supply customers with what they want or need without requiring them to ask for it (Georgiadis et al, 2005). Business server has to learn a customer's personality automatically from interaction with and observation on the customer. The personality information can be learnt with artificial intelligence technology, especially machine learning. Transactions that the customer makes are recorded, and trends of customer's typical behaviours are analysed for customer's profile. For example, if a customer often buys online movies at weekends from a business, the business will only provide movie advertisements on Fridays and weekends. Data mining technique can also be applied to learn common behaviours of many people, and use the knowledge of common behaviours for specific persons. For example, a customer often buys DVD movies from a site, and the business has consistently shows advertisements of DVD movies for the customer. At a certain time, the customer orders a blur-ray disk player. If a common behaviour known by data mining technique is that blue-ray disk player owners seldom buy DVD movies, the site should not show DVD advertisements any more but blue-ray disk instead. This indicates that customer profiles must be maintained. As more knowledge of the personal and common behaviours is acquired over time, the site will be better able to accommodate the customer's personal preferences and interest, and provide him/her with the right information at right time.

3.2.2. Push Technology

Location-based and environment-based (where people are and what they are doing) access to consumers' mobile devices is important and possible for mobile marketing. Impulses to buy products and services are generated as consumers move around their environment and interact with the physical world. An impulse trigger formed by well informed marketers allows consumers to quickly refer to their memory and make the purchase decision (Satchu, 2008). One example is the scenario of local navigation and interest alert described in Section X.3.1.2, where the customer got an advertising message of his/her interested store. In this example, Bluetooth technology is used for determination of the location. Similarly, de Castro and Shimakawa (2006) proposed a new method of personalising mobile advertisement by considering not only the user's location but also his/her interest. Most likely a customer makes a decision in the moment to make a purchase. Another example can be made by extending the scenario of city tour bus in Section X.3.1.2. At a location, advertising message for relevant books, CDs or DVDs and souvenirs about the location can be sent to the tourists. In this example, the location is identified by GPS technology.

Mobile services are usually characterised by mobility, reachability, localisation and identification (Okhrin and Richter, 2005). Mobile technology is powerful for personalisation-based and location-based marketing.

3.3. Shopping

The ability to shop and buy using a mobile device is still in its infancy (O'Donnell, 2007). In a recent study of mobile applications, Larry Freed, president and CEO of ForeSee Results, uncovered that the emergence of mobile as a fourth channel could ultimately have more of an impact on brick-and-mortar shopping than online (Gaffney, 2009). A major use of mobile devices in shopping is to acquire information. In a retail store, a customer is often referred to the Web sites of products for detailed features and specifications. In many cases, the store will lose the customer, as the customer may go to others stores after they know the product information from the Web. A mobile device is a solution to the problem. In Section 10.3.1.2, RFID technology was introduced for looking after children during shopping. Similarly, with RFID technology or Infrared technology, a customer can do shopping without assistance and under no pressure to buy. Using a mobile device such as a mobile phone with Bluetooth, a customer can get interesting information from a RFID tag attached to a sample product.

A mobile phone with a camera is often a tool for impulse purchase. For example, people often read magazines while waiting in clinics. Some products are advertised with QR (quick response) code, which is a two-dimensional bar code, for the Web site of the product. If someone finds a product in a magazine and wants to buy it, this person can scan the QR code with the camera of a mobile phone, and the phone is directly directed to the Web site of the product. In this case, an impulse purchase may be made. Giant QR codes are sometimes placed side by side with outdoor advertisements. People can do online purchase on the road without typing and searching or do "window shopping" to get information. To scan QR codes, the mobile phone needs QR reader software, which can be freely downloaded from the Web. Figure 10.4 is the QR code of the Wikipedia main page.

Figure 10.4: QR code

Although successful in selling digital products such as software, music and movies, online shopping has been less successful in selling goods that normally require physical presence, such as cars, clothes, toiletries, or household appliances (Chin and Swatman, 2005). For these products, people may do shopping on the Web to find product information and make comparison, and make purchase at brick-and-mortar stores. Before purchase of a product in a store, a customer often wants to know if the same or similar product can be purchased at lower prices at other stores or on the Web. In this case, the customer can make a comparison between products and prices, and between shopping online or at the brick-and-mortar stores. Some comparison shopping search engines are listed at http://searchenginewatch.com/2156331 to help shoppers check prices at various online stores or locate e-commerce outlets by category. Some mobile retailing sites register merchants as members and help shoppers find and compare products provided by the members. Buyers may pay to buy products online while they are standing in the store.

In the same study of ForeSee, it was found that people are using phones more often to actually call someone to get an opinion or to send a picture of an item and, more often than not, the opinion they get encourages them to buy the item. "Perhaps stores should consider 'phone-a-friend' promotions to encourage this kind of shopping behaviour." The store should get information materials ready including text, images and URL for a shopper to send to friends by mobile devices.

Information is the focus in mobile shopping. Jon Stine, director of Cisco's Internet Business Solutions Group, states that retailers can no longer afford to ignore the internal and external benefits that mobile devices bring. They should be prepared to sell, but also be prepared to inform (Gaffney, 2009).

Mobile payment with electronic wallet is possible with a mobile device. A client-side electronic wallet stores customer's information in his/her own computer. One of its disadvantages is that it is not portable (Schneider, 2007). If the wallet is stored in a mobile phone, the owner can make a payment in any place at any time. The payment with electronic cash becomes optional at a brick-and-mortar store. The electronic wallet can also be a mobile personal data repository, which is more powerful than smart cards.

3.4. Information Integration and Sharing

Business is conducted between stakeholders including business partners, customers, buyers, sellers and distributors. Success of a business relies on a well-managed chain of activities involving all of the stakeholders and workforce within businesses. Businesses crave instant communication to get ahead of the competition. The need for swift and accurate information anytime and anywhere is crucial to competitive advantages. Information integration and sharing among all stakeholders is crucial for effective and efficient management of the activities.

3.4.1. Value Chain Management

Because of the distributed nature of marketing, sale, delivery, service, transportation and warehousing, these activities may be done in the field and/or in the office at any time by different people. This leads to the problem of inconsistent, inaccurate, redundant or out-of-date data in different types of data repositories. For example, sale people at different locations may not be able to access the updated instant inventory. This may result in that customers have to unnecessarily wait while plenty of products are piled up in the warehouse or products cannot be delivered to some customers as agreed upon because of insufficient quantity of products stored in the warehouse. Many companies have made great effort in marketing campaigns, but company call centres push their potential clients who need urgent services to competitors at the last minute, because the call centres do not know the information of the "waiting list" and unnecessarily require potential clients to wait for the maximum processing time. A solution to this problem is an integrated business management system with a single data warehouse.

GPS determines the location of a vehicle at any time and transmits the location data regularly to the data warehouse. The data can be distributed to or accessed by all relevant stakeholders including product suppliers, the business company and customers by wired connection or wireless connection. Wireless barcode scanner or RFID technology can be used to capture product data at the central depot and demand points, and therefore paper work can be omitted. Dynamic fleet routing is possible with the updated information from the integrated data warehouse.

In a Wi-Fi wireless networking system, a mobile inventory taking device can get the data of inventory levels in warehouses or retail spaces and transmit the data to the integrated data warehouse.

At customer premises or anywhere else, sale people can take orders by accessing the data warehouse with mobile phones for instant inventory or vehicle transportation information. The order details are transmitted to the data warehouse to update the data. Sale people may also access the data warehouse for customer profiles and current promotions to negotiate special prices with customers. A quote or invoice can be generated at the company server and sent to customers by email or fax from the server. Sale people can also download the quote or invoice to their mobile phones and send it to a customer electronic storage device such as a computer or mobile phone, or a wireless printer by means of Bluetooth connection.

The wireless connection accelerates the entire process (Okhrin and Richter, 2005), decreases operating cost, improves customer satisfaction, and obtains more opportunities for better competitive advantages.

3.4.2. Workforce Management

In some businesses, employees work in or out of offices, therefore coordination among them is necessary. Mobile technology can be deployed to provide cross-organisational solutions to the problem of collaboration in cooperative activities. Collaboration requires individuals and groups to communicate, coordinate, integrate, and distribute work. Some examples of specific collaborative activities performed in the workplace include scheduling meetings and other events, retrieving and managing information about a co-worker or client, and communicating with a co-worker or client by calling, messaging, or e-mailing them (O'Connell and Bjorkback 2006). Beside an integrated data warehouse that can be accessed by all the individuals, also needed is an interaction mechanism based on the context in which cooperative activities are completed.

Interaction can be synchronous or asynchronous. The asynchronous communication includes email, voice mail, etc. Telephone call, instant messaging, meetings, and shared whiteboards are examples of synchronous communication services. In synchronous communication, unified communication is important. It requires that different forms of communication tools or methods are integrated to complete complex communication. The following are two scenarios of integrating different mobile devices, which are based on the information on IBM Web site (http://www.zurich.ibm.com/fluid/scenarios.html).

A PDA can access a database on a server to download data (e.g. maintenance history) by a wireless LAN (Wi-Fi). The user finds it difficult to log the current maintenance details because of the small display and keypad of the PDA. If a laptop or a desktop computer is available, the PDA can be connected with the computer by means of Bluetooth. The user can use the computer to enter data, and every keystroke at the computer is immediately reflected on the PDA.

A team leader is having a phone meeting through a wireless WAN (3G) with other two team members to schedule a trip to another city for maintenance for a client. During the meeting, someone else makes a phone call to the team leader, and the call is transmitted to the voice mail server. The intellectual agent at the server identifies that this is an urgent call. The agent converts the speech to text and sends the text to the leader's phone. Reading the text message, the leader cancels the meeting because the text tells that the client postpones the maintenance.

The time keeping system of the student of Southern Cross University in Section 3.1.2 is another example of unified communication. A mobile phone gets location data (GPS) and transmits the data to the office computer (WiMAX). The office computer calculates the working time (telemetrie) of all relevant workers and generates an invoice, which can be sent to client's mobile phone by email or in other methods.

In the self-diagnose example in Section 3.1.2, the scenario can become as follows. A maintainer uses a mobile phone to start the self-diagnose program (mobile remote control), and gets the diagnose result (Bluetooth). If the maintainer cannot identify the problem, he/she sends the result by email to the service department (3G) and makes a phone call to get advices from the department.

Commercial information systems are available for mobile services and supply chain. For example, Oracle Mobile Field Service enables customer service agents to access and update key information via both handheld and laptop devices. The agents can access complete data about customer, product, and service request; manage schedules; order spare parts; record material, costs and labour; and enter counter readings. Benefits of the system include improved service levels, reduced service costs, faster billing cycles, and optimised inventory levels. To meet the needs of mobile workforce, Cisco offers a comprehensive set of mobile solutions that are integral to Cisco Unified Communications products. The mobile solutions offer a variety of intelligent endpoints, including wireless IP phones, mobile phones, and smartphones. People communicate in the way they want to, whether they are in the office, on the road or at home.

Customised mobile information systems are often created by scenario-based design. The scenarios are described in the perspective of specific business activities, technical background (e.g. wireless network/connection, information security, mobile devices, etc.), social background (e.g. business culture, privacy concern, etc.) and limitations of wireless mobile technologies, which will be introduced in Section 4. In many cases, mobile devices are used in conjunction with other office tools to mediate the activities and tasks needed to do work. Therefore these devices must be adapted for integration with texts and other applications that support collaborative work (O'Connell and Bjorkback, 2006).

4. Limitations of Mobile Devices

The rapid advancement of wireless technologies and mobile devices has created new business opportunities. Many services that were previously deliverable via fixed network connections can now be delivered via mobile data infrastructures (O'Brien, 2007). The m-business extends the experience that people have from e-business. However, m-business is not the "next generation" of e-business because of the limitations of mobile devices. Many of the limitations to mobilising business applications are the same today as they were ten years ago (Wellman, 2007). Some of the limitations can be removed in the future, while others can never be.

Lack of unified operating system

Technology platform vendors provide different operating systems (OS) and micro-browsers for mobile devices. There are BlackBerry, Windows Mobile, Palm OS, Symbian, Linux and J2ME. Each of them has its own characteristics. M-business managers have to choose a suitable OS to deploy to mobilise the workforce. Currently, Symbian is the world leading mobile OS provider, but, like twenty-five years ago, Microsoft and Apple are the prominent contenders (Cohen, 2008). Once an OS establishes its dominant position, most software developers will develop software, including mobile Web browsers that run on the OS. Businesses should consider this issue for a long run plan.

Narrow bandwidth

Compared with the broadband Internet connection for desktop computers, the current bandwidth available for mobile devices is relatively narrow. Data transmission rate is slower and often inconsistent. The narrow bandwidth restricts the transmission of large documents or files.

Less powerful processor

The central processing units (CPUs) in mobile devices are less powerful in computing capacity than those in desktop computers. For work that requires heavy computation, there will be long processing delay. It restricts the execution of programs with complex algorithms. Major computational work need to be done on servers.

Low memory capacity

Because of the low level of memory capacity, many mobile devices provide limited amounts of available random-access memory (RAM) to the browsers. Therefore, complex Web pages may not be properly displayed, and large documents may not be entirely downloaded to the handheld devices and presented to users directly.

Small screen and limited keypad

Mobile devices share two significant design limitations: small screen, which is much smaller than that of a desktop computer, and limited keypad functionality, which only includes numeric keys and a few additional keys. Moreover, most mobile devices do not offer functionality comparable to the mouse of a desktop computer. These limitations restrict the amount of contents that can be displayed, data entry and navigation.

Limited battery run-time

Unlike desktop computers, which have continuous power supply, mobile devices use batteries. The limited run-time of batteries is a concern of consumers, manufactures of mobile devices and businesses that provide services.

Beside the technical limitations, social constraints such as privacy concern and acceptance of mobile technology are also considered issues in the development of m-business. Organisations need to reshape their business processes and newly design their workflows to capture all opportunities of mobile technology (Okhrin and Richter, 2005), and to avoid the limitations and constraints.

While this chapter was being formatted for the publication, it was reported on a Web site that "Students at the MIT Media Lab have developed a wearable computing system that turns any surface into an interactive display screen" (Zetter, 2009). The system consists of two parts, a mobile phone and an input/output device, which includes an ordinary webcam and a battery-powered 3M projector with an attached mirror. According to the video demonstration on the Web site, the size of the input/output device is smaller than the mobile phone. Costing less than US$350, this setup can project information from the phone onto any surface. It allows the user to input with gestures. For example, if the user draws a circle on his/her wrist, the face of a watch with current time pops up on his/her wrist. The user can project a phone pad onto his/her

Figure 10.5: E-newspaper

palm and dial a number on the palm without removing the phone from his/her pocket. The system can also read RFID tags to know, for example, the information about products. Figure 10.5 shows that a user is watching a Web video displayed by the wearable computing system on a newspaper. This system provides a solution to the problem of small screen and limited keypad by projecting a virtual touch-screen on any surface. Hopefully, many other limitations of mobile devices will be removed soon. Businesses should be ready for the application of innovations.

References

Barnes, S.J. (2003) Location-Based Services: the State of the Art, e-Service Journal, Vol. 2, No. 3, pp. 59-70.

Business Technology (2008) Wireless Communication: A Look at Bluetooth, Wi-Fi, 3G & WiMAX, [On-line] Available at http://www.leasingideas.com/blog/business-technology/wireless-communication-a-look-at-bluetooth-wi-fi-3g-wimax/ (accessed January 29, 2009).

Chin, C. and Swatman, P. (2005) The Virtual Shopping Experience: Using Virtual Presence to Motivate Online Shopping, Australasian Journal of Information Systems, Vol. 13, No. 1, pp. 239-253.

Cohen. S. (2008) Mobile Warfare, China International Business, Vol. 250, pp. 33-35.

De Castro, J.E. and Shimakawa, H. (2006) Mobile Advertisement System Utilizing User's Contextual Information, Proceedings of the 7th International Conference on Mobile Data Management, Nara, Japan, p. 91.

EDA Geek News Staff, (2007) Samsung Announces Embedded RFID Reader Chip for Mobile Devices, [On-line] Available at http://edageek.com/2007/11/27/samsung-rfid-ic/ (accessed January 23, 2009).

Gaffney, J. (2009) New Reports Show Mobile Shopping Nearing Big Impact on Store Experience, [On-line] Available at http://www.retailtouchpoints.com/home/cross-channel-strategies/199-new-reports-show-mobile-shopping-nearing-big-impact-on-store-experience.html (accessed January 25, 2009).

Georgiadis, C.K., Mavridis, I. and Manitsaris, A. (2005) Context-Based Humanized and Authorized Personalization in Mobile Commerce Applications, International Journal of Computing & Information Sciences, Vol. 3, No. 2, pp. 1-9.

Germanakos, P., Tsianos, N., and Mourlas, C. (2005) Building an Adaptive Web-based Educational Environment Considering the User Perceptual Preference Characteristics, Proceedings of the 3rd International Conference on Open and Distance Learning: 'Applications of Pedagogy and Technology' (ICODL2005), Patra, Greece, pp. 508-521.

Getting, B. (2007) Basic Definitions: Web 1.0, Web. 2.0, Web 3.0, [On-line] Available at http://www.practicalecommerce.com/articles/464-Basic-Definitions-Web-1-0-Web-2-0-Web-3-0, (accessed February 11, 2009).

Laudon, K.C. and Traver, C.G., (2009) E-commerce: Business, Technology, Society, 5th ed. Upper Saddle River: Pearson/Prentice Hall.

Long, L. and Long, N. (2005) Computers: Information Technology in Perspective, 12th ed. Upper Saddle River: Pearson/Prentice Hall.

Mobile Marketing Association, (2009a) Global Code of Conduct, [On-line] Available at http://www.mmaglobal.com/codeofconduct.pdf (accessed January 19, 2009).

Mobile Marketing Association, (2009b) Mobile Advertising Overview [On-line] Available at http://mmaglobal.com/mobileadoverview.pdf (accessed January 19, 2009).

Molloy, F. (2008) The End of the Web?, Fast Thinking, Vol. 13, pp. 69-71.

O'Brien, P. (2007) Ubiquitous Service Delivery - Another New Marketspace?, Public Lecture in Business Informatics, [On-line] Available at http://www.ec.tuwien.ac.at/trends2007 (accessed January 30, 2009).

O'Connell, R. and Bjorkback, S. (2006) An Examination of Mobile Devices in the Workplace, ENG 512, Department of Technical Communication, North Carolina State University, Raleigh, North Carolina.

O'Donnell, J. (2007) Shop by Phone Gets New Meaning, [On-line] Available at http://www.usatoday.com/money/industries/retail/2007-12-18-young-shoppers-cellphone_N.htm (January 19, 2009).

Okhrin, I. and Richter, K. (2005) Mobile Business: Framework, Business Applications and Practical Implementation in Logistics Companies, Arbeitsberichte Mobile Internet Business, 1.

Satchu, A. (2008) The Impulse Trigger and the Planned Purchase Tiger, [On-line] Available at http://www.bizcovering.com/Marketing-and-Advertising/The-Impulse-Trigger-and-the-Planned-Purchase-Tiger.107251 (accessed January 23, 2009).

Schneider, G. (2007) Electronic Commerce, 7th ed. Boston: Thomson Course Technology.

Smith, N., Ferreira, L. and Mead, E. (2000) E-Business Trends, Working Paper 2 of the E-Business and Transport Project for the National Transport Secretariat, Queensland University of Technology, Australia.

Turban, E., King, D. and Lang, J. (2009) Introduction to Electronic Commerce, 2nd ed. Upper saddle River: Prentice Hall.

Turban, E., King, D., McKay, J., Marshell, P., Lee, J. and Viehland, D. (2008) Electronic Commerce: A Managerial Perspective, Upper saddle River: Prentice Hall.

Walsh, K.R. (2002) Reducing Distance in E-Commerce Using Virtual Reality, In: Lowry, P.B., Cherrington, J.O. and Watson, R.J. (Eds.), E-business Handbook, Boca Raton: St. Lucie Press.

Wellman, S. (2007) Mobile Business Expo: Mobile Business Applications Are Here and They're Delivering Value, [On-line] Available at http://www.informationweek.com/blog/main/archives/2007/10/mobile_business_6.html (accessed January 27, 2009).

Zetter, K. (2009) MIT Students Turn Internet into a Sixth Human Sense, [On-line] Available at http://blog.wired.com/business/2009/02/ted-digital-six.html, (accessed February 11, 2009).

CHAPTER 11

THEORIES AND FACTORS AFFECTING ELECTRONIC COMMERCE ADOPTION IN SMALL AND MEDIUM ENTERPRISES (SMES): A REVIEW

Sabah Al-Somali, Roya Gholami & Ben Clegg

Operations &Information Management Group, Aston Business School

The adoption[1] of electronic commerce by Small and Medium Enterprises (SMEs) has increasingly gained the attention of academics, governments and international bodies like the World Trade Organisation (WTO). E-commerce has resulted in fundamental changes to the traditional working practices of SMEs. Recently, many studies have explored critical factors influencing the successful adoption of e-commerce. The objective of this chapter is to provide an exhaustive review of prior theoretical literature on the factors that impact the successful adoption of e-commerce in SMEs and identification of the stages of the adoption process in organisation. Four groups of factors are discussed including technological, organizational, entrepreneurial and environmental factors.

1. Introduction and Background

In the increasingly interconnected global economy, e-commerce which relies on various information and communication technologies (ICT), has increasingly become a global economic phenomenon, with revenue from e-commerce rising to an estimated $US8.5 trillion in 2005 (Uzoka 2008).

[1] Adoption generally refers to an individual's or organisation's decision to make full use of an innovation as the best course of action available, while rejection is the decision to not to adopt (Rogers, 1995).

The term 'electronic commerce' is usually defined as business activities taking place through the increasing standardisation of transactions of goods or services on the Internet, the improved usage of the Internet and related technologies (Hanson 2000).

A number of e-commerce studies in SMEs have been conducted in recent years and have indicated that SMEs did not take a proactive approach in adopting information system (IS) or e-commerce technologies in their business activities and value chain (Alexander 1999; Al-Qirim 2007; Levy et al. 2002; Levy and Powell 2002; Mcdonagh and Prothero 2000; Oliver and Damaskopoulos 2002).

Moreover, e-commerce development in organisations is a phased process in which firms are found to move gradually through series of stages beginning with e-mail, progressing through website development, e-commerce and finally transforming the organisation. Indeed, adoption of advanced e-commerce technologies, especially those involving online transactions and integration with internal business processes are costly, complicated and required ICT skills. On the other hand, the adoption of simple Internet–based technologies such as simple brochure web sites is found to be relatively inexpensive and easy, which makes the adoption decision less controversial (Hong and Zhu 2006).

2. Defining SMEs

Generally speaking, SMEs are found to be managed directly by their owner(s) who provide most of the finance and make most of the principal decisions (Cameron and Massey 1999). Moreover, Cameron and Massey (1999) note that countries and agencies use different criteria in defining SMEs. For example, the North American Industry Classification System depending on the industry in question uses measures such as number of employees and total turnover. The European Union (EU) has created a uniform definition that includes independent companies with fewer than 250 employees and having turnovers of less than 50 million Euro (European Commission 2004). Independent enterprises are ones that are not owned by other enterprises or several enterprises, where independents have 25% or more of the capital or voting rights.

Subsequently, SMEs continue to be important contributors to the economy of the nation where they form a significant proportion of economic development and stability, not only in terms of the crucial role in creating jobs and numbers of people they employ, but in what they contribute to the gross domestic product (GDP) as a whole. For instance, in the United States, small businesses generate two-thirds of the new jobs, produce 39% of the gross national product (GNP) and generate more than half of the technological innovation (Bruque and Moyano 2007; Kuan and Chau 2001). In Europe, 99.8% of the firms are SMEs, responsible for two-thirds of the turnover and business employment (Carayannis et al. 2006). In Southern Europe, SMEs generate 70% of the employment in Spain (European Commission 2005)

3. Organisational Assimilation of E-commerce

The adoption of worldwide Internet use has resulted in the dynamic growth of e-commerce and the creation of applications that drive innovation into business processes. Moreover, the adoption and use e-commerce is found to contribute to the creation of competitive advantages (Del Aguila-Obra et al. 2002).

Organisational assimilation of e-commerce has been measured by the degree of different technological activities such as the use of the Internet, e-mail for inter-organisational communication, website presence and online payments (Hong and Zhu 2006). Subsequently, e-commerce development in organisations is a phased process in which firms are found to move gradually through series of stages beginning with e-mail, progressing through website development, e-commerce and finally transforming the organisation. *Figure* 11.1 illustrates that firms goes from Level 1— very basic or no online capabilities to Level 4— complete transactions through buying, selling and receive payments on the web-site (Price Water House Coopers 1999; Sergeant 2000; Martin and Matlay 2001).

This adoption ladder has four levels of e-commerce capabilities. *Level 1* represents SMEs with very basic or no online capabilities (non-adopters), while *level 2* represents SMEs that use e-mail for internal and external communication, but with no advanced capabilities. *Level 3* includes SMEs that have a web site but they do not conduct business transactions online. These websites are often static brochure that serves principally to establish their presence on the web and are mainly used as a promotional tool. Finally Level *4* constitutes SMEs that can take orders, make complete transactions and receive payment on their web site.

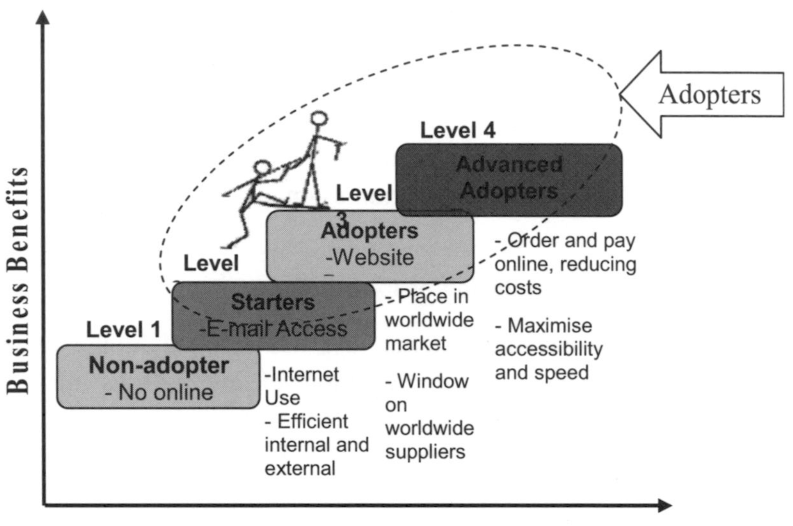

Figure 11.1: E-commerce and Internet-based technologies adoption ladder (Source: PriceWaterHouseCoopers 1999; Nachira et al. 2002; Martin and Matlay 2001)

It is worth noting that the 'adoption ladder' approach which is favoured by the UK government's Department of Trade and Industry (DTI) details the elements of organisational sophistication that are seen as successive steps on the ladder. More importantly, it implies that business benefits derive directly from the organisational change and increasing ICT sophistication that the Internet facilitates (Sergeant, 2000; Martin and Matlay 2001).

Adoption of advanced e-commerce technologies, especially those involving online transactions and integration with internal business processes are costly, complicated and required ICT skills. On the other hand, the adoption of simple Internet–based technologies such as simple brochure web sites is found to be relatively inexpensive and easy, which makes the adoption decision less controversial (Hong and Zhu 2006). Al-Qirim (2005) noted that e-commerce adoption in SMEs can be categorised into three groups: (1) 'starters' (adopters of Internet and email); (2) 'adopters' (adopters of at least one of the following e-commerce technologies: Intranet, Extranet/Virtual Private Network (VPN), Internet-based Electronic Data Interchange (EDI) and websites) and (3) 'extended adopters' or 'advanced adopters' (simultaneous adopters of several advanced technologies).

4. Theoretical Background

Some efforts in academia have been devoted to studying enterprise information system (IS) adoption and has been a topic of interest to researchers (e.g.Tornatzky and Klein 1982; Fichman, 1992; Premkumar & Ramamurthy 1995; Chau & Tam 1997; Lai 1999; Kurnia & Johnston 2000; Gallivan 2001; Hollenstein 2004) as well as e-business and e-commerce adoptors (e.g. Grandon and Pearson 2003; Ching and Ellis 2004; Wymer and Regan 2005; Molla and Licker 2005a, 2005b ; Kartiwi and MacGregor 2007). Moreover, researchers have draw theories and models from areas such as economics, computer science, psychology and management to have more insight to all issues related to enterprise systems adoption (Dewar and Dutton 1986; Attewell 1992; Loch and Huberman 1999; Kambil et al. 2000; bethuyne 2002; Zhu and Weyant 2003). Generally, enterprise adoption of IS and e-business can be analyzed and categorized on the basis of four theoretical foundations and frameworks:

(1) The Innovation Diffusion Theory (Rogers 1995; Beatty et al. 2001; Mehrtens et al. 2001),

(2) Organizational Innovation Theory (Technology-Organization-Environment Model) (Tornatzky and Klein 1982; Tornatzky and Fleischer 1990; Depietro et al. 1990; Damanpour 1991; Kuan and Chau 2001; Xu et al. 2004; Zhu et al. 2003),

(3) Institutional theory (Abrahamson and Rosenkopf 1993; King et al. 1994; Scott 1995; Toe et al. 2003; Chatterjee et al. 2002;Gibbs and Kraemer 2004),
(4) Resourced-based view (RBV) theory (Barney 1991; Barney and Arikan 2001; Zhu and Kraemer 2005).

It is worth noting that researchers found that enterprise adoption of ICT and e-business cannot be understood without careful attention to these four theories and the individual, organizational and environmental contexts in which it takes place (Tornatzky and Klein 1982; Boynton and Zmud 1987; Damanpour 1991; Frambach 1993; Chandrashekaran and Sinha 1995). The following sections discuss the four research approaches in further detail.

4.1. Innovation Diffusion Theory

Rogers (1995) introduced the Innovation Diffusion theory (IDT) and it represents an approach to technology acceptance and use. Moreover, it has been the basis of many studies to explain the adoption and diffusion of ICT. It is generally used in the study of how, why, and at what rate innovations are accepted by individuals or other units of adoption (Roger 1995). Generally, IDT explains the innovation decision process, the determining factors of rate of adoption and different categories of adopters. This theory covers the area of economic, social, communication, and behavioral issues, and has therefore been adapted to research in all of these areas, which makes it difficult to attach it down to a single purpose or field.

According to IDT, The innovation-diffusion process is one through which an individual (or other decision-making unit) passes through: (1) from first knowledge of an innovation, (2) to forming an attitude towards the innovation (persuasion), (3) to a decision to adopt or reject, (4) to implementation of the new idea, and (5) to confirmation of this decision Rogers (1995). There are also five important innovation attributes that explain the different rates of adoption by users, namely relative advantage, compatibility, complexity, trialability, and observability. Further, Rogers (1995) defines relative advantage as "the degree to which an innovation is perceived as being better than existing one"; compatibility as "its consistency with existing social norms or values, past experiences and needs"; complexity as "the degree to which the new technology is easy to use and learn"; trialability as "the degree to which an innovation may be experimented with prior to actually using it on a limited basis"; and observability as " the extent to which a new technology's outcomes are clear and visible to others".

4.2. Organizational Innovation Theory (Technology-Organization-Environment Model)

Organizational innovation has been consistently defined as the adoption of an idea or behaviour that is new to organization (Damanpour 1991). An innovation can be a new product or service, a new technology, or a new administrative practice or system or new program relating to organizational members. Generally, the adoption of innovation is basically intended to contribute to the performance or effectiveness of the adopting organization. Tornatzky and Fleischer (1990) identify three elements of a firm's context that influence the process by which it adopts and implements technological innovations and those are:

(1) **Technological context** - in which it describes both the internal and external technologies relevant to the business.
(2) **The organisational context** - which is defined in terms of several descriptive measures such as business size, nature of the business, the managerial structure, the quality of its human resources, and the amount of slack resources available internally.
(3) **The environmental context** - which is the arena that a business conducts its operations: its industry, competitors, access to resources supplied by others and dealings with government.

4.3. Institutional Theory

Institutional theory tries to explain the processes by which structures, including schemas, rules, norms, and routines, become established as authoritative guidelines for social behaviour. It inquires into how these elements are created, diffused and adopted over space and time; and how they force one unit in a population to resemble other units that face the same environment fall into decline and disuse (Scott 1995; Abrahamson and Rosenkopf 1993; King et al. 1994). Furthermore, institutional theory has captured the attention of a wide range of scholars across the social science to examine the structure and behavior of organizations (Abrahamson and Rosenkopf 1993; King et al. 1994; Scott 1995; Toe et al. 2003; Chatterjee et al. 2002; Gibbs and Kraemer 2004).

Scott (1995) posits that institutions consist of three pillars (structures): cognitive, normative and regulative structures. The cognitive pillar presents the rules that constitute the nature of reality and the frames through which meaning is made. For instance, symbols, signs and words have their effect to make sense of the ongoing stream of happenings by shaping the meaning we attribute to objects and activities. The second pillar comprises normative structure by which compliance is obtained through social obligation and it specifies how things should be done through defining goals or objectives (e.g. wining the game or adopting a technology). The third pillar provides the basis of coercive power and it presents institutions constrains and regularizes behaviour. Moreover, regulative processes involve the capacity to establish rules, inspect or overview others 'conformity to them and rewards or punishments in an attempts to influence future behaviour (Scott 1995). All these pillars have been identified by one or another social theorist as vital components of institutions.

4.4. Resourced-based View Theory (RBV)

The Resource-based View, like any theory, draws on prior theoretical work in developing its predictions and prescriptions (e.g. Dynamic capabilities, Knowledge based theory of the firm, Resource-dependency theory, Theory of competitive strategy, Evolutionary theory, and Organizational knowledge creation) (Barney and Arikan 2001). It posits that firms create value by combing various resources that are economically valuable, difficult to copy, or imperfectly mobile across firms. Moreover, those resources are found to be protected by some form of isolating mechanism preventing their diffusion throughout industry (Barney 1991). Obviously, resources that are valuable and rare can lead to the creation of competitive advantage. That advantage can be sustained over longer time periods if and only if the firm is able to protect against resource imitation, transfer, or substitution.

Generally speaking, in the IS literature, the resource-based view (RBV) has been used to analyze IT capabilities (Mata et al., 1995; Broadbent et al., 1999; Stuart and Podolny 1996). Also empirical studies using the theory have strongly supported the RBV (Klassen and Whybank 1999; Li and Ye 1999) and it was used to understand how IT business value resides more in the organization's skills to leverage IT than in the technology itself (Clemons and Row 1991; Ross et al. 1996).

5. Critical Factors Affecting an Electronic Commerce Adoption in Small and Medium Enterprises (SMEs)

In addition to the above theoretical perspectives there is also growing body of literature addressing more pragmatic e-commerce adoption issues in the context of small and medium sized enterprises (SMEs) (see for example Webb and Sayer 1998; Poon and Swatman 1999; Jacobs and Dowsland 2000; Keeling et al. 2000; Poon 2000; Doherty et al. 2001; Elsammani et al. 2001) . These studies offer further insights regarding the favourable conditions for e-commerce adoption and more importantly the critical factors influencing the successful adoption of e-commerce in SMEs (Tan et al. 2007; Al-Qirim 2007; Zhu et al. 2003). The following sections discuss the critical factors that are found to influence the successful adoption of e-commerce within the categories of technological characteristics, organizational characteristics, entrepreneurial issues and environmental issues. The following sections discuss each of these factors as illustrated in Figure 11.2.

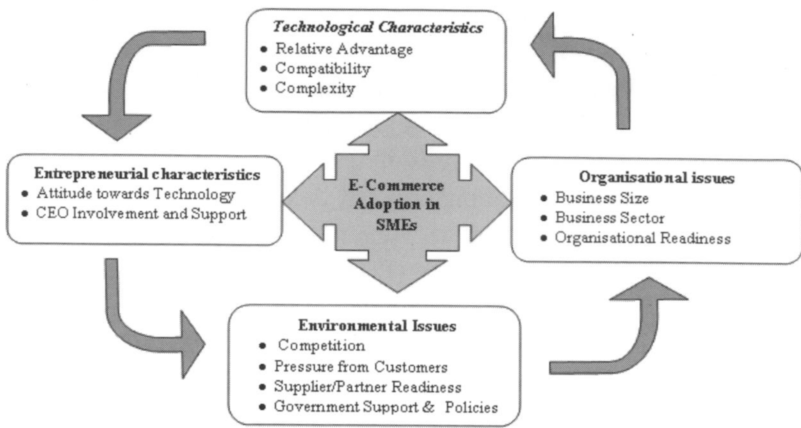

Figure 11.2: Critical Factors Affecting an Electronic Commerce Adoption in SMEs

5.1. Technological Characteristics

Certain technological characteristics have been identified as contributing to the success of an e-commerce project as identified in figure 2. The first technological characteristic is 'relative advantage' or a perceived benefit which refers to the level of recognition of the perceived business benefits that e-commerce adoption can provide. Indeed an organisation will only choose to adopt an innovation if it perceives that doing so will provide comparatively greater benefits than existing methods. Relative advantage or perceived e-commerce benefits have been widely identified as one of the most critical adoption factors and almost all studies acknowledge this benefit as a reason for adoption. Prior studies have found relative advantage to be a significant predictor of innovation adoption and a key variable correlated with adoption (Cragg and King 1993; Premkumar and Ramamurthy 1995; Tan and Teo 1998; Beatty et al. 2001; Lertwongsatien and Wongpinumwatana 2003).

The second technological trait, 'compatibility' is defined as "the degree to which an innovation is perceived as consistent with existing values, past experiences and needs of potential adopters" (Rogers 2003, pg. 240). Compatibility is one of the most frequently studied factors in innovation adoption (Tornatzky and Klein 1982). Moreover, compatibility with existing attitudes, beliefs, value systems, and IT infrastructure ensures less resistance to adoption and lesser risk to the adopter (Teo et al. 1998). Firms would choose to use e-commerce if it is compatible with the organisation's practices, culture, values, and IT infrastructure, therefore requiring minimal adjustments and changes (Lee and Kim, 2007). Compatibility of the new technology with existing business processes and systems is anticipated to influence the adoption decision; less compatible technologies decrease the likelihood of adoption (Rogers, 1995). Indeed an innovation which is perceived to be incompatible with business processes will eventually be rejected (May et al., 2001), therefore business processes and new adopted technologies must be closely matched (Iacovou et al. 1995, Chau and Tam 1997, Zhu et al. 2003).

'Complexity' is the third technological factor which refers to the "degree to which an innovation is perceived as relatively difficult to understand and use" (Rogers 2003, pg. 257). Complexity of an innovation acts as a major barrier to potential adopters of IS innovation. IT and Internet–based technologies require substantial technical know-how in order to realise successful implementation and operation (Lee and Kim 2007). Moreover, Lee and Kim (2007) assert that small organizations may see Internet-based information systems (IIS) as complex and may lack the technical capability to develop IIS. The perceived complexity of e-commerce applications decreases the chance of adoption (Rogers 1995).

5.2. Organisational Characteristics

Organisational characteristics have been the most widely investigated and often used as a key determinant of technological innovation adoption. Firstly, a number of previous studies have shown that the organisational size influences the use of technology and researchers report a positive relation between organisation size and the decision to adopt IT technologies (Straub and Beauclair, 1988; Thong, 1999; Yoa et al., 2003; Fallon and Moran, 20001 Crespi et al.,2004). Fallon and Moran (2000) report significant links between the size of the small business in terms of the number of employees and the extent of Internet adoption.

Thong et al. (1996) and DeLone (1988) note that business size can affect several crucial organisational processes and the way that small firms deal with adoption and implementation issues can differ substantially. Moreover, Davies (1979) and Levy and Powell (2002) note that larger SMEs are found to be in a better position to adopt EC than smaller ones. Conversely, Bajwa et al. (2005) and Bajwa and Lewis (2003) suggest that size may not be a significant predictor of adoption of some inexpensive collaboration tools like email and web-based tools. Moreover, Seyal and Rahman (2003) found that organisational size was not statistically significant in the likelihood to adopt e-commerce adoption.

The second organisational characteristic is business sector or the industry to which the firm belongs. Business sector affects the adoption decision and may cause some firms to be innovators and others to be laggards (Cobham 1999; Caselli and Coleman 2001, Sadowski et al. 2002; Pontikakis et al. 2006). Moreover, Shore (2001) notes that the industry within which an organisation operates may be instrumental in determining the degree to which an organisation participates in e-commerce. For example, service-oriented firms tended to adopt e-commerce far more than their manufacturing counterparts (MacGregor 2004). Moreover, MacGregor (2004) indicates that the majority of SMEs who have used and adopted the portal also tend to be service-oriented businesses.

The third organisational characteristic of primary importance is organisational readiness which is the firm's technological capabilities (computing), financial resources available for e-commerce adoption and employees' IT knowledge. Generally speaking, organisational readiness and the degree to which IT infrastructure is sophisticated have often been identified as predictors of successful IT adoption (Iacovou et al. 1995). IT infrastructure or technological resources include hardware and software resources while financial resources refer to the installation costs, implementation of any subsequent enhancements, and ongoing expenses during usage such as communication charges, usage fees, etc. (Iacovou et al. 1995).

Organisational readiness has been shown to be important in e-commerce adoption because SMEs typically lack the technical and financial resources necessary for e-commerce and other IT investment (Gemino et al. 2006). Mehrtens et al. (2001) state that SMEs with high levels of IT are more likely to adopt the Internet. Furthermore, Wan and Tsa (2002) investigated the factors involved in the adoption of e-commerce in Taiwanese manufacturing and service industries. Their analysis revealed that organisational readiness reflects a firm's technological capabilities, or the level of knowledge and skills. This suggests that the more resources there are in a firm, the more successful its e-commerce application. On the other hand, organisations without such capacity will be less able to adopt innovation and thus demonstrate lower readiness.

Furthermore, Wan and Tsa (2002) stress that, in terms of e-commerce, SMEs need to acquire the technical skills and knowledge related to the Internet in order to reduce costs and improve efficiency. Technical skills and knowledge include namely website design, programming skills, Internet security knowledge and electronic data interchange skills (Taylor et al., 2004). Financial resources were also seen to be important factors influencing the likelihood to adopt innovation. Research by Harrison et al. (1997) and Chwelos et al. (2001) posit that the organisational readiness is composed of two constructs, namely computing and financial resources and both were found to directly affect the adoption of e-commerce in SMEs. It is worth noting that previous studies have concluded that firms' technological capabilities, financial resources and employees' IS knowledge were among the most important organisational characteristics affecting innovation adoption (Cragg and King 1993; Iacovou et al.1995; Harrison et al. 1997; Scupola 2003).

5.3. Entrepreneurial Issues

The successful adoption of an e-commerce requires decision-maker or entrepreneurial input. The first entrepreneurial issue is the need for CEO involvement and support which is found to be a key requisite for successful implementation and adoption of any technology (Lederer and

Mendelow 1988). Top management vision, commitment, and support have emerged as key variables in past research on implementation and adoption success in IS (Sanders and Courtney 1985) and in innovation adoption literatures (Zmud, 1984; Premkumar and Ramamurthy 1995; Ramamurthy et al. 1999; Lee and Kim 2007). In addition, support from top management such as CEOs, senior management and IT technical support employees has consistently been cited as a key variable in both the innovation and IS implementation literatures (Kwon and Zmud 1987; Grover 1993; Ramamurthy et al. 1999; Lee and Kim 2007). According to Al-Qirim (2006), in small business, the CEO is not only involved in adoption decisions but also in the entire e-commerce project (e.g., selecting suppliers and supervising the project). In addition, management information system (MIS) research confirms that the introduction of new or different systems is less likely to success without the support of top management (Zmud 1984; Doll 1985; Delone 1988; Lucas et al. 1990; Dong 2001; Wixom and Watson 2001).

The second entrepreneurial issue is CEO 'attitude' towards technology. Attitude is comprised of the person's beliefs and behaviour leading certain outcomes and it refers to the degree of an individual's favourable or unfavourable reaction towards a given behaviour (Fishbein and Ajzen 1975). In SMEs where there are few management layers, the decision-makers are usually the CEOs of organisations who exercise great power to directly control the decision-making process. Moreover, when CEOs have positive attitudes toward innovation adoption, they will ideally ensure that all required resources will be available when required (Rai and Patnayakuni 1996). Harrison et al. 1997) conclude that attitudes toward adoption (i.e., perceived positive and negative anticipated consequence of adoption) strongly influence a small business executive's decision to adopt IT in order to help his/her firm compete. Thong and Yap (1995) studied CEO's attitudes towards IT adoption in small business and their empirical results indicated that these attitudes were a crucial facilitator for innovation adoption by small businesses. In general, research has found that adopting decision-makers tend to be younger, better educated, and more outward-looking, or cosmopolitan, than non-adopters (Kimberly 1978; Ozanne and Churchill 1971; Robertson and Wind 1983; Rogers 1983).

5.4. Environmental Issues

Another set of factors are the (industrial) environmental issues where in many cases, a firm may adopt a technology due to influences exerted by its business partners and/or its competitors and where the decision has a little or nothing to do with the technology and the organisation *per se* (Kuan and Chau 2001).

The first environmental issue identified in the literature relate to competitive pressures. Peers pressure from the industry is found to force many firms to reactively implement e-commerce in which firms facing significant competition tend to attribute more value to IS innovations (Zhu et al. 2004). Numerous studies have highlighted the role of competition intensity in the adoption literature and it has long been recognised as an important driver for adopting innovations (Iacovou et al. 1995; Kuan and Chau 2001; Kowtha and Choon 2001; Mirchandani and Motwani 2001; Mehrtens et al. 2001; Zhu et al. 2003). Lin and Lin (2008) point out that competitive pressure is a key determinant of e-business adoption in which e-business is expected to be adopted most successfully in highly competitive environments and firms that are first-movers in deploying e-business have tended to derive the greatest advantages.

The second environmental issue which is considered to be an important category is customer pressure on firms to adopt e-commerce technologies. Harrison et al. (1997) found that external pressure from customers had a strong influence on IT adoption. Moreover, Mehrtens et al. (2001) report that Internet adoption by SMEs is influenced by external pressure from customers, and not from competitors.

The third environmental issue is supplier or partner readiness in which considerable empirical support exists for the importance of firms' suppliers or business partners' readiness in successfully implementing internet–based technologies, since partner relationships are significant determinants of inter-organisational systems adoption and implementation (Chau and Tam 1997; Lin and Lin 2008) suggest that a powerful supplier or customer may pursue IS strategies to encourage its trading partners to use e-commerce because value can be maximised only when many business partner are using e-commerce. Simatupang et al. (2002)

also argue that the greater supplier and business partner expertise, the greater the likelihood businesses will engage in e-commerce adoption and linkages.

The fourth environmental issue is existence of government support and policies. Generally, governments have a critical role in fostering technological innovation, where regulation can both stimulate and discourage the adoption of innovations (Scupola 2003). Some studies discussed the government's role in the adoption of technological innovation and have found that government promotion and investment, especially in SMEs, is a major enabler of e-commerce; national policies such as trade and telecommunication liberalization and the existence of e-commerce regulation are also likely to have a big impact on e-commerce, by making IT more affordable to firms and increasing pressure on firms to adopt e-commerce (Iacovou et al. 1995; Damsgaard and Lyytinen 1996; Molla 2005; Kuan and Chau 2001; Scupola 2003; Gibbs et al. 2003). For example, in the United States, an executive order was issued in response to the paper reduction act, which required federal agencies to convert to electronic commerce (U.S. Small Business Administration 1996). Governments can contribute to e-commerce adoption and implementation by conducting informational campaigns to increase awareness, provide financial subsidies and also by increasing the knowledge of English and facilitating the access to related technologies on the local market, as evidenced by government activities in southern Italy (Scupola 2003).

It is noteworthy that a number of studies examined the different characteristics that separate technological innovation adopters from non-adopters in SMEs (Iacovou et al. 1995, Chau and Tam 1997, Zhu et al. 2003) in which factors affecting adoption are found to be perceived differently by adopters and non-adopters. For example, in their study of e-commerce adoption by SMEs, Wymer and Regan (2005) found that competitive pressure was the most important factor for adopters and it also showed the most significant difference between adopters and non-adopters. Moreover, Black et al. (2001) found that adopters were more likely than non-adopters to recognize relative advantages in terms of improved accessibility, convenience, and cost. Kuan and Chau (2001) conducted a study in Hong Kong to understand factors distinguishing

EDI adopters from non-adopters. They conclude that adopters perceive a higher government pressure and a lower industry pressure than non-adopters and perceived benefits were distinguishing adopter from non-adopter firms. Jeon et al. (2006) note that CEO's innovativeness and attitude towards technology are higher for e-commerce adopting firms, compared to non-adopters.

6. Comparing E-commerce Adoption in SMEs and Large Firms

Most will agree that there are fundamental differences between large and small businesses and how they run their operations (Cragg and King 1993; Harrison et al. 1997; Thong 1999) and there has been much written about how firm size effects aspects of business activity (Tellis 1989; Chen and Hambrick 1995; Murphy et al. 1998; Raymond et al. 1998). It is believed that large firms have some advantages over smaller organisation such as the availability of resources to facilitate innovation and adoption, the ability to observe the risk associated with early stages of innovation adoption the ability to achieve economies of scale more easily (Poon 1999; Zhu et al. 2003). In contrast, smaller businesses have much simpler organisational structures and decision-making processes (represented by the personality of the owner/CEO) which often speed up adoption. On the other hand a lack of financial resources and specialized skills (experts), short term planning and niche target marketing (Poon 1999; Thong 1999) can hinder new technology adoption in SMEs.

There is now a rapidly growing body of literature addressing the contrast in SME and large organization technology adoption (see Keeling et al. 2000; Mcdonagh and Prothero 2000; Poon 2000; Agrawal et al. 2001; Hoffman and Novak 2000), which are summarised in Table 11.1.

It has been suggested by Lynn et al. (1999) and Clayton (2000) that smaller companies are adopting e-commerce in order to compete more effectively with their competitors. Indeed, e-commerce can give SME's a better chance to compete in their markets and will soon become a competitive necessity for survival. On the other hand, larger firms are likely to adopt e-commerce in order to simplify internal business processes or operations which are found to be more complex than those

Table 11.1: E-commerce adoption in SMEs and Large firms

Criteria/Category	SMEs	Large Firms	Source
E-commerce adoption intentions	Many SMEs use e-commerce to: • generate revenues or reduce costs. • expand their market reach • enhance their services • improve their competitive position • find new customers and improve relationship with their customers • respond to suppliers	• Large companies use e-commerce for a wide range of activities such as: • Entering into a dialogue with customers. • Streamlining internal business processes • Improving relationships with suppliers.	- Daniel and Storey (1997); - Butler and Peppard (1998); - Watson et al. (1998); - Kenny and Marshall (2000) - Poon (2000); Porter (2001); - Keeling et al. (2000); - Daniel and Grimshaw (2002)
E-commerce benefits	• SMEs may benefit from the increased market reach that e-commerce provides them. • E-commerce is found to offer SMEs comparatively more advantages to have access to information about customers and suppliers that was previously unavailable – either internationally or regionally	Whilst larger companies are likely to benefit particularly from the ability to simplify complex processes and the ability to address their larger supplier base	- Hamill and Gregory (1997); - Poon and Jevons (1997) - Kaplan and Sawhney (2000); - Wise and Morrison, (2000).
E-commerce requirements	SMES do have the advantage that they have the flexibility for trying new approaches because their processes, structures and systems are simpler than larger firms	The adoption of e-commerce in large companies may require additional considerations such as: 1. Formal e-commerce strategy development processes 2. The development of an appropriate culture 3. Organisational restructuring	- Chang and Powell, (1998); - Pollard and Hayne (1998); - Keeling et al. (2000) - Daniel and Grimshaw (2002)

of smaller businesses (Dutta and Segev 1999; Porter 2001) and to improve relationships with customers and suppliers (Butler and Peppard 1998; Kenny and Marshall 2000; Ferrari 2000, Kaplan and Sawhney 2000; Wise and Morrison 2000; Wilson et al. 2001).

In regards to the benefits that e-commerce provides for both small and large firms, Small companies view e-commerce as an opportunity for improving their performance and increasing their market reach, whilst larger companies are likely to benefit mainly from the ability to address their larger supplier base (Daniel and Grimshaw 2002; Poon 2000; Poon and Swatman 1999).

Interestingly, Lynn et al. (1999) in their comparative study examine the adoption and effectiveness of new media such as the Internet and intranets in small and large companies found that large firms appeared to be obtaining less benefit from their e-commerce adoption as compared to their smaller counterparts. Moreover, they note that smaller companies were making more use of such technologies for contacting their customers than their larger counterparts (Lynn et al. 1999).

It is worth mentioning here that e-commerce offers an opportunity for SMEs to enhance their current services and make them comparable to those of larger companies. Indeed without e-commerce, the services provided by SMEs to their customers can not always compare to those that large businesses can offer. Daniel and Grimshaw (2002) found that the use of e-commerce for responding to competitors, providing enhanced customer services and improving relations with suppliers was driving the uptake by smaller businesses to a greater extent than their larger counterparts. The study also found that smaller businesses believed that they had achieved greater benefits from their e-commerce services. However, in general it was found that large firms tend to be leaders in adopting e-commerce, as they possess the IT resources *and* capability to leverage IT investments over a large revenue base and long time frame (Thatcher et al. 2006).

7. Conclusion

Enterprise adoption of innovation such as e-commerce is a very important and essentially a complex issue faced by decision-makers today. Moreover, enterprises continue to heavily adopt and implement technological innovation in order to create and sustain competitive advantages. Hence, a solid understanding of the main determinants of information and communication technology (ICT) and e-commerce adoption and implementation is of utmost significance.

This chapter has sought to provide a comprehensive review of the key theoretical foundations and practical insights about enterprise ICT and e-commerce adoption studies. In particular, this chapter reviewed the theories of innovation diffusion theory, organisational innovation theory, institutional theory and resourced-based view. Together, these theories provide a comprehensive basis for explaining and describing factors that impact the adoption of e-commerce in SMEs. These factors were categorised into four groups namely, technological, organisational, entrepreneurial and environmental factors. It is important to note that significant differences are found to be between adopters and non-adopters in terms of internal resources such as technological and financial resources and external environments.

Subsequently, this chapter also provided comprehensive comparisons of the difference between large and small businesses in terms of e-commerce adoption intentions and realised benefits. To large companies it would appear that e-commerce is viewed as an opportunity for simplifying complex internal processes and, hence, reducing costs. Conversely, e-commerce is found to offer SMEs comparatively more advantages to:

- quickly obtain data about consumers' patterns and behaviours
- serve current and new customers better, hence offering more value to them
- provide flexible advertisements at relatively low cost.
- offer entirely new services and products.

Indeed, e-commerce can give SME's a better chance to compete in their markets and will soon become a competitive necessity for survival. SMEs may access new markets and deal with many more suppliers than before (Chen 1999; Kersten et al. 2000). Finally, this research calls for a conceptual contingency framework to be developed that is specifically tailored for the needs of SMEs at differing levels of e-readiness and adoption.

References

Abrahamson, E. and Rosenkopf, L. (1993) Institutional and Cometitive Bandwagons: Using mathematical Modeling as a Tool to Explore Innovation Diffusion, Academy of management Review, Vol. 18, No. 3, pp. 487-517.

Agrawal, V; Arjona, L. D. and Lemmens, R (2001) e-Performance: the path to rational exuberance, McKinsey Quarterly, Vol. 1, pp. 31–43.

Alexander, A. (1999)Tuning small business for e-commerce: consultants say business consulting is essential, even in e-commerce, Accounting Technology, Vol. 15, No. 11, pp. 48–53.

Al-Qirim, N. (2007)The adoption of eCommerce communications and applications technologies in small businesses in New Zealand, Electronic Commerce Research and Applications, Vol. 6, No. 4, pp.462-473

Al-Qirim, N. (2007a) Research Trilogy into eCommerce Adoption in Small Businesses in New Zealand: A Concluding Focus Group Approach, Electronic Markets, Vol. 17, No. 4, pp. 263-285

Al-Qirim, N.(2005) An Empirical Investigation of an e-commerce Adoption-Capability Model in Small Businesses in New Zealand, Electronic Markets, Vol. 15, No. 4, pp. 418 – 437.

Al-Qirim, N. (2006) Personas of E-commerce Adoption in Small Business in New Zealand, Journal of Electronic Commerce in Organizations (JECO), Vol. 4, No. 3, pp. 18-45.

Attewell, P. (1992) Technology Diffusion and Organisational learning: The case of Business Computing, Organisation Science, Vol. 3, No. 1, pp. 1-19.

Beatty, R.C, Shim, J.P and Jones, M.C. (2001) Factors influencing corporate web site adoption: a time-based assessment, Information & Management, Vol.38, pp. 337–354.

Barney, J.B. (1991) Firm resources and sustained competitive advantage, Journal of Management, Vol. 17, pp. 99–120.

Barney, J. B. and Arikan, A. M. (2001) The resource-based view: Origins and implications. In Handbook of Strategic Management, Hill MA, Freeman RE, Harrison JS (eds). Blackwell: Oxford, U.K.; 124–188.

Bethuyne, G. (2002) The Timing of Technology Adoption by Cost-Minimizing firm, Journal of Economics, Vol. 76, No. 2, pp. 123-154.

Boynton, A.C., and Zumud, R. W. (1987) Information Technology Planning in the 1990's: Directions for practice and research, MIS Quarterly. Vol. 11, No. 1, pp. 59-71.

Broadbent, M., Weill, P., and Neo, B.S. (1999) Strategic context and patterns of IT infrastructure capability, Journal of Strategic Information Systems, Vol. 8, No. 2, pp. 157-187.

Bruque, S. and Moyano, J. (2007) Organisational determinants of information technology adoption and implementation in SMEs: The case of family and cooperative firms, Technovation, Vol. 27, No. 5, pp. 241-253.

Butler, P. and Peppard, J. (1998) Consumer purchasing on the Internet: processes and prospects, European Management Journal, Vol.16, No. 5, pp. 600–610.

Cameron, A. and Massey, C.(1999) Small and Medium-Sized Enterprises: A New Zealand perspective. Auckland, New Zealand: Addison Wesley Longman New Zealand Ltd.

Carayannis, E. G., Popescu, D., Sipp, C. and Stewart, M.(2006). Technological learning for entrepreneurial development (TL4ED) in the knowledge economy (KE): case studies and lessons learned, Technovation, Vol. 26, No. 4, pp. 419–443

Chandrashekaran, M. and Sinha, R. (1995) Isolating the determinants of Innovativeness: A split-population Tobit (SPOT) duration Model of Timing and Volume of first and repeat purchase, Journal of Marketing Research, Vol. 32, pp. 444-456.

Chang, L. and Powell, P. (1998) Towards a framework for business process re-engineering in small and mediumsized enterprises, Information Systems Journal, Vol. 8, No. 3, pp. 199–215.

Chatterjee, D., Grewal, R. and Sambamurthy, V. (2002) Shaping up for e-Commerce: institutional enablers of the organisational assimilation of web technologies, MIS Quarterly, Vol. 26, No. 2, pp. 65–89.

Chau, P.Y.K and Tam, K.Y (1997) Factors affecting the adoption of open systems: an exploratory study, MIS Quarterly. Vol. 21, No. 1, pp. 1–21.

Chen, K. (1999) Factors that motivate internet users to use Business-to-customer Electronic commerce, UMI. PhD Thesis, Ohio: Cleveland State university, USA

Chen, M. J. and Hambrick, D.C. (1995) Speed, stealth and selective attack: how small firms differ from large firms in competitive behaviour, Academy of Management Journal, Vol. 38, No. 2, pp. 453–82.

Ching, H., L. and Ellis, P. (2004) Marketing in Cyberspace: What factors Drive E-commerce Adoption?, Journal of Marketing Management, Vol. 20, No. 3/4, pp. 409-429.

Chwelos, P., Benbasat, I. and Dexter, A (2001) Research report: empirical test of an EDI adoption model, Information Systems Research, Vol. 12, No. 3, pp. 304–321.

Clayton, K. (2000) Microscope on micro businesses, Australian CPA, Vol. 70, No. 2, pp. 46–47.

Clemons, E. K. and M. C. Row (1991) Sustaining IT advantage: the role of structural differences, MIS Quarterly, Vol. 15, No. 3, pp. 275-292.

Cobham, A. (1999) The Financing and Technology Decisions of SMEs: Finance as a Determinant of Investment, Finance and Trade Policy Research Centre, University of Oxford: Oxford.

Cragg, P. and King, M. (1993) Small-firm computing: motivators and inhibitors, MIS Quarterly, Vol. 17, No. 1, pp. 47-60.

Crespi,G., Mahdi, S. and Patel, P. (2004) Adoption of e-commerce technology: Do network and learning externalities matter? Department for Business, Enterprise and Regulatory Reform. Available from: http://www.berr.gov.uk/files/file21912.pdf [Accessed on 6 th July 2008]

Damanpour, F. (1991) Organisational Innovation: A Meta-Analysis of Effects of Determinants and Moderators, Academy of Management Journ*al*, Vol. 34, No. 3, pp. 555-590.

Damsgaard, J. and Lyytinen, K.(1996) Government Strategies to Promote The Diffusion of Electronic Data Interchange (EDI): What we know and what we don't know, Information Infrastructure and Policy, Vol. 5, No. 3, pp. 169-190.

Daniel, E.M. and Storey, C. (1997) On-line banking: strategic and management challenges, Long Range Planning, Vol. 30, No. 6, pp. 890–898.

Daniel, E.M. and Grimshaw, D.J (2002) An exploratory comparison of electronic commerce adoption in large and small enterprises. Journal of Information Technology, Vol. 17, pp. 133-147

Davies, S. (1979) The Diffusion of Process Innovations, Cambridge: Cambridge University Press.

Del Aguila-Obra, A.R., Bruque-Camara, S., Padilla-Meléndez, A. (2002) Internet usage and competitive advantage: the impact of the Internet on an old economy sector. Internet Research, Vol. 12, No. 5, pp.391-401.

DeLone, W.H.(1988) Determinants of success for computer usage in small business, MIS Quarterly, Vol. 12, No. 1, pp. 51–61.

Depietro, R.; Wiarda, E.; and Fleischer, M.(1990) The Context for Change: Organisation, Technology, and Environment.In L. G. Tornatzky and M. Fleischer (eds.), The Processes of Technological Innovation. Lexington, MA: Lexington Books, pp. 151-175.

Dewar, R.D. and Dutton, J.E. (1986) The adoption of Radical and Incremental Innovations: An Empirical Analysis, Management Science, Vol. 32, No. 11, pp. 1422-1433.

Doherty, N., Hughes, F. and Ellis-Chadwick, F. (2001) An investigation into the factors affecting the level of e-commerce uptake amongst SMEs. In Roberts, M., Moulton, M., Hand, S. and Adams, C. (eds) Sixth Annual Conference of UKAIS, Portsmouth, April (Zeus Press, Manchester), pp. 251–257.

Dong, L. (2001).Modeling top management influence on ES implementation, Business Process Management Journal, Vol. 7, pp. 243-250.

Dutta, S. and Segev, A. (1999) Business transformation on the Internet, European Management Journal, Vol. 17, No. 5, pp. 466–76.

Elsammani, Z., Scown, P. and Hackney, R. (2001) A case study of the impact of a diffusion agent on SMEs adoption of Web presence. In Roberts, M., Moulton, M.,

Hand, S. and Adams, C. (eds) Sixth Annual Conference of UKAIS, Portsmouth, April. (Zeus Press, Manchester), pp. 562–76.

European Commission (2005) Gateway to the European Union. Available from: http://www.europa.eu.int [Accessed on 15 th April 2008]

European Commission (2004) SME definitions, the European Commission Available from: http://europa.eu.int/comm/enterprise/enterprise_policy/sme_definition/index_en.htm. [Accessed on 14 th May 2008]

Ferrari, R. (2000) Exchanges promise big competitive potential, Supply Chain Management Review, November/ December, pp. 23–26.

Fichman, R.G. (1992) Information Technology Diffusion: A review of Empirical Research, Proceedings of the Thirteenth International Conference on Information Systems, pp. 195-206.

Fishbein, M. and Ajzen,I. (1975) Belief, Attitude, Intention, and Behavior: An Introduction to Theory and Research. Addison-Wesley: Reading, MA.

Frambach, R.T. (1993) An Integrated Model of Organisational Adoption and Diffusion of Innovation, European Journal of Marketing, Vol. 27, No. 5, pp. 22-41.

Gallivan, M., J. (2001) Organisational adoption and assimilation of complex technological innovations: development and application of a new framework, SIGMIS Database, Vol. 32, No. 3, pp. 51-58.

Gibbs,J., Kraemer, K.L. and Dedrick, J (2003) Environment and policy factors shaping global e-Commerce diffusion: a cross-country comparison, The Information Society. Vol. 19, pp. 5–18.

Grandon, E., Pearson, J.M. (2003) Strategic Value and Adoption of Electronic Commerce: An Empirical Study of Chilean Small and Medium Businesses, Journal of Global Information Technology Management, Vol. 6, No. 3, pp. 22-43.

Grover,V.(1993) An empirically derived model for the adoption of customer-based interorganisational systems, Decision Sciences, Vol. 2, No. 3, pp. 603-640.

Hamill, J. and Gregory, K. (1997) Internet marketing in the internationalisation of UK SMEs, Journal of Marketing Management, Vol. 13, No. 1, pp. 9–28.

Hanson, W. (2000) Principles of Internet Marketing, Cincinnati: South-Western College Publishing.

Harrison DA, Mykytyn Jr PP and Riemenschneider CK (1997) Executive decisions about adoption of information technology in small business: theory and empirical tests. Information Systems Research, Vol. 8, pp. 171–195.

Hoffman, D.L. and Novak, T.P. (2000) How to acquire customers on the Web. Harvard Business Review, Vol. 74, No. 3, pp. 179–88.

Hollenstein,H. (2004) Determinants of the adoption of Information and Communication Technologies (ICT): An empirical analysis based on firm-level data for the Swiss business sector, Structural Change and Economic Dynamics, Vol. 15, No. 3, pp. 315-342

Hong, W. and Zhu, K. (2006) Migrating to internet-based e-commerce: Factors affecting e-commerce adoption and migration at the firm level, Information & Management. Vol.43, No. 2, pp. 204-221.

Iacovou, C., Benbasat, I. and Dexter, A. (1995) Electronic data interchange and small organisations: adoption and impact of technology. MIS Quarterly, Vol. 19, No. 4, pp. 465–485

Jacobs, G. and Dowsland, W. (2000) The dot-com economy in Wales: the long road ahead. In Beynon-Davies, P.; Williams, M.D. and Beeson, I (eds) UK Academy of Information Systems Conference, Swansea (McGraw-Hill, Maidenhead, UK), pp. 590–600.

Jeon, B.N., Han, K.S. and Lee, M. J. (2006) Adoption of e-business: the case of SMEs in Korea, Applied Economics, Vol. 38, pp. 1905–1916

Kambil, A., Kamis, A., Koufaris, M. And Henry, C. Lucas, J. (2000) Influences on the corporate adoption of Web technology, Communications of ACM, Vol. 43, No. 11, pp. 264-271.

Kaplan, S. and Sawheny, M. (2000) E-hubs: the new B2B marketplaces, Harvard Business Review, Vol. 74, No. 3, pp. 97–103.

Kartiwi, M.; MacGregor, R. C., (2007) Electronic commerce Adoption Barriers in Small to medium enterprises (SMES) in developed and developing countries: A cross-Country comparison, Journal of Electronic Commerce in Organisations, Vol. 5, No. 3, pp. 35-51.

Keeling, K., Vassilopoulou, K., McGoldrick, P. and Macaulay, L. (2000) Market realities and innovation in small to medium enterprises: facilitators and barriers to the use of electronic commerce, New Product Development and Innovation Management, Vol. 2, No. 1, pp. 57–70.

Kenny, D. and Marshall, J. (2000) Contextual marketing: the real business of the Internet, Harvard Business Review, Vol. 78, No. 6, pp. 119–125.

Kersten, G. E., Noronha, S.J. and Teich,J. (2000)Are All E-Commerce Negotiations Auctions?. Fourth International Conference on the Design of Cooperative Systems,Sophia-Antipolis, France. Available from: http://www.cs.uu.nl/docs/vakken/ec/auctions_negotiation.pdf [accessed on 02-11-2008]

Kimberly, J. R. (1978) Hospital adoption of innovation: The role of integration into external informational environment, Journal of Health and Social Behaviour, Vol., 19, (December), pp. 361-373

King, J. L., Gurbaxani, V., Kraemer, K.L., McFarlan, F.W., Raman, K.S., and Yap, C.S. (1994) Institutional factors in Information Technology innovation, Information Systems research, Vol. 5, No. 2, pp. 139-169.

Klassen, R.D., and Whybank, D.C. (1999) The impact of environmental technologies on manufacturing performance, Academy of management Journal, Vol. 42, No. 6, pp. 599-615

Kowtha, N.R. and Choon, T.M.I. (2001) Determinants of website development: a study of electronic commerce in Singapore, Information and Management. Vol. 39, No. 3, pp. 227–242.

Kuan, K and Chau, P. (2001) A perception-based model of EDI adoption in small businesses using technology–organization–environment framework, Information & Management, Vol. 38, pp. 507–521

Kurnia, S. and Johnston, R.B. (2000) The need for a process view of inter-organisational systems adoption, Journal of Strategic Information Systems, Vol. 9, Issue 4, pp. 295-319.

Kwon, T. H. and Zmud, R. W (1987) Unifying the fragmented models of information systems implementation, In Critical Issues in Information Systems Research, R. J. Boland and R. A. Hirschheim, Eds. New York: Wiley, pp. 257-252.

Lal, K., (1999) Determinants of the adoption of Information Technology: a case study of electrical and electronic goods manufacturing firms in India, Research Policy, Vol. 28, pp. 667–680

Lederer, A.L. and Mendelow, A.L (1988) Convincing top management of the strategic potential of information systems, MIS Quarterly, Vol. 12, No. 4, pp. 526–536.

Lee, S. and Kim, K. (2007) Factors affecting the implementation success of Internet-based information systems, Computers in Human Behavior, Vol.23, No.4, pp 1853-1880.

Lertwongsatien, C. and Wongpinumwatana, N. (2003) E-commerce adoption in Thailand: An empirical study of small and medium enterprises (SMEs), Journal of Global Information Technology management, Vol. 6, No. 3, pp. 67-83.

Levy, M., Powell, P. and Yetton, P. (2002) The dynamics of SMEs information stations, Small Business Economics, Vol. 19, No. 4, pp. 341–354.

Levy, M. and Powell, P. (2002) SMEs Internet Adoption: Toward a Transporter Model, Proceedings of the Fifteenth Bled Electronic Commerce Conference (Reality: Constructing the Economy), Bled, Slovenia, June 17–19, pp. pp. 507–521.

Li, M. and Ye, L.R. (1999) Information technology and firm performance: Linking with environmental, strategic and managerial contexts, Information and Management, Vol. 35, No. 1, pp. 3-51

Lin, H. and Lin S.(2008) Determinants of e-business diffusion: A test of the technology diffusion perspective, Technovation, Vol. 28, pp. 135-145.

Loch, C.H. and Huberman, B. A. (1999) A punctuated-Equilibrium Model of Technology Diffusion, Management Science, Vol. 45, No. 2, pp.160-177.

Lucas, H.C. Jr, Ginzberg, M.J., Schultz, R.L. (1990) Information Systems Implementation: Testing a Structural Model. Ablex Publishing Corporation: Norwood, NJ.

Lynn, G., Maltz, A., Jurkat, P. and Hammer, M. (1999) New media in marketing redefine competitive advantage: a comparison of small and large firms Journal of Services Marketing, Vol. 13, No. 1, pp. 9–18.

Martin, L. and Matlay, H. (2001) Blanket" approaches to promoting ICT in small firms: some lessons from the DTI ladder adoption model in the UK', Internet Research: Electronic Networking Applications and Policy, Vol. 11, No. 5, pp. 399-410.

Mata, F. J., Fuerst, W. L. and Barney, J. B. (1995) Information technology and sustained competitive advantage: a resource-based analysis, MIS Quarterly, Vol. 19, No .4, pp. 487-505.

May, C., Gask, L., Atkinson, T., Ellis, N., Mair, F. and Esmail, A (2001) Resisting and promoting technologies in clinical practice: the case of telepsychiatry, Socila Science and medicine, Vol. 52, No. 12, pp. 1889-1901.

Mcdonagh, P. and. Prothero, A. (2000) Euroclicking and the Irish SME: prepared for e-commerce and the single currency, Irish Marketing Review, Vol. 13, No.1 ,pp. 21–33.

Mehrtens, J. Cragg, P. and Mills, A. (2001) A model of Internet adoption by SMEs, Information & Management, Vol. 39, pp. 165–176.

Mirchandani, A.A. and Motwani, J. (2001) Understanding small business electronic commerce adoption: an empirical analysis, Journal of Computer Information Systems (Spring), pp. 70–73.

Molla, A. (2005) Exploring the reality of eCommerce benefits among businesses in a developing country. University of Manchester, Precinct Centre: Manchester, UK. Available from: http://www.sed.manchester.ac.uk/idpm/research/publications/wp/di/documents/di_wp22.pdf [Accessed 09 th June 2008]

Molla, A. and Licker, P.S. (2005a) Ecommerce adoption in developing countries: a model and instrument. Information & Management, Vol. 42, pp. 877–899

Molla, A. and Licker, P.S. (2005b) Perceived E-Readiness factors in E-Commerce adoption: an empirical investigation in a developing country, International Journal of Electronic Commerce, Vol.10, No. 1, pp. 83–110.

Murphy, P.M., Daley, J.M. and Knemeyer, A.M. (1998) Comparing logistics management in small and large firms: an exploratory study, Transportation Journal, Vol. 38, No. 4, pp.18–25.

Nachira, F., Chiozza, E., Ihonen, H., Manzoni, M. And Cunningham, F. (2002) Towards a network of digital business ecosystems fostering the local development. Available from: www.digital-ecosystems.org/doc/discussionpaper.pdf [Accessed on 26 th May 2008]

Oliver, J. and Damaskopoulos,P. (2002) SMEs eBusiness readiness in five Eastern European countries: results of a survey. In: Proceedings of the Fifteenth Bled Electronic Commerce conference (Reality: Constructing the economy), Bled, Slovenia, June 17–19, 2002, pp. 584–599.

Ozanne, U. B. and Churchill Jr., G. A. (1971) Five dimensions of the industrial adoption process, Journal of Marketing Research, Vol. 8, (August),pp. 322-328

Pierce, J.L. and Delbecq, A.L. (1977) Organizational structure, individual attitudes and innovation, Academy of Management Review, Vol. 2, No. 1, pp. 27–37.

Pollard, C.E. and Hayne, S.C. (1998) The changing face of information systems issues in small firms, International Small Business Journal, Vol. 16, No. 3, pp. 70–87.

Poon, S. (2000) Business environment and Internet commerce benefit: a small business perspective, European Journal of Information Systems, Vol. 9, No. 2, pp. 72–81.

Poon, S. and Jevons, C. (1997) Internet-enabled international marketing: a small business network perspective, Journal of Marketing Management, Vol. 13, No. 1, pp. 29–41.

Poon, S. and Swatman, P.M.C. (1999) An exploratory study of small business Internet commerce issues, Information and Management, Vol. 35, No. 1. pp. 9–18.

Pontikakis, D., Lin, Y. and Demirbas, D. (2006) History matters in Greece: The adoption of Internet-enabled computers by small and medium sized enterprises, Information Economics and Policy., Vol. 18, No. 3, pp. 332-358.

Porter, M. (2001) Strategy and the Internet, Harvard Business Review, Vol. 75, No. 3, pp. 63–78.

Premkumar, G. and Ramamurthy, K. (1995) The Role of Interorganisational and Organisational Factors on the Decision Mode for Adoption of Interorganisational Systems. Decision Sciences, Vol. 26, No. 3, pp. 303-336.

PriceWaterhouseCoopers, (1999) SME E-commerce Study, Asia Pacific Economic Cooperation (APEC). Final Report, September 24.

Ramamurthy, K., Premkumar, G., & Crum, M. R. (1999) Organizational and interorganizational determinants of EDI diffusion and organizational performance: A causal model, Journal of Organizational Computing & Electronic Commerce, Vol. 9, No. 4, pp. 253-285.

Rai, A. and Patnayakuni, R. (1996) A structural model for CASE adoption behaviour, Journal of Management Information System, Vol. 13, No. 2, pp. 205-234.

Raymond, L and Magnenet, T.N (1982) Information System in Small Business: Are they used in Management Decision?, American Journal of Small Business, Vol. 16, No. 4, pp. 20-27.

Robertson, T. S. and Wind, Y. (1983) Organizational cosmopolitanism and innovativeness, Academy of Management Journal, Vol.26, No. 2, pp.332-338.

Rogers, E.M. (2003) Diffusion of innovations (5th Ed.), New York: The Free Press.

Rogers, E.M. (1995) Diffusion of innovations (4th Ed.), New York: The Free Press.

Rogers, E.M. (1983) Diffusion of Innovations, 3rd ed. New York: Free Press

Ross, J., Beath, C. and Goodhue (1996) Developing long-term competitiveness through IT assets, Sloan Management Review, Vol. 38, No. 1, pp. 31-42

Scott, W.R. (1995), Institutions and Organisations. Thousand Oaks, Sage, CA .

Sergeant, J. (2000) Presentation by the e-envoy of UK Online, cited in Martin, L. and Matlay, H. 2001.

Shore, B. (2001) Information sharing in global supply chain systems, Journal of Global Information Technology Management, Vol. 4, No. 3, pp. 27-50.

Simatupang, T.M., Wright, A.C., Sridharan, R. (2002) The knowledge of coordination for supply chain integration, Business Process Management Journal, Vol. 8, No. 3, pp. 289-308

Straub Jr., D.W. and Beauclair, R.A. (1988) Current and Future Uses of Group Decision Support System Technology: Report on a Recent Empirical Study, Journal of Management Information Systems, Vol. 5, No. 1, pp. 101-116.

Stuart, T. E. and Podolny, J.M. (1996) Local search and the evolution of technological capabilities, Strategic management Journa, Vol. 17 (Special summer Issue), pp. 21-38.

Tan, M. and Teo, T.S.H (1998) Factors influencing the adoption of the internet, International Journal of Electronic Commerce, Vol. 2, No. 3, pp. 5-18.

Tan, J., Tyler, K. and Manica, A. (2007) Business- to – business adoption of ecommerce in China, Information & Management, Vol. 44, pp. 321-351.

Taylor, M. J., Mcwilliam, J., England, D. and Akomode, J. (2004) Skills required in developing electronic commerce for small and medium enterprises: case based generalization approach, Electronic Commerce Research and Applications, Vol.3, No. 3, pp. 253-265.

Tellis, G.J. (1989) The impact of corporate size and strategy on competitive pricing, Strategic Management Journal, Vol. 10, No. 8, pp. 569–585.

Teo, H. H., Wei, K.K. and Benbasat, I. (2003) Predicting Intention to Adopt Interorganisational Linkages: an Institutional Perspective, MIS Quarterly, Vol. 27, No. 1, pp. 19-49.

Teo, T, Tan, M. and Buk, W. (1998) A contingency model of internet adoption in Singapore, International Journal of Electronic Commerce, Vol. 2, No. 2, pp. 95–118.

Thatcher, S.M.B., Foster, W. and Zhu, L. (2006) B2B e-commerce adoption decisions in Taiwan: The interaction of cultural and other institutional factors. Electronic Commerce Research and Applications, Vol. 5, pp. 92–104

Thong, J. (1999) An integrated model of information systems adoption in small business, Journal of Management Information Systems, Vol. 15, No. 4, pp. 187–214.

Thong J.Y.L and Yap C. S. (1995) CEO Characteristics, Organizational Characteristics and Information Technology Adoption in Small Business, Omega, International Journal of Management Science, Vol. 23, No. 4, pp. 429-442.

Tornatzky, L.G. and. Fleischer, M (1990) The Process of Technological Innovation, Lexington Books, Lexington, MA.

Tornatzky, L.G. and Klein, K.J.(1982) Innovation characteristics and innovation adoption–implementation: a meta analysis of findings, IEEE Transactions on Engineering Management, Vol. 29, No. 11, pp. 28–45

U.S. Small Business Administration (1996).Electronic commerce/electronic data interchange, pp. 1–9.

Uzoka, F-M.E. (2008) Organisational influences on e-commerce adoption in developing country context using UTAUT, International Journal of Business Information Systems, Vol. 3, No. 3, pp. 300-316.

Watson, R.T., Akselsen, S. and Pitt, L.F. (1998) Attractors: building mountains in the □ at landscape of the World Wide Web, Californian Management Review, Vol. 40, No. 2, pp. 36–56.

Webb, B. and Sayer, R. (1998) Benchmarking small companies on the Internet, Long Range Planning., Vol. 31, No. 6, pp. 815–827.

Wise, R. and Morrison, D. (2000) Beyond the exchange: the future of B2B, Harvard Business Review, Vol. 74, No. 6, pp. 86–96.

Wilson, H.N., Daniel, E.M., Sutherland, F., McDonald, M.H.B. and Ward, J. (2001) Profiting from eCRM in Action: Making the New Marketing Work (FT Pearson Press, London).

Wierenga, B. and Oude Ophuis, P.A.M. (1997) Marketing decision support systems: adoption, use and satisfaction, International Journal of Research in Marketing, Vol. 14, No. 3, pp. 275–290.

Wixom, B.H., Watson, H. (2001) An empirical investigation of the factors affecting data warehousing success, MIS Quarterly, Vol. 25, pp. 17-41.

Wolfe, R.A.(1994) Organizational Innovation: Review, Critique and Suggested Research Directions, Journal of Management Studies, Vol. 31, No. 3, pp. 405 – 431.

Wymer, S. and Regan, E. (2005) Factors Influencing e-commerce Adoption and Use by Small and Medium Businesses, Electronic Markets, Vol. 15, No. 4, pp. 438-453.

Yoa, J.E., Xu, X., Liu, C. and Lu, J. (2003) Organization Size: A significant predictor of IT innovation adoption, Journal of Computer Information Systems, Vol. 43, No. 2, pp. 76-82.

Xu, S, Zhu, K. and Gibbs, J.(2004) Global technology, local adoption: a cross-country investigation of Internet adoption by companies in the United States and China, Electronic Markets, Vol. 14, No. 1, pp. 13–24

Zhu, K, Kraemer, K. and Xu, S. (2003) Electronic business adoption by European firms: a cross-country assessment of the facilitators and inhibitors, European Journal of Information Systems, Vol. 12, No. 4, pp. 251-268.

Zhu, K., Kraemer, K. L., Xu, S and Jason L. Dedrick. (2004) Information technology payoff in e-business environments: An international perspective on value creation of e-business in the financial services industry, Journal of Management Information Systems, Vol. 21, No. 1, pp 17-54.

Zhu, K. and Weynat, J.P. (2003) Strategic Decissions of new Technology Adoption under Asymmetric Information: A Game-Theoretic Model, Decision Science, Vol. 34, No. 4, pp. 643-675.

Zmud R. W (1984) An examination of push-pull theory applied to process innovation in knowledge work, Management Science, Vol. 30, No. 6, pp. 727-738.

CHAPTER 12

FACTORS OF COMMERCIAL WEBSITE SUCCESS IN SMALL AND MEDIUM ENTERPRISES: AN INDONESIAN STUDY

Vera Pujani & Jun Xu

Graduate College of Management, Southern Cross University, Australia

Mohammed Quaddus

Graduate School of Business, Curtin University of Technology, Australia

This study examined a model of website success, which was built on DeLoan and McLean's (1992, 2003) information system success model. The data were collected via surveying 550 Indonesian small and medium enterprises (SMEs) and were analyzed through partial least square (PLS) approach. The results indicate that quality of website and trust are significant factors that influence use of the website, which, in turn, has influence on organizational performance. In the meantime, quality of website and website use are found to have significant impact on website users' satisfaction, which, in turn, is positively associated with organizational performance. The results of this study provide practical suggestions to organizations that are embarking on e-commerce websites in Indonesian and across the globe.

1. Introduction

The utilisation of new technologies, especially Internet technology, has been identified as an innovative way to perform global business and gain a competitive advantage (Negash, Ryan & Igbaria 2003; Teo & Pian 2004). As Internet usage by various companies has broadened, company sales have increased through the selling of products and services in the cyber market (Tamimi, Sebastianelli & Rajan 2005). The total e-commerce revenue in Asian countries is predicted to reach up to US$535.3 trillion in 2010, an increase of 67.7% from 2000. For the period of 2006-2010 countries like Japan, South Korea, China, India are projected to have revenue growth of 54%, 48.6%, 13.9% and 18.8% respectively (eMarketer 2006). In Indonesia the estimated transaction volume of online shopping in 2010 is US$144 million (Rp 1324 trillion), with an increase of 52% from 2006 (Marketing Megazine 2007).

The use of e-commerce has brought both potential benefits and negative effects for organisations. E-commerce technologies are able to assist organisations in gaining their objectives by increasing their revenue stream, improving market exposure, decreasing operating costs, cutting the length of product life-cycles, improving supplier management, extending global reach, increasing customer loyalty and increasing value chains (Dou, Nielson & Tan 2002; Raharjo 1999; Sellito, Wenn & Burgess 2003; Teo & Choo 2001). As one of the main e-commerce applications, the web site is viewed as a revolutionary way to deliver services, educational programs, and daily business, especially for strategic, informational and transactional purposes (Raymond 2001; Sandy & Burgess 2003; Sellito, Wenn & Burgess 2003). Negative effects may occur in terms of *social impacts* (i.e., social isolation, loss of individuality or privacy concerns, impact on local, social and political value) and *economic impacts* (i.e., taxation issues, global trade concerns) (Sharma & Gupta 2003).

In Indonesia, the utilisation of e-commerce is still underdeveloped. Concerns such as insufficient information technology infrastructure, lack of financial support, limitations in education and English language capabilities have been identified as major e-commerce constraints in Indonesia (Pimchangthong et al. 2003; Raharjo 1999; Setiyadi, 2002). Nevertheless, some information communication technology (ICT) indicators have shown a significant improvement. In Indonesia, from 1996-1999, use of personal computers has increased by 17.85%, the number of Internet hosts by 24.11% and the number of online users by 42.52% (Orbeta 2002). In addition, the total number of Indonesian Internet domains has grown from 1,479 in 1998 to 21,762 in 2004 (APJII 2005). Furthermore, Indonesia has the rapidest growth in terms of the number of Internet users among ASEAN countries (see Table 12.1).

Table 12.1: Internet Users in ASEAN

Countries	Internet users (June 30, 2007 Data)	Penetration (% Population)	% users in Asia	User Growth (2000-2007*)
Indonesia	20,000,000	8.9 %	4.6 %	900.0 %
Singapore	2,421,800	66.3 %	0.6 %	101.8 %
Thailand	8,420,000	12.5 %	1.9 %	266.1 %
Malaysia	13,528,200	47.8 %	3.1 %	265.6 %
Philippines	14,000,000	16.0 %	3.2 %	600.0 %
Total Asia-Users	**436,758,162**			
Total World-Users	**1,173,109,925**			

(Source: adapted from Internet World Stats 2007)

The population in Indonesia is unevenly spread. Over 200 million Indonesian people are living across approximately 12,000 islands, with 60% of them on Java Island (Setiyadi 2002). Most Indonesian regions are separated by ocean. Development in Indonesian is slow, and the economic growth is unbalanced. Therefore, geographical problems are the main issues of performing business activities in Indonesia. The advantages of e-commerce and websites of being unconstrained by geographic location, give hope to solving the geographic problems which Indonesian businesses face. Furthermore, small and medium enterprises (SMEs) are identified as the backbone of economic growth in Indonesia. They make significant contributions to Indonesian development, and constitute the largest number of businesses (Indonesia Cooperative Department 2006). They are the backbone of Indonesian Economy and are perceived as a rescue valve in the recovery process of the national economy during the post-economic crisis (Berry et al. 2002; Grandon, & Pearson 2003). Indonesian SMEs have contributed a total of 53.5% of domestic product (product domestic pruto (PDB)) in 2006 (Rp 1.491,06 trillion) (Indonesia Cooperative Department 2006). Therefore, any research into SMEs in Indonesia will be of great assistance to the Indonesian economy.

On the other hand, while the enormous growth of the Internet has the profound impact on business activities of large companies which enjoy the benefits of experiences, stronger foundations and greater resources

(Bandyo-padyay 2002, p. 261), the adoption of Internet technologies in small and medium enterprises is still a recent phenomenon (Seyal & Rahman 2003). Given the fact that the majority of businesses in Indonesia are small and medium enterprises and the unique characteristics of SMEs (e.g., resources, size, structure), there is a strong need for understanding e-commerce in Indonesian SMEs. However there is a lack in the literature on e-commerce practices in Indonesian SMEs.

This research aims to make contribution to close this gap via examining website success in Indonesian SMEs. The primary focus of this research centers around the following three research questions:

(i) What are the factors that influence the website use in Indonesian SMEs?
(ii) What are the factors that influence user satisfaction about Indonesian SMEs' websites?
(iii) What are the relationships between use, user satisfaction and organizational performance of website in Indonesian SMEs?

This chapter is organized as follows. The following section presents relevant background. The research model and hypotheses are presented next. This is followed by the demographic information of the national survey. The data analysis through partial least square approach is also presented in this section. Conclusions regarding research questions and implications for theory and practice are discussed next. The paper finishes with summary, limitations and future research directions.

2. Background

2.1. Measuring Website Success

The utilization of new technology, in particular information technology (IT)/information systems (IS), has rapidly increased during the past half century (Martinsons & Chong 1999). On the contrary, the rapid IT development is not followed by the success of IT utilities and IS implementation (Lim 1998; Serafeimidis 1997). There are more failures and disappointments than successes (Whyte & Bytheway 1996). Organizations are seriously questioning about the gains and benefits arising from IT investment (Drury & Farhoomand 1998; Myers, Kappelman & Prybutok 1997). One of the reasons of information technology project failure is the gap between academic theories, conceptual frameworks and actual practices in organisations (Serafeimidis 1997). Another reason could be misalignment between business and IT in the strategic planning process (Garrity & Sandress 1998). Also there is a lack of well-established literature on IS evaluation (Myers, Kappelman & Prybutok 1997). Therefore, more practical research on better understanding IS/IT implementation is needed (Garrity & Sanders 1998).

One important perspective in understanding IS/IT implementation is measuring IS/IT success (Rai, Sandra & Welker 2002), which is a very challenging task since the success is normally temporal and can mean different things for different beholders (Gunson et al. 2004). The IS/IT success measures are a multidimensional concept, which can be measured at different levels (e.g., individual, group, organization, society, country) and at different aspects (e.g., economic, financial, behavioral, and perceptual) (Molla & Licker 2001). In addition, problems do exist in defining and understanding the concept of IS/IT success (Garrity & Sanders 1998; Myres, Kappleman & Prybutok 1997). There is a need for more studies to enhance the understanding of information system success and understanding how to evaluate IS/IT projects.

One important literature is the information system success model, developed by DeLone and McLean (1992; 2003), which consists of factors such as information system (IS) quality, use, user satisfaction, organizational benefits, and success connotations based on stakeholder perspectives,. DeLone and McLean (1992, 2003) suggest that the IS success is a multidimensional construct of technological, behavior and organizational factors. The validity of their model has been proven by many IS/IT research around the world. Their study has been the foundations of many later IS success studies.

The majority of e-commerce success models have been developed and tested in western context and developed countries, thus there is a need for e-commerce success model for firms in developing countries to reflect the changes in situation (Lertwongsatien & Wongpinunwatana, 2003). While there exist some studies regarding e-commerce success in

SMEs in developing countries including Indonesia (i.e., Lertwongsatien & Wongpinunwatana, 2003, Beeharry & Schneider, 1996; Korpela 1996; Foong 1999; Jain, 1997, Pimchangthong et al. 2003; Achjari & Quaddus 2002), there is a silence on the factors and models for website success in Indonesian SME context. To address this gap, this research developed a model of website success based on DeLone and McLean's information system success model (1992, 2003).

2.2. The Research Model & Hypotheses of the Study

The research model as shown in Figure 12.1 was framed on DeLone and McLean's information system model (1992, 2003). This model also incorporates such factors of features of website and trust. The research model suggests external factors such as quality of website, features of website and trust will have positive influence on the customers' use of website (i.e., for communicating with customers, vendors/suppliers, and business partners) and their satisfaction towards website (reflected by measures such as repeat visits, repeat purchase and complaints), which in turn have impact on the firm's organizational performance (referring to operational, financial and strategic benefits which the company receives from website usages).

Some dimensions of quality of website include ease of navigation, ease of transaction, customisation, download time, entertainment, personalisation, completeness of the information, up-to-date information, accurate information, price information, responsiveness to the customer's orders and questions, after-sales services, and shipping & handling of the product. Features of website refers to perspectives of contact details including contact information of the firm, webmaster and management team, company information, site map, table of content of the site, product information, special offer highlights, search function, FAQ section, online customer services, feedback form, online community, online advertisement banners, online ordering & payment facilities, links to other websites, language options, and website's own email services. Trust factor looks at things such as user authentication systems, secure transaction systems (e.g. SSL, or SET), third-party assurance/services (e.g. CA (Certificate Authority), VeriSign, or TRUSTe,) practices of informed consent in data collection and use, provision of relevant government regulations, presence of clear transaction rules and disclaimers, visible privacy policy, and trust building activities. In the mean time, website use by consumers has positive influence on their satisfaction towards website.

Based on the literature review, the following hypotheses were proposed (also see Figure 12.1). Due to space limitations the development of hypotheses are not described fully in the chapter.

- Hypothesis 1: Quality of website is positively associated with website use
- Hypothesis 2: Quality of websites is positively associated with user satisfaction of the website
- Hypothesis 3: Trust is positively associated with use of website
- Hypothesis 4: Quality of website is positively associated with user satisfaction of the website
- Hypothesis 5: Features of website is positively associated with user satisfaction of the website.
- Hypothesis 6: Trust is positively associated with user satisfaction of the website.
- Hypothesis 7: Website use is positively associated with user satisfaction of the website
- Hypothesis 8: Website use is positively associated with organizational performance
- Hypothesis 9: User satisfaction of the website is positively associated with organizational performance

3. Research Methodology

This study has been conducted using a quantitative approach. A combination of mail and 'drop and collect' surveys to collect primary data from Indonesian small and medium enterprises owning commercial websites were undertaken. The questionnaires were distributed to six selected provinces on Java Island which were chosen according to time and cost considerations. Before the formal survey, a pilot study was performed to test the questionnaires on ten respondent samples. The main purpose of the pilot study was to improve data validity and reliability. Thus, the results of the pilot study were used as input to improve and redesign the questionnaires to be used in the final survey. The questionnaire consisted of a number of structured questions in two main parts. Part A consisted of the questions related to the demographic profiles of respondents and Part B related to the respondents' perceptions of the website success variables. This research employed the multivariate techniques of data analysis, namely Structural Equation Modeling (SEM). Also, the Partial Least Square (PLS), one of the various SEM tools used to analyze data, was applied. PLS has the ability to simultaneously examine comprehensive relationships, and allows movement from an exploratory position to confirmatory analysis (Chin & Newsted 1999).

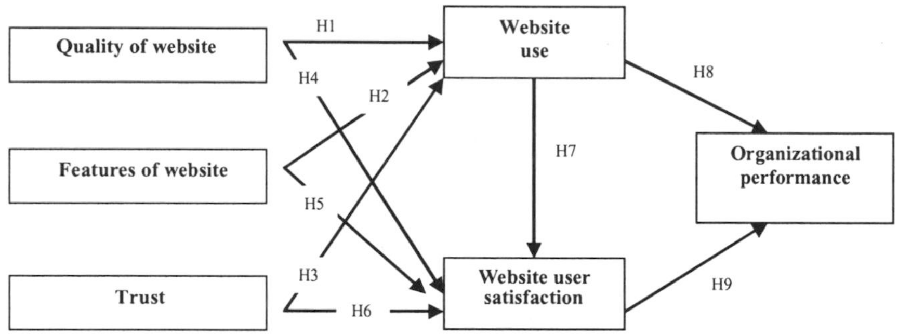

Figure 12.1: The Research Model

The respondents of this study included small and medium enterprises (SMEs) in Indonesia which were operating commercial websites. The questionnaires were distributed by mail and drop-and-collect surveys to one person at managerial level of each SME. 550 questionnaires were distributed to 550 businesses located in six different regions in Java Island including Jakarta, West Java, Central Java, Yogyakarta, East Java and Bali provinces. In the end, 129 valid responses were received.

4. Results

4.1. Respondent Characteristics

This section details the demographic data collected from the responses to the questions on personal and organisational information, and website characteristics and features.

4.1.1. Personal Information

The personal characteristics of the respondents were grouped into gender, age, current position in the organisation and educational level.

Gender

As depicted in Table 12.2, the majority of the respondents to the survey were male (89.1 percent), with 10.9 percent female.

Table 12.2: Personal information by gender

Gender	Frequency	Percent (%)
Male	115	89.1
Female	14	10.9

Age

As shown in Table 12.3, 64.8 percent (83 out of 128) of respondents were aged between 30 and 49; 67.9 percent were over 30 years old, 23.4 percent were over 40 years old and the remaining 3.1 percent were over 50 years old.

Table 12.3: Personal information by age

Age	Frequency	Percent (%)
< 30	41	32.0
30 - 39	57	44.5
40 - 49	26	20.3
50 - 60	4	3.1

Current Organisational Position

Table 12.4 shows that the most common position held in the organisation by research respondents was the dual position of owner and head of the company (31.8 percent). The owner-only position was held by 25.6 percent of respondents. Another four positions (company head, IS manager, marketing manager and others) were occupied by less than 18 percent of respondents. These results are typical of SMEs which are generally family businesses, with the owner managing the company.

Table 12.4: Personal information by position in organisation

Position	Frequency	Percent (%)
Owner	33	25.6
Company Head	18	14.0
Owner & Company Head	41	31.8
IS manager	8	6.2
Marketing Manager	7	5.4
Others	22	17.1

Level of Education

As seen in Table 12.5, 91.7 percent of respondents had at least a high school degree, 69.7 percent of respondents had a bachelor degree, and 10.8 percent had a post-graduate degree. This data illustrates that most respondents were educated people.

Table 12.5: Personal information by level of education

Highest education attained	Frequency	Percent (%)
Junior High School	3	2.3
Senior High School	11	8.5
Diploma 1 Year	7	5.4
Diploma 2/3 years	18	14.0
Bachelor degree	76	58.9
Master degree	11	8.5
Doctoral Degree	3	2.3

4.1.2. Organisational Information

Organisational information was categorised into three areas: (Tables 12.6–12.8) including number of employees, business sector, and company income (Indonesian Dollar Rupiah/ IDR).

Number of Employees

As Table 12.6 shows, 95.8 percent of the SMEs represented by the survey respondents employed less than 150 workers, while 91.9 percent of SMEs represented employed less than 100 workers and 81 percent employed less than 50. These results were commensurate with the definition of SMEs used as a basis for this research, as being organisations which employ less than 200 workers.

Table 12.6: Organisational information by number of employees

Number of Employees	Frequency	Percent (%)
< 5	50	38.8
5 - 50	57	42.2
50 - 100	14	10.9
100 - 150	5	3.9
150 - 200	3	2.3

Business Sector

As shown in Table 12.7, the main industry sectors of the SMEs represented by survey respondents were: computer/IT (27.1 percent); trading (23.3 percent); manufacturing (17.1 percent) and other sectors – a combination of banking, property, hospitality, engineering and others (32.5 percent). These results illustrate that a variety of industry sectors were included in this research.

Table 12.7: Organisational information by business sector

Business Sectors	Frequency	Percent (%)
Manufacturing	22	17.1
Banking/Finance	1	0.8
Trading	30	23.3
Computer/IT service	35	27.1
Property	10	7.8
Travel/Hospitality	4	3.1
Engineering/Construction	4	3.1
Others	23	17.8

Company Income

Two main groups of company income (in Indonesian Dollar Rupiah or IDR) are shown in Table 12.8. While 64.3 percent (81 out of 129) of respondent SMEs had an income of less than IDR500million, 35.7 percent (48 out of 129) of respondent SMEs had an income of more than IDR500million.

Table 12.8: Organisational information by company income

Company Income (IDR)	Frequency	Percent (%)
< 100 million	48	38.1
100 - 500 million	33	26.2
500 - 1000 million	12	9.5
1000 - 1500 million	10	7.9
1500 - 2000 million	3	2.4
2000 - 2500 million	4	3.2
2500 - 3000 million	2	1.6
3000 - 3500 million	3	2.4
3500 - 4000 million	11	8.7

4.1.3. Website Information

The website information collected from respondents is provided in twelve categories: age of website, contributions of the website, hosting costs (Indonesian Dollar Rupiah/IDR), language used, customers, level of investment in the website, type of website, number of visitors, number of orders, actual purchases, customer revisits and customer repurchases (Tables 12.9 – 12.20).

Age of Website

Table 12.9 shows that most respondents (67 percent) had operated company websites for over 1 year, 48 percent for over 2 years, and 35.6 percent for over 3 years. The duration of the operation of these websites illustrates the early adoption of commercial websites by Indonesian SMEs.

Table 12.9: Website information by age of website

Duration of Website Use	Frequency	Percent (%)
< 6 months	21	16.3
6 - 12 months	21	16.3
1 - 2 years	25	19.4
2 - 3 years	16	12.4
3 - 4 years	10	7.8
4 - 5 years	14	10.9
> 5 years	22	17.1

Contributions of Website

From Table 12.10 it can be seen that 73.4 percent of respondents reported that their website contributed more than 5 percent to the company, while 60.1 percent of respondents reported that their website contributed more than 10 percent and 42.3 percent of respondents reported that their website contributed more than 20 percent.

Table 12.10: Website information by contribution

Website Contributions	Frequency	Percent (%)
< 5 %	34	26.6
5 - 10 %	17	13.3
10 - 20 %	23	17.8
20 - 30 %	8	6.3
30 - 40 %	5	3.9
40 - 50 %	8	6.3
50 - 60 %	8	6.3
> 60 %	25	19.5

Hosting Costs

The costs for hosting the websites are presented in Table 12.11. The majority of SMEs (85.1 percent) represented by respondents paid less than IDR1million and only a small number of SMEs represented by respondents (14.9 percent) paid more than IDR1million.

Table 12.11: Website information by hosting costs

Hosting Costs (IDR) (Rp,000)	Frequency	Percent (%)
< 100	49	38.6
100 - 500	42	33.1
500 - 1000	17	13.4
1.0 - 1.5 million	6	4.7
1.5 - 2.0 million	6	4.7
2.5 - 3.0 million	1	0.8
> 3.0 million	6	4.7

Language Used

As is presented in Table 12.12, the main language of the SME websites of the survey respondents was a combination of Indonesian and English at 40.3 percent. Indonesian only was used by 39.5 percent, while English and other languages (e.g. Mandarin or the local language) were used by 17.1 and 1.6 percent respectively.

Table 12.12: Website information by language used

Language Used	Frequency	Percent (%)
Indonesian	51	39.5
English	22	17.1
Indonesian & English	52	40.3
Other	2	1.6

Website Customers

The majority of respondents (Table 12.13) had customers only from Indonesia (49.2 percent). The next largest percentage (46.9 percent) of SMEs had website customers from around the world, including Indonesia, and 3.9 percent of respondents had customers from overseas only. This illustrates that Indonesian websites not only focus on the domestic market but also on the global market, indicating they have utilised their websites to expand their market.

Table 12.13: Website information by customers

Website Customers	Frequency	Percent (%)
Indonesian	63	49.2
Foreigners	5	3.9
Indonesian & foreigners	60	46.9

Level of Investment in the Website

Table 12.14 presents the extent of investment made by Indonesian SMEs in their websites. It was found that the majority of respondent SMEs (96.1 percent) invested less than IDR200million in the implementation of their website; and a small number of respondents (2.9 percent) invested more than IDR200million.

Table 12.14: Website information by level of investment

Website Investment (IDR)	Frequency	Percent (%)
< 5 million	94	73.4
5 - 50 million	17	13.3
50 - 200 million	12	9.4
200 - 300 million	1	0.8
300 - 400 million	2	1.6
400 - 500 million	1	0.8
> 500 million	1	0.8

Type of Website

As seen in Table 12.15, most of the respondents (84.5 percent) used their company websites to perform business with individual consumers (business-to-customer). Of these, 46.5 percent operated purely business-to-customer websites, and 38 percent used their websites for business-to-customer and business-to-business operations. Purely business-to-business websites were operated by 10.9 percent of respondents and 4.7 percent of respondent SMEs operated other types of websites, such as portals or search engines.

Table 12.15: Website information by type of website

Website Type	Frequency	Percent (%)
Business-to-customer	60	46.5
Business-to-business	14	10.9
Both business-to-customer and Customer-to-business	49	38.0
Others	6	4.7

Number of Website Visitors per Week

The number of visitors to Indonesian SME websites is depicted in Table 12.16. These results showed that 54 percent of the respondent SMEs have weekly website visits of more than 50 visitors, 24.1 percent had more than 100 visitors and 13.9 percent had more than 200 visitors.

Table 12.16: Website information by weekly visitors

Weekly Visitors	Frequency	Percent (%)
< 50	59	46.0
50 - 100	38	29.9
100 - 200	13	10.2
200 - 300	7	5.5
300 - 400	1	0.8
400 - 500	1	0.8
> 500	8	6.3

Number of Website Orders per Week

The number of orders received via websites is presented in Table 12.17. Most respondents received weekly orders via their websites in the range of less than 10 to 50 orders (85.9 percent). Weekly orders in the range of

50 to 150 were received via the websites by 9.4 percent of respondents and 4.7 percent of respondents received more than 150 orders per week.

Table 12.17: Website information by weekly orders

Weekly Orders	Frequency	Percent (%)
< 10 orders	83	64.8
10 - 50	27	21.1
50 - 100	11	7.8
100 - 150	2	1.6
150 - 200	3	2.3
200 - 250	1	0.8
> 250	2	1.6

Percentage of Actual Purchases

The percentage of visitors who purchased via SME websites is illustrated in Table 12.18. Among respondents, 84.3 percent believed that up to 30 percent of their website visitors made on-line purchases whereas 74.9 percent of the respondents believed that up to 20 percent of their website visitors purchased on-line, and 38.6 percent of respondents believed that up to 5 percent of their websites visitors purchased on-line.

Table 12.18: Website information by actual purchases

Actual Purchases	Frequency	Percent (%)
< 5 %	49	38.6
5 - 10 %	27	20.5
10 -15 %	12	9.4
15 - 20 %	8	6.3
20 - 25 %	8	6.3
25 - 30 %	4	3.1
> 30 %	20	15.7

Customer Revisits

The visitors who 'hit' an Indonesian SME website more than once are defined as revisit users. As shown in Table 12.19, 82.8 percent of respondents believed that up to 30 percent of their website visitors were revisit users, while 60.6 percent of respondents believed that up to 10 percent of their website visitors were revisit users, and the remaining respondents (34.4 percent) believed that up to 5 percent of their website visitors were revisit users.

Table 12.19: Website information by revisit users

Revisit Users	Frequency	Percent (%)
< 5 %	42	34.4
5 - 10 %	32	26.2
10 - 15 %	10	8.2
15 - 20 %	6	4.9
20 - 25 %	4	3.3
25 - 30 %	7	5.7
> 30 %	21	17.2

Customer Repurchases

Customers who purchased more than once via a website were identified as repurchasing customers. As shown in Table 12.20, 86 percent of respondents believed their repurchasing customers were not more than 30 percent of their customers, and 81 percent of the respondents believed that their repurchasing customers were not more than 20 percent of their customers. Only 46.4 percent of respondents believed that their repurchasing customers were not more than 5 percent of their customers.

Table 12.20: Website information by repurchasing customers

Repurchasing Customers	Frequency	Percent (%)
< 5 %	56	46.4
5 - 10 %	22	18.5
10 - 15 %	8	6.6
15 - 20 %	9	7.4
20 - 25 %	3	2.5
25 - 30 %	6	5.0
> 30 %	17	14.0

The above information collected from the respondents represented an initial picture of Indonesian commercial websites, especially those of SMEs. This information will give a clear depiction of the commercial websites in Indonesia.

4.1.4. Website Features

The features of company websites were presented in the survey in twenty-two categories, as shown in Table 12.21. The data shows that half of the respondents provide seven main website features: the company address, an overview of the company, e-mails to the marketing staff, highlights of new products, e-mails to the webmaster, on-line order facilities, and website links, and were in the range of 96.1-53.1 percent of respondents. The seven lowest percentages of features provided were: privacy policy, language options, on-line payment facilities, on-line community, advertising banners, terms and conditions and FAQs, and were in the range 20.9-36.4 percent of respondents. This information illustrates the features displayed on SME websites in Indonesia, based on the highest percentage of features provided. Most of these features demonstrate that the commercial websites of Indonesian SMEs are used for information purposes rather than transactional purposes.

Table 12.21: Respondents by website feature

Website Features	**Respondent (%)**
Company phone/address	96.1
Overview of company	83.7
E-mail to marketing staff	83.1
New product highlights	61.2
Online orders	58.1
E-mail to webmaster	57.4
Links to other websites	53.1
Guest book	45.0
Special offer highlights	44.2
E-mail to technical staff	43.4
News	42.6
Search facilities	41.9
Feedback forms	41.9
Online customer service	39.5
E-mail service	38.3
FAQs	36.4
Terms and conditions	33.3
Advertising banners	30.2
On-line community	28.7
On-line payment facilities	27.9
Language options	23.3
Privacy policy	20.9

According to the literature, the website features provided by Indonesian SMEs categorise those websites as simple websites. Teo and Pian (2004) classed this type of website as level 1, or web presence applications. This level provides in-process and static websites which are more electronic brochures than business integration systems (Sandy & Burgess 2003). Similarly, Scharl, Gebauer & Bauer (2001) categorised this level of website as a *basic interaction* consisting of some low-level information feedback.

The survey data included personal and organisational information, and website characteristics and features. This demographic data showed that the use of commercial websites by Indonesian SMEs was still at the level of early adoption.

4.2. Response Bias

The comparison of two survey groups was conducted to identify any possible significant difference between response samples to the mailed survey and the drop-and-collect surveys. Questionnaires had been distributed in six locations in Java Island (seventy-three of the 129 respondents (56.6 percent) as the drop-and-collect group). The comparison between the mail group and the drop-and-collect group was conducted using the t-test of independent samples assuming equal error variances. The t-test results of the comparison between the mail and drop-and-collect groups using the demographic data which including personal, organisational and website data. In general, there are no major differences between these two groups of survey.

4.3. Data Analysis Using the PLS Approach

We used standard PLS procedure to analyse the data. This involves analysing the data in two stages. In the first stage the measurement model is tested for reliability and validity. The model may be fine tuned to conform to the reliability and validity issues (Barclay et al. 1995, Igbaria et al. 1997). In the second stage the whole model is run again to test the hypotheses.

It is noted that PLS is specially appropriate for small sample analysis (Chin & Newsted, 1999). According to Barclay et al. (1995) PLS requires a minimum sample size that is ten times the greater of: (i) the number of items comprising the most complex formative construct, or (ii) the largest number of predictors leading to an endogenous (dependent) construct. We don't have any formative construct in our research model and in our case the largest number of predictors leading to an endogenous construct (Website User Satisfaction) is four. Thus this study requires a minimum sample size of 40. Therefore 129 usable responses in our case is quite appropriate for data analysis using PLS.

Assessment of Measurement Properties

The results of the examination of the individual item reliability assessed by examining the loadings of the items (a minimum value of 0.6 was used as criterion to accept the reliability of individual items as Chin (1998) suggested) and internal consistency of the latent variables that was measured following the procedure of Fornell and Larcker (1981) with the cut-off point of 0.7 of the constructs of the model, shows all the variables are reliable and all the constructs are internally consistent. In the meantime, discriminant validity of the latent variables was tested using the procedure of Fornell and Larcker (1981) and found all the latent variables are different from each other.

Table 12.22: Structural Model for this research

	Proposed effect	**Path coefficient**	**Observed t-value**	**Sig. Level (1-tail)**
H1: Quality	+	0.307	3.134	0.001
H2: Feature	+	-0.082	0.590	*ns**
H3: Trust	+	0.412	3.853	0.001
H4: Quality	+	0.267	2.630	0.01
H5: Feature	+	-0.049	0.432	*ns*
H6: Trust	+	0.074	0.684	*ns*
H7: Use	+	0.519	8.057	0.001
H8: Use	+	0.319	3.395	0.001
H9: User Satisfaction	+	0.429	4.641	0.001
	R^2 for Use=0.324), R^2 for User satisfaction=0.497, R^2 for Organizational Benefits=0.464			

(* ns: not significant)

The Structural Model and Tests of Hypotheses

Table 12.22 shows the results of the structural model. It is observed that among the hypotheses H2, H5, and H6 are not supported (insignificant t-values) while the hypotheses H1, H3, H4, H7, H8, and H9 are supported (significant t-values). The model explains 32.4% of the variance of use, 49.7% of user satisfaction, and 46.4% organizational benefits, which are quite good.

5. Discussion of Results

5.1. Conclusions of the Research Findings

This section presents a discussion of the results of the statistical analysis of the collected data. The hypotheses tests were performed to answer the research questions through t-value estimations of PLS outputs. Of the nine hypotheses, six were identified as having statistical significance and therefore were supported by the research data: H1, H3, H4, H7, H8, and H9. The remaining three hypotheses (H2, H5, and H6) were identified as having no supporting statistical evidence. Details of the analysis results in relation to each research question are provided in the following sections, interpreting the results and elaborating on the effect of the success of e-commerce websites in Indonesian SMEs.

5.1.1. Findings for Research Question 1

Impact of Quality on Website Use (H1)

The first hypothesis (H1: *Quality of websites is positively associated with use by Indonesian SMEs*) proposed that the quality of a website had a positive relationship with the use of the website. The result of this study found a significant relationship between qualities and website use. This result was consistent with previous studies (i.e., Chen, Gillenson & Sherrell 2004; D'Angelo & Little 1998; Darvern, Te'eni & Moon 2000). The direct affect of quality on website use was quite robust. Given the fact that the quality of a website is a vital factor, Indonesian SMEs need to operate quality websites for the success of their e-commerce activities. Indonesian SMEs' websites should be easy to use and enable customers to perform online activities (such as online search, online shopping, online communication), and is very critical for informative websites (many Indonesian SMEs' website are such websites) to provide accurate, complete, timely and updated information.

Impact of Features on Website Use (H2)

The second hypothesis (H2: *Features of websites are positively associated with website use by Indonesian SMEs*) tested the effect of features on website use. This study found that there was no significant evidence to support this hypothesis, and indicated in the context of Indonesian SMEs, features are not viewed as a key dimension in using websites. This result was not consistent with prior research (Abel, White & Hahn 1997; Kim, Shaw & Schneider 2003; Lee, Katerattanakul & Hong 2005). Analysis of the demographic data on the features of websites of surveyed Indonesian SME found that most Indonesian SME websites were only using their web sites for informative purposes (i.e., online catalogues) and for communication purposes. Therefore, unsurprisingly, the features were not important to them.

Impact of Trust on Website Use (H3)

The third hypothesis (H3: *Trust is positively associated with website use by Indonesian SMEs*) examined the effect of trust on website use. Based on the results of the hypothesis testing, there is a statistical significance supporting this hypothesis. This result was consistent with various empirical studies (Fenech 2000; Heidjen & Verhagen 2004; Lee, Katerattanakul & Hong 2005). This study revealed that trust was a key factor, specifically for SME websites in Indonesia. This result is in line with the literature (i.e., McKnight, Choudhury & Kacmar 2002; Wang & Emurian 2004). In this study trust is defined as institutional-based trust which built trustworthiness from the point of view of the website users or customers. Despite the task of building online trust is a formidable task because trust is a complex and abstract concept (Wang & Emurian 2004),

Indonesian SMEs websites should work on security and privacy issues to enhance users' trust.

5.3.2. Findings for Research Question 2

Impact of Qualities on User Satisfaction (H4)

This hypothesis (H4: *Quality of websites are positively associated with user satisfaction of Indonesian SME websites)* assumed that the quality of the website will influence the user's satisfaction when using the websites. This study proved significant relationships between the quality of websites and user satisfaction. Such finding is in line with previous studies (i.e., Jiang & Rosenbloom 2004; Muylle, Moenaert and Despostin 2004; Negash, Ryan and Igbaria 2003).

Impact of Features on User Satisfaction (H5)

The fifth hypothesis (H5: *Features of websites are positively associated with user satisfaction of Indonesian SME websites*) tested the features of websites as a valuable factor influencing user satisfaction. However, the result demonstrated no significant effects between features and user satisfaction of websites, indicating a lack of evidence to support the hypothesis that features are a key determinant of user satisfaction. This finding does not support previous studies (i.e., Feinberg & Kadam 2002; Muylle, Moenaert and Despontin 2004; Palmer 2002). This result can be explained by the fact that most Indonesian websites still operate for informative purposes (electronic brochures), so that revisitors and repurchasers are probably are not influenced by the features provided within the websites. Furthermore, Indonesian users of websites are generally aiming to find a particular product or service within the Indonesian market and understand that Indonesian e-commerce websites are still in a stage of early development and generally do not offer advanced features. Therefore, website features are not considered a crucial requirement by Indonesian users and they are satisfied with technologically simple Indonesian websites. Accidental surfing may also be a factor in the relative lack of importance users place on website features. As argued by Dholakia and Rego (1998) users browse websites for a variety of purposes, such as searching for special information; random web-surfing; participation in contests and raffles (lottery); and word-of-mouth information from other web enthusiasts. Therefore, users who revisit websites are not necessarily users who have been previously-satisfied by the features of a website. Given these particular user situations, the features of websites are not important determinants in encouraging users to browse or revisit websites in Indonesia.

Impact of Trust on User Satisfaction (H6)

Trust was hypothesised as having a positive correlation to website user satisfaction (H6: *Trust is positively associated with user satisfaction of Indonesian SME websites*). However, the finding of this study shows that trust is not an influential factor on user satisfaction, and is inconsistent with prior studies (e.g. Negash, Ryan & Igbaria 2003; Pavlou 2002; Szymanski & Hise 2000). One possible explanation for this non-significant effect is that Indonesian SME websites generally have a low number of online orders, purchases, revisits and repurchases. Therefore the majority of respondents of this study may believe that trust attributes such as facilities for security, regulations and privacy are not a priority requirement on their websites. Also, the trust measures tend to relate to the conduct of on-line business transactions, whereas most respondents of this study still conducted off-line business transactions, since Indonesian customers still prefer to use phone orders and bank transfer payments rather than website facilities for their transactions. This can be seen by the fact that only 28 percent of research respondents had online payment facilities. Furthermore, website revisits may be from accidental or random visitors who browse websites from search engines, and not due to dedicated searching for information from a particular site which has been previously visited. Another possible explanation for this result is that revisiting and repurchasing customers may be business customers (partners) who have entered into a contract or business collaboration before undertaking on-line transactions, in which case the business transactions would require regular revisits and purchases. It also can be seen from the respondent data that almost 49 percent of respondents run business-to-business websites, where 38 percent are a mix of business-to-customer and business-to-business and 10.9 percent are business-to-business only. In other words, website trust may not be a particular effect of or requirement for this kind of business relationship.

Impact of Use on User Satisfaction (H7)

The influence of use on user satisfaction was tested with hypothesis 7 (H7: *Website use is positively associated with user satisfaction of Indonesian SME websites*). This study proved statistically that website use has a significant correlation with user satisfaction. This result also supports numerous previous studies (i.e., McGill, Hobbs & Klobas 2003; Gelderman 1998), indicating that website use is identified as a relevant factor in creating user satisfaction with a website. This result demonstrated that Indonesian SMEs' efforts in building the satisfaction of their website users by providing e-commerce functions (i.e., 58 percent of respondents offered online ordering facilities and 28 percent offered online payment facilities), are able to encourage their customers to revisit and repurchase via their website. In addition, by using their websites, Indonesian SMEs are able to communicate, collaborate, and transact with customers (individuals and businesses) to maintain their business relationships. Therefore, through effective responses and relationships with users, SMEs are able to encourage their website customers to re-transact via their website.

5.3.3. Findings for Research Question 3

Impact of Use on Organisational Benefits (H8)

The concluded support for H8 (H8: *Website use is positively associated with organisational benefits of Indonesian SME websites)* is consistent with previous research (i.e., Lii, Lim & Tseng 2004; Teo & Choo 2000; Teo & Pian 2004). This result shows a statistically significant correlation between website use and organisational benefits. It suggests that Indonesian SMEs believed they can gain benefits from owning commercial websites.

Impact of User Satisfaction on Organisational Benefits (H9)

User satisfaction has also been identified as an essential factor in gaining organisational benefits through website usage, proven in this study by the results of testing hypothesis 9 (H9: *User satisfaction is positively associated with organisational benefits of Indonesian SME websites*). The results of this research show a significant correlation between uses and organisational benefits, which supports the study of Gelderman (1998). When website users revisit and repurchase via a company website, the associated organisational benefits will be acquired continually. In spite of the lack of number of online transactions via websites, Indonesian SMEs still consider the importance of user satisfaction with their websites and the concomitant organisational benefits. Therefore, Indonesian SME website operators confirmed in this study that the satisfaction of their customers with their websites is a crucial factor in achieving organisational benefits.

6. Implications of this Research

The results of this study have both theoretical and practical implications. In this research, a website success model was developed from the information systems success model of DeLone and Mclean (1992; 2003) and their e-commerce success model (2004). Two new independent factors of features and trust are added into the DeLone and McLean's models and tested. The results of the study lend the support to DeLone & Mclean's models by proving the significant relations between quality, use, user satisfaction and organizational benefits. And this study further unveiled the significance of trust in website success. Small and medium enterprises who are embarking on e-commerce or have adopted e-commerce could use those factors and the variables within those factors to examine and guide their e-commerce initiatives. In the meantime, as per the analysis of demographic information of participating SMEs in Indonesia, it can be concluded that Indonesian SME websites are at the early adoption stage of e-commerce and are primarily use websites for informative and communication purposes.

In order to gain benefits from commercial websites, Indonesian SMEs need to work on such areas as ensuring website quality, working on trust building, marketing effectively, acquiring customers, and maintaining customers' loyalty. In the meantime, Indonesian government should deploy more pro-e-commerce policies, invest on ICT infrastructure, and provide assistance to SMEs (including financial support and education courses by collaborating with education services providers).

7. Sumamry, Limitations and Future Research Directions

7.1. Summary

This study developed and tested a model of website success in Indonesian SMEs. The results of this study enhance our understanding of e-business practices in Indonesian SMEs, provide e-business organizations and relevant parties in Indonesia suggestions regarding implementing successful commercial websites in Indonesia SMEs. The results of this study could also adapted for assisting SMEs in other countries when they are embarking on e-business or are enhancing their existing e-business operations.

7.2. Limitations of this Research

Dissimilar Survey Groups

For the purposes of data comparison, the survey was conducted in two different groups, one receiving a drop-and-collect questionnaire and the other a mailed questionnaire. The drop-and-collect survey was only undertaken in two locations, while the mail survey was conducted in five provinces, so there are minor differences between respondents of the mail and drop-and-collect groups. The majority of commercial websites in Jakarta and West Java provinces (the drop-and-collect respondents) tend to be operated by SMEs in a greater variety of industries than the other provinces. Most of the mail survey respondents had commercial websites in the hospitality and manufacturing industries. Therefore, a comparison of the mail and drop-and-collect survey groups identified some slightly significant differences. In addition, the number of sample sizes of the two groups was unequal and the number of responses to this research was not controlled and did not gather equal numbers of responses from the two survey groups. The sample size of the mail survey was 53 and that of the drop-and-collect survey was 69. This condition was not properly examined by a comparative study of the two groups.

Unfamiliar Website Terms

Because most Indonesian SME websites are electronic brochures with no on-line transactions, several questions, in particular related to attributes (features, trust and use), could not be answered as the knowledge of respondents relating to websites is still limited. Therefore, some respondents skipped the related questions or left parts of questions blank, especially in relation to website terms such as those measuring website features. This situation may also have arisen because the measures of website features did not have significant effects on the use and user satisfaction of commercial sites. However, this limitation would be a relevant consideration for future research.

Limited Time and Costs

Due to limited resources (finances, time and access to databases) the researchers conducted this survey in six provinces of Java Island only. However, Indonesia is widely spread across thousands of islands. Therefore, a limitation of this research is that limited resources prevented an exhaustive study of all SME websites in Indonesia.

7.3. Suggestions for Future Research

Formative Construct

This study used the PLS technique for data analysis. Based on the literature, the PLS has the advantage of being able to examine research constructs for both reflective and formative constructs. In this research, the model was identified as having reflective construct only, however, the quality, features and trust attributes may also be defined as formative constructs, adjusted for construct indicators or measures. Future research may benefit from consideration of the formative specifications of the website success model.

Second-order Measures

This research only studied a high-level model of website success. Several items were dropped from the quality and features constructs, as having dissimilar meanings. These dropped items probably are able to form new constructs from their original construct. Therefore, in the future, second-order factors of the quality and features constructs could be further studied.

Survey Area Expansions

In addition, while browsing for company websites, the researcher found the majority of the websites on are Java Island. Therefore, the Indonesian government should develop programs to promote e-commerce to companies or SMEs located off Java Island. Collaboration between national and local bodies as well as academic research would provide assistance to local SMEs to undertake e-commerce activities, in particular the development of commercial websites. Furthermore, the researcher obtained positive responses during the pilot study and the collected data indicated that SME managers are enthusiastic about website implementation. Some participants of the pilot study explained when they realized the potential benefits of e-commerce, they lack of knowledge and skills for effective implementation of e-commerce initiatives. Therefore, local SMEs require government assistance in promote and develop e-commerce solutions.

Non-commercial Websites

This research examined the website success model for commercial purposes only. The same website success model could be applied to non-commercial websites, e.g. educational and government websites. In general, success in using websites is believed to involve combinations of perspectives such as technological, behavioural, and marketing which may be applicable for other website types.

References

Abel, EG., White, MD. & Hahn (1997) Identifying user-based criteria for web pages, Internet Research: Electronic Networking Applications and Policy, Vol. 7, No. 4, pp. 252-262.

Achjari, D. & Quaddus, M. (2002) Roles of Formal/Informal Network and Perceived Compatibility in the Diffusion of WWW: The case of Indonesia banks, Proceedings of the 36th Hawaii International Conference on System Science (HICSS-36) (IEEE Computer Society Press, Maui).

APJII (2005) Assosiasi Penyedia Jasa Internet Statistic tersedia : www.apjii.org, akses 27 Maret 2006.

Asia Foundation (2002) SMEs and e-commerce, Online, Available: http://www.asiafoundation.org/pdf/SMEsurvey_Indo.pdf' (Accessed 20 Nov 2004).

Bagozzi, R.P. (1994) Principles of Marketing Research, Basil Blackwell, Massachusetts, USA.

Bandyo-padhyay, N. (2002) E-commerce: Context, Concepts and Consequences, McGraw-Hill, New York.

Barclay, D., Higgins, C. & Thompson, R. (1995) The partial Least Squares (PLS) approach to causal modeling: Personal computer adoption and use as an illustration, Technology Studies, Vol. 2, No. 2, pp. 285-309.

Beeharry, A. & Schneider, GM. (1996) Creating a campus network culture in a newly developing economy, Information Technology for Development, Vol. 7, No. 1, pp. 3-16.

Chen, L., Gillenson, ML. & Sherrell, DL. (2004) Consumer acceptance of virtual stores: a theoretical model and critical success factors for virtual stores, Database for Advances in Information Systems, Vol. 35, No. 2, pp. 8-31.

Chin, W.W., (1998) Issues and opinion on structural equation modeling, MIS Quarterly, Vol. 22, No. 1, pp. vii-xvi

Chin, W.W., & Newsted, PR. (1999) Structural Equation Modeling analysis with small samples using Partial Least Squares, in Rick Hoyle (Ed.)', Statistical Strategies for Small Sample Research, Sage Publications, pp. 307-341.

Costa, E. D. (2001) Global e-commerce strategies for small businesses, MIT Press, Cambridge, Mass

D'Angelo, J. & Little, S. (1998) Successful web pages: what are they and do they exist?, Information Technology and Libraries, Vol. 17, No. 2, pp. 71-81.

DeLone, W.H., & McLean, E R. (1992) Information systems success: the quest for the dependent variable, Information Systems Research, Vol. 3, No. 1, pp.60-95.

DeLone, W.H., & McLean, E R. (2003) The DeLone and McLean model of information systems success: A ten-year update, Journal of management Information Systems, Vol. 19, No. 4, pp. 9-30.

DeLone, W.H., & McLean, E R. (2004) Measuring e-commerce success: applying the Delone & McLean Information Systems success model, International Journal of Electronic Commerce, Vol. 9, No. 1, pp. 31-47.

Dholakia, U. M. & Rego, L. (1998) What makes commercial web page popular? An empirical investigation of webpage effectiveness, European Journal of Marketing, Vol. 32, No. 7/8, pp. 724-736.

Dou, W., Nielson, U.O. & Tan, C.M. (2002) Using corporate websites for export marketing, Journal of Advertising Research, Sept/Oct, pp. 105-118.

Drury, D.H. & Farhoomand, A.F. (1998) A hierarchical structural model of information system success', INFOR, Vol. 36, No. 1/2. pp. 25-40.

eMarketer (2006) Usage Patterns, Online, Available: http://www.emarketer.com/ [accessed 20 September 2007]

Feinberg, R., & Kadam, R. (2002) E-CRM Web service attributes as determinants of customer satisfaction with retail web sites, International Journal of Service Industry Management, Vol. 13, No. 5, pp. 432-451.

Fenech, T. (2000) Attitude and security do count for shopping on the World Wide Web, Online, Available: http://130.195.95.71:8081/www/ANZMAC2000/CDsite/papes/f/Fenech1.pdf. (accessed 14 August 2004)

Foong, Soon-Yau (1999) Effect of & user personal and systems attributes on computer-based information system success in Malaysian SMEs', Journal of Small Business Management, Vol. 37, No.3, pp. 81-87.

Fornell, C. and Larcker, D. F. (1981) Evaluating Structural Equation Models with Unobservable Variables and Measurement Error, Journal of Marketing Research, XVIII, (February 1981), pp. 39-50.

Garrity, E.J, & G.L. Sanders (1998) Introduction to Information Systems Success Measurement," in Information Systems Success Measurement, Idea Group Publishing, Harrisburg, PA, edited by E.J. Garrity and G.L. Sanders, 1998, pp. 1-12.

Geissler, G., Zinkhan, G., & Watson, RT. (2001) Web home page complexity and communication effectiveness, Journal of the Association for information Systems, Vol. 2, No. 2, pp. 1-46.

Gelderman, M. (1998) The relationships between user satisfaction, usage of information systems and performance, Information & Technology, Vol. 34, No. 1, pp. 11-18.

Gunson, J., De Blasis, J-P., Esteves, J. & Pastor, J. (2004) Information system implementation: model to determine what constitutes success and failure, Online, Available: http://hec.info.uniqe,ch/researchers_publications/cahiers/2004.05.pdf (accessed 14 February 2005).

Heart, T & Pliskin, N. (2002) Business-to-business eCommerce of information systems: Two cases of ASP-to-SME eRental, INFOR, Vol. 40. No. 1, pp. 23- 35.

Heijden, H., & Verhagen, T. (2004) Online store image: conceptual foundation and empirical measurement, Information & Management, Vol. 41, pp. 609-617.

Holck, J. (2003) 4 Perspectives on Web Information Systems, Proceeding of the 36th Hawaii International Conference on System Science, Online, Available: http://web.cbs.dk/staff/holck/ (accessed 30 June 2004).

Igbaria, M, Zinatelli, N, Cragg, P and Cavaye, A. L. M. (1997) Personal Computing Acceptance Factors in Small Firms: A Structural Equation Model, MIS Quarterly, September, pp. 279-302.

Indonesia Cooperative Department (2006) Indikator makro ekonomi usaha kecil dan menengah tahun 2006, Online, Available: http://www.depkop.go.id/berita_resmi/index.htm (accessed 10 October 2007).

Internet World Stats (2007) Internet users, Online, Available: http://www.nternetworldstats.com (accessed 20 September 2007).

Jain, R. (1997) Key constructs in successful IS implementation: South-East Asian experience, Omega, International Journal Management Science, Vol. 24, No. 3, pp. 267-284.

Janda, S., Trochia, P., & Gwinner, K., (2002) Consumer perceptions of internet retail service quality, International Journal of Service Industry Management, Vol. 13, No. 5, pp. 412-431.

Jiang, P., & Rosenbloom, B. 2004, 'Customer intention to return online: price perception, attribute-level performance, and satisfaction unfolding overtime', European Journal of Marketing, vol. 39(1/2), pp.150-174.

Kim, S.E, Shaw, T. & Schneider, H. (2003) Web site design benchmarking within industry groups, Internet Research, Vol. 13, No. 1, pp. 17-26.

Korpela, M (1996) Traditional culture or political economy? on the root causes of organizational obstacles of IT in developing countries, Information Technology for Development, Vol. 7, No. 1, pp. 29-42.

Lee, SM., Katerattanakul, P. & Hong, S. (2005) Framework for user perception of effective e-tailing web sites, Journal of Electronic Commerce in Organizations, Vol. 3, No. 1, pp. 13-34.

Lertwongsatien, C. & Wongpinunwatana, N. (2003) E-commerce adoption in Thailand: an empirical study of small and medium enterprises (SMEs), Journal of Global Information Technology Management, Vol. 6, No.3, pp. 67-83.

Lii, Ys., Lim, H., & Tseng, L. (2004) The effects of web operational factors on marketing performance, Journal of American Academy of Business, Vol. 5, No. 1/2, pp. 486-494.

Lim, SK. (1998) A Frame work to evaluate the information level, in Information Systems Success Measurement, Idea Group Publishing, Harrisburg, PA, edited by E.J. Garrity and G.L. Sanders, 1998, pp. 13-22.

Marketing Megazine (2007) A number of online transactions, Online, Available www.spireresearch.com (accessed 10 October 2007).

Martinsons, M. G, & Chong, P.K.C, (1999) The influence of human factors and specialist involvement on information systems, Human Relations, Vol. 52, No. 1, pp. 123-152.

McGill, T., Hobbs, V. & Klobas, J. (2003) User-developed application and information systems success: a test of DeLone and McLean's model, Information Resource Management Journal, Vol. 16, No. 1, pp. 24-45.

McKnight, D., Choughury, V., & Kacmar, C. (2002) Developing and validating trust measures for e-commerce: an integrative typology', Information, Systems Research, Vol. 13, No. 3, pp. 334-361.

Molla, A., & Licker, P.S. (2001) E-commerce systems success: an attempt to extend and respecify the Delone and MacLean model IS success, Journal of Electronic Commerce Research, Vol. 2, No. 4, pp. 131-141.

Muylle, S., Moenaert, R., & Despontin, M. (2004) The conceptualization and empirical validation of web site user satisfaction, Information & Management, Vol. 41, pp. 543-560.

Myers, B.L, Kappelman, L.A., & Prybutok, V.R (1997) A comprehensive model for assessing the quality and productivity of the information systems function: toward a theory for information systems assessment, Information Resources Management Journal, Vol. 10, No. 1, pp. 6-25.

Negash, S., Ryan, T., & Igbaria, M. (2003) Quality and effectiveness in web-based customer support systems, Information & Management, Vol. 40, pp. 757-768.

Nunnally, J.C., & Bernstein, I.H. (1994) Psychometric Theory , McGraw-Hill series in Psychology, USA.

Orbeta, A., C. (2002) E-commerce in Southeast Asia: A review of developments, challenges, and issues, in Information Technology in Asia, by Yue, Siow, Chia & Lim, Jerome, Jamus, Institute of Southeast Asian Studies, Singapore, p. 111-146.

Palmer, J.W. (2002) Web site usability, design and performance metrics, Information Systems Research, Vol. 13, No. 2, pp.151-167.

Pavlov, P.A. (2002) Institution-based trust in interorganizational exchange relationships: the role of online B2B marketplaces on trust formation, Journal of Strategic Information Systems, Vol. 11, pp. 215-243.

Pimchangthong, D., Plaisent, M., & Bernard, P. (2003) Key issues in information systems management: a comparative study of academics and practitioners in Thailand, Journal of Global Information Technology management, Vol. 6, No. 4, pp. 27-44.

Raharjo, B. (1999) Implementing ecommerce in Indonesia, Online, Available: http://budi.insan.co.id/articles/1999-02.pdf (accessed 2 April 2004).

Rai, A., Sandra, S., L. & Welker, R.B. (2002) Assessing the validity of IS success models: An empirical test and theoretical analysis, Information System Research, Vol. 13, No. 1, pp.50-69.

Raymond, L. (2001) Determinants of web site implementation in small business, Internet Research, Vol. 11, No. 5, pp. 441-422.

Sandy, G., & Burgess, S. (2003) A decision chart for small business web site content, Logistics Information Systems, Vol. 16, No. 1, pp. 36-47.

Sarosa, S., & Zowghi, D. (2003) Strategy for adopting information technology for SMEs: experience in adopting email within an Indonesia furniture company, Electronic Journal of Information System Evaluation, Vol. 6, No. 2, pp.165-176, Online, Available: http://www.ejise.com (accessed 22 March 2004).

Scharl, A., Gebauer, J. & Bauer, C. (2001) Matching process requirements with information technology to assess the efficiency of the web information systems, Information Technology and Management, Vol. 2, No. 2, pp. 193-210.

Sellito, C., Wenn, A., & Burgess, S. (2003) A review of the web sites of small Australian wineries: motivations, goals and success, Information Technology and Management, Vol. 4, No. 4, pp. 215-232.

Serafeimidis, V. (1997) Information systems investment evaluation: conceptual and operational explorations, unpublished PhD thesis, London School of Economics and Political Science

Setiyadi, Mas W.R. (2002) E-commerce for rural and SMEs development in Indonesia, Online, Available: http://www.ecommerce.or.th/APEC- workshop2002/ ppt/slide/wigrantoro.pdf (accessed 2 April 2004).

Seyal, Afzal,H. & Rahman, Mohd, N., A. (2003) A preliminary investigation of e-commerce adoption in small & medium enterprises in Brunei, Journal of Global Information Technology Management, Vol. 6, No. 2, pp. 6-26.

Sharma, S., & Gupta, J. (2003) Socio-Economic influences of e-commerce adoption, Journal of Global Information Technology management, Vol.6, No. 3, pp. 3-21.

Szymanski, D., & Hise, R. (2000) E-satisfaction: an initial examination, Journal of Retailing, Vol. 76, No. 3, pp. 309-316.

Tagliavini, M., Ravarini, A. & Antonelli, A. (2001) An evaluation model for electronic commerce activities within SMEs, Information Technology and Management, Vol. 2, No. 2, pp. 211-230.

Tamimi, N., Sebastianelli, R. & Rajan, M. (2005) What do online customers value?, Quality Progress, Vol. 38, No. 7, pp. 35-39.

Teo, T., & Choo, W. (2000) Assessing the impact of using the internet for competitive intelligence, Information & Management, Vol. 39, pp. 67-83.

Teo, T. & Pian (2004) A model for web adoption, Information & Management, Vol. 41, pp. 457-468.

Turban, E., King, D., Viehland, D. & Lee, J. (2006) Electronic Commerce 2006: A Managerial Perspective, International edn. Upper Saddle River, NJ: Prentice

Wang, YD., & Emurian, H. (2004) An overview of online trust: concepts, elements, and implications, Computer in Human Behavior, Vol. 21, pp.105-125.

Whyte, G. & Bytheway, A. (1996) Factors affecting information systems success, International Journal of Service Industry Management, Vol. 7, No. 1, pp. 74-93.

CHAPTER 13

E-COMMERCE ADOPTION IN SMALL ENTERPRISES: AN AUSTRALIAN STUDY

Jahjah Hallal & Jun Xu

Graduate College of Management, Southern Cross University, Australia

Mohammed Quaddus

Graduate School of Business, Curtin University of Technology, Australia

E-commerce is becoming one of the most significant business tools. Small enterprises should be encouraged to actively consider the adoption of e-commerce to improve business performance and explore new opportunities arising from the Internet, especially when the use of computing equipment and the adoption of the Internet among Australian population is growing rapidly. This study examined factors influencing e-commerce adoption in Australian small enterprise. Ten factors were found to be significantly influencing the adoption of the e-commerce. These predictors are relative advantage, compatibility, complexity, trialability, observability, decision maker competency, organisation's capacity, business type, organisation size, and contextual characteristics. Small enterprises should look at those ten factors very closely when they are embarking on e-commerce. In the meantime, the findings of this study provide suggestions (i.e., working on ten significant factors identified in this study) for relevant parties of e-commerce (including policy makers, small enterprises network associations, societies of the Internet and e-commerce, and e-commerce marketing practitioners) when they are promoting e-commerce among small enterprises who haven't yet adopted e-commerce.

1. Introduction

E-commerce, which including "buying and selling products and services, serving customers, collaborating with business partners, and conducting electronic transactions within an organization" (Turban et al. 2008, p. 4) via the Internet, has gained a lot of popularity in the past decade. It has been viewed as a new business philosophy (Fillis et al. 2003), and has greatly influenced organizations' competitive strategies and their business performance (Davies & Garcia-Sierra 1999; Porter 2001). It has offered small enterprises many opportunities and benefits (i.e., being a global player, reaching a much wider customer base, reducing operating costs) (Coviello & McAuley 1999; Keoth et al. 1998; Santarelli & D'Altri 2003).

In Australia, e-commerce has grown rapidly in recent years. The statistical figures obtained from Australian bureau of statistics indicate that e-commerce activities have generated a revenue of A$ 56.7 billion dollars in 2005-2006 (ABS 2005-2006, cat. no. 8129.0) (see Table 13.1). However low percentages of Australian businesses who placed orders or received orders via the Internet (i.e., 37.3% and 20.9% in 2005-2006 respectively as displayed in Table 13.1) indicate significant business opportunities have yet to be tapped into. In the meantime, 45% or 6.9 million Australian adults shopped online in 2006-2007 while there were only 15% or around 2.2 million Australian adults who are online shoppers in 2002 and 31% or 4.7 million in 2003-2004 (ABS 2004, cat. no. 8146.0, cited in DCITA 2005; ABS 2007, cat. no. 8146.0).

Table 13.1: Business orders for goods and services via the Internet From 2002-2003 to 2005-2006 in Australia

Details	2002-2003	2003-2004	2004-2005	2005-2006
Proportion of businesses who placed orders via the Internet (%)	27.8	31.3	32.7	37.3
Proportion of businesses who received orders via the Internet (%)	13.3	12.0	12.2	20.9
Internet revenue ($b)	24.3	33.3	39.6	56.7

(Source: adapted from Business Use of Information Technology (ABS 2005-2006, cat. no. 8129.0))

However despite such a favourable e-commerce environment (i.e., more consumers are shopping online, and access to the Internet is relatively inexpensive and readily available for businesses), the small business sector in Australia is still reluctant to adopt this new business practice (Muecke 2000; Yellow Pages Business Index 2001). Many small enterprises still refuse to go along with the move, and continue to focus on more conventional means of carrying out their business activities, or at least, they have been slow in employing this phenomenon (e-commerce) in their business practices (Crawford 1998, p. 20) The statistical figures for the year 2005-2006 showed that while 88.8% of small businesses were using computers in their business operations, and 81.3% of them had access to the Internet , only 29.8% of small businesses have a web presence (ABS 2007, cat. no. 8129.0). One of the reasons for slow adoption of e-commerce in Australian small enterprises is that many of them have the difficulty in realising the suggested benefits of e-commerce (Cronin 1996).

As a result, there is a need for understanding small businesses' slow adoption of e-commerce. In the meantime, literature is also very sparse on e-commerce adoption by small firms. This study seeks to close this gap via examining adoption of e-commerce in Australian small enterprises. In particular, this research will investigate the following research questions: (1) what is the current status of e-commerce adoption among small enterprises in Australia?; (2) what factors are influencing the adoption of e-commerce in Australian small enterprises?.

This chapter is organized as follows. The following section presents relevant background. The research model and hypotheses are presented next. This is followed by the demographic information of the national survey. The data analysis through logistic regression is also presented in this section. Discussions regarding research questions are delivered next. The paper finishes with conclusions and future research directions.

2. Background

2.1. Small Enterprises (SEs)

In this study, we adopted the Australian Bureau of Statistics (ABS 2002) definition of SEs, which refers small businesses as businesses with more than four and less than 20 employees. Small businesses in Australia range from manufacturing through to intermediaries (wholesalers) and services, and they are in general privately owned. They play a significant role in Australia's economy.

In spite of the fact that medium and small enterprises are sharing many common characteristics such as an organic organisational formation, absence of standardisation and formal working affairs, a flat organisational structure, and staff development (Ghobadian and Gallear 1996), small enterprises have many additional unique characteristics. Most small firms are 'operated by a single owner/manager' (Storey 1994), where owner and manager are the same person. Thus, the firm and management factors join to act as one, due to the high locus of control exerted by the key decision maker (Boone, De-Brabander & Hellemans 2000). Small enterprises' managers tend to be more rigid, conventional and outmoded in their business practices, and akin to track many less intricate decision making processes (Jocumsen 2002). More interestingly, due to their size, small businesses have distinct advantages, including more flexible in introducing innovations (Levy 1998; Scozzi, Garavelli & Crowston 2005; Julien & Raymond 1994; Storey 1994), good internal communications and a dynamic entrepreneurial management style (Rothwell, cited in Scozzi, Garavelli & Crowston 2005), and more capable technical people (Scozzi, Garavelli & Crowston 2005).

2.2. E-commerce Adoption

While there are many studies of innovation adoption, a consensus among researchers of innovation adoption is technological superiority alone is not enough to guarantee the adoption of innovation (Pool 1997; Surry & Ely n.d.) and that a complex set of social, economic, technical, organisational, and individual factors interact to influence an organization's adoption decision (Segal 1994; Surry & Ely n.d.). In addition, it is suggested that there is no one-size-for-all adoption process due to the nature of the innovation, the innovators and the environmental context within which the organisation is placed (Chiasson & Lovato 2001; Pease & Rowe 2005; Poku & Vlosky 2002; Wejnert 2002). Consequently, researchers have called for the development of a special category of theories to be based on a specific class of technology (Fichman 2000; Power 2005) that reflects the adoption process. When one studies the determinants of innovation adoption in the organization, it is necessary to take into consideration the various aspects of the business environment of the organisation (Thong 1999). Therefore, to study the adoption of e-commerce within small enterprises, the theory applied ought to take into consideration all potential constructs that might influence the decision to adopt e-commerce. And it may need to use more than one theory.

Hence, to find out what are the key determinants that influence small enterprises' decision to adopt e-commerce, various studies on adoption and diffusion of innovation were reviewed. Table 13.2 present some factors influencing innovation adoption identified from the literature. The constructs in the table are represented in the dimensions of organisational characteristics, decision maker's characteristics, innovation technology characteristics, and the organisation contextual characteristics. Accordingly, these four factors are used in this study for investigating factors influencing e-commerce adoption in Australian small enterprises.

Table 13.2: The potential determinants of innovations adoption

Past Studies	Identified Determents of Innovations Adoption
Kwon and Zmud (1987)	User community characteristics, organisational characteristics, technology characteristics, task characteristics, and environmental characteristics.
Tornatzky and Fleischer (1990)	Technology characteristics, organisational characteristics, and environmental characteristics.
Rogers (1995, 2003)	Technology characteristics, decision makers' characteristics, organisational internal characteristics, organisation external characteristics.
Grover (1993)	Organisational characteristics, policy characteristics, environmental characteristics, support characteristics, and system-related characteristics.
Thong (1999)	Decision makers' characteristics, innovation technology characteristics, organisation characteristics, and organisation environmental characteristics.

(Source: developed for this research based on pervious studies)

2.3. The Research Model

A research model of electronic commerce adoption in small enterprises is developed as the findings from an extensive review of literature (see Figure 13.1), which suggests E-commerce characteristics (including relative advantages, compatibility, complexity, trialability, observability), Decision maker's characteristics (i.e., decision maker's competence, formal education, ethical background), Organizational characteristics (such as organizational capacity, business type, business size, time in business), and Contextual characteristics have direct impact on small enterprises' decision to adopt electronic commerce.

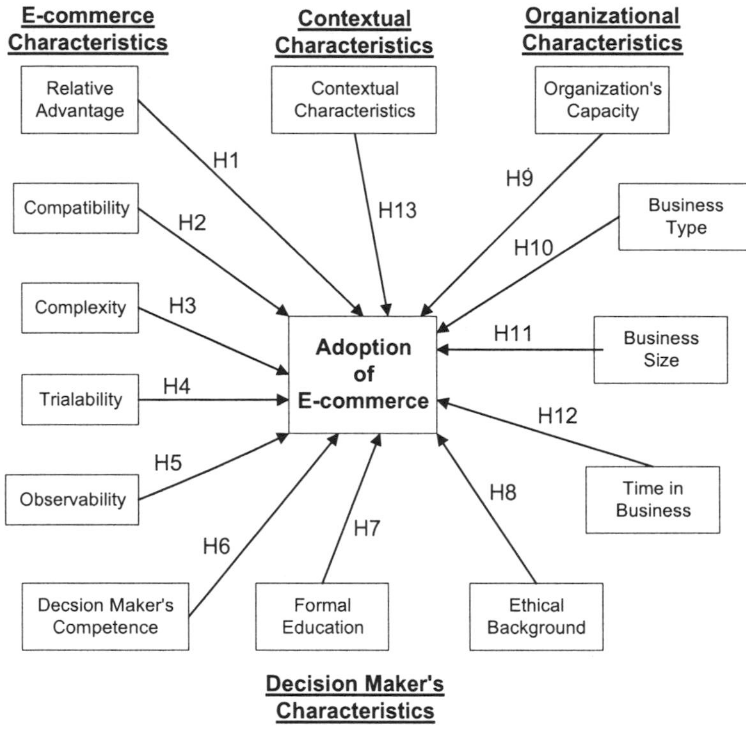

Figure 13.1: The research model

There are thirteen hypotheses in the model:

- H1: The relative advantage of e-commerce positively influences the adoption decision of e-commerce.

- H2: The compatibility of e-commerce positively influences the adoption decision of e-commerce.
- H3: The complexity of e-commerce negatively influences the adoption decision of e-commerce.
- H4: The traliability of e-commerce positively influences the adoption decision of e-commerce.
- H5: The observability of e-commerce positively influences the adoption decision of e-commerce.
- H6: The decision maker's competence positively influences the adoption decision of e-commerce.
- H7: The decision maker's formal education positively influences the adoption decision of e-commerce.
- H8: The decision maker's ethnical background influences the adoption decision of e-commerce.
- H9: The organisation's capacity positively influences the adoption decision of e-commerce.
- H10: The organisation's business type influences the adoption decision of e-commerce.
- H11: The organisation's business size positively influences the adoption decision of e-commerce.
- H12: The organisation's time in business positively influences the adoption decision of e-commerce.
- H13: The contextual characteristics positively influence the adoption decision of e-commerce.

3. Research Design

This study uses a quantitative framework relying exclusively on primary data, utilising a questionnaire survey as a method to collect data needed to find the appropriate answer/s for its proposed hypotheses. The convenience sample method was employed in selecting the participants' small enterprise organisations for the considerations of costs and convenience. Samples were chosen from all seven states of Australia and included various types of businesses (i.e., Manufacturing, Construction, Wholesales Trade, Retails Trade, Accommodation, Transport, Storage, Communication, Finance, Insurance, Property Services, Education, Health, Cafes, Restaurants, and Personal and other services). The number

Table 13.3: The chosen sample size for each state

State	Number of Businesses '000	Number of sample units
New South Wales	57.5	368
Victoria	43.3	277
Queensland	29.3	187
South Australia	13.2	84
Western Australia	17.5	112
Tasmania	4.4	28
Northern Territory	1.7	11
Australian Capital Territory	2.9	18
Total	169.4	1085

(Source: developed for this research based on data abstracted from ABS (2002, cat. no. 1321.0))

of samples from each state was proportional to the number of businesses in each state (Refer to Table 13.3).

The pilot-tested questionnaire was distributed to 1085 managers of small enterprises. Choosing the manager as the sampling unit for each small enterprise appears to have been appropriate, because the questionnaire mainly investigated the action of the decision maker (owner or manager) in the specific enterprise. In addition, based on the literature review most firms were operated by a single owner/manager.

4. Results

4.1. Demographic Information

Gender

Table 13.4 shows that there were 207 respondents in total, which are distributed into three categories (female, male, and missing). Approximately two-third (67.6 percent) of the respondents were male, 31.9 percent were female and 0.5 percent selected not to identify their gender. This result reflects male dominance in small business sectors.

Table 13.4: Participants' gender

Gender	Frequency	Percent (%)
female	66	31.9
male	140	67.6
missing	1	0.5
Total	207	100.0

Age

Table 13.5 shows that the majority of the participants (79.2 percent) were between 31 and 50 years old. The highest proportion was the third category with 42.5 percent (between 41-50 years), and the lowest proportion recorded for first and last categories with respectivily1.9 percent (up to 30 years) and 4 percent (61 and over).

Table 13.5: Participants' age

Age	Frequency	Percent (%)
up to 30 years	4	1.9
31-40	76	36.7
41-50	88	42.5
51-60	35	16.9
61 and over	4	1.9
Total	207	100.0

Education level

As shown in Table 13.6 below over two-third (70.6 percent) of the participants have attained at least a certificate or college degree, with 41.3 having a certificate or college degree, 26.1 have completed a university degree and only 3.4 percent reported that they attained postgraduate degree.

Table 13.6: Participants' education level

Education Level	Frequency	Percent (%)
up to year 10	13	6.3
high school	47	22.7
certificate or college degree	85	41.1
university/college degree	54	26.1
postgraduate degree	7	3.4
missing	1	0.5
Total	207	100

Participants' employment position

As shown in Table 13.7 below, most of the respondents have reported that they are owners (87.0 percent), 9.7 percent are managers and only 1.4 percent other. This result reflected one of the unique characteristic of the small enterprises that being the owner and the manager is the same person.

Table 13.7: Participants' employment position

Position	Frequency	Percent (%)
manager	20	9.7
owner	180	87.0
other	3	1.4
missing	4	1.9
Total	207	100

Years in current company

As shown in Table 13.8 the majority (56.5 percent) of the participants had spent more than 11 years in their current business field, avidly followed by 31.9 having work experience in their current businesses' field between 6 – 10 years. Only a small proportion (11.6 percent) has just 5 years of experience or less.

Table 13.8: Participants' years in current company

Years in Current Company	Frequency	Percent (%)
up to 2 years	7	3.4
2-5 years	17	8.2
6-10 years	66	31.9
11-15 years	41	19.8
more than 15 years	76	36.7
Total	207	100

Participants by years in current position

Table 13.9 below showed that, similar to frequency analysis of the participants by years in current position, we could claim that almost of the respondents (56 percent) have been in current company for 11 years and over, followed by (33.3) of participants who have been in current company between six to ten years. Only 10.6 percent of participants have been for six years or less in current company. This information unveiled that overwhelming proportion 89.4 percent (with experience of 6 years

Table 13.9: Participants' working years in the current position

Years in the Current Position	Frequency	Percent (%)
up to 2 years	5	2.4
2-5 years	17	8.2
6-10 years	69	33.3
11-15 years	40	19.3
more than 15 years	76	36.7
Total	207	100

and over) of participants is familiar with their companies' current business activities and needs.

Participants' background

As shown in the Table 13.10 overwhelming majority of the participants who have chosen to participate in this survey are Australian or have been born in Australia, while only 12.1 percent of the participants were born overseas.

Table 13.10: Participants' ethnicity background (Place of birth)

Place of Birth	Frequency	Percent (%)
overseas	25	12.1
Australia	180	87.0
missing	2	1.0
Total	207	100

Participating companies' industrial classification

Table 13.11 shows that most of industries were part of the survey, four sectors have accounted for 54 percent of participating companies, including 14.0 percent by Accommodation, cafes and restaurants, 15.9 percent by Construction, 13.0 percent by Manufacturing, and 11.1 percent by Retail trade. 46 percent of participants were distributed

Table 13.11: Participating companies' industrial classification

Industry	Frequency	Percent (%)
Accommodation, cafes and restaurants	29	14.0
Communication services (incl. postal serv.)	12	5.8
Construction	33	15.9
Cultural and recreation services	3	1.4
Education	7	3.4
Finance and insurance	12	5.8
Health and community services	7	3.4
Manufacturing	27	13.0
Personal and business services	19	9.2
Property and business services	17	8.2
Retail trade	23	11.1
Transport and storage	3	1.4
Wholesaling trade	9	4.3
Other	6	2.9
Total	207	100

between the other ten industries. Four industries have not been represented in the study include Agriculture, Forestry and Fishing, Electricity, Gas and Water supply, and Mining. This can be justified on account of the nature of these businesses. For example, most of companies in the last three industries would be large and so no chance for them to be part of this survey. Another reason could be the distinctive nature of industries such as agriculture, forestry and fishing.

Number of employees

As shown in the Table 13.12 over one third (42.0 percent) of the participants surveyed were organisations with 6-10 employees, followed by about third (32.9 percent) of organisations with 16-19 employees, and 25.1 percent of organisations with 11-15 employees.

Table 13.12: Number of employees

Number of Employees	Frequency	Percent (%)
6-10	87	42.0
11-15	52	25.1
16-20	68	32.9
Total	207	100.0

Number of years in business

Table 13.13 shows that overwhelming majority (93.2 percent) of companies have been in business for 6 years and over, over half of participants surveyed (62.3 percent) reported that they have been in business for more than 11 years. Only 6.8 percent of participating companies have been in business for less than 5 years.

Table 13.13: Number of years in business

Number of Years in Business	Frequency	Percent (%)
up to 3 years	3	1.4
3-5	11	5.3
6-10	64	30.9
11-20	81	39.1
over 20 years	48	23.2
Total	207	100.0

Membership of a network association

Table 13.14 below shows that the majority (67.6 percent) of participating companies were members of network associations, while only (30.9 percent) of surveyed companies reported that they are not members of any network associations.

Table 13.14: Membership of a network association

Membership of a Network Association	Frequency	Percent (%)
no	64	30.9
yes	140	67.6
missing	3	1.4
Total	207	100.0

Location of participating companies

Table 13.15 below shows the geographical distribution of participating companies. The analysis showed that New South Wales come first with 43 percent, followed secondly by Victoria by 22.2 percent, while the third place held by Queensland with 14.5 percent. On the other hand, South Australia, Western Australia, Tasmania, ACT and Northern Territory were a place for only 20.3 percent of surveyed companies. Overall the distribution of participating companies is quite in line with the distribution of businesses in Australia.

Table 13.15: Location of participating companies

State	Frequency	Percent (%)
New South Wales	3	1.4
Victoria	89	43.0
Queensland	2	1.0
South Australia	30	14.5
Western Australia	13	6.3
Tasmania	11	5.3
Northern Territory	46	22.2
Australian Capital Territory	13	6.3
Total	207	100.0

Business growth

Table 13.16 below illustrates the growth of the surveyed organisations. The data revealed that 91.4 percent of the participating companies were generally in good condition in terms of business growth. 21.3 percent reported that they are in a stable condition. Around two third (66.2 percent) were growing at a moderately rate, and 3.9 percent were having high growth rate. Only 1 percent was in a decreasing condition.

Table 13.16: Business growth

Business Growth	Frequency	Percent (%)
High	8	3.9
Moderate	137	66.2
Stable	44	21.3
Decreased	2	1.0
missing	16	7.7
Total	207	100.0

Revenue

Table 13.17 below pointed out that 77.3 percent of the surveyed firms were generating revenue in excess of A$1M or more. Also, the analysis revealed that 63.8 percent generated revenue from A$1,000,000-2,999,999, followed by 14 percent with an annual revenue of over A$3M. The firms with annual revenue of less A$1M have accounted for no more than 19.8 percent. Only a small proportion (2.9 percent) has chosen not to disclose their annual revenue.

Table 13.17: Annual revenue before tax

Annual Revenue before Tax	Frequency	Percent (%)
up to A$1,000,000	41	19.8
A$1,000,000-2,999,999	132	63.8
A$3,000,000-4,999,999	18	8.7
more than A$5,000,000	10	4.8
missing	6	2.9
Total	207	100.0

4.2. E-commerce Information Profile

Purposes of e-commerce adoption

Participants were asked to specify the rationale of their firms' motivations of adopting e-commerce based on the five main aspects include increasing customer base, marketing, improving relationship with suppliers, selling products and services, and improving relationship with customers. Two most important motivations reported are increasing customer base and marketing with 77.8 percent and 76.3 percent respectively. Next 39.1 percent and 36.2 percent reported improving relationship with customers and selling products and services as their firms' motivations of adopting e-commerce. Only 15 percent reported that improving relationship with suppliers as their incentive to adopt e-commerce.

E-commerce adoption primary focus

Table 13.18 below shows that almost half of participants' surveyed reported that the main purpose for their decision to adopt e-commerce was making business with customers (48.8 percent), followed by making business with both customers and businesses (46.4 percent). Only a small proportion of participants (2.4 percent) reported that their main purpose for adopting e-commerce was making business with other businesses. This means that most of participating organisations see that making business with customers as one of the top priority target for their decision to adopt e-commerce.

Table 13.18: E-commerce adoption primary focus

E-commerce Adoption Primary Focus	Frequency	Percent (%)
making business with customers	101	48.8
making business with other businesses	5	2.4
making business with both customers and businesses	96	46.4
missing	5	2.4
Total	207	100.0

Years of e-commerce adoption

Table 13.19 showed that about half (45.9 percent) of participating firms have adopted e-commerce for 3-5 years, followed by 25.1 percent for

Table 13.19: Years of e-commerce adoption

Years of E-commerce Adoption	Frequency	Percent (%)
up to 1 year	8	3.9
from 2-3 years	45	21.7
from 3-5 years	95	45.9
6 years and over	52	25.1
missing	7	3.4
Total	207	100.0

over 6 years, and 21.7 percent for a period between 2-3 years. Only 3.9 percent have adopted e-commerce for less than one year.

E-commerce revenue

As shown in Table 13.20, in response on the question of how much of revenue is approximately generated from e-commerce almost half of participating firms (46.8 per cent) reported that they generated revenue between 11-30 percent from e-commerce. While approximately one third (31.9 percent) generated 6-10 percent, 15.5 percent generated less 5 percent, and only 3.4 percent generated over 31 percent of their revenue from e-commerce.

Table 13.20: E-commerce revenue

E-commerce Revenue	Frequency	Percent (%)
1-5%	32	15.5
6-10%	66	31.9
11-20%	34	16.4
21-30%	63	30.4
31% and over	7	3.4
missing	5	2.4
Total	207	100.0

4.3. Logistic Regression Analysis

The information attained from the descriptive analysis has provided us with general information regarding current status of the SEs population. However, this information is not sufficient to report the various factors that have driven these firms to embrace the e-commerce. For this reason additional statistical analysis reporting is needed. Accordingly, we have conducted a logistic regression analysis, where direct entry method was used to test the influence of the proposed constructs on the small enterprises decision to adopt e-commerce. Direct logistic regression was preformed to assess the impact of a number of factors illustrated in the theoretical model on the organization's adoption of e-commerce. The model has four main independent factors, e-commerce technology characteristics, decision-maker characteristics, organisational or internal characteristics and contextual or environmental characteristics.

The proposed hypotheses were tested via direct logistic regression. Based on the results of the hypotheses testing, hypotheses H1, H2, H3, H4 and H5 of e-commerce characteristics (relative advantage, compatibility, complexity, triability and observability), hypothesis H6 of decision maker's competency, hypotheses H9, H10 and H11 of organisational characteristics (the organisation's capacity, the type of business, and the business size), and hypothesis H13 of contextual characteristics, were found to display a significant influence on the participating small enterprises' decision to adopt e-commerce. Meanwhile, hypotheses H7, H8, and H12 were rejected by the analysis, since the findings of this study showed that H7, H8, and H12 had non-significant influence on adoption decision of e-commerce in Australian small enterprises. The adoption model below (Figure 13.2) illustrates the significant determinants of e-commerce adoption in Australian small enterprises.

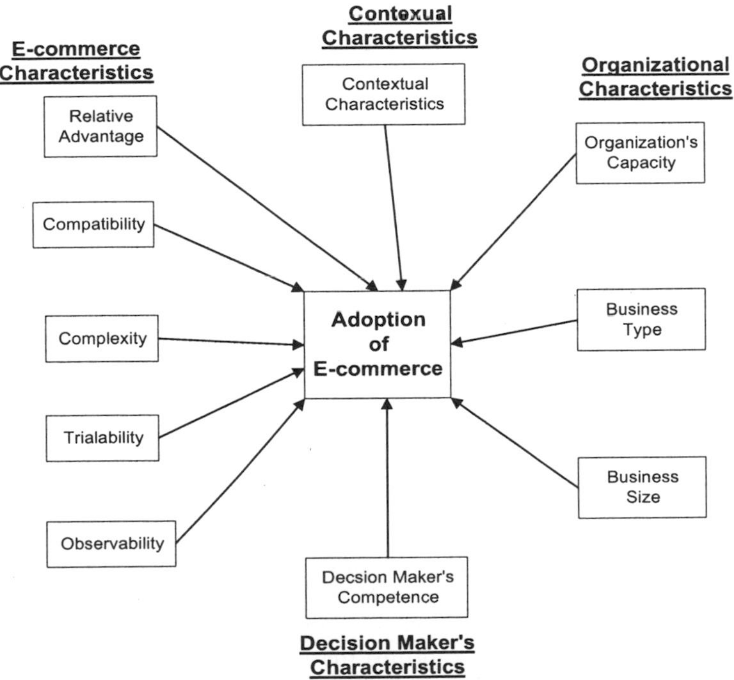

Figure 13.2: The significant determinants of e-commerce adoption in Australian small enterprises

5. Discussions

5.1. Addressing Research Question 1

The main characteristics of the SEs decision makers

It is found that there is domination of males (68%) in e-commerce adoption decision making in the Australian small enterprises. The majority (79.2 percent) of them were between 31 and 50 years old. Interestingly, overwhelming proportion of them are owners (88.7 percent). This result accentuates one of the most distinctive characteristics of the small business that being the owner and the manager is the same person. Also, the findings revealed that almost all of the participants are well educated, they have at least achieved a certificate or college degree (66.5 %). Also, the findings unveiled that participants have a high level of familiarity with their business activities and needs, as 89.4 % reported an experience of 6 years and over. Lastly, the overwhelming majority (87.8%) of the participants are Australian or were born in Australia.

What is the primary focus of e-commerce adoption in Australian SEs?

The overwhelming majority of Australian SEs (95.2%) surveyed have recognised the great role of e-commerce in strengthening their business relationship with customers, whether they are individuals or other businesses. The findings uncovered that doing business with customers (wether they are individuals or other businesses) were the main focus of the e-commerce adoption by participating small enterprises. Hence, SEs will be more likely to adopt e-commerce if they are aware about potential benefits of e-commerce.

What are the most common features of the SEs who adopted e-commerce?

Results of this research showed information related to the characteristics of the participating companies. The outcome revealed that most of the surveyed SEs have been in business for more than six years. Most of them have membership of network associations. In addition, the data showed the majority of surveyed firms who have adopted e-commerce have over A$ 1 million revenue and enjoy moderate growth rate. In future, the efforts of promoting e-commerce in Australian small enterprises should target at those firms with those characteristics.

5.2. Addressing Research Question 2

E-commerce characteristics:

Relative advantage H1

The findings showed that relative advantage played a significant role in influencing the adoption of e-commerce in Australian SEs. This result is in agreement with previous studies of innovation adoption (i.e., Abell & Lim 1996; Agarwal & Prasad 1997; Auger & Gallaugher 1997). The crucial role of the relative advantages of innovation in stimulating the acceptance of the new idea is based on the argument that an organisation will not adopt any new technologies, unless there is a clear perceived advantage, or there is an immediate disadvantage that pushes them to do so (Clarke 1997). This implies that small business organisations will adopt e-commerce if they can see e-commerce can give them some advantages in areas such as improving relations with customers and suppliers, increasing customer base, marketing, and selling products and services.

Compatibility H2

The findings of this research showed that compatibility played an essential role in influencing SEs decision to adopt e-commerce. This result is in correspondence with literature on the adoption of innovation (i.e., Loh & Ong 1998; Rogers 1995; Tornatzky & Klein 1982; Rogers 1995). It suggests that e-commerce should be compatible with current practices, needs, and existing IS/IT systems of adopting firms.

Complexity H3

The perceived simplicity (non complexity) of e-commerce was found to be a significant predictor in influencing small enterprises' decision to adopt e-commerce. Participating small enterprises decision to adopt e-commerce had based on a belief that e-commerce is: (1) easy to implement, (2) easy to operate, (3) and will not cause any perplexity or serious problem for their daily business's operation. This finding is in agreement with results of previous studies (i.e., Agarwal & Prasad 1997; Greve 1998; Loh and Ong 1998). It implies that it is highly unlikely for Australian small enterprises to adopt e-commerce if it is complicated and difficult to use.

Trialability H4

Trialability was found to be one of the significant factors influencing the adoption decision of e-commerce in Australian SEs. This finding is in agreement with previous studies results (i.e., Greve 1998; Rogers 1995 p. 243; Weiss & Dale 1998). It suggests small enterprises are more likely to adopt e-commerce if they can try and have some experience of e-commerce when they are embarking on e-commerce.

Observability H5

Observability was found to be a significant factor influencing the adoption decision of e-commerce in Australian small enterprises. This finding is in agreement with prior studies (i.e., Chaves 1996; Hedstrom, cited in Wejnert 2002; Rogers 1995, p.244). It suggests that small enterprises should spend sufficient time in examining potential benefits/costs, issues, and concerns associated with e-commerce adoption before they finalise their adoption decision.

Decision Maker Characteristics:

Decision maker's competence (H6)

The decision maker's competence was found to play a significant role in influencing the decision of adopting e-commerce in Australian small enterprises. The finding is in line with past research (i.e., Lefebvre & Lefebvre 1996; Standing, Vasudavan & Borbely 1998;Tornatzky & Klein 1982). It implies that when small enterprises are adopting e-commerce, their decision makers should assess the firm's readiness for e-commerce and calculate expected benefits/costs of adoption e-commerce by studying information from various sources, such as peers, consultants, media, academic and professional publications, industry associations, and relevant government agencies.

Decision maker's formal education (H7)

Decision maker's formal education was not found to be a significant predictor of the adoption of e-commerce. The result of this study is not in line with the findings of prior studies (i.e., Power 2005). One possible explanation is the unique structure of small enterprises whose owners and managers very often are the same person.

Decision Maker's ethnical background (H8)

The findings of this study revealed that decision maker's ethnic background was not found to play any significant role in influencing SEs decision of adopting e-commerce. This result doesn't support the results of previous studies (i.e., Takada & Jain 1991; Herbig & Palumbo 1994). One possible explanation why decision maker's ethnical background does not play a greater role in small enterprises' decision-making of e-commerce adoption is the unique structure of small enterprises whose owners and managers very often are the same person. Nonetheless, the influence of decision maker's ethnic background on the adoption of e-commerce in Australian SEs must remain the subject for further enquiry.

Organisational characteristics:

Organisational capacity (H9)

The organisational capacity was found to play a significant role in influencing small enterprises' decision to adopt e-commerce. This result is in agreement with prior studies (i.e., Utomo & Dodgson 2001, The organisation ability to offer the appropriate financial resources required (Chau, cited in Sarosa & Zowghi 2003; Fink 1998; Armstrong & Collopy 1996; Kohli & Jaworski 1990). It indicates that when small enterprises are adopting e-commerce, they need to allocate sufficient resources, equip people with adequate capabilities (i.e., via training and learning), and develop pro-e-commerce culture & policies.

Organisation's business type (H10)

The business type of small enterprises was found to play a significant role in influencing small enterprises' decision to adopt e-commerce in Australia context. This finding is in corresponding with previous studies (i.e., Jutla et al. 2002; Martin & Matlay 2001; Simpson & Docherty 2004). This implies that some industries (i.e. some sectors of whole trade, retail trade or services) are more likely to view e-commerce as a strategic necessity and are more willing to adopt e-commerce.

Organisation's business size (H11)

The business size was found to play a significant role in influencing small enterprises' decision to adopt e-commerce. This result is in corresponding with past studies (i.e., Bodorick et al., cited in Simpson & Docherty 2004; Daniel & Myers 2000). The significant result revealed by the findings of this study suggests that the size of small enterprises play a key role in influencing their decision to adopt e-commerce.

Organisation's time in business (H12)

The organisation's time in business was not found to play a significant role in influencing small enterprises' decision to adopt e-commerce. The outcome of this study finding is not in line with previous studies (i.e., Bodorick et al., cited in Simpson & Docherty 2004; Daniel & Myers 2000). The non-significant result could be attributed to the unique nature of small enterprises, and/or the existence of other organisational factors (i.e., organisation's capacity, organisation's business type, organisation's business size and others) that have more influence on the decision making of e-commerce adoption in Australian SEs. Nonetheless, the influence of business size on the adoption of e-commerce in Australian SEs must remain subject for further enquiry.

Organisation contextual characteristics (H13)

Contextual characteristics were found to play a significant role in influencing participating small enterprises' decision to adopt e-commerce. This finding is in line with previous research (i.e., Julien et al. 1996; Raymond 2001; Poon 2000; Drew 2003; Sarosa & Zowghi 2003). It suggests that small enterprises' e-commerce adoption could be driven by the needs of being more competitive in the marketplace and strengthening their relationships with customers, suppliers, and business partners. And it also indicates that the government's efforts (i.e., policies, investment on e-commerce infrastructure) play a very important role in encouraging small enterprises to adopt e-commerce.

6. Conclusions & Future Research Directions

This study and its findings have enriched the existing literature on e-commerce adoption, through directing its focus on examining the factors affecting the adoption of e-commerce in Australian small enterprises. This research has looked into thirteen factors that influence the adoption decision of e-commerce in Australian small enterprises on the national level. Future research could study those factors in individual states in Australia to see differences and similarities of e-commerce adoption in different states. Meanwhile the authors believe that the factors involved in this study may not include all the factors that affect small enterprises' decision to adopt e-commerce. Future studies could include other factors which may influence small enterprises' adoption of e-commerce.

In addition, in this research the small enterprises with more than 4 and less than 20 employees were under investigation. Future studies targeting businesses with 20 to 50 and 51 to 100 employees would be desirable to see to what extend that the differences in the business size would affect the factors of e-commerce adoption. In this case, the developed model could be used to demonstrate if the results claimed here are valid for other business sizes. It is also interesting to conduct the same research in other countries to study the impact of country characteristics (i.e., political, economic, social and technological factors) on small enterprises' adoption of e-commerce. Furthermore, this research used a quantitative approach to investigate the factors that affecting e-commerce adoption. Future studies could apply qualitative research methodology (i.e., via interviews, case studies, action research) or combined approach to have better understanding from multiple perspectives. Finally, this research has looked at small enterprises from various industries. In future, research on e-commerce adoption in small enterprises in specific industries could be pursued to have deeper understanding of e-commerce adoption in specific industries and examine the differences and similarities of e-commerce adoption across different industries.

References

ABS (2002) 1321.0 Small businesses in Australia, viewed 21 July 2006, <http://www.abs.gov.au/Ausstats/abs@.nsf/e8ae5488b598839cca25682000131612/97452f3932f44031ca256c5b00027f19!OpenDocument>.

ABS (2004) 8127.0 Characteristics of Small Business, viewed 10 July 2006, <http://www.abs.gov.au/Ausstats/abs@.nsf/0/1b9f7811c6b830eaca256ff100037bae?OpenDocument >

ABS (2007) 8129.0 Business Use of Information Technology, 2005-06, viewed 10 December 2007, <http://www.abs.gov.au/ausstats/abs@.nsf/5087e58f30c6bb25ca2568b60010b303/9c7742890adec989ca2568a900139423!OpenDocument>.

Abell, W. & Limm, L. (1996) Business use of the Internet in New Zealand: an exploratory study, viewed 12 April 2006, <http://ausweb.scu.edu.au/aw96/business/abell/>.

Al-Qirim, N. (2003) Electronic Commerce in small to medium sized enterprises: Frameworks, Issues, and Implications', in Electronic commerce in small to medium-sized enterprises: Frameworks, issues and implications, pp. 1-16, ed. N Al-Qirim, Idea Group Inc, Hershey, PA.

Agarwal, R. & Prasad, J. (1997) The Role of Innovation Characteristics and Perceived Voluntariness in the Acceptance of Information Technology, Decision Sciences, Vol. 28, No. 3, pp. 557-582.

Armstrong, A. & Hagel, J. (1996) The Real Value of Online Communities, Harvard Business Review, Vol. 74, No. 3, pp. 134-141.

Armstrong, J.S. & Collopy, F. (1996) Competitor Orientation: Effects of Objectives and Information on Managerial Decisions and Profitability, Journal of Marketing Research, Vol. 33, May, pp. 188-199.

Auger, P. & Gallaugher, J.M. (1997) Factors affecting the adoption of an Internet -based sales presence for small businesses, The Information Society, Vol. 13, No. 1, pp. 55-74.

Attewell, P. (1992) Technology diffusion and organizational learning: the case of business computing, Organizational Science, Vol. 3, No. 1, pp. 1-19.

Baskerville, R. & Pries-Heje, J. (2001) A multiple-theory analysis of a diffusion of information technology case, Information Systems Journal, Vol. 11, No 3, pp.181-212.

Boone, C., De-Brabander, B. & Hellemans, J. (2000) Research note: CEO locus of control and small firm performance, Organization Studies, Vol. 21, No. 3, pp. 641-646.

Bradley, S.P., Jerry, A.H. & Richard, L.N. (eds) (1993) Globalization, Technology, and Competition, Harvard Business School Press, Boston.

Chaves, M . (1996) Ordaining women: the diffusion of an organizational innovation, The American Journal of Sociology, Vol. 101, No. 4, pp. 840-73.

Chiasson, M.W. & Lovato C.Y. (2001) Factors Influencing the Formation of a User's Perceptions and Use of a DSS Software Innovation, Database for Advances in Information Systems, Vol. 32, No. 3: pp. 16-35.

Clarke, R. (1997) What's Holding Up: EC in Australia, viewed 20 Feb 2005, <http://www.anu.edu.au/people/Roger.Clarke/EC/Impeds97.html>.

Coviello, N. & McAuley, A. (1999) Internationalisation and the smaller firm: a review of contemporary empirical research, Management International Review, Vol. 39, No. 3, pp. 223-240.

Crawford, J. (1998) Networked Enterprise Web Strategy: A Project to get smaller enterprises online, Department of Industry, Science and Tourism, Australia, viewed Sept 05 2006, <http://www. noie.gov.au/publications/NOIE/SME/newsbk.pdf >.

Cronin, M.J. (1996) The Internet strategy handbook: lessons from the new frontier of business, Harvard Business School Press, Boston.

Daniel, E. & Myers, A. (2000) Levelling the playing-field: electronic commerce in SMEs, viewed 18 Nov 2006, <http://mn-isweb-1.som.cranfield.ac.uk/publications/ISRC_2001_SME-Report.pdf>.

Davies, AJ & Garcia-Sierra, AJ 1999, 'Implementing electronic commerce in SMEs - three case studies, BT Technology Journal, vol.17, no. 3, pp. 97-111.

Deeter-Schmelz, D.R. & Kennedy, K.N. (2004) Buyer-seller relationships and information sources in an E-commerce world, Journal of Business and Industrial Marketing, Vol. 19, No. 3, pp. 188-196.

Dos Santos, B.L. & Peffers, K. (1998) Competitor and vendor influence on the adoption of innovative applications in electronic commerce, Information & Management, Vol. 34, pp. 175-184.

Drew, S. (2003) Strategic uses of e-commerce by SMEs in the east of England, European Management Journal, Vol. 21, No. 1, pp. 79-88.

Emory, W. & Cooper, D.R. (eds) (1991) Business research methods, 4th edn, R.D. Irwin, Homewood.

Fichman, R.G. (2000) The diffusion and assimilation of information technology innovations', in Framing the Domain of IT Management: Pinnaflex Educational Resources, ed. R.W. Zmud, Cincinnati, OH.

Fillis, I., Johansson, U. & Wagner, B. (2003) A conceptualisation of the opportunities and barriers to e-business development in the smaller firm, Journal of Small Business and Enterprise Development, Vol. 10, No. 3, pp. 336-344.

Fink, A. (2002) The survey handbook, 2nd edn, Sage Publications, Thousand Oaks.

Geiger, S. & Martin, S. (1999) The Internet as relationship marketing tool-some evidence from Irish companies, Irish Marketing Review, Vol. 12, No. 2, pp. 25-36.

Ghobadian, A. & Gallear, D.N. (1996) Total quality management in SME's, Omega, Vol. 24, No.1, pp. 83-106.

Greve H.R.(1998) Performance, Aspirations and Risky Organizational Change', Administrative Science Quarterly, Vol. 43, March, pp. 58-86.

Grover, V. (1993) An empirically derived model for the adoption of customer-based interorganizational systems, Decision Sciences, Vol. 24, No. 3, pp. 603-40.

Herbig, P.A. & Palumbo, F. (1994) The effect of culture on the adoption process: a comparison of Japanese and American behavior, Technological Forecasting and Social Change, Vol. 46, pp. 71-101.

Jaworski, B.J. & Kohli, A.K. (1993) Market orientation: antecedents and consequences, Journal of Marketing, Vol. 57, No. 3, pp. 53-70.

Jeffcoate, J., Chappell, C. & Feindt, S. (2002) Best practice in SME adoption of e-commerce, Benchmarking: An International Journal, Vol. 9, No. 2, pp. 122-132.

Jocumsen, G. (2004) How do small business managers make strategic marketing decisions? A model of process, European Journal of Marketing, Vol. 38, No. 5/6, pp. 659-674.

Jones, C., Hecker, R. & Holland, P. (2003) Small firm Internet adoption: opportunities forgone, a journey not begun, Journal of Small Business and Enterprise Development, Vol. 10, No. 3, pp. 287-297.

Julien, P.A. & Raymond, L. (1994) Factors of new technology adoption in the retail sector, Entrepreneurship Theory and Practice, Vol. 18, No. 4, pp. 79-90.

Julien, P.A., Raymond, L., Jacob, R. & Ramangalahy, C. (1996) Patterns and determinants of technological scanning: an empirical investigation of manufacturing SMEs, in, Frontiers of Entrepreneurship Research, ed. PD Reynolds et al., Babson College, Babson Park, MA, pp. 584-98.

Jutla, D., Bodorick, P. & Dhaliwal, J. (2002) Supporting the e-business readiness of small and medium-sized enterprises: approaches and metrics, Internet Research: Electronic Networking Applications and Policy, Vol. 12, No. 2, pp. 139-164.

Kalakota, R. & Robinson, M. (2001) E-Business 2.0: Road-map for Success, Addison-Wesley, Harlow.

Keogh, W., Jack, S.L., Bower, J. & Crabtree, E. (1998) Small, technology-based firms in the UK oil and gas industry: innovation and internationalisation strategies, International Small Business Journal, Vol. 17, No. 1, pp. 57-68.

Kirby, D. & Turner, M. (1993) IT and the Small Retail Business, International Journal of Retail and Distribution Management, Vol. 21, No. 7, pp. 20-27.

Koh, S.C.L. & Maguire, S. (2004) Identifying the adoption of e-business and knowledge management within SMEs, Journal of Small Business and Enterprise Development, Vol. 11, No. 3, pp. 338-348.

Kohli, A.K. & Jaworski, B.J. (1990) Market orientation: the construct, research propositions, and managerial implications, Journal of Marketing, Vol. 54, No. 2, pp. 1-18.

Kwon, T.H. & Zmud, R.W. (1987) Unifying the fragmented models of information systems implementation, in Critical issues in information systems research, eds RJ Boland & R Hirschheim, John Wiley & Sons, New York.

Lanz, J 2002, ‚Worst Information Technology Practices in Small to Mid-Size Organizations', The CPA Journal, vol 72, No 4, pp 71-74.

Lefebvre, E. & Lefebvre, L. (1996) Information and telecommunication technologies: The impact of their adoption on small and medium-sized enterprises, viewed May 03 2006, <http://www.idrc.ca/books/focus/807/807.html>.

Levy, M. (1998) SME flexibility and the role of information systems, Small Business Economics, Vol. 11, No. 2, pp. 183-96.

Loh, L. & Ong, Y. (1998) The adoption of Internet -based stock trading: aconceptual framework and empirical results, Journal of Information Technology, Vol. 13, pp. 1-94.

Love, P.E.D., Irani, Z., Li, H., Cheng, E.W.L. & Tse, R.Y.C. (2001) An Empirical Analysis of The Barriers to Implementing E-Commerce in Small medium Sized Construction Contractors in The State of Victoria, Australia, Construction Innovation, Vol. 1, No.1, pp 31-41.

Martin, L. & Malay, H. (2001) Blanket" approaches to promoting ICT in small firms: some lessons from the DTI ladder adoption model in UK, Internet Research: Electronic Networking Application and Policy, Vol. 11, No. 5, pp. 399-410.

Muecke, T. (2000) Electronic Commerce and Australian Small Business: Next Steps, Speech to National Small Business Forum, Main Committee Room, Parliament House, Canberra, 3 November, viewed 27 Feb 2005, <http://www.setel.com.au/publications/public/subs/051.htm>.

Narver, J.C. & Slater, S.F. (1990) The effect of market orientation on business profitability', Journal of Marketing, Vol. 54, October, pp. 20-35.

Pease, W. & Rowe, M. (2005) Diffusion of Innovation-The Adoption of Electronic Commerce by Small and Medium Enterprises (SMES) - A Comparative Analysis, Australian Journal of Information Systems, Vol. 13, No. 1, pp. 287-294,

Poku, K. & Vlosky, R.P. (2002) A Model of the Impact of Corporate Culture on Information Technology Adoption, viewed 22 Jan 2006,

Porter, M.E. (1980) Competitive Strategy: Techniques for Analyzing Industries and Competitors, The Free Press, New York, <http://www.rnr.lsu.edu/lfpdc/publication/papers/ITAdoption.pdf>.

Porter, M. (2001) Strategy and the Internet , Harvard Business Review, Vol. 79, No.3, pp. 62-78.

Pool, R. (1997) Beyond engineering: How society shapes technology, University Press, Oxford.

Poon, S. (2000) Business environment and Internet commerce benefit: a small business perspective, European Journal of Information Systems, Vol. 9, No. 2, pp. 72-81.

Poon, S. and Swatman, P. (1997) The Internet for Small Businesses: An Enabling Infrastructure for Competitiveness, Paper presented to the fifth Internet Society Conference, viewed 10 July 2006, <http://www.isoc.org/HMP/PAPER/126/html/paper.html>.

Power, D. (2005) Determinants of business-to-business e-commerce implementation and performance: a structural model, Supply Chain Management: An International Journal, Vol. 10, No. 2, pp. 96-113.

Raymond, L. (2001) Determinants of Web site implementation in small businesses, Internet Research: Electronic Networking Applications and Policy, Vol. 11, No. 5, pp. 411-424.

Rogers, E. M. (1995) Diffusion of Innovations, 4th edn, Free Press, New York.

Rogers, E. M. (2003) Diffusion of Innovations, 5th edn, Free Press, New York.

Santarelli, E. & D'Altri, S. (2003) The Diffusion of E-commerce at the Firm Level: Theoretical, Implications and Empirical Evidence', Small Business Economics, Vol. 21, No. 3, pp. 273-279.

Sarosa, S. & Zowghi, D. (2003) Strategy for Adopting Information Technology for SMEs: Experience in Adopting Email within an Indonesian Furniture Company, Electronic Journal of Information Systems Evaluation, Vol. 6, No. 2, pp. 165-176.

Scozzi, B., Garavelli, C. & Crowston, K. (2005) Methods for modeling and supporting innovation processes in SMEs, European Journal of Innovation Management, Vol. 8, No. 1, pp. 120-137.

Segal, H.P. (1994) Future imperfect: the mixed blessings of technology in America, The University of Massachusetts Press, Amherst.

Simpson, M. & Docherty, A.J. (2004) E-commerce adoption support and advice for UK SMEs, Journal of Small Business and Enterprise Development, Vol. 11, No. 3, pp. 315-328.

Standing, C., Vasudavan, T. & Borbely, S. (1998) Re-engineering travel agencies with the world wide web, Electronic Markets, Vol. 8, No. 4, pp. 40-3.

Storey, D.J. (1994) Understanding the Small Business Sector, Routledge, London.

Surry, W.D. & Ely, D.P. n.d., Adoption, Diffusion, Implementation, and Institutionalization of Educational Technology, viewed 22 May 2005, <http://www.southalabama.edu/coe/best/surry/papers/adoption/chap.htm>.

Takada, H. & Jain, D. (1991) Cross-national analysis of diffusion of durable goods in Pacific rim countries, Journal of Marketing, Vol. 54, pp. 48-54.

Timmers, P. (2000) Electronic Commerce- strategies & models for business-to-business trading, John Wiley & Sons, New York, NY.

Thong, J.Y.L. (1999) An integrated model of information systems adoption in small business, Journal of Management Information Systems, Vol. 15, No. 4, pp. 187-214.

Tornatzky, L.G. & Fleischer, M. (1990) The processes of technological innovation, Lexington Books, Lexington, MA.

Tornatzky, L.G., & Klein, R.J. (1982) Innovation characteristics and innovation adoption-implementation: A meta-analysis of findings, IEEE Transactions on Engineering Management, Vol. 29, pp. 28-45.

Utomo, H. & Dodgson, M. (2001) Contributing Factors to The Diffusion of IT Within Small and Medium-sized Firms in Indonesia, Journal of Global Information Technology Management, Vol. 4, No. 2, pp. 22-37.

Wejnert, B 2002, 'Integrating models of diffusion of innovations: A conceptual framework', Annual Review of Sociology, vol. 28, pp. 297-326.

Weiss, J.A. & Dale, B.C. (1998) Diffusing against mature technology : Issues and strategy, Industrial Marketing Management, Vol. 27, No. 4, pp. 293-304.

Wolfe, R.A. (1994) Organizational Innovation: Review, Critique and Suggested Research Directions, Journal of Management Studies, Vol. 31, No. 3, pp. 405-431.

Whitely, D. (2000) E-Commerce Strategy, Technologies and Applications, McGraw-Hill, London.

Section 3

Outlook of E-Business

CHAPTER 14

FUTURE OF E-BUSINESS, SUCCESS FACTORS, AND E-BUSINESS OPPORTUNITIES

Jun Xu

Graduate College of Management, Southern Cross University, Australia

Mohammed Quaddus

Graduate School of Business, Curtin University of Technology, Australia

Even though there are still many issues and concerns to be dealt with, the future of e-business is bright. Future e-business growth will come from various areas of all types of e-business. In addition, there are also many e-business opportunities associated with emerging business trends. Organizations can enhance their e-business operations or embark on new e-business initiatives by closely examining those future growth areas and emerging opportunities. Furthermore, organizations could also better manage their e-business projects and better prepare for future e-business initiatives by understanding success/critical factors of e-business.

1. The Future of E-business

While there exist differences in predictions for e-business future (i.e., in terms of growth rates, revenue, contribution to overall economy, development stages and progresses of e-business in different industries, the future of current e-business heavy players, the dominant business models on the Internet in the future), there are general consensus and optimism about the future of e-business (i.e., Turban et al. 2008; Laudon & Traver 2008).

The future of e-business is bright even though e-business organizations are still facing issues and challenges such as security &

privacy concerns, intellectual property issues, taxation issues, Internet governance challenges, standardization challenges, Internet access, net neutrality & digital divide problems, globalization of e-business, e-business for small and medium enterprises, and development of future Internet technologies (i.e., Internet-2, IPV 6 projects, multilingual domain name registration system), among many others. E-business is becoming a very important method of reaching customers, providing services, improving operations of organizations, trading among organizations and collaborating with business partners. The future growth of e-business will come from various areas of all types of e-business including growth and new opportunities in B2B, B2C, C2C, mobile business, e-government, e-publishing, e-learning, social networks, intra-organizational activities, etc (see Table 14.1).

Table 14.1: Some future E-business growth opportunities

E-business types	Examples of future growth opportunities
B2B	While the current B2B activities have the emphasis on upstream part of the supply chain (i.e., e-procurement, collaborative demand forecasting and planning) and downstream part of the supply chain (i.e., selling to customers via web sites; collaborative information sharing with retailers and wholesalers), more attention could be given to the middle part of the supply chain (i.e., co-creation, co-design, co-research & development, knowledge trading marketplace with business partners and suppliers); Better B2B trust services; Wider adoption of B2B bartering services (especially when businesses are short of cash during bad times); among many others.
B2C	While the B2C e-business is getting more and more popular, better and more innovative services could be offered to various stages of consumers' online shopping process (i.e., virtual shop assistant who give more personalized services; common 3-D display of products); More personalized web sites which will adjust content of the site and sequence of web pages according to identified & perceived needs and interests of consumers; Coordinated customer services by both e-assistant and human assistant (i.e., a human assistant will be alerted and approach a visitor via video pop-up box or text invitation to communicate with him/her if the online system thinks the visitor is experiencing difficulties in finding required information); Online voice shopping system (consumers can shop online by talking to the site); Better B2C trust services; among many others.

Table 14.1: *Continued*

E-business types	Examples of future growth opportunities
C2C	Growth in support services for C2C (i.e., more online payment & finance systems (applications such as PayPal's payment processing system, person-to-person lending services from Zopa); Online bartering services especially when consumers want to spend as less cash as possible in raining days; Online exchanges for individuals' intangible assets (i.e., ideas, knowledge, skills, inventions); among many others.
Mobile Business	Many opportunities in various areas of B2B, B2C, C2C, E-government, E-learning, E-publishing, Social Networks, and Intra-organizational activities since so far mobile phone and other wireless devices have been heavily used for telecommunication purposes (i.e., making and answering phone calls, sending and replying messages in audio, text or video formats).
E-government	Wider adoption and diffusion of online government services to citizens, businesses, other governments and government agencies since many countries are still in the early adoption stage of e-government; Better monitoring of citizens (i.e., check illegal plants via Google maps); More comprehensive e-applications for enhancing national security and dealing with terrorism; and so on.
E-learning	Wider adoption and diffusion of online universities, online corporate universities, e-training, online exam preparation programs, and other online learning applications since many education providers and businesses are still learning to deal with various issues of e-learning (i.e., teaching and learning process on the Internet) and master the skills of balance the online and offline channels.
E-publishing	Many contemporary publications (i.e., newspapers, magazines, journals, textbooks) will be moved online since they are updated very regularly (e.g., daily, monthly, yearly) while some books and publications (like classic novels or books as a gift given by friends or family members or books with special meaning) and publications will still having the option of hard copy since the information inside or the publication itself has the long-lasting effect or/and purpose (but then technologies such as print-on-demand systems will be adopted to print a small volume or even a copy of book). And there are also opportunities in integrating radio and television broadcasting (a kind of publishing) with Internet publishing (i.e., with self-publishing/broadcasting sites such as youtube.com), and other opportunities.

Table 14.1: *Continued*

E-business types	Examples of future growth opportunities
Online communities & Social networks	Online adverting growth in online communities and social networks via better understanding and enhanced techniques of generating revenue within them and more acceptance of online advertising with online communities and social networks from advertisers and consumers; Market research and other knowledge co-creation (via large number of members) opportunities; Online third-party detective/referral services (i.e., checking characters and reputation via reading the behavior within online communities and social networks and cross-checking with other online and offline sources) or online neighborhood watch programs; Turning online members into offline community members and vice versa; Business opportunities arising from offline gatherings of online members; among many others.
Intra-organizational Activities	Adopting effective Google-alike search engines for internal knowledge search; Applying internal wikis, blogs, social networks and other web 2.0 applications to enhance collaboration and communication within the organization; Enhancing knowledge sharing via establishing comprehensive Amazon-style knowledge recommendation systems (i.e., people look for this knowledge also examines that knowledge) and advanced E-bay type knowledge auction/swap/exchange platforms; among many others.

(Source: developed for this study based on Turban et al. 2008; Laudon & Traver 2008; The Authors' Own Knowledge)

The dot.com failures happened in the late 20th century have given us many lessons to learn and valuable experiences. Many e-businesses have bettered their business models (i.e., not solely relying on advertising-driven business models), improved their ways of running the business (i.e., working on innovations and products/services needed for customers instead of focusing on too much on fame and money even though sufficient financial support and generating revenue are critical for any e-business), and adjusted/fine tuned their organizations (i.e., organizational culture, structure) to be more pro-e-business.

When economic situations (like the current one and the economic downturn in mid-2001 around the dot.com bubble) have negative impacts (i.e., reduced consumer spending, more difficult to get funding) on all businesses including e-business firms (especially for e-start-ups), there are also plenty of opportunities (i.e., people will tend to stay home more, spend long hours online and do more online shopping to cut down their spending and get good bargains online; businesses (especially small and medium businesses) will use the Internet more for procurement (i.e., booking travels, purchasing advertising spaces, buying office suppliers) online and for communication and providing services (i.e., online training to the staff, video conferences with staff from different geographic locations, providing answers to frequently asked questions and issues, using online communities to enable customers to help each other to reduce the costs for services provided by human beings in business premises or/ and in call centers). Furthermore, for winning businesses who are looking at long term sustainable success they will keep on investing in innovations all the time since they understand it will take some time before innovative ideas to be commercialized and the economy will recover sooner or later (Nicholas 2008).

2. E-business Success Factors

The Internet is amazing! It has changed the way we do the business and has rewritten the rules for business and transformed many industries, e.g., book, travel, music, accommodation, Internet phone, real estate, and so on. And it has great impacts on our lifestyle, on society, and on politics, and on the way we see the world and ourselves in it. However like any other innovations, there are successes and failures of e-business.

By reviewing success & failure factors of e-business projects we can have better understanding of e-business practices, better prepare for future e-business initiatives, better predict emerging trends and opportunities of e-business, and achieve better productivity with reduced risks and costs by avoiding reinventing the wheels and repeating the same mistakes. Some success factors include:

Managing supply chain by creation of business partners & strategic alliance

Through creating business partners and strategic alliances, e-business organizations can concentrate on their core business and core competences. In reality, not many organizations have the capacity to do all the jobs along the supply chain consisting of upstream, internal, and downstream parts. Many firms will not have required resources and expertise to deal with every part of their supply chains and need to emphasize on one or two parts of their supply chains, and let their strategic alliances & business partners to do the remaining part(s). For example, e-business organizations can use Australia Post, Fedex, UPS and other delivery services providers for packaging, delivery, and warehousing services. Major petroleum companies (i.e., BP and Shell) may be one of the very few exceptions. They try to work on all the parts of their supply chains: oil & gas exploration (upstream activities), oil refining & petrochemical processing (internal activities), and petrol stations (downstream activities).

Selection of products & services

Arguably, the ultimate goal of e-business is to digitize everything we do (or as much as possible) in the offline world, and the Internet provides a global market in which in theory you can sell whatever you want. However the reality is not the same. For example, only certain products (such as software, documents, music, and videos, are particularly well suited for online business because they can be distributed to customers electronically, resulting in instant delivery and with very low distribution costs. In fact, Turban et al. 2008 (p. 713) argued "EC success stories abound, primarily in specialty and niche markets". And effective online pricing strategies (i.e., aligning with organization's pricing strategies, not causing conflict with offline prices, not being too low or too high) are a must for the successful e-tailing.

In addition, when e-business organizations are making the decision on products and services they also may need to take into consideration of industry condition (i.e., whether using e-business is becoming an industry standard? or are you willing to become the industry standard (such practice could be very expensive)?, market competition (i.e., are there many players in the market?), and consumer characteristics (i.e., are consumers ready for your e-business initiatives? how about consumers' quality and speed of their Internet access? how is their acceptance and attitude towards your e-initiatives or/and towards e-business as a whole (shaping consumers' e-culture may take longer time than you thought to establish)?.

Once organizations have decided to sell certain products and services online, they should be able to produce a large range of products with cheaper prices. For example, the major pillars of Amazon's success could be said as: a great product selection (i.e., having much more books than any other brick-and-mortar bookshops since there is no need for physical places for displaying books), cheaper prices (i.e., without the costs of running physical shops), and convenience (24X7X365 availability-the shop will never be closed).

Excellent customer services

E-business organizations should provide customized and personalized services to each individual customer (the dream of mass customization and one-to-one relationship comes to reality. We should thank the Internet !). When e-business organizations are able to communicate with their customers via multiple touch points, the important thing for customers is to receive quality and consistent customers services across the board no matter who they are dealing with (machines or human beings) and how thy are dealing with online and offline channels. We believe e-business organizations should provide dynamic online human assistance initiated by them (i.e., when the system informs the human assistant that a customer may be having difficulties in finding what he/she is after, human assistant should approach the customer (via text or video invitation) to provide friendly services and try to have the customer' business). E-business organizations also should provide customers with excellent online assistances (i.e., useful and use friendly tools for searching information, comparing products & services, online purchasing decision making, arranging delivery and tracking status of delivery, after-sales communication) to enhance their online shopping experiences. In the virtual environment, ensuring customers' privacy rights and secure online transactions are paramount to win their trust and their business, and more importantly their repeat business. One area that is becoming increasingly important is customer care, without addressing customer care effectively all the spending on marketing will be wasted (French 2007). Furthermore O'Brien & Marakas 2006 (p. 251) suggest that (1) it costs six times more to sell to a new customer than to sell to an existing one; (2) a typical dissatisfied customer will tell 8 to 10 people about his/her experience; (3) a company can boost its profit 85% by increasing its annual customer retention by only 5%; (4) the likelihood of selling to a new customer are 15%; an old customer 50%; and (5) 70% of complaining customers will do business with the company again if it takes care of a service mishap.

Trust, Usefulness & User friendliness

E-business organizations need to ensure their e-business systems are trustworthy, useful, and user friendly. Just building awareness is not enough, they must also build trust. This may be done by tying oneself to well-known global or local brands. Customers have to trust you before they are willing to give a credit card number and personal data. To gain trust online, e-business firms need to adopt secure transaction systems (i.e., SSL), put a clear privacy policy in place, strictly implement the privacy policy, provide excellent customer services, implement review and feedback systems, act on the collected feedback timely, use third-part assurance services, and so on. They also can tie themselves to well-known global and local brands to enhance customers' trust. Their e-business systems need to provide good functionalities (i.e., fast uploading/downloading speed, accurate and complete information, effective online order & payment facilities, good search engines, useful links, attractive interface, innovative website design), and they must be user friendly (i.e., easy to navigate and use, ease to find relevant information, match with users' existing IT skills and gears, etc).

Leveraging multiple channels

So far the majority of e-business organizations are click-and-mortar businesses. Some previously pure online businesses (i.e., online banks) also look at establishing offline operations or having strategic relations with traditional businesses or e-businesses with physical presence. In the meantime, it is beneficial for pure e-business organizations to cooperate with brick-and-mortar businesses (i.e., displaying their products in the physical shops, co-promoting their products and services with shops (especially well-established shops), promoting shops' products online at their sites, using shops' supply chain facilities).

The integration of the marketplace and marketspace or the integration of offline and online operations is a very important challenge for the future of e-business. The most noticeable integration of the two concepts is in the click-and-mortar organization. Some organizations will use e-business as just another selling channel (a complement channel). Others will use e-business for only some products and services. A major problem for the click-and-mortar approach is how the two channels can best cooperate in: planning, advertising, logistics, resource allocation and alignment of e-business strategy with strategic plans of the organization. Organizations have to carefully deal with conflict with existing distribution channels and the coexistence of both channels.

Regarding building customer awareness, the web is may not be a good medium for it. If potential customers have never heard of one before it goes online, it can't assume they will find it and trust it when they find it. It is important to build awareness through offline channels. This is true for the local as well as the international market. In addition, the best advertising approach so far is the combination of online and offline channels, especially in the beginning stage. On the other hand, e-business firms need to be aware that many customers search information online before they purchase in the shop (Economist Intelligence Unit 2009). Word-of-mouth and referrals may play very important roles in the beginning stage of an e-initiative.

Having appropriate E-business strategy planning & implementation process in place

The authors believe that one of the important reasons that many failures of e-business projects is the lack of systematic and strategic planning (Turban et al. 2008; Laudon & Traver 2008; McNurlin & Sprague 2004). Many organizations have embarked on e-business projects without thoroughly understanding internal environment (i.e., current operations, internal needs and problems, strengths and weaknesses) and external environment (i.e., the market, the needs of customers, opportunities, competition & threats, the government policies and emerging regulations). And very often they have not gone through a strategic planning and implementation process (i.e., not going through all four steps of e-business strategic planning process (including initiation, formulation, implementation and assessment) suggested by Turban et al. (2008), and have skipped some activities in those four steps (i.e., bypassing things such as testing, training, documentation, change management, risk management, project management; missing involvement from users and alignment between business and information technology function). A good e-business strategy planning process helps organizations learn about themselves and its external operating environment, reduce risks associated with e-business projects (i.e., customers' rejection of proposed e-business initiatives, falling behind competitors' similar e-business initiatives, obsolescence arising from missing emerging technologies, hurdles in e-business system development process), and make required changes/adjustments (i.e., to business strategies, processes, organizational culture, organizational structure , business processes), shape right e-business strategy that guide the direction of and implementation of the organization's e-business initiatives, and greatly facilitate the adoption, success and sustainable success of e-business initiatives.

Sound business model and business practices

Many e-business failures have fell hard on the assumption of once you build it money will come. As a result, many e-business organizations have neglected its core stuff (their products and services as well as values created for customers), and have overly spent resources (money, time and human resources) on marketing and branding. And many of them also rely too heavily on generating revenue from advertising, or/and underestimate the total costs of ownership of an e-business (in other words, no sufficient funding has been secured before they start up their e-businesses). The total cost of ownership of an e-business may include tangible/quantifiable costs (costs that can be quantified costs (e.g., cost of hardware and software, employee salaries) and intangible/qualitative costs (i.e., loss of customer goodwill or employee morale caused by errors and disruptions arising from the installation of a new e-business application) and direct costs (i.e., capital investments) and indirect costs (i.e., training, conversion, license updating and maintenance). When many factors can contribute to the success and failure of e-business, one fundamental principle is any successful business does follow sound business practices (i.e., effective accounting & finance practices, right structure, good products & customers services, good management team). In summary, e-business is just another kind of businesses. When it comes to achieve sustainability and viability of an e-business, the emphasis should be more on business and less on E.

Being a global player

Globalization provides the opportunity for e-business organizations to serve not only their traditional geographic markets, but potentially the global market. But there are some challenges and issues they have to face. On top of common e-business issues (i.e., issues we have discussed above in this section), e-business organizations expanding into a foreign market also need to have thorough understanding the operating environment of the market and take into consideration of political (i.e., relevant regulations, privacy laws), technological (i.e., broadband infrastructure, Internet adoption rates, mobile phone adoption rates), economic factors (i.e., taxation practices, national payment systems networks, cross-border fund transfer differences, economic situations), and social factors (i.e., language, culture). Without thorough understanding of local operating environment, blindly applying best practices in home country of a foreign e-business would only lead to failures and lessons. For example, the three Internet giants of E-bay, Yahoo and Google all have been struggling in the Chinese market as a result of their lack of understanding the operating environment in China and the Chinese way of doing business. And a combined approach of having both centralization and decentralization should be taken. A centralization approach focuses on organizations' strategic objectives and on gaining more control while a decentralization approach works on localizing their offers, complying with local regulations, and meet local expectations (i.e., local buyers will expect the international provider to use local practices in terms of warranties, money-back guarantees, refunds).

Being the best player in your field

Companies like E-bay (online marketplace), Yahoo (Internet directory/ Portal), and Apple computer (software and hardware products) "got there first" and leveraged their first-mover/early adopter competitive advantage. When the first mover strategy can give e-business organizations advantages of establishing their brands and building strong user base before competition comes in, such advantages cannot guarantee them the sustainable success. For example, companies such as Citibank (ATM), Sony (video tape), Chemdex (B2B digital exchange), Netscape (Internet browser), lost their first-mover advantages to late movers. And firms such as Intel (microchip), America Online (Internet marketing), Google (online search engine), are some good examples of companies who were later movers but gained success over earlier adopters by being the best (Turban et al. 2006, p. 592). In the long run, best-mover advantage not first-mover advantage determines the market leader. E-business organizations need to be the best in the areas/industries they are competing in and constantly generate new/better products and services to win and retain their customers. Some e-business organizations who so far have been very successful in this strategy include: Alibaba, Amazon, Google, Apple, Microsoft, and so on.

We have discussed some success factors of e-business. But many other factors influencing the success of e-business (i.e., organizational factors, external environment & influences, knowledge management, organizational learning, etc) have not been included here for reasons such as page limitation, lack of established literature. In the next chapter, we develop a model to explore factors influencing adoption, success and sustainable success of e-business. All the factors and variables in the model could have the impact (either directly or indirectly) on the success of e-business initiatives. Future research testing the model could confirm or disconfirm the proposed impact of factors and variables in the developed model.

How about e-business factors in small and medium businesses? Being Small is beautiful or not so beautiful when it comes to e-business? Small and medium enterprises (SMEs), particularly small businesses, can obtain many benefits from participating in e-business (i.e., opportunities in marketing, business expansion, cost cutting, and tighter strategic alliances), but they will need to be pro-active in preparing for and embarking on e-business. On the other hand, inhibiting factors which keep SMEs from getting actively involved in e-business could include inability to compete on large scale, potential huge entry costs for some types of business, lack of resources, and lack of required in-house expertise, and so on. Support for SMEs wishing to venture into e-business is potentially available from several areas. Individual countries and industries may have different arrangements. Potentially, though, there is help available in the form of government support schemes (i.e., e-businessguide (www.e-businessguide.com.au)–an initiative of the Australian Government for providing information and resources about e-business for small businesses in Australia and for those who advise them), industry support initiatives (i.e., small business solutions from chamber of commerce and industry in Western Australia (http://www.cciwa.com/Small_business_solutions_1.aspx) and other associations), from IT vendors (i.e., IBM's small and medium business center (http://www-304.ibm.com/jct03004c/businesscenter/smb/us/en/). In addition, in order to successfully implement e-business, small business need to work on areas such as appropriate capital investment, effective, secure electronic payments, flexible payment methods, appropriate logistical services and inventory control, effective web site design, and so on.

3. Emerging Business Trends and E-business

It is always extremely hard to predict the future. Many experts, gurus and successful entrepreneurs have tried their luck and failed. It is not because they are not intelligent (in fact they are super-smart people), the future just cannot be accurately predicted when the only certainty in the future is uncertainty. Has anyone predicted the wide diffusion of the Internet and the successes of Google, Yahoo, Amazon, E-bay, Dell and other e-business organizations?.

One way we can discuss the future e-business is looking at future trends and corresponding opportunities for e-business. The following Table 14.2 presents some discussion as per this approach.

Table 14.2: Some future trends and corresponding opportunities for E-business

Trends	Examples of E-business Opportunities
Rapid growth of world population (especially in developing countries)	E-learning opportunities to help people (especially in developing countries) get educated cheaply, easily and quickly facilitated by scholars and academics from all over the world connected by the Internet as well as donated knowledge stored in digital formats (an online world university for developing countries-education is an effective solution to poverty); Using the Internet to distribute knowledge (especially in the areas of health, farming, manufacturing, technology development-knowledge is the key for better tomorrow); Online communities to help improve living standards in developing countries (people sharing their experiences of and giving support (financial and non-financial) to the poor); Online marketplaces (preferably set up by relevant widely recognized official organizations) to coordinate and ensure sufficient products and services supplied at low prices to the poor); Using wireless devices (mostly mobile phones) to alert people about diseases and natural disasters when the access to the Internet is difficult or expensive to get; Social networks (via wired or wireless devices) to connect kids in developing countries with kids in developed countries so that they can be friends and help each other; among many others.
Aging population (longer-living population) in the developed world	Collaborative e-health care for the elderly via connecting doctors, specialists, nurses, patients & their relatives all together, who are in different locations of the world, by applying wired and wireless (Internet-enabled) multimedia communication devices; Collaborative drug development by tapping into both internal and external expertise through applications such as wikis, social networks, online knowledge marketplaces; Using artificial intelligence applications (i.e., robots) to perform certain or/and assist in surgeries and take care of patients with the regular checking and updates from doctors, specialists, and nurses connected via networks; Wider adoption of tracking devices (i.e., enhanced radio frequency identification applications) to monitor the

Table 14.2: *Continued*

Trends	Examples of E-business Opportunities
	movement and condition of patients, Letting the elder search the web regularly to slow down the aging of their brains as suggested by latest research results cited in Kleinig (2009), among many others.
Faster pace of technological innovation	Adopting open e-hub structure where the organization, its customers, suppliers, and business partners can work together on developing new products and services; Purchasing required knowledge and new technologies via buy-side e-knowledge marketplaces (reverse auction approach); Internal wikis, discussion forums, online expert directories/yellow pages, online conferences & brainstorming sessions, best-practices databases and other knowledge management systems to help manage the organization's knowledge and foster innovation (especially tacit knowledge); among many others.
More globalized and integrated economy	Buying and selling products and services globally via both B2B and B2C e-business models (for large, medium and small enterprises), Connecting buyers and sellers from all over the world via online marketplaces; Better collaboration and cooperation between governments via e-government applications; among many others.
The greatly increased importance of managing knowledge assets and carriers (also creators, distributors, users) of those knowledge assets	Online training programs and corporate universities to disseminate and share both internal and external organizational knowledge and enhance individuals' knowledge base; Knowledge management systems to assist in creating, storing, organizing, distributing, using, and monitoring the use of knowledge from internal and external sources; Online talent registration, recruitment and management systems and networks to recruit and manage domestic and overseas talents; Private or public online marketplaces for trading knowledge assets; among many others.
The greatly enlarged role of technology in economy and society	E-assistants who check your emails, answer your phone calls, and arrange your diaries; Virtual consultants who can provide good advices on questions such as what and where should I eat, wear, and do today by learning from your online behavior and do a much better job than today's search engines; Smart houses in which all the appliances are connected, controlled by all-in-one device (i.e., TV, computers, hi-fi systems, air-conditioners, wash machines and others in one's home are centrally controlled by one mobile phone), and charged by usage (including computing and Internet surfing) via one device (i.e., one's mobile phone) which indicate all the

Table 14.2: *Continued*

Trends	Examples of E-business Opportunities
	usage of different devices in the house); Mobile living supported by pervasive and wearable devices (i.e., clothing with electronic tags and wearable mobile which can make phone multimedia calls, surf the Internet , enjoy entertainments, locate the positions, taking photos, recording videos, and interact all the devices at the home and in the office, etc); World games everywhere and everyday (i.e., playing bowls in the local bowls club but competing with players all the world via publishing your scores to the world via the Internet in real time); Voting online; Applying for visas and passports online; Working on better Internet technologies (beyond Internet 2 and IPV 6 projects); among many others.
The greatly increased control by the government	More closely monitoring your behaviors and read your minds via examining your online movements and cross-checking with your offline activities; Better administration for local governments (i.e., using applications such as Google Map to check whether residents have any illegal buildings, etc); E-toll to collect revenue from passing vehicles; Compulsory online payment systems to collect fines, taxes, and fees from residents; Compulsory online development applications; Online DNA and Biometric databases; Online water usage systems to monitor water usage in households; among many others.
The greater importance of education	Online universities and colleges; Virtual classrooms, examinations and simulations (i.e., 3D applications such as Second Life); Global assignments and projects connecting students in different continents; A world degree which you earn by studying different subjects or a world subject which you complete by studying different modules of similar subjects or different subjects with various universities across the globe ; Online learning communities to facilitate our life-long learning and enhance communications regarding learning issues between the developed and the developing worlds; among many others.
The greatly increased power of consumers	More personalized and localized online services (i.e., more and more companies will likely to have online services in Chinese as a result of the very large number of Internet users in China); Wider adoption of mass customization via online channel; Better understanding of online customer behaviors via development of better technologies and techniques to dig the huge amount data sitting in the data warehouse; Development of better

Table 14.2: *Continued*

Trends	Examples of E-business Opportunities
	technologies to collect and manage customers' demands; Development of more advanced technologies to assist various stages of customers' online decision making process (including more effective information search-at the moment large amount of information on the Internet could not be effectively accessed); More advanced voice-based e-business systems; among many others.
The greatly increased value and scarcity of time (time is essence and a commodity)	Serving customers' time by providing products and services online to customers (i.e., via B2B and B2C sites); Reducing time from ideas to product development to manufacturing to testing the product to reaching the market via connecting all the relevant parties working together simultaneously; Trading time in online time marketplaces; among many others.
The greater emphasis on working on issues of climate change	Wider adoption of shared infrastructure and implementation of such initiatives as service oriented architecture, grid computing, cloud computing, web services, semantic web, web science, and virtualization to more effectively use our technological infrastructure and reduce emission (i.e., fewer computers and data centers); Development of better Internet technologies and systems (Internet enabled) to capture and calculate carbon emissions and prints for each computing device and each business activity of online and offline channels; Online marketplaces for trading carbon emission permits; Widely promote applications such as e-ink, e-paper, e-book and other paperless publishing applications; Charging the battery of computing and communication devices (wired and wireless) by solar energy; Adopting all-in-one device (i.e., including computer, mobile phone, remote control, TV, Hi-fi system, Radio); Alternative computer box and screen (i.e., your watch or mobile phone is the computer box and your glasses are the screen); among many others.
The greater interest on space and the life outside the earth	E-simulations and online training for life in space; Using the Internet (i.e., via applications such as wikis) to create and distribute knowledge of the space and the life outside the earth; Creating an e-space or an e-universe for better understanding of the space and the universe, and applying gained knowledge in developing future e-business; among many others.

(Source: developed from Haag et al. 2008, pp. 431-435; Stephenson & Pandit 2008; Laudon & Traver's 2008, pp. 40-42; The Authors' Own Knowledge)

4. Conclusions

This chapter discusses the future of e-business by looking at some future e-business growth opportunities for various types of e-business organizations. This chapter also presents and explains some success factors for e-business initiatives. Such factors will provide assistance to organizations who are embarking on e-business or who have adopted e-business. In addition, this chapter also presents some e-business opportunities associated with emerging business trends.

References

Amaravadi, C. S. (2003) The world and business computing in 2051, Journal of Strategic Information Systems, Vol. 12, pp. 373-386.

Economist Intelligence Unit (2009) The World in Figures: Industries (E-commerce), The World in 2009, The Economist, pp. 120.

French, T. D. (2007) Confronting proliferation in online media: An interview with Yahoo's senior marketer, The McKinsey Quality, June 2007, pp. 1-9.

Haag, S., Baltzan, P. & Phillips, A. (2008) Business Driven Technology, 2nd edition, McGraw-Hill Irwin, Boston, U.S.A.

Kleinig, J. (2009) Internet stimulates elderly, The Australian, January 13, 2009, Online, Available at: http://www.australianit.news.com.au/story/0,24897,24905688-15306,00.html (accessed on January 13, 2009).

Laudon, K.C. & Traver, C.G. (2008) E-commerce: Buisness, Technology, Society 2008, 4th edn, Addison Wesley, Boston, USA.

McNurlin, B.C. & Sprague, R.H. (2004) Information Systems Management in Practice, 6th edn, Pearson Education, New Jersey.

Nicholas, T. (2008) Innovation lessons from the 1930s, The McKinsey Quarterly, December, pp. 1-10.

O'Brien, J.A. & Marakas, G.M. (2006) Management Information Systems, 7th edn. Boston: Irwin/McGraw-Hill.

Stephenson, E. & Pandit, A. (2008) How companies act on global trends: A McKinsey global survey, The McKinsey Quarterly, March, pp. 1-10.

Turban, E., King, D., McKay, J., Marshall, P., Lee, J. & Viehland, D. (2008) Electronic Commerce 2008: A Managerial Perspective, International edn, Prentice Hall, Upper Saddle River, NJ.

CHAPTER 15

ACHIEVING SUSTAINABLE E-BUSINESS SUCCESS: DEVELOPMENT AND APPLICATION OF A MODEL OF E-BUSINESS ADOPTION, SUCCESS AND SUSTAINABLE SUCCESS

Jun Xu

Graduate College of Management, Southern Cross University, Australia

Mohammed Quaddus

Graduate School of Business, Curtin University of Technology, Australia

This chapter develops a model of adoption, success and sustainable success of e-business. It presents various factors and variables in detail. Hypotheses established from the model are presented which can be tested via empirical study. The proposed model has both theoretical and practical implications. It can be adapted for e-business implementations in various organizations in national and international arena.

1. Introduction

As a result of the relative newness of e-business, fast changing Internet technologies, and the hypes & myths of successes and failures of e-business/e-commerce organizations we have seen in the past decade or so, there is a need for better understanding factors influencing success and sustainable success of e-business. On the contrary to the wide adoption of the Internet, the more affordable computing gears, and the rapidly growing popularity and publicity of doing business on the Internet, there is a lack of established literature of factors influencing adoption, success and sustainable success of e-business, especially in the domains of success and sustainable success of e-business.

One notable exception is Molla & Licker's (2001) e-commerce success model, which is built on Delone & Mclean's information systems model (1992) and takes into consideration of the nature of the virtual environment and the characteristics of online operations. The Molla and Licker's (2001) e-commerce success model consists of factors of e-commerce system quality, content quality, trust, support and service, use, e-commerce customer satisfaction, and e-commerce success, and it proposes that e-commerce system factors such as system quality, content quality, trust, support & service will influence e-commerce success in an indirect way, with their influencing being mediated by both use and customer e-commerce satisfaction. It also postulates that customers' use of e-commerce affects their e-commerce satisfaction, which in turn influences e-commerce success.

In the meantime, there exist studies investigating factors affecting the adoption of e-business from different perspectives, including the external environment (i.e., Gibbs et al. 2002; Molla 2004; Gunasekaran & Ngai 2005; Stylianou et al. 2003; Tan & Ouyang 2004), organisational factors (i.e., Gibbs et al. 2002; Gunasekaran & Ngai 2005; Molla 2004; Teo & Ang 1999; Lu 2003), senior/top management factors (i.e, Barnes et al. 2004; Epstein 2005; Gibbs et al. 2002; Gunasekaran & Ngai 2005; Molla 2004; Sabherwal et al. 2004; Stylianou et al. 2003), e-business/e-commerce strategies (Epstein 2004; Gunasekaran & Ngai 2005; Hart 2003; Harvey 2000; Rogers 2001; Steinfield 2004), and consumer characteristics (i.e., Dillon & Reif 2004; Gibbs et al. 2002; Ratchford et al. 2001; Teo 2001). In addition, other innovation diffusion theories (i.e., Rogers' (1995) theory of innovation; Xu & Quaddus' (2005) model of knowledge management systems diffusion in an organization) and technology acceptance models (i.e., Davis's (1989) technology acceptance model; Xu & Quaddus's (2007) model of adoption and continued use of knowledge management systems) could be useful for explaining the adoption, success and sustainable success of organizations' e-business initiatives.

In this chapter, the authors aim to address the gap in the literature by proposing a model of e-business adoption, success and sustainable success. In the following sections, the proposed model will be discussed, followed by discussion of implications for theory and practices. Conclusions and future plan are presented in the final section.

2. The Model of E-business Adoption, Success and Sustainable Success

Building on the literature as we discussed in the previous section, the chapter proposed of a model of e-business adoption, success and sustainable success, which consists of three parts: (1) step 1: adoption decision making stage; (2) step 2: achieving success stage; and (3) step 3: achieving sustainable success stage (see Figure 15.1).

In the adoption decision making stage (step 1), the model suggests that internal factors (such as organizational factors, knowledge management, learning & innovation), external factors (such as external environment, external influences), and e-business factors (such as e-business strategy planning, expected trust, expected benefits, expected characteristics of e-business system) will have direct influence on the adoption decision of e-business. In the achieving success stage (step 2), it suggests that factors related to the organization's efforts in embracing e-business including organizational adjustments and ongoing knowledge management, learning, and implementation and factors concerning the performance of e-business system and evaluation of e-business activities including realized characteristics of e-business system, realized benefits, gained trust, e-business strategy implementation will have direct impact on the e-business success. In the achieving sustainable success stage (step 3), it postulates that by successfully repeating activities of step 1 for reviewing and embarking new e-business initiatives and activities of step 2 for enhancing gained e-business success, organizations will be able to achieve sustainable e-business success. In the meantime, the model is not a static model, and a constant feedback process through closely monitoring and evaluating an e-business project is built into the model (see Figure 15.2). Such feedback process allows going back and re-working on previously completed steps. In the following sections various factors of the proposed model are described in detail.

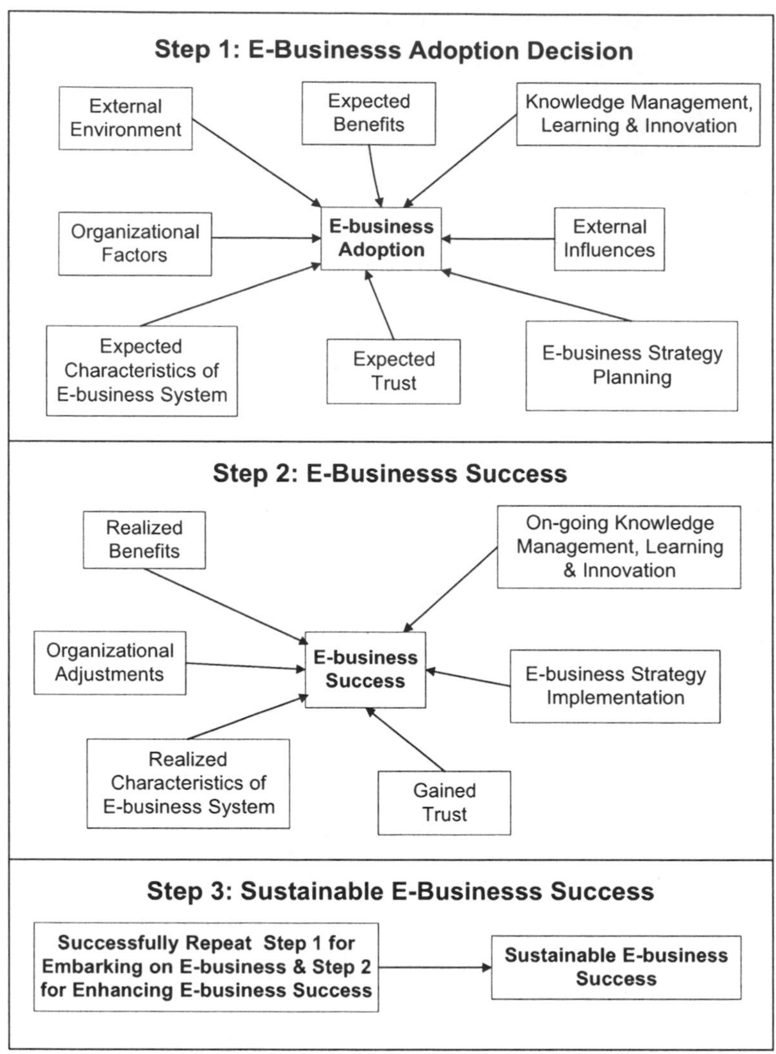

Figure 15.1: A Model of Sustainable Success of E-business
(Source: developed for this study)

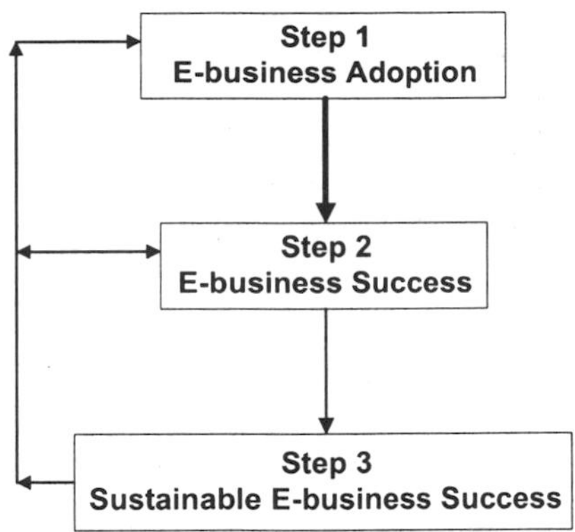

Figure 15.2: Sustainable E-business Success Cycle
(Source: developed for this study)

External Environment Factors

In the proposed model, external environment factors include dimensions of competitive pressure/competition, regulations & policies, opportunities arising from development of information technology infrastructure & advances of Internet technologies, economic conditions, and social environment (see Table 15.1).

Table 15.1: External environment factors

Dimensions	Brief Explanation
Competitive Pressure/ Competition	Organizations' e-business activities could be initiated by tough competition in the market place.
Regulations and Policies	Organizations' e-business activities could be initiated by relevant/favorable regulations and policies (i.e., policies for electronic communication & transaction, taxation, privacy, environment sustainability, and climate change issues).
Opportunities Arising from Development of Information Technology Infrastructure and Advances of Internet Technologies	Organizations' e-business activities could be initiated by opportunities arising from development of information technology infrastructure (i.e., the diffusion of broadband, the availability of online payment systems, the accessibility & the affordability of access to the Internet and required hardware and software, etc) and rapid advances of Internet technologies.
Economic Conditions	Organizations' e-business activities could be initiated by the economic conditions (both domestic and international).

Table 15.1: *Continued*

Dimensions	Brief Explanation
Social Environment	Organizations' e-business activities could be initiated by favorable social environment (including things such as languages, cultures, religions, customs & traditions, lifestyle, and demographic patterns & trends, etc)

(Source: developed for this study)

External Influences

External influences in the proposed model are represented by factors of following the trend/fashion and/or the lead by industry's leaders, influence from external consultants & experts, customer expectation and demand, market opportunities, and peer business influence (see Table 15.2).

Table 15.2: External influences

Dimensions	Brief Explanation
Following the trend/fashion and/or the lead by industry's leaders	Organizations' e-business activities could be initiated by increased popularity of e-business in the industry or/and by following the lead by industry leaders.
Influence from External Consultants & Experts	Organizations' e-business activities could be initiated by recommendations from external consultants and experts.
Customer Expectation and Demand	Organizations' e-business activities could be initiated by customers' increasing demand for value-for-money products and services.
Market Opportunities	Organizations' e-business activities could be initiated by market opportunities (i.e., tapping into larger markets or new markets in other cities and countries).
Peer Business Influence	Organizations' e-business activities could be initiated by the influence from peer businesses that have adopted e-business (i.e., having seen the benefits and costs of embarking e-business).

(Source: developed for this study)

Knowledge Management, Learning & Innovation

In the proposed model, knowledge management, learning & innovation factors consist of creation of knowledge, capture of knowledge, storage & organization of knowledge, dissemination and sharing of knowledge, application of knowledge, existence of culture for knowledge management, existence of structure for knowledge management, existence of processes for managing knowledge, existence of tools for managing knowledge, existence of strategies for managing knowledge, co-creation attitude, learning desire and activities, learning ability & knowledge building, research & development investments, innovation efforts, innovation environment, innovativeness and talent management (see Table 15.3).

Table 15.3: Knowledge management, learning & innovation

Dimensions	Brief Explanation
Creation of Knowledge	Organizations' e-business activities could be initiated by their activities of creating knowledge (both tacit and explicit) from internal and external sources (i.e., learning changes in the market).
Capture of Knowledge	Organizations' e-business activities could be initiated by their activities of collecting knowledge (both tacit and explicit) from internal and external sources.
Storage & Organization of Knowledge	Organizations' e-business activities could be initiated by their efforts of storing and organizing knowledge (both tacit and explicit) from internal and external sources.
Dissemination and Sharing of Knowledge	Organizations' e-business activities could be initiated by their efforts of distributing and sharing knowledge (both tacit and explicit) from internal and external sources.
Application of Knowledge	Organizations' e-business activities could be initiated by their efforts of applying knowledge (both tacit and explicit) from internal and external sources (i.e., better and faster responding to the changes in the market).
Existence of Culture for Knowledge Management	Organizations' e-business activities could be initiated by their pro-knowledge management culture.
Existence of Structure for Knowledge Management	Organizations' e-business activities could be initiated by their pro-knowledge management structure.
Existence of Processes for Managing Knowledge	Organizations' e-business activities could be initiated by their systematic knowledge management processes.
Existence of Tools for Managing Knowledge	Organizations' e-business activities could be initiated by their appropriate knowledge management systems.
Existence of Strategies for Managing Knowledge	Organizations' e-business activities could be initiated by their knowledge management strategies.
Co-creation Attitude	Organizations' e-business activities could be initiated by pro-co-creation initiatives with business partners, suppliers, customers and even competitors instead of sticking to the not-invented –here attitude.
Learning Desire and Activities	Organizations' e-business activities could be initiated by their desire and activities of learning the internal and external environments.

Table 15.3: *Continued*

Dimensions	Brief Explanation
Learning Ability & Knowledge Building	Organizations' e-business activities could be initiated by activities of developing collective and individual learning ability and efforts of knowledge building.
Research & Development Investments	Organizations' e-business activities could be initiated by their investments in research and development activities.
Innovation Efforts	Organizations' e-business activities could be initiated by their efforts of producing new products and services all the time (in both good and bad times).
Innovation Environment	Organizations' e-business activities could be initiated by their innovation environment where people are encouraged and supported for being innovative and creative.
Innovativeness	Organizations' e-business activities could be initiated by their willingness to try new ideas and technologies (i.e. e-business).
Talent Management	Organizations' e-business activities could be initiated by their efforts of better talent management (including recruiting, training and retaining talented people (or people with required knowledge or people who are eager to create new knowledge) and their knowledge).

(Source: developed for this study)

Organizational Factors

The concept of organizational factors are made of dimensions of nature of business, established brand and reputation, size of business, business growth/strategic direction, age of business, top management support, people's support, the need for problem solving, strategic alliance and supply chain improvement, business processes, organizational structure, organizational culture, information technology infrastructure and expertise for developing e-business applications, management's experience and knowledge of e-business, and people's experience and knowledge of e-business (see Table 15.4).

Table 15.4: Organizational factors

Dimensions	Brief Explanation
Nature of Business	Organizations' e-business activities could be initiated by their nature of business (i.e., some businesses may have more needs for e-business than others or have more suitable products & services for e-business).

Table 15.4: *Continued*

Dimensions	Brief Explanation
Established Brand and Reputation	Organizations' e-business activities could be initiated by their established brand and reputation.
Size of Business	Organizations' e-business activities could be initiated by their size of business (i.e., small business may be more willing to embark on e-business than their larger counterparts as a result of relatively low entry costs, constrained resources (especially human resources) and their flexibility).
Business Growth/Strategic Direction	Organizations' e-business activities could be initiated by their needs of business growth/strategic direction (i.e., expanding their business domestically or/and internationally).
Age of Business	Organizations' e-business activities could be initiated by the age of business (i.e., newly established businesses may be more willing to try e-business).
Top Management Support	Organizations' e-business activities could be initiated and facilitated by top management (i.e., providing resources and leadership for the implementation of e-business).
People's Support	Organizations' e-business activities could be initiated by or encouraged by their people.
The Need for Problem Solving	Organizations' e-business activities could be initiated by the need for solutions of problems.
Strategic Alliance and Supply Chain Improvement	Organizations' e-business activities could be initiated by the need for establishing strategic alliance and supply chain improvement.
Business Processes	Organizations' e-business activities could be initiated the need for business process improvement or facilitated by pro-e-business business processes.
Organizational Structure	Organizations' e-business activities could be initiated the need for the change in organizational structure or facilitated by pro-e-business organizational structure.
Organizational Culture	Organizations' e-business activities could be initiated the need for the change in organizational culture or facilitated by pro-e-business organizational culture.
Information Technology Infrastructure and Expertise for Developing E-business Applications	Organizations' e-business activities could be initiated or facilitated by their information technology infrastructure and expertise.
Management's Experience and Knowledge of E-business	Organizations' e-business activities could be initiated or facilitated by management's experience and knowledge of e-business.

Table 15.4: *Continued*

Dimensions	Brief Explanation
People's Experience and Knowledge of E-business	Organizations' e-business activities could be initiated or facilitated by people's experience and knowledge of e-business.

(Source: developed for this study)

E-business strategy planning

E-business strategy planning covers perspectives of e-business strategy, e-business strategic planning process, e-business model, sufficient analysis and planning, implementation plan, and post-implementation maintenance & evaluation (see Table 15.5).

Table 15.5: E-business Strategy Planning

Dimensions	Brief Explanation
E-Business Strategy	Organizations' e-business activities could be facilitated by having an appropriate e-business strategy (i.e., how and what the online channel can contribute to the organization's performance).
E-Business Strategic Planning Process	Organizations' e-business activities could be facilitated by having gone through strategic planning process (i.e., including strategy initiation, formation, implementation and assessment as suggested by Turban et al. (2008)).
E-Business Model	Organizations' e-business activities could be facilitated by having an appropriate e-business model (focusing on generating revenue and creating value for an organization, its customers and its business partners).
Sufficient Analysis and Planning	Organizations' e-business activities could be facilitated by having gone through sufficient analysis and planning when they are deciding specific business strategies.
Implementation Plan	Organizations' e-business activities could be facilitated by having established a comprehensive implementation plan for chosen e-business strategy.
Post-implementation Maintenance and Evaluation	Organizations' e-business activities could be facilitated by having established a comprehensive plan for post-implementation activities and a detailed set of processes and tools to examine the performance of choose e-business strategy.

(Source: developed for this study)

Expected characteristics of E-business system

This construct focuses on the expectation of e-business system's ease of use and its performance, including such dimensions as ease of use, cheap to learn & use, speed, accessibility, availability, regular maintenance & updates, and systems integration (see Table 15.6).

Table 15.6: Expected characteristics of E-business system

Dimensions	Brief Explanation
Ease of Use	Organizations' e-business activities could be facilitated by expected ease of use of the e-business system (i.e., making finding information easy by providing online search facility, frequently ask questions (FAQ) section, website map, navigation assistance/guide, etc) for both internal (i.e., employees) and external stakeholders (customers, business partners and suppliers)).
Cheap to Learn and Use	Organizations' e-business activities could be facilitated by expected non-expensive learning and use of the e-business system for both internal (i.e., employees) and external stakeholders (customers, business partners, and suppliers).
Speed	Organizations' e-business activities could be facilitated by expected fast speed (i.e., uploading, downloading and navigation speed) of the e-business system.
Accessibility	Organizations' e-business activities could be facilitated by expected easy access by every authorized user.
Availability	Organizations' e-business activities could be facilitated by expected 24/7 availability of the e-business system.
Regular Maintenance and Updates	Organizations' e-business activities could be facilitated by expected regular maintenance and updates.
Systems Integration	Organizations' e-business activities could be facilitated by expected integration with the organization's existing systems and with systems of customers, business partners, and suppliers.

(Source: developed for this study)

Expected Benefits

This construct is looking at potential benefits arising from adopting e-business in organizations and is represented by following dimensions: better/ new products and services, efficiency, effectiveness, time & cost reduction, net benefits, relationships with customers, relationships with suppliers and business partners, relationships with government agencies, relationships with competitors, enlarging market share, achieving market leader position, increasing revenue, improving profit, better image, responsiveness to changes in the market (see Table 15.7).

Table 15.7: Expected benefits

Dimensions	Brief Explanation
Better/ New Products and Services	E-business is able to help organizations create better/new services and innovations.
Efficiency	E-business is able to help organizations enhance the efficiency of their internal operations (i.e., simplifying workflows, speeding the projects).
Effectiveness	E-business is able to help organizations do the right things (i.e., working on the right projects, markets).
Time & Cost Reduction	E-business is able to help organizations save time and money for them (i.e., via improved communication, enhanced business businesses, reduced costs in marketing & other operation areas, etc).
Net Benefits	E-business is able to create net benefits (more benefits than costs) for organizations.
Relationships with Customers	E-business is able to help organizations enhance their relationships with customers and provide them with better products & services.
Relationships with Suppliers and Business Partners	E-business is able to help organizations enhance their relationships with suppliers and business partners and help improve their supply chains.
Relationships with Government Agencies	E-business is able to help organizations enhance their relationships with government agencies, strengthen their relationships with them, and reduce unexpected events.
Relationships with Competitors	E-business is able to help organizations enhance their relationships with their competitors and achieve a win-win situation (co-opetition is made possible).
Market Share	E-business is able to help organizations enhance their market share.
Market Leader Position	E-business is able to help organizations achieve/enhance their market leader position (i.e., enjoying large market share, more experience, established online brand)
Revenue	E-business is able to help organizations generate more revenue.
Profit	E-business is able to help organizations produce more profit.
Image	E-business is able to help organizations create better image in the market.
Responsiveness to Changes in the Market	E-business is able to help organizations enhance their responsiveness to changes in the market.

(Source: developed for this study)

Expected Trust

Trust is the most formidable barrier to doing business on the Internet (Wang & Emurian 2004). Many customers are reluctant to conduct business online as a result of the lack of human-to-human interaction, which play a very important role in building trust towards an e-business organization. In the proposed model, trust of e-business can be expected from such dimensions of security, quality of products and services, provision of third party assurance services, privacy policy, intellectual property management, terms and conditions, online communities, online feedback/reputation systems, providing opportunities to talk to human beings, and providing information of the organization (see Table 15.8).

Table 15.8: Expected trust

Dimensions	Brief Explanation
Security	Organizations' e-business activities could be facilitated by expected trust arising from security of the e-business system (i.e., secured online shopping and payment processes, secured communication with customers, business partners and suppliers, and secured intra-organization communication).
Quality of Products and Services	Organizations' e-business activities could be facilitated by expected trust arising from quality products and services (i.e., providing online services such as search functions they offer).
Provision of Third Party Assurance Services	Organizations' e-business activities could be facilitated by expected trust arising from providing third-party assurance/services to guarantee a peaceful mind for their online customers (such as CA (Certificate Authority), VeriSign, or TRUSTe).
Privacy Policy	Organizations' e-business activities could be facilitated by expected trust arising from presenting detailed and visible privacy policy (concerning the collection and use of customers' data), which is clearly comply with relevant government regulations.
Intellectual Property Management	Organizations' e-business activities could be facilitated by expected trust arising from visible and effective intellectual property management.
Terms and Conditions	Organizations' e-business activities could be facilitated by expected trust arising from presenting detailed and visible terms and conditions clauses including refund and dispute resolution procedures and policies.
Online Communities	Organizations' e-business activities could be facilitated by expected trust arising from establishing online communities for their relevant stakeholders (i.e., for customers, business partners, and suppliers) and tapping into crowd intelligence created in the online communities.

Table 15.8: *Continued*

Dimensions	Brief Explanation
Online Feedback/Reputation Systems	Organizations' e-business activities could be facilitated by expected trust arising from establishing online feedback/reputation systems for their relevant stakeholders (i.e., for customers, business partners, and suppliers) regarding their views on organizations' products and services and tapping into crowd intelligence created in the systems.
Providing Opportunities to Talk to Human Beings	Organizations' e-business activities could be facilitated by expected trust arising from providing contact numbers of the organization which will be answered by relevant/key people in the organization instead of the machine, especially when customers are having issues with the organization.
Providing Information of The Organization	Organizations' e-business activities could be facilitated by expected trust arising from providing sufficient information on the company (i.e., who we are, what we do, the history of the organization, organizational structure, members of senior managers, culture, mission, vision, strategic objectives, strategic alliances, career services & opportunities, financial information (i.e., share prices, annual reports))

(Source: developed for this study)

E-business Adoption

Organizations' adoption of e-business can be reflected in their uses of e-business for internal operations & communications, interaction with suppliers and business partners, interaction with customers, interaction with government agencies, interaction with competitors, using the Internet as a new business channel, and channel integration (see Table 15.9).

Table 15.9: E-Business adoption

Dimensions	Brief Explanation
Internal Operations & Communications	Organizations will adopt e-business for enhancing internal operations and communications.
Interaction with Suppliers and Business Partners	Organizations will adopt e-business for enhancing interaction with suppliers and business partners.
Interaction with Customers	Organizations will adopt e-business for enhancing interaction with customers.
Interaction with Government Agencies	Organizations will adopt e-business for enhancing interaction with government agencies.

Table 15.9: *Continued*

Dimensions	Brief Explanation
Interaction with Competitors	Organizations will adopt e-business for enhancing interaction with competitors.
Using the Internet as a New Business Channel	Organizations will adopt e-business for establishing a new/additional business channel.
Channel Integration	Organizations adopting e-business will integrate its new online initiatives with its existing offline operations.

(Source: developed for this study)

Realized Benefits

This construct is similar to realized benefits as shown in Table 15.7. However the variable definitions are different now as the construct emphasizes on realized benefits (see Table 15.10)

Table 15.10: Realized benefits

Dimensions	Brief Explanation
Better/New Products and Services	E-business has helped organizations create better/new services and innovations.
Efficiency	E-business has helped organizations enhance the efficiency of their internal operations (i.e., simplifying workflows, speeding the projects).
Effectiveness	E-business has helped organizations do the right things (i.e., working on the right projects, markets).
Time & Cost Reduction	E-business has helped organizations save time and money for them (i.e., via improved communication, enhanced business businesses, reduced costs in marketing & other operation areas, etc).
Net Benefits	E-business has created net benefits (more benefits than costs) for organizations.
Relationships with Customers	E-business has helped organizations enhance their relationships with customers and provide them with better products & services.
Relationships with Suppliers and Business Partners	E-business has helped organizations enhance their relationships with suppliers and business partners, and has helped improve their supply chains.
Relationships with Government Agencies	E-business has helped organizations enhance their relationships with government agencies, strengthen their relationships with them, and reduce unexpected events.
Relationships with Competitors	E-business has helped organizations enhance their relationships with their competitors and achieve a win-win situation (co-opetition is made possible).

Table 15.10: *Continued*

Dimensions	Brief Explanation
Market Share	E-business has helped organizations enhance their market share.
Market Leader Position	E-business has helped organizations achieve/enhance their market leader position (i.e., enjoying large market share, more experience, established online brand).
Revenue	E-business has helped organizations generate more revenue.
Profit	E-business has helped organizations produce more profit.
Image	E-business has helped organizations create better image.
Responsiveness to Changes in the Market	E-business has helped organizations enhance their responsiveness to changes in the market.

(Source: developed for this study)

Ongoing Knowledge Management, Learning & Innovation

This construct is similar to perceived benefits as shown in Table 15.3. However definitions of variables/dimensions are different as shown in Table 15.11, as it represents organizations' ongoing commitments in knowledge management, learning & innovation (see Table 15.11).

Table 15.11: Ongoing knowledge management, learning & innovation

Dimensions	Brief Explanation
Creation of Knowledge	Organizations' e-business activities could be enhanced by their on-going efforts of creating knowledge (both tacit and explicit) from internal and external sources (i.e., learning changes in the market).
Capture of Knowledge	Organizations' e-business activities could be enhanced by their on-going efforts of collecting knowledge (both tacit and explicit) from internal and external sources.
Storage & Organization of Knowledge	Organizations' e-business activities could be enhanced by their on-going efforts of storing and organizing knowledge (both tacit and explicit) from internal and external sources.
Dissemination and Sharing of Knowledge	Organizations' e-business activities could be enhanced by their on-going efforts of distributing and sharing knowledge (both tacit and explicit) from internal and external sources.
Application of Knowledge	Organizations' e-business activities could be enhanced by their on-going efforts of applying knowledge (both tacit and explicit) from internal and external sources (i.e., better and faster responding to the changes in the market).
Existence of Culture for Knowledge Management	Organizations' e-business activities could be enhanced by their on-going pro-knowledge management culture.

Table 15.11: *Continued*

Dimensions	Brief Explanation
Existence of Structure for Knowledge Management	Organizations' e-business activities could be enhanced by their ongoing effort of having pro-knowledge management structure.
Existence of Processes for Managing Knowledge	Organizations' e-business activities could be enhanced by their ongoing effort of having systematic knowledge management processes.
Existence of Tools for Managing Knowledge	Organizations' e-business activities could be enhanced by their on-going effort of having appropriate knowledge management systems.
Existence of Strategies for Managing Knowledge	Organizations' e-business activities could be enhanced by their on-going existence of knowledge management strategies.
Co-creation Attitude	Organizations' e-business activities could be enhanced by their ongoing effort of having pro-co-creation initiatives with business partners, suppliers, customers and even competitors instead of sticking to the not-invented –here attitude.
Learning Desire and Activities	Organizations' e-business activities could be enhanced by their ongoing desire and activities of learning the internal and external environments.
Learning Ability & Knowledge Building	Organizations' e-business activities could be initiated by activities of developing collective and individual learning ability and knowledge building.
Research & Development Investments	Organizations' e-business activities could be enhanced by their ongoing investments in research and development activities.
Innovation Efforts	Organizations' e-business activities could be enhanced by their ongoing efforts of producing new products and services all the time (in both good and bad times).
Innovation Environment	Organizations' e-business activities could be enhanced by their ongoing efforts of maintaining an environment where people are encouraged and supported for being innovative and creative.
Innovativeness	Organizations' e-business activities could be enhanced by their ongoing efforts of trying new ideas and technologies.
Talent Management	Organizations' e-business activities could be enhanced by their ongoing efforts of better talent management (including recruiting, training and retaining talented people (or people with required knowledge or people who are eager to create new knowledge) and their knowledge).

(Source: developed for this study)

Organizational Adjustments

This construct reflects organizations' adjustments to various parts of the organization (as shown in Table 15.4) for the purpose of embracing their e-business initiatives, including enhanced top management support, better organizational culture, adjusted organizational structure, improved business processes, updated information technology infrastructure and expertise, updated management's knowledge and skills of e-business, updated people's knowledge and skills of e-business, refined portfolio of

Table 15.12: Organization adjustments

Dimensions	Brief Explanation
Enhanced Top Management Support	Organizations' e-business activities could be enhanced by more top management support.
Better Organizational Culture	Organizations' e-business activities could be enhanced by better environment for e-business.
Adjusted Organizational Structure	Organizations' e-business activities could be enhanced by appropriately restructuring the organization for fostering e-business (i.e., creating a separate unit, a new company for e-business).
Improved Business Processes	Organizations' e-business activities could be enhanced by making business processes better.
Updated Information Technology Infrastructure and Expertise	Organizations' e-business activities could be enhanced by having updated information technology infrastructure and expertise which are relevant and critical to e-business.
Updated Management's Knowledge and Skills of E-business	Organizations' e-business activities could be enhanced by updated management's knowledge and skills of e-business.
Updated People's Knowledge and Skills of E-business	Organizations' e-business activities could be enhanced by updated people's knowledge and skills of e-business.
Refined Portfolio of Products and Services	Organizations' e-business activities could be enhanced by refined portfolio of products and services offered in online and offline operations (i.e., some products are only offered online while others are only offered in physical shops, etc).
Refined Pricing Strategies	Organizations' e-business activities could be enhanced by refined pricing strategies for products and services offered in online and offline operations (i.e., could be the same prices or not).
Refined Brand Portfolio	Organizations' e-business activities could be enhanced by refined brand portfolio (i.e., could have a new brand for its online business or not).

(Source: developed for this study)

products & services, refined pricing strategies, and refined brand portfolio (see Table 15.12).

E-business Strategy Implementation

This construct looks at the organization's implementation of its e-business strategy by reviewing whether such dimensions discussed in Table 15.5 previously have been done (see Table 15.13).

Table 15.13: E-business strategy implementation

Dimensions	Brief Explanation
E-Business Strategy	Organizations' e-business activities could be enhanced by successfully implementing and continually ensuring an appropriate e-business strategy (i.e., how and what the online channel can contribute to an organization's performance).
E-Business Strategic Planning Process	Organizations' e-business activities could be enhanced by successfully implementing and continually reviewing their strategic planning process (i.e., including strategy initiation, formation, implementation and assessment as suggested by Turban et al. (2008)).
E-Business Model	Organizations' e-business activities could be enhanced by successfully implementing its business model and continually ensuring having an appropriate e-business model (focusing on generating revenue and creating value for the organization, its customers and its business partners).
Sufficient Analysis and Planning	Organizations' e-business activities could be enhanced by ensuring sufficient analysis and planning have been done when they are deciding specific business strategies.
Implementation Plan	Organizations' e-business activities could be enhanced by successfully implementing a comprehensive implementation plan for chosen e-business strategy.
Post-implementation Maintenance and Evaluation	Organizations' e-business activities could be enhanced by successfully carrying out a comprehensive plan for post-implementation activities and using a detailed set of processes and tools to examine the performance of choose e-business strategy.

(Source: developed for this study)

Realized Characteristics of E-business System

This construct is similar to expected characteristics of e-business system as shown in Table 15.6. However definitions of dimensions are different as shown in Table 15.14, as it represents realized characteristics of e-business system (see Table 15.14).

Table 15.14: Realized characteristics of E-business system

Dimensions	Brief Explanation
Ease of Use	Organizations' e-business activities could be enhanced by realized ease of use of the e-business system (i.e., making finding information easy by providing online search facility, frequently ask questions (FAQ) section, website map, navigation assistance/guide, etc) for both internal (i.e., employees) and external stakeholders (customers, business partners, and suppliers).
Cheap to Learn and Use	Organizations' e-business activities could be enhanced by realized non-expensive learning and use of the e-business system for both internal (i.e., employees) and external stakeholders (customers, business partners, and suppliers).
Speed	Organizations' e-business activities could be enhanced by realized fast speed (i.e., uploading, downloading and navigation speed) of the e-business system.
Accessibility	Organizations' e-business activities could be enhanced by achieved easy access by every authorized user.
Availability	Organizations' e-business activities could be enhanced by achieved 24/7 availability of the e-business system.
Regular Maintenance and Updates	Organizations' e-business activities could be enhanced by achieved regular maintenance and updates.
Systems Integration	Organizations' e-business activities could be enhanced by achieved integration with the organization's existing systems and with systems of customers, business partners and suppliers.

(Source: developed for this study)

Organizational Factors

This construct is similar to perceived benefits as shown in Table 15.8. However definitions of variables/dimensions are different as shown in Table 15.15, as it represents gained trust (see Table 15.15).

Table 15.15: Gained trust

Dimensions	Brief Explanation
Security	Organizations' e-business activities could be enhanced by gained trust arising from having effectively implemented security of the e-business system (i.e., secured online shopping and payment process, secured communication with customers, business partners and suppliers, and secured intra-organization communication).
Quality of Products and Services	Organizations' e-business activities could be enhanced by gained trust arising from having delivered quality products and services (i.e., providing online services such as search functions they offer).

Table 15.15: *Continued*

Dimensions	Brief Explanation
Provision of Third Party Assurance	Organizations' e-business activities could be enhanced by gained trust arising from having provided third-party assurance/services to guarantee a peaceful mind for their online customers (such as CA (Certificate Authority), VeriSign, or TRUSTe).
Privacy Policy	Organizations' e-business activities could be enhanced by gained trust arising from presenting detailed and visible privacy policy (concerning the collection and use of customers' data), which is clearly comply with relevant government regulations, and having implemented such policy.
Intellectual Property Management	Organizations' e-business activities could be enhanced by gained trust arising from visible and effective intellectual property management policy and having implemented such policy.
Terms and Conditions	Organizations' e-business activities could be enhanced by gained trust arising from presenting detailed and visible terms and conditions clauses including refund and dispute resolution procedures and policies, and having implemented them.
Online Communities	Organizations' e-business activities could be enhanced by gained trust arising from having established online communities for their relevant stakeholders (i.e., for customers, business partners, and suppliers) and having tapped into crowd intelligence created in the online communities.
Online Feedback/ Reputation Systems	Organizations' e-business activities could be enhanced by gained trust arising from having established online feedback/reputation systems for their relevant stakeholders (i.e., for customers, business partners, and suppliers) regarding their views on organizations' products and services and having tapped into crowd intelligence created in the systems.
Providing Opportunities to Talk to Human Beings	Organizations' e-business activities could be enhanced by gained trust arising from having provided contact numbers of the organization which will be answered by relevant/key people in the organization instead of the machine, especially when customers are having issues with the organization.
Providing Information of The Organization	Organizations' e-business activities could be enhanced by gained trust arising from having provided sufficient information on the company (i.e., who we are, what we do, the history of the organization, organizational structure, members of senior managers, culture, mission, vision, strategic objectives, strategic alliances, career services & opportunities, financial information (i.e., share prices, annual reports)).

(Source: developed for this study)

E-business Success

Previously we discuss various areas that e-business can be applied (as shown in Table 15.9), this construct measures how successful organizations have been in using e-business since its adoption by monitoring performance of e-business in those areas and other additional areas (including success in achieving expected benefits, success in making organizational adjustments, success in achieving e-business system characteristics, success in achieving expected trust, success in implementing e-business strategy, and success in achieving ongoing knowledge management, learning and innovation) (see Table 15.16).

Table 15.16: E-Business success

Dimensions	Brief Explanation
Success in the Use of E-business in Internal Operations & Communications	Organizations' e-business success can be evidenced in their successful use of e-business for enhancing internal operations.
Success in the Use of E-business in Interacting with Suppliers and Business Partners	Organizations' e-business success can be evidenced in their successful use of e-business for enhancing their interaction with suppliers and business partners.
Success in the Use of E-business in Interacting with Customers	Organizations' e-business success can be evidenced in their successful use of e-business for enhancing their interaction with customers.
Success in the Use of E-business in Interacting with Government Agencies	Organizations' e-business success can be evidenced in their successful use of e-business for enhancing their interaction with government agencies.
Success in the Use of E-business in Interacting with Competitors	Organizations' e-business success can be evidenced in their successful use of e-business for enhancing their interaction with competitors.
Success in Dealing with Channel Conflict	Organizations' e-business success can be evidenced in their good balance of online and offline channels.
Success in Integration	Organizations' e-business success can be evidenced in their smooth efforts of making online operations a part of the organization.
Success in Achieving Expected Benefits	Organizations' e-business success can be evidenced in their success in making organizational adjustments.
Success in Making Organizational adjustments	Organizations' e-business success can be evidenced in their success in achieving expected benefits.

Table 15.16: *Continued*

Dimensions	Brief Explanation
Success in Achieving E-business System Characteristics	Organizations' e-business success can be evidenced in their success in achieving expected e-business characteristics.
Success in Achieving Expected Trust	Organizations' e-business success can be evidenced in their success in achieving expected trust.
Success in Implementing E-business Strategy	Organizations' e-business success can be evidenced in their success in implementing e-business strategy.
Success in Achieving Ongoing Knowledge Management, Learning and Innovation	Organizations' e-business success can be evidenced in their success in achieving ongoing knowledge management, learning and innovation (i.e., benefits such as being leading e-businesses, established online brands, achieving critical mass of users arising from innovative e-business initiatives, maintaining competitive advantages resulting from first-mover strategy by keeping on providing new/better products and services).

(Source: developed for this study)

Sustainable E-business Success

While Table 15.16 presents measures of successful performance of e-business in organizations, such measures have to be constantly checked to ensure the sustainability of the success of e-business (see Table 15.17).

Table 15.17: Sustainable E-Business Success

Dimensions	Brief Explanation
Sustainable Success in the Use of E-business in Internal Operations & Communications	Organizations' sustainable e-business success can be evidenced in their sustainable success in using e-business for enhancing internal operations and communications.
Sustainable Success in the Use of E-business in Interacting with Suppliers and Business Partners	Organizations' sustainable e-business success can be evidenced in their sustainable success in using e-business for enhancing their interaction with suppliers and business partners.
Sustainable Success in the Use of E-business in Interacting with Customers	Organizations' sustainable e-business success can be evidenced in their sustainable success in using e-business for enhancing their interaction with customers.

Table 15.17: *Continued*

Dimensions	Brief Explanation
Sustainable Success in the Use of E-business in Interacting with Government Agencies	Organizations' sustainable e-business success can be evidenced in their sustainable success in using e-business for enhancing their interaction with government agencies.
Sustainable Success in the Use of E-business in Interacting with Competitors	Organizations' sustainable e-business success can be evidenced in their sustainable success in using e-business for enhancing their interaction with competitors.
Sustainable Success in Success in Dealing with Channel Conflict	Organizations' sustainable e-business success can be evidenced in their sustainable efforts of balancing online and offline channels.
Sustainable Success in Success in Integration	Organizations' sustainable e-business success can be evidenced in their sustainable efforts of making online operations a part of the organization.
Sustainable Success in Achieving Expected Benefits	Organizations' sustainable e-business success can be evidenced in their sustainable success in achieving expected benefits.
Sustainable Success in Making Organizational adjustments	Organizations' sustainable e-business success can be evidenced in their sustainable success in making organizational adjustments.
Sustainable Success in Achieving E-business System Characteristics	Organizations' sustainable e-business success can be evidenced in their sustainable success in achieving expected e-business characteristics
Sustainable Success in Achieving Expected Trust	Organizations' e-business sustainable success can be evidenced in their sustainable success in achieving expected trust.
Sustainable Success in Implementing E-business Strategy	Organizations' e-business sustainable success can be evidenced in their sustainable success in implementing e-business strategy.
Sustainable Success in Achieving Ongoing Knowledge Management, Learning and Innovation	Organizations' e-business sustainable success can be evidenced in their sustainable success in achieving ongoing knowledge management, learning and innovation (i.e., benefits such as being leading e-businesses, established online brands, achieving critical mass of users arising from innovative e-business initiatives, maintaining competitive advantages resulting from first-mover strategy by keeping on providing new/better products and services).

(Source: developed for this study)

3. Implications

3.1. Implications for Research

This chapter presents a model of e-business adoption, success and sustainable success which includes and consists of 17 constructs and 159 factors/variables. As far as the authors' knowledge, so far there is no e-business adoption and success models being so comprehensive and covering different stages of adoption and success of e-business. Even though some concepts of the proposed model are not unique (for example, concepts such as expected/realized benefits & expected/ realized characteristics of e-business system are to some extent equivalent to Rogers' (1995) concepts of relative advantage, complexity, Davis' (1989) perceived usefulness and perceived ease of use, and Xu & Quaddus' (2007) perceived/realized benefits and perceived/realized user friendliness; concepts of gained trust/realized trust are overlaps with trust concepts in the previous studies (i.e., Ba & Pavlou 2002; Heijden & Verhagen 2004; Lee et al. 2005); concept of external influences share common thoughts with concept of external inspiring suggested by Xu & Quaddus (2005)), the constructs and the factors within each construct and their meanings are different from earlier studies and are more specific to e-business and are specially designed for this study.

Future research could investigate factors influencing adoption, success and sustainable success of e-business (i.e., by asking questions such as (a) what are the factors influencing organizations' decision to adopt e-business?; (b) what are the factors influencing organizations' e-business success?; (c) what are the factors influencing organizations' sustainable e-business success?)), and examine the whole model by establishing hypotheses for each of the paths in the proposed model (i.e., a longitudinal study covering 3 steps of the model via quantitative research approach through collecting data in the form of questionnaire survey). Some hypotheses arising from the model include:

For adoption stage:

- H1: External environment positively influences the adoption of e-business.
- H2: Organizational factors positively influence the adoption of e-business.
- H3: Expected characteristics of e-business system positively influence the adoption of e-business.
- H4: Expected benefits positively influence the adoption of e-business.
- H4: Knowledge management, learning and innovation positively influence the adoption of e-business.
- H6: External influences positively influence the adoption of e-business.
- H7: E-business strategy planning positively influences the adoption of e-business.
- H8: Expected trust positively influences the adoption of e-business.

For achieving e-business stage:

- H9: Realized benefits positively influence the success of e-business.
- H10: Organizational adjustments positively influence the success of e-business.
- H11: Realized characteristics of e-business system positively influence the success of e-business.
- H12: Gained trust positively influences the success of e-business.
- H13: E-business strategy implementation positively influences the success of e-business.
- H14: Ongoing knowledge management, learning & innovation positively influence the success of e-business.

For achieving sustainable e-business success:

- H15: Organizations' continued efforts in searching for and then embarking on new e-business opportunities and in sustaining gained e-business successes positively influence sustainable success of e-business.

Alternatively they also can study one part of the model (i.e., by looking at each step separately). In the meantime, future studies also can conduct comparison studies by examining various dimensions of factors in the model (i.e., looking at organizational construct and then examining the impacts of such factors as business size, nature of business and other variables on the adoption, or/and success, or/and sustainable success of e-business; looking at external environment factors and then studying the differences and similarities of e-business practices in different industries and economies, among many others).

3.2. Implications for Practice

The model, including both of its constructs and factors, can be applied as a checklist for organizations to find out how they fare in terms of adopting e-business, achieving e-business success and sustaining e-business success, with respect to those constructs and factors. It also can serve as a detailed implementation guide for those organizations who are thinking about or embarking on e-business. Furthermore e-business related organizations and industries (i.e., e-business reviewers, e-business rating organizations, e-business marketing and design firms, e-business investment firms) can use the model to evaluate e-businesses they are interested in. In addition, government agencies also can use the comprehensive model to develop policies, shape strategies and form action plans to more effectively and efficiently support firms' e-business initiatives (especially small and medium enterprises) and encourage e-entrepreneurship.

Tables 15.18-15.27 present an example of using the model to predict the future success of e-business. For the illustration purpose, those tables only discuss second stage of model, and the discussion is very exploratory in nature since complete information regarding those companies is not available to the authors at the point of time when the authors are writing up this chapter. However such exploratory discussion should to some extent illustrate how the proposed model can be applied in real world practices.

Table 15.18: Likely future success of some current leading E-business organizations selected by the authors: Alibaba

Self-selected E-businesses: Alibaba	
Contributions/Benefits of E-business	A leading B2B online marketplace
User Friendliness of E-business System	Very good (especially simple to use and easy to find required information)
Trustworthiness	High (but lack of dynamic online interaction with customers by human assistants initiated and supported by Alibaba; privacy could be an issue; and delivering quality information to customers could be a challenges when it has very large amount of information from large number of users)
Organizational Environment/ Factors	Very good organizational facilitating environment (especially an excellent top management team with complementary skills and having a visionary leader of Jack Ma)
E-business Strategy	Good (but one of the big challenges is to become successful in markets outside the China)
Knowledge Management, Learning & Innovation	Very good (can be evidenced by being able to respond fast to the market changes and produce well-received products and services, such as Gold Suppliers, Trade Manager, TrustPass)
Likelihood of Future Success	Very likely (but they may need to explore other parts of the B2B supply chain and other markets outside China)

(Source: developed for this study)

Table 15.19: Likely future success of some current leading E-business organizations selected by the authors: Amazon

Self-selected E-businesses: Amazon	
Contributions/Benefits of E-business	A leading online retailer
User Friendliness of E-business System	Very good (especially simple to use and easy to find required information)
Trustworthiness	High (but lack of dynamic online interaction with customers by human assistants initiated and supported by Amazon; privacy could be an issue (i.e., arising from tracking customers' online movements)
Organizational Environment/ Factors	Very good organizational facilitating environment (especially an excellent top management team with complementary skills and having a visionary leader of Jeff Bezos)
E-business Strategy	Good (but one of the big challenges is to become successful in markets outside the America (i.e., in China))

Table 15.19: *Continued*

Self-selected E-businesses: Amazon	
Knowledge Management, Learning & Innovation	Very good (can be evidenced by being able to respond fast to the market changes and produce well received products and services (i.e., excellent online recommendation systems, excellent ability to understand customers thus providing personalized services, Kindle(a e-book reader), and self-publishing services))
Likelihood of Future Success	Very likely (but they may like to explore more opportunities in B2B supply chains) and other B2C areas (i.e., selling virtual goods which are becoming popular (especially in online games and 3D online communities such as Second Life) in recent years and have an approximate US$ 1.5 billion a year market (Linden Lab 2009))

(Source: developed for this study)

Table 15.20: Likely future success of some current leading E-business organizations selected by the authors: E-bay

Self-selected E-businesses: E-bay	
Contributions/Benefits of E-business	A leading C2C e-business
User Friendliness of E-business System	Good (but there exist complains such as deleting sellers below certain ranking; sellers being banned from leaving negative feedback, dysfunctional seller tools, site stability, poor search results for buyers Balk (2008))
Trustworthiness	Could be High (but lack of dynamic online interaction with customers by human assistants initiated and supported by E-bay; privacy could be an issue; reputation of sellers and buyers could be another challenge (i.e., delivering on time, delivering what buyers purchased; certain issues surrounding Paypal (i.e., performing functions of and enjoy benefits (such as interest from money sitting in the accounts) of financial institutes while it is not a financial institute))
Organizational Environment/ Factors	Good organizational facilitating environment (Even though they have an excellent top management team with complementary skills, there is a need for stability in the top management (quite a few executives have left the company))
E-business Strategy	Good (but one of the big challenges is to become successful in markets outside the America (i.e., in China); also not so sure about the future of pure C2C online marketplace. Social networks and online communities also can be the venue where people can trade things; and the consumer's shift toward fix pricing transactions could be another challenge)

Table 15.20: *Continued*

Self-selected E-businesses: E-bay	
Knowledge Management, Learning & Innovation	Very good (can be evidenced by being able to respond fast to the market changes and produce well received products and services, i.e., its pioneered C2C online auction marketplace; offering Paypal in E-bay)
Likelihood of Future Success	Likely if they can keep critical mass of users in the system, make the systems more useful and user friendly; keep the top stable and powerful, and effectively cope with competition from B2C e-businesses and online communities & social networks, and the consumer's shift to fix-pricing transactions rather than online auctions

(Source: developed for this study)

Table 15.21: Likely future success of some current leading E-business organizations selected by the authors: Wikipedia

Self-selected E-businesses: Wikipedia	
Contributions/Benefits of E-business	A leading online publishing business and online community
User Friendliness of E-business System	Very good (especially simple to use and easy to find required information)
Trustworthiness	High (but lack of dynamic online interaction with customers by human assistants initiated and supported by Wikipedia; quality control is an issue; privacy could be an issue as well)
Organizational Environment/ Factors	Very good organizational facilitating environment (especially its use of community model in the management, i.e., all the members of board of trustees are volunteers).
E-business Strategy	Good (but not sure about how long the revenue model of sponsoring by donation can last for?; Can Wikipedia survive for a long time like charity organizations or religion associations (both of them are primarily funded by donations)?; How can it maintain contributors' long term loyalty? And another concern could be the lack of business skills of top management)
Knowledge Management, Learning & Innovation	Very good (can be evidenced by being able to respond fast to the market changes and produce well-received products and services, i.e., offering in many languages, largest free public knowledge management system/mass intelligence system)
Likelihood of Future Success	Likely if they can maintain the loyalty of users and create additional revenue channels

(Source: developed for this study)

Table 15.22: Likely future success of some current leading E-business organizations selected by the authors: Youtube

Self-selected E-businesses: Youtube	
Contributions/Benefits of E-business	A leading online video sharing business and social network
User Friendliness of E-business System	Good (sometime could be slow depend on the bandwidth)
Trustworthiness	High (but lack of dynamic online interaction with customers by human assistants initiated and supported by Youtube; privacy could be an issue)
Organizational Environment/ Factors	Good organizational facilitating environment (But the founders may not have required management experience and they may not be as lucky as Bill Gates and Michael Dell-both of them are self-trained (of course with some help from others) successful leaders and have smoothly transited from amateur leaders to professional leaders with no major disruption to the company)
E-business Strategy	Not so clear since so far it has not been able to monetize the opportunities from its large user base even though the founders may believe money will come later when the content and technology are right
Knowledge Management, Learning & Innovation	Good (but sharing video may not be so innovative comparing to other innovations from other leading e-businesses (i.e., less knowledge content than Wikipedia so far)
Likelihood of Future Success	Likely if they can figure out how to generate sufficient revenue (winning public popularity only may not make them a successful firm), and how to maintain the loyalty of its users (people may become not so exciting in contributing user-generated videos after some initial excitements)

(Source: developed for this study)

Table 15.23: Likely future success of some current leading E-business organizations selected by the authors: Google

Self-selected E-businesses: Google	
Contributions/Benefits of E-business	A leading search engine business
User Friendliness of E-business System	Very good (especially easy to search with key words; fast results delivery; user friendly home page without any advertisement; providing the Internet platform on which one only needs a computer, an Internet connection point, and a browser for all of one's online activities)
Trustworthiness	High (but lack of dynamic online interaction with customers by human assistants initiated and supported by Google; privacy could be an issue, especially with applications such as Gmail, Google map)

Table 15.23: *Continued*

Self-selected E-businesses: Google	
Organizational Environment/ Factors	Very good organizational facilitating environment (especially an excellent top management team with complementary skills, i.e., combination of Eric Schmidt's extensive management skills and two co-founders' superb knowledge of products and technical skills)
E-business Strategy	Good (but one of the big challenges is to become successful in markets outside the America, i.e., in China)
Knowledge Management, Learning & Innovation	Very good (can be evidenced by being able to respond fast to the market changes and produce well-received products and services, i.e., search engine, Gmail, Google map, and especially its pro-innovation environment, i.e., giving people 20% of their time to pursue the projects they are interested in)
Likelihood of Future Success	Very likely if they keep on the way they are innovating now (but they may like to look at other areas of organizing and presenting information for human beings, i.e., virtual assistants)

(Source: developed for this study)

Table 15.24: Likely future success of some current leading E-business organizations selected by the authors: Yahoo

Self-selected E-businesses: Yahoo	
Contributions/Benefits of E-business	A leading online portal
User Friendliness of E-business System	Very good (especially simple to use and easy to find required information)
Trustworthiness	High (but lack of dynamic online interaction with customers by human assistants initiated and supported by Yahoo; privacy could be an issue)
Organizational Environment/ Factors	Good organizational facilitating environment (but there exists an instability of top management, i.e., CEO has been replaced a few times in recent years; other concerns (as suggested by Carlson 2008) include lack of product leadership (too many disparate businesses), self-isolated leadership, tolerating a non-performing culture, and matrix organizational culture)
E-business Strategy	Good (but one of the big challenges is to become successful in markets outside the America (i.e., in China); also not sure about the future of Internet portals which may be taken over by search engines (since search engines may give people a better central point or gateway to enter the wonderland of information on the Internet)

Table 15.24: *Continued*

Self-selected E-businesses: Yahoo	
Knowledge Management, Learning & Innovation	Very good (can be evidenced by being able to respond fast to the market changes and produce well received products and services, i.e., its search engine, its online portal, Yahoo mail, Yahoo Personals)
Likelihood of Future Success	Likely if they can win the competition from search engines and decide its core business and competence (or create new core business and new competence), keep its top stable and powerful, and work on the four issues of product leadership, leadership, culture and structure mentioned by Carlson (2008)

(Source: developed for this study)

Table 15.25: Likely future success of some current leading E-business organizations selected by the authors: Dell

Self-selected E-businesses: Dell	
Contributions/Benefits of E-business	A leading online computer vendor
User Friendliness of E-business System	Very good (especially simple to use and easy to find required information)
Trustworthiness	High (but lack of dynamic online interaction with customers by human assistants initiated and supported by Dell; privacy could be an issue)
Organizational Environment/ Factors	Good organizational facilitating environment (but there exists an instability of top management, especially after Michael Dell stepped down)
E-business Strategy	Good (but one of the big challenges could be finding additional revenue channels, especially when PCs are becoming commodities and margin is dramatically shrinking)
Knowledge Management, Learning & Innovation	Very good (can be evidenced by being able to respond fast to the market changes and produce well-received products and services, i.e., it pioneered online direct selling model, its personalization and customization facilities)
Likelihood of Future Success	Likely if they can be successful in creating revenue from other areas (i.e., services) and from tapping into new territories (i.e., wireless devices)

(Source: developed for this study)

Table 15.26: Likely future success of some current leading E-business organizations selected by the authors: Microsoft

Self-selected E-businesses: Microsoft	
Contributions/Benefits of E-business	The largest software services provider
User Friendliness of E-business System	Good (different versions of operation systems and applications, and integration with systems and applications from other vendors could cause headaches)
Trustworthiness	High (but lack of dynamic online interaction with customers by human assistants-so interaction is initiated and supported by Microsoft; privacy could be an issue)
Organizational Environment/ Factors	Good organizational facilitating environment (but there exists an unpredictability of top management after the departure of Bill Gates)
E-business Strategy	Good (but one of the big challenges is to cope with the emerging open source movement, and to be more successful on the Internet is another challenge-so far it has not been able to find ways to deal with Google's dominance on the Internet)
Knowledge Management, Learning & Innovation	Very good (especially can be evidenced by being able to respond fast to the market changes and produce well-received products and services, i.e., its windows operating systems, office applications, MSN, hotmail)
Likelihood of Future Success	Likely if they can cope with open source movement (i.e., cloud computing pushed by Google and others) and develop & implement better strategy for competing on the Internet)

(Source: developed for this study)

Table 15.27: Likely future success of some current leading E-business organizations selected by the authors: Apple

Self-selected E-businesses: Apple	
Contributions/Benefits of E-business	A leading online entertainment and mobile devices company
User Friendliness of E-business System	Very good (especially simple to use and easy to find required information)
Trustworthiness	High (but lack of dynamic online interaction with customers by human assistants initiated and supported by Apple ; privacy could be an issues)
Organizational Environment/ Factors	Good organizational facilitating environment (but there exists an instability of top management, i.e., too much attention has been given to CEO Steven Jobs' Health)
E-business Strategy	Good (but one of the big challenges is to become successful in markets outside the America (i.e., i-tunes in China)

Table 15.27: *Continued*

Self-selected E-businesses: Apple	
Knowledge Management, Learning & Innovation	Very good (especially can be evidenced by its popular products and services such as I-phone and I-tunes)
Likelihood of Future Success	Very likely if they are able to keep surprising the world with innovative products and services, maintain their strengths in online & mobile entertainment as well as associated devices, and keep having leaders in the top who are as innovative and visionary as Steve Jobs

(Source: developed for this study)

4. Conclusions & Future Plan

This chapter develops a model of e-business adoption, success and sustainable success. The developed model could provide assistance to organizations who are embarking on e-business or to organizations who have adopted e-business. The authors' immediate plan is to test the model with some leading e-businesses in Australia before further testing with international leaders in e-business (i.e., those e-business organizations mentioned in the Table 15.18). Such research may involve researching both e-business organizations and their e-business users.

References

Ba, S, & Pavlou, P. (2002) Evidence of the effect of trust building technolohy in electronic markets: price premiums and buyer behavior, MIS Quarterly, Vol. 26, No. 3, pp. 243-268.

Balk, D. (2008) 2008: The year eBay lost its mojo, Seeking Alpha, Online, Available at: http://seekingalpha.com/article/111564-2008-the-year-ebay-lost-its-mojo?source=article (accessed on December 23, 2008).

Barnes, D., Hinton, M. and Mieczkowska, S. (2004) Managing the transition from bricks-and-Mortar to click-and-Mortar: A business process perspective. Knowledge and Process Management, Vol. 11, No 3, pp. 199-209.

Carlson, N. (2008) Four reasons for Yahoo's four-year slump, CNN Money, Online, Available at: http://money.cnn.com/news/newsfeed/siliconalley/media/2008_12_four_seasons_for (accessed on December 30, 2008).

Davis, F. D. (1989) Perceived usefulness, perceived ease of use, and user acceptance of information technology, MIS Quarterly, Vol. 13, No. 3, pp. 319-340.

DeLone, W.H., & McLean, E R. (1992) Information systems success: the quest for the dependent variable, Information Systems Research, Vol. 3, No. 1, pp. 60-95.

DeLone, W.H., & McLean, E R. (2003) The DeLone and McLean model of information systems success: A ten-year update, Journal of Management Information Systems, Vol. 19, No. 4, pp. 9-30.

Dillon, T.W. & Reif, H.L. (2004) Factors influencing consumers' e-commerce commodity purchases, Information technology, Learning and Performance Journal, Vol. 22, No. 2, pp. 1-12.

Epstein, M.J. (2005) Implementing successful e-commerce Initiatives, Strategic Finance, Vol. 86, No. 9, pp. 22-29.

Gibbs, J., Kraemer, K.L.& Dedrik, J. (2002) Environment and Policy Factors Shaping e-commerce Diffusion: A Cross-Country Comparison. Centre for Research on Information Technology and Organisation, University of California.

Gunasekaran, A. and Ngai, E.W.T. (2005) e-commerce in Hong Kong: an empirical perspective and analysis, Internet Research, Vol. 15, No. 2, pp. 141-159.

Hart, M. (2003) Harvard Business School Case Selections from the Field Series: Inside Retailing, Renmin University of China.

Harvey, M. (2000) Elements of e-commerce success, Folio: The Magazine for Magazine Management, pp. 192-197.

Heijden, H., & Verhagen, T. (2004) Online store image: conceptual foundation and empirical measurement, Information & Management, Vol. 41, pp. 609-617.

Lee, S.M., Katerattanakul, P. & Hong, S. (2005) Framework for user perception of effective e-tail web sites, Journal of Electronic Commerce in Organizations, Vol. 3, No. 1, pp. 13-34.

Linden Lab (2009) Linden Lab goes shopping, buys virtual goods marketplaces to integrate web shopping with Second Life, Online, Available at: http://lindenlab.com/pressroom/releases/01_20_09 (accessed on March 23, 2009).

Lu, J. (2003) A model for evaluating E-commerce based on cost/benefit and customer satisfaction, Journal of Information Systems Frontiers, Vol. 5, No. 3, pp. 265-277.

Molla, A. 2004 The impact of eReadiness on eCommerce Success in Developing Countries: firm-level evidence, Institute for Development Policy and Management.

Molla, A., & Licker, P.S. (2001) E-commerce systems success: an attempt to extend and respecify the Delone and MacLean model IS success, Journal of Electronic Commerce Research, Vol. 2, No. 4, pp. 131-141.

Ratchford, B.T., Talukdar, D. and Lee, M.S. (2001) A model of consumer choice of the The Internet as an information source, International Journal of Electronic Commerce, Vol. 5, No. 3, pp. 7-21.

Rogers, E. M. (1995), Diffusion of Innovations (Fourth Edition), The Free Press, New York, USA.

Roger, J. (2001) Six keys to B2C e-commerce success, Insurance & Technology, Vol. 26, No. 8, pp. 49-54.

Sabherwal, R., Jeyaraj, A., Chowa, C. (2004) Information system success: Dimensions and Determinants, College of business administration, University of Missouri.

Steinfield, C. (2004) Does Online and offline channel integration work in practice? Department of Telecommunication, Michigan State University.

Stylianou, A.C, Robbins, S.S. and Jackson, P. (2003) Perceptions and attitudes about e-commerce development in China: an exploratory study, Journal of Global Information Management, Vol. 11, No. 2, pp. 31-47.

Tan, Z.X. and OuYang, W. (2004) Globalization of e-commerce: Diffusion and Impacts of the Internet and e-commerce in China, Centre for Research on Information Technology and Organisations, University of California.

Teo, T.S. (2001) Demographic and Motivation Variables Associated with The Internet Usage Activities, Internet Research: Electronic Network Applications and Policy, Vol. 11, No. 2, pp. 125-137.

Teo, T.S. and Ang, J.S. (1999) Critical success factors in the alignment of IS plans with business plans, International Journal of Information Management, Vol. 19, No. 2, pp. 173-185.

Turban, E., King, D., McKay, J., Marshall, P., Lee, J. & Viehland, D. (2008) Electronic Commerce 2008: A Managerial Perspective, International edition, Prentice Hall, Upper Saddle River, NJ.

Xu, J. & Quaddus, M. (2005) A Six-Stage Model for the Effective Diffusion of Knowledge Management Systems, The Journal of Management Development, Vol. 25, No. 4, pp. 362-373.

Xu, J. & Quaddus, M. (2007) Exploring the Factors Influencing End Users' Acceptance of Knowledge Management Systems: Development of a Research Model of Adoption and Continued Use, Journal of Organizational and End-Users Computing, Vol. 19, No. 4, pp. 57-79.